Black Poachers, White Hunters

A Social History of Hunting
in Colonial Kenya

EDWARD I. STEINHART

Professor of History
Texas Tech University

James Currey
OXFORD

EAEP
NAIROBI

Ohio University Press
ATHENS

James Currey Ltd
73 Botley Road
Oxford
OX2 0BS

East African Educational Publishers
Kijabe Street, PO Box 45314
Nairobi

Ohio University Press
The Ridges, Building 19
Athens, Ohio 45701, USA

© Edward I. Steinhart 2006
First published 2006

1 2 3 4 5 10 09 08 07 06

British Library Cataloguing in Publication Data
Steinhart, Edward I.
Black poachers, white hunters : a social history of hunting
in colonial Kenya. - (Eastern African studies)
1. Big game hunting - Social aspects - Kenya 2. Hunters -
Kenya - Social conditions 3. Big game hunting - Kenya -
History 4. Poaching - Kenya - History 5. Game protection -
Kenya - History 6. Kenya - race relations
I. Title
799.2'6'096762

ISBN 10: 0-85255-961-5 (James Currey Cloth)
ISBN 13: 978-085255-961-1 (James Currey Cloth)
ISBN 10: 0-85255-960-7 (James Currey Paper)
ISBN 13: 978-085255-960-4 (James Currey Paper)

Library of Congress Cataloging-in-Publication Data
available on request

ISBN 0-8214-1663-4 (Ohio University Press Cloth)
0-8214-1664-2 (Ohio University Press Paper)

Typeset in 10/11 pt Baskerville
by Long House Publishing Services, Cumbria, UK
Printed and bound in Great Britain
by Woolnough, Irthlingborough

Black Poachers, White Hunters

EASTERN AFRICAN STUDIES

Revealing Prophets
Edited by DAVID M. ANDERSON
& DOUGLAS H. JOHNSON

East African Expressions
of Christianity
Edited by THOMAS SPEAR
& ISARIA N. KIMAMBO

The Poor Are Not Us
Edited by DAVID M. ANDERSON
& VIGDIS BROCH-DUE

Potent Brews
JUSTIN WILLIS

Swahili Origins
JAMES DE VERE ALLEN

Being Maasai
Edited by THOMAS SPEAR
& RICHARD WALLER

Jua Kali Kenya
KENNETH KING

Control & Crisis in Colonial Kenya
BRUCE BERMAN

Unhappy Valley
Book One: State & Class
Book Two: Violence
& Ethnicity
BRUCE BERMAN
& JOHN LONSDALE

Mau Mau from Below
GREET KERSHAW

The Mau Mau War
in Perspective
FRANK FUREDI

Squatters & the Roots
of Mau Mau 1905-63
TABITHA KANOGO

Economic & Social Origins
of Mau Mau 1945-53
DAVID W. THROUP

Multi-Party Politics in Kenya
DAVID W. THROUP
& CHARLES HORNSBY

Empire State-Building
JOANNA LEWIS

Decolonization & Independence
in Kenya 1940-93
Edited by B.A. OGOT
& WILLIAM R. OCHIENG'

Eroding the Commons
DAVID ANDERSON

Penetration & Protest in Tanzania
ISARIA N. KIMAMBO

Custodians of the Land
Edited by GREGORY MADDOX, JAMES
L. GIBLIN & ISARIA N. KIMAMBO

Education in the Development
of Tanzania 1919-1990
LENE BUCHERT

The Second Economy in Tanzania
T.L. MALIYAMKONO
& M.S.D. BAGACHWA

Ecology Control & Economic Development
in East African History
HELGE KJEKSHUS

Siaya
DAVID WILLIAM COHEN
& E.S. ATIENO ODHIAMBO

Uganda Now • Changing Uganda
Developing Uganda • From Chaos to Order
Religion & Politics in East Africa
Edited by HOLGER BERNT HANSEN
& MICHAEL TWADDLE

Kakungulu & the Creation
of Uganda 1868-1928
MICHAEL TWADDLE

Controlling Anger
SUZETTE HEALD

Kampala Women Getting By
SANDRA WALLMAN

Political Power in Pre-Colonial Buganda
RICHARD J. REID

Alice Lakwena & the Holy Spirits
HEIKE BEHREND

Slaves, Spices & Ivory in Zanzibar
ABDUL SHERIFF

Zanzibar Under Colonial Rule
Edited by ABDUL SHERIFF &
ED FERGUSON

The History & Conservation of Zanzibar
Stone Town
Edited by ABDUL SHERIFF

Pastimes & Politics
LAURA FAIR

Ethnicity & Conflict in the Horn of Africa
Edited by KATSUYOSHI FUKUI
& JOHN MARKAKIS

Conflict, Age & Power in
North East Africa
Edited by EISEI KURIMOTO
& SIMON SIMONSE

Property Rights & Political
Development in Ethiopia & Eritrea
SANDRA FULLERTON JOIREMAN

Revolution & Religion in Ethiopia
ØYVIND M. EIDE

Brothers at War
TEKESTE NEGASH &
KJETIL TRONVOLL

From Guerrillas to Government
DAVID POOL

Mau Mau & Nationhood
Edited by E.S. ATIENO ODHIAMBO
& JOHN LONSDALE

A History of Modern Ethiopia, 1855-199
(2nd edn) BAHRU ZEWDE

Pioneers of Change in Ethiopia
BAHRU ZEWDE

Remapping Ethiopia
Edited by W. JAMES, D. DONHAM,
E. KURIMOTO & A. TRIULZI

Southern Marches of Imperial Ethiopia
Edited by DONALD L. DONHAM
& WENDY JAMES

A Modern History of the Somali (4th edn
I.M. LEWIS

Islands of Intensive Agriculture
in East Africa
Edited by MATS WIDGREN
& JOHN E.G. SUTTON

Leaf of Allah
EZEKIEL GEBISSA

Dhows & the Colonial Economy
of Zanzibar 1860-1970
ERIK GILBERT

African Womanhood in Colonial Kenya
TABITHA KANOGO

African Underclass
ANDREW BURTON

In Search of a Nation
Edited by GREGORY H. MADDOX
& JAMES L. GIBLIN

A History of the Excluded
JAMES L. GIBLIN

Black Poachers, White Hunters
EDWARD I. STEINHART

Crisis & Decline in Bunyoro*
SHANE DOYLE

Ethnic Federalism*
DAVID TURTON

Emancipation without Abolition in
German East Africa*
JAN-GEORG DEUTSCH

* forthcoming

Contents

List of Maps & Photographs   vi
Acknowledgements   vii

Introduction   1
Hunting in Kenya

Part I
The African Hunters   15

1
Kenya's People of the Bow   17

2
Hunters & Farmers in Kwale & Meru   30

3
Hunting Transformations in Kitui 1860–1939   42

Part II
The White Hunters   59

4
Class & Tradition in the Making of the Hunt   61

5
The Settler Hunters 1903–39   91

Part III
Black & White Together   111

6
Safari Hunting 1909–39   113

7
New Technologies, Changing Values   138

Contents

Part IV
Gamekeepers & Poachers

147

8
The Kenya Gamekeepers & Conservation 1895–1925 149

9
International Preservationists & the National Park Idea 1925–45 174

10
National Parks & the Poaching Crisis 1946–63 189

Conclusions & Epilogue 206

Bibliography 218
Index 243

◆◆◆◆◆◆◆◆◆◆◆◆◆◆◆◆◆◆◆◆◆◆◆◆◆◆◆◆

List of Maps & Photographs

Map
Eastern Kenya 8

Photographs

3.1 Philip Percival and Kamba Trackers, *c.* 1915 57
6.1 Vivien Percival and Colonel Roosevelt, 1909 117
6.2 Philip Percival on the Duke of Connaught's Safari, 1906 135
8.1 Archie Ritchie: Game Warden 160

Acknowledgements

Any work of history accumulates a burden of debt. But a work of oral history, requiring field research, and one such as this so long in gestation, becomes as debt encumbered as a 'Global South nation'. The extraordinary expenses of field research along with archival work have put me deep in the debt of the Social Science Research Council's Africa Committee and the American Council of Learned Societies. Small grants from the American Philosophical Society, the National Endowment for the Humanities and Texas Tech University's various research funds and a TTU Faculty Development Leave have also contributed to both conducting the field work and shorter periods of library research as well as allowing time for writing up the materials. Colleagues and staff of Texas Tech University, Old Dominion University in Virginia and the Davis Center for Historical Studies at Princeton University have afforded me the support with which to write and the stimulation of colleagues with whom I could discuss, debate and rethink my ideas.

In addition to these institutions, I have also accumulated debts to archives and libraries and their staff whose generous assistance makes these debts heartfelt. Foremost among them, the National Archives of Kenya and its Chief Archivist, Kasila Musembi, are owed an unimaginable debt. When I first began to search the archives for material from the Kenya Game Department and the Wildlife Service, I drew a near blank. Only the timely and crucial intervention of Mr Musembi and his archives staff with the Kenya Wildlife Headquarters where the materials were still stored in 1987, the transfer and quick cataloging of those materials allowed me to proceed with the research at all. My gratitude was and is inexpressible. Once the papers I needed were transferred and accessioned, the assistance of Richard Ambane and the other staff of the archives reading room was graciously and efficiently given.

Others within Kenya who were unstinting in their efforts on my behalf include the staffs of the Kenya Wildlife Service at Langata, the Wildlife Research Library in Nairobi, the librarians and staff of the British Institute in Eastern Africa, the University of Nairobi Library and the Institute of African Studies of the University of Nairobi. The Institute of African Studies and its late Director, Professor Gideon Were, as my official host and sponsor, deserve an extra payment of interest on my debt.

In Britain, the personal attention and help I received from the staff of the Public Records Office at Kew, the Official Papers Library, the School of Oriental and African Studies Library, the Royal Commonwealth Society Library and Rhodes House Library added immeasurably to my debt. I also profited from access to the photographic collections of the American Museum of Natural History in New York, although the photographs published here are previously unpublished materials from the National Archives of Kenya. The archives staff, once again deserve my highest praise and thanks.

In conducting the field research, I necessarily threw myself on the kindness of people who often were strangers to me at first. In England, David Anderson and his family have often provided me a place of welcome. In Nairobi, Caroline Agola, Celia Nyamweru, Naomi Kipury, Jane and Atieno Odhiambo and Ruth Sang and their families provided the comforts of home, including often the stimulation of their children's bright wits and warm friendship. Drs John and Grace Bennett often provided hospitality in the form of hot coffee and free medical advice. More formally, the wardens and staffs of Ufungamano House in Nairobi and London House in Mecklenburg Square, London, provided room and board during extended periods of research. In the field, the homes of the late James de Vere Allen, Maluki and Mary Mwinzi and the families of Mucee Kairanya, Joseph Mugao Kibunjia, John Nkinyangi and Steven Nyaa became the bases from which I could search out and conduct interviews in the Kwale, Kitui and Meru Districts of Eastern and Central Kenya. It should also be noted that without the research and language assistance of Mucee Kairanya, David Maore, Kalinga Mgandi and Steven Nyaa this work could never have been finished. Additional assistance with translations from Julius Kaluki, Samson Koome and Salim Mwahaga is also gratefully acknowledged. Elaine Dawson of Norfolk, Virginia, provided word processing assistance and expertise. The editors at James Currey – James himself, Douglas Johnson and Lynn Taylor – showed great patience and skill in the editing of the manuscript. My thanks are also offered to the anonymous reader for the trenchant and helpful comments.

And finally, those who are to remain blameless: those many friends and colleagues, who have read, commented, listened, advised and encouraged. This list must begin with my partner and kindest critic, Dr Anita Clair Fellman, whose love has seen me through the last decade of writing, re-writing, polishing, editing and amending the text. It continues with my ex-wife and good friend, Suzi Duffy, who bore many of the early burdens of research absences and obsessions. Even a partial list of helpful and supportive colleagues must include James de Vere Allen, David Anderson, Heike Behrend, Paul Deslandes, Phyllis Ferguson, Dan Flores, Jean Hay, Drew Isenberg, Karim Janmohammed, Aneesa Kassam, Corinne Kratz, John Lonsdale, Gregory Maddox, Maureen Malowany, Stuart Marks, M. Catherine Miller, David Newbury, Francois Ngolet, Ronald Rainger, Nigel Rothfels, Lynn M. Thomas, Robert Tignor, David and Amy Troyansky and Luise White. My apologies to those many others whose names I have omitted. Finally, to those countless and too often nameless Kenyans who made me welcome in their midst and as a guest in their homes and country, I offer my thanks for their generosity of spirit and kindness of heart.

Introduction
Hunting in Kenya

In May 1977, the government of Kenya banned all legal hunting of wildlife in its efforts to cope with a poaching crisis that was spreading across the African continent.[1] In so doing, all licensed hunting by Africans, white Kenyans, and visitors to Kenya was made illegal, ending a period of almost a century during which Kenya had become 'a sportsman's paradise'. Less obvious was the fact that for many centuries before the period of big game hunting made Kenya famous as a destination for sportsmen and trophy collectors from Europe, Asia, and America, Kenya's game-laden plains and forests had been the rich, rewarding hunting grounds of her indigenous African population. The government decree of 1977 had put an end to that as well. Although it may well be that the twenty-first century may see a restoration of limited hunting as a legal activity for licensed hunters willing to pay high prices for their trophies and their memories, the fabled era of hunting by 'great white hunters' has ended and, in a changed world, can never be resurrected. Moreover, hunting by Kenyan Africans, with or without licences, has also become largely a thing of the past. It is the purpose of this book to examine the history of hunting during Kenya's colonial era from the late nineteenth to the mid-twentieth century. The narrative is intended to illuminate the complex patterns of cultural and social conflict and interaction that emerged in the struggle to lay claim to the rights and privileges, the rewards of wealth and prestige that hunting bestowed on its successful practitioners, both black and white. In the course of this narrative the reader will encounter many different kinds of hunters and many different relationships between hunters and their prey, between human animals and the natural world.

---

[1] J. K. Mutinda, Director, Wildlife Conservation and Management Department, 'Government Ban on All Hunting of Game Animals', Wildlife Research Section WRS/PROJ/IV, 2(a).

What follows is an account of three particular kinds of hunting: hunting by Africans prior to and during the colonial era; hunting by European visitors, settlers, and others who came to Kenya from the late nineteenth century; and lastly, hunting by those whose stated mission was to preserve and protect wildlife: the gamekeepers and conservationists. In doing so, I hope to underscore three important insights into the history of hunting in colonial Kenya.

First, I will uncover the significant role that hunting played in the lives of Kenya's farmers and herders from beneath layers of denial and occultation. It will be shown that those who came to be described as farmers or peasants, herders, or 'pure' pastoralists were also inheritors of a variety of hunting practices and techniques, values, and traditions. They, as well as the country's scattered and sparse population of hunter-foragers, hunted for food, for sport, and as a regular part of their social and cultural lives. However, only the hunting done by Kenya's supposed 'pure' hunter-gatherers has received scholarly attention. The root of the problem has been the persistent undervaluation of hunting by subsistence farmers in the ethnographic and historical literature on African agricultural societies and of the role that hunting has played in producing both economic and cultural values.

Second, the colonization of Kenya in the 1890s by British imperial statesmen and soldiers, and its settlement by mostly British gentlemen and ladies, would lay the basis for the creation of new forms of hunting. The attempts to re-create on African soil, with African prey, the practices and values of nineteenth-century European hunts, complete with their class-ridden meanings and messages, will lay the basis for our examination of a distinct colonial and settler hunting practice in Kenya. The connections between hunting and imperialism's self-image and representations has recently been explored at length by David Cannadine, who underscores the role of class in the creation of that image.[2] Kenya's white hunters made a unique contribution to the hunting traditions of the twentieth century in introducing the 'big game safari'. The hunting safari developed as an organized expedition in search of big game, combining African commercial caravan organization and leadership with European ideas of the Hunt. It would become not only Kenya's distinctive contribution to twentieth-century sport hunting, it was also a truly cross-cultural or 'trans-cultural' creation of both the European hunters and those African hunters who were exploited for their labour and their knowledge, but demeaned in the process.

The big game safari promoted the image of Kenya abroad as a veritable Garden of Eden. At the same time, it created and reinforced an image of African inferiority and subordination that was at the heart of the imperial and colonial ideology. The central insight here regards the differential evaluation and conflicting images of hunting among African and European inhabitants of colonial Kenya as a potent source of political and cultural conflict between the two hunting traditions and their

[2] *Ornamentalism. How the British Saw Their Empire* (Oxford: Oxford University Press, 2001).

representatives. Beginning with the efforts to trace the roots of the hunting tradition that would be translocated to Kenya from late nineteenth-century Europe, I will try to show how various groups of white hunters, both visitors and residents, would borrow freely from their African subjects, teachers, and companions in developing the unique East African safari hunting synthesis. The heyday of this tradition in the interwar period of the 1920s and 1930s would make Kenya the best example of empire as 'a vast system of outdoor recreation for the upper classes' of Europe and America. By laying claim to the 'hunting safari' as a cultural attribute of the rich and powerful, the great white hunters would also complete the alienation of Africans from their traditional and visible practices of hunting, silencing their independent voices and turning them increasingly and tragically into the 'black poachers' of colonial imagination and this book's title.

Finally, it would fall to another group who would claim sovereignty over the world of nature and wildlife, the conservationists, to complete the transformation of African hunters into criminal poachers and to engineer their elimination from the hunting scene in Kenya. The role of conservation ideology and the emergence in Kenya of a colonial and imperial movement for the creation of national parks will provide the narrative basis for our third insight. I will argue that the ethos of game conservation for the benefit of future hunting opportunities, introduced to Kenya in the early decades of colonial rule, was gradually supplanted by an ethos of wildlife preservation in 'total sanctuaries'. This new ideal of wildlife preservation would, over time, impinge on both European and African hunting traditions in colonial Kenya. The result of this new way of thinking about wildlife and wilderness would climax in the first major colonial African anti-poaching campaign to succeed in its objectives − the elimination of poachers from a national park. It would also bring about the eventual triumph of the preservationist ideal in the creation of Kenya's postcolonial approach to hunting and wildlife, culminating in the 'total ban' on hunting in Kenya in 1977.

This is the 'master' narrative that I set out to write and that still shapes the structure of the story I tell. If it reflects a Marxian perspective in both its dialectical outlines and its emphasis on class, I make no apology for my training and commitments. However, much of the content and import of what I hoped to convey in presenting this research was changed as I learned more of the quotidian struggles of African and European hunters and conservationists to maintain and advance their own complex understanding of the proper relationship of hunters to prey, of lords and masters to peasants and workers, and of men and women to both the natural world they found and the social world they created through that struggle. In the end, I believe the reader will find that the outlines of a dialectical 'master narrative' have left ample room for presenting the rich diversity of the experience of hunting in colonial Kenya.[3]

---

[3] For a statement of the fallen status of master or universal narratives, see Steven Feierman, 'Africa in History', in *After Colonialism*, ed. Gyan Prakash (Princeton: Princeton University Press, 1995), 40–65.

Hunting and gender

Despite the diversity of hunting experience, there is one area in which the image of hunting, both African and white, has remained singular: the area of gender. This book is about male hunting, because, with few exceptions that will be examined in the text, I see hunting in Kenya to have been a male activity from which the participation of women was restricted or forbidden. This is a brash statement to make in the current context of concern over the significance of gender in both the content and analysis of historical phenomena such as imperialism and colonialism, so close to the heart of this study. Therefore let me explain why women play a marginal role in this study and why I do not focus on hunting as constitutive of male identity.

When I first undertook the research on hunting, the idea that men and not women hunted was virtually axiomatic. Despite some exceptions among the European nobility and Kenya's settler elite, where class may have trumped gender and 'ladies' were permitted to participate in hunting organized by men of their class, such as fox hunts and shooting parties, women's place was not in the hunting field. And the received knowledge from African ethnography at that time similarly excluded 'women, especially women in hunting-gathering societies', from the study of hunting.[4] As my research progressed, I began to examine the assumptions behind this generalization, and in my interviews and readings searched out counter instances of women with weapons in pursuit of game. My failure to find this evidence in any substantial or probative amounts is due to several causes.

First, it may have to do with the failures inherent in my field research method. I employed only male assistants, whose responsibilities included arranging interviews with individuals knowledgeable in local history and with reputations for hunting. Moreover, I never pressed them to gender my sample of interview subjects. This may have reflected both the assumptions and biases of the assistants and my own failure to question them or to ask questions that might have elicited information on hunting by women. It certainly did reflect the assumptions of the informants we did select. Questions about the role of women in hunting among African hunting and farming communities were met with responses that ranged from the incredulous to the derisive. In one case, when the wife of a hunter had been a party to an interview and was drawn in with a question regarding her participation in the hunt, the response, after the laughter stopped, was to say that her role began when the prey was to be prepared for the pot and cooked.[5] Recent studies of the relationship between women and hunting among 'pure' hunter-gatherers like the San (Basarwa) of southern Africa as well as the Aka and Bambuti of the

[4] A. Estioko-Griffin and P. Bion Griffin, 'Woman the Hunter: The Agta', in *Woman the Gatherer*, ed. Frances Dahlberg (New Haven: Yale University Press, 1981), 121.
[5] Interview B/2 Kitonga Kusewa, 14 April 1987.

Congo basin[6] were more encouraging of finding evidence than for the farmer-hunters. Unfortunately, my failure to locate any existing communities of the Waata hunter-gatherers in eastern Kenya, who had suffered an ethnocidal assault in the 1950s, left me at the mercy of previous observers of these communities and hunting fellowships. And these sources were silent on any roles that women had played in the Waata hunt.[7] Thus, either through my fault as researcher or through the bias of my oral and other sources, I discovered no evidence of hunting by Kenyan African women.

One partial exception to this statement might be made. In Meru district, I did obtain testimony that women among the Tharaka, a group of recently settled hunter-farmers, would 'trap birds with string' and might take up weapons to defend their fields and crops from raiders such as rodents or baboons (but not elephants). This would involve their chasing them and killing them when possible. However, both in the understanding of the informant and of the researcher, this did not constitute real hunting. Neither in the sense of hunting large dangerous animals nor as the organized pursuit of game for food or sport did the killing of small animals by women add up to a hunt. It was conceived of as an outgrowth of the work of cultivation, more akin to weeding and chasing away birds and pests, than to hunting *per se*.[8] Even this evidence was sparse and tended to confirm the exclusion of women from both small local hunting parties and the larger expeditions.

A second cause of the failure to examine the role of women in hunting is based on the unquestionable male bias of the writers on white hunting examined in the representation of the white hunting tradition as it developed in Europe and particularly Britain and as it was re-created in colonial Kenya. When women are found in the hunting fields, the clear subtext is that these were exceptional, even aberrational women in colonial society. Thus we find that, when Isak Dinesen (Baroness Karen Blixen) or Beryl Markham wrote of their own hunting experience, it is often to

---

[6] E.g. Megan Biesele, *Women Like Meat* (Johannesburg: Witswatersrand University Press, 1993); and Susan Kent, 'Cross-cultural Perceptions of Farmers as Hunters and the Value of Meat', in *Farmers as Hunters*, ed. Susan Kent. (Cambridge: Cambridge University Press, 1989). Susan Kent (personal communications on numerous occasions between 1992 and 2003) provided valuable information on the San/Basarwa. On the 'pygmy' female hunters, see A. Noss and B. Hewlett, 'The Contexts of Female Hunting in Central Africa', *American Anthropologist* 103, 4 (2001), 1024–41; and R. Bailey and R. Aunger, Jr., 'Net Hunters vs. Archers: Variations in Women's Subsistence Strategies in the Ituri Forest', *Human Ecology* 17, 3 (1989), 273–98. Despite these efforts, the research record on women as hunters remains sparse.

[7] See below Chapters 1 and 10 on Waata hunting and poaching.

[8] Interview C/7 John Livingston Mate, 11 September 1987. A suggestive exception is the role of women in net hunting among the Bambuti of the Ituri forest in eastern Congo – suggestive because while net hunting is significant, there is still a prohibition against women using lethal weapons, e.g. bows and arrows. Bailey and Aunger, 'Net Hunters'; and Colin Turnbull, *The Forest People* (New York: Simon and Schuster, 1962), 94–108. For statements on the current state of knowledge on women in hunting-foraging societies, see entries on Africa and gender relations in Richard Lee and Richard Daly, eds, *The Cambridge Encyclopedia of Hunters and Gatherers* (Cambridge: Cambridge University Press, 1999).

underline their distance and marginality within the settler community. Not infrequently, hunting by women was enough of a breach of hunting expectations and etiquette to warrant being hidden, as in the case of the hunting by Osa Johnson of the American wildlife film production team.[9] Even a casual acquaintance with the fictional and descriptive writings of hunters like Ernest Hemingway and Robert Ruark will reveal a deep-seated antipathy to women and a veneration of the hunt as a proof of manliness and male dominance. Indeed, the 'accidental' death of Hemingway's Francis Macomber is eloquent testimony to the hostility of the great white hunters and their professional white hunter guides to the presence of women on safari. More important than the blatant exclusion and demeaning of the place of women in the masculine hunting fields of the Kenyan safari, is the more ominous silence of most firsthand sources, such as the travel and hunting accounts, on any possible contributions of women to the hunt beyond the encouragement and admiration they might offer the men.[10]

The third and final explanation for the absence of a sustained treatment of women or gender issues cannot be blamed on my sources or methods, but lies in my desire to focus attention on issues of class as the key determinant of both African hunting practice and the relations between African and white hunting as it developed in the colonial context. I do briefly examine the constitutive role of hunting in the gender education and socialization of Kenyan boys and frequently underscore the attitudes of machismo and hyper-masculinity displayed by the white hunters. But I have chosen to highlight the class socialization and attitudes of privilege and entitlement as being more central to the history of struggle over hunting in colonial Kenya than questions of gender construction or relations. This is not to underplay the importance of gender in the construction of the colonial world, as has been usefully explored by other authors who have had gender as their focus.[11] Read together, our work can convey the complex roles of class and gender in the cultural practices of modern colonial societies.

---

[9] Isak Dinesen, *Out of Africa and Shadows on the Grass* (New York: Vintage, 1985); Beryl Markham, *West with the Night* (Boston: Houghton Mifflin, 1942). On Osa Johnson, see below, pp. 142–3.

[10] See below, on Hemingway, pp. 128–30, especially 129–30, on the role of women in his fictional hunting accounts. On Robert Ruark, see below, p. 136. For a survey of the early hunting and travel literature, see Chapter 4.

[11] Among the most prominent recent works on gender and colonialism in Africa and globally, see J. Allman, S. Geiger and N. Musoke, eds, *Women in African Colonial Histories* (Blooming-ton: Indiana University Press, 2002); A. Burton, ed. *Gender, Sexuality and Colonial Modernities* (London: Routledge, 1999); B. Bush, *Imperialism, Race and Resistance: Africa and Britain, 1919–1945* (London: Routledge, 1999); Catherine Coquery-Vidrovitch, *African Women: A Modern History* (Boulder: Westview Press, 1997); Clare Midgley, ed. *Gender and Imperialism* (New York: Manchester University Press, 1998); and R. Pierson and N. Chaudhuri, eds, *Nation, Empire, Colony: Historicizing Gender and Race* (Bloomington, Indiana University Press, 1998).

The outline of hunting history

In Part I, we will reconstruct the history of African hunting in a cross section of the eastern region of what would become colonial Kenya. Kwale, Kitui, and Meru districts were selected for this study for three reasons. First, they are contiguous, running in a roughly north–south direction and extending from the eastern slopes of Mt. Kenya, the historical centre of the country, to the Indian Ocean coast and the Tanzanian border. They would come under colonial control at approximately the same time, had each experienced prior contact with coastal trade and influence, and were inhabited principally by Bantu-speaking farmers, who kept some cattle and small stock and, most importantly, hunted to supplement their agro-pastoral activities. It was expected that this would make them a useful 'controlled comparison', through which certain variables could be isolated and held constant while others could be examined for their impact on the divergent courses that the three districts took both before and under colonial rule. Second, the region was chosen because a national park or major game reserve is located within each of the districts. The parks vary in their importance and influence on the history of the district, with the Shimba Hills National Park in Kwale district created after the colonial era with which we are concerned. The importance for this study of the presence of the parks in each district is that it attests to the fact that game animals were present in numbers worth preservation throughout the 65-year colonial period and beyond. The destruction of wildlife, then, would not become a limiting factor in the comparison we wish to make over the entire period, including local hunter responses to the presence of these sanctuaries. Finally, the three districts were selected for the practical reason of minimizing the diversity of languages and allowing the author to make use of his limited linguistic skills in Bantu languages.

The first chapter examines what I argue is a core hunting tradition and technique introduced to Kenya by hunter-foragers known as Waata, or Waliangulu. They are believed to have originated among non-Bantu speakers of the northern Kenyan, Somali, and Ethiopian borderlands, where they can still be found. Within Kenya, these bow-and-arrow hunters would themselves never be very numerous, but would see their hunting techniques adapted by the neighbouring Bantu-speaking farmers, including the various Mijikenda peoples, the Akamba, Tharaka, and the Wameru, all living to the south and west of the Waata homelands. The following chapter, 'Hunters and Farmers in Kwale and Meru', focuses on the Digo, Duruma, Meru, and Tharaka hunters of those two districts, who adopted and adapted the Waata hunting kit and grafted it onto their own economic and cultural practices as subsistence hunters and farmers. Finally, Chapter 3 will examine in depth the transformation of this subsistence hunting praxis, first under the influence of the ivory trade with the Kenyan coast, and then with the intrusion of European colonial control. The emergence of long-distance

7

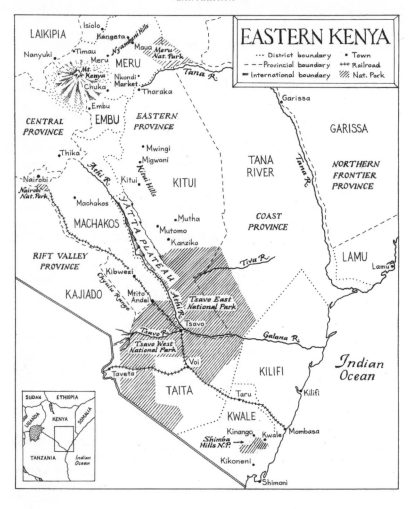

Map 1 *Eastern Kenya* (drawn by Amy Troyansky)

trade coincided with the emergence of long-distance, specialized, elephant hunting, especially among the Kamba people of Kitui district. Originally elephants were hunted for food as well as for their tusks, then increasingly for their ivory only. This hunting transition closes Part I and provides the groundwork for our examination of the introduction of European and particularly British hunting culture in Part II, The White Hunters.

Part II begins with Chapter 4's survey of the long history of British hunting as it developed out of the peculiar class system of medieval and early modern English society. It continues with a prosopographic examination of the European hunters who came to Kenya in the late nineteenth century as bearers of this tradition, introducing what I refer to as 'Imperial Hunting'. This includes those who came solely to hunt and continues with those who hunted as a corollary to their activities as explorers, colonial administrators, police, and soldiers. Chapter 5 continues the story of the imperial hunt with an examination of the first generation of permanent settlers, some of whom came to Kenya to hunt, others to farm. Regardless of their social standing, 'many British settlers ... sought to recreate a full-scale replica of the elaborately graded social hierarchy they had left behind at home'.[12] This replica included, as we will see, a wide variety of hunting activities from 'riding to hounds' and the weekend 'shooting party' to the killing of 'vermin' in protection of property.

Part III examines the processes by which African and imperial hunting traditions interacted and fused into a new 'transcultural' entity: the hunting safari.[13] The roots of the hunting safari can be dated back over a millennium to the trading safari of African, Arab, and Swahili merchants. This caravan commerce, especially in ivory, which linked coast and hinterland, was briefly examined in Chapter 3. In Chapter 6, 'Safari Hunting', the processes of grafting the European hunting ethos onto these commercial roots is examined as a wide variety of European hunters seek and obtain the guidance and organizational assistance of African, Arab, Swahili, and white settlers and officials in mounting their hunting expeditions. Variations of the early hunting safari, exemplified by Theodore Roosevelt's paradigmatic excursion of 1909, are examined, including the safaris of scientific specimen collectors, royal and aristocratic 'champagne' adventurers, and the celebrity literary notables. By the 1930s, the safari had become an international institution, the most glamorous and glittering example of empire as a system of outdoor recreation for the upper classes. Chapter 7 introduces the professionalization of the hunting safari during the 1920s and 1930s that sees the emergence of the figure of the Professional White Hunter. It continues the story with a discussion of some of the technological changes, such as automotive and air transport and the use of lightweight cameras, that will lead to the increasing professionalization and democratization of the hunting safari.

Part IV, Gamekeepers and Poachers, brings the story of hunting

---

[12] Cannadine, *Ornamentalism*, 14.

[13] See M. L. Pratt, *Imperial Eyes* (London: Routledge, 1992), 1–11, for an explication of this concept.

located within each of the districts of colonial Kenya to a dramatic climax. Beginning with an examination of the early history of game keeping and conservation in Kenya in Chapter 8, it narrates the little known story of Kenya's contribution to international conservation efforts between the wars in Chapter 9. The culmination of both local and international conservation efforts came with the establishment of Kenya's first national parks and the triumph of a new environmental ideal of wildlife preservation, explored in Chapter 10. Both Africans and whites – settlers, visitors, and professionals – would find their hunting practices, ideas, and ideals challenged. During the last decade of the colonial era, those who would suffer the first onslaught of the new conservation policies would be Kenya's original hunters, the Waata, and their most successful followers, the Kamba of Kitui district. This confrontation between hunters and hunters-turned-conservationists in Kenya's Tsavo National Park would bring the age-old practices of elephant hunting in eastern Kenya to an end, and sound the death knell of the hunting safari in soon-to-be independent Kenya.

Hunting and historiography

While the struggle between Africans and settlers over land has captured the attention of Kenya's historians for three generations, the continuing struggle over the control of animals, especially wildlife, has been largely ignored. With the exception of romantic studies of the great white hunters, such as Errol Trzebinski's biography of Denys Finch Hatton, there are few, if any, serious historical or sociological monographs examining either African hunters or the whites and Africans who devoted themselves to hunting or game conservation.[14] To my knowledge, this is the first study to examine the history of hunting and wildlife conservation in Kenya that looks at both white and African hunters and gamekeepers.

Before I claim an undeserved precedence, I should point out that this study inherits a valuable intellectual debt from several contemporary Africanist scholars. I include this acknowledgement of debt here rather than in the formal acknowledgements because I believe that each of these scholars has been seminal, not just for this work, but in significantly reshaping the fields of African and imperial cultural and environmental history. Their contributions must be acknowledged in order to place my own intended contributions in a clear framework.

John MacKenzie's *The Empire of Nature*, looks seriously at the history of hunting in Africa and India and offers a compelling overview of the

---

[14] Two doctoral dissertations pioneered the study of East African game conservation: Nora Kelly, 'In Wildest Africa: The Preservation of Game in Kenya, 1895–1933', Ph.D. dissertation, Simon Fraser University, 1978; and Thomas Ofcansky, 'A History of Game Preservation in British East Africa, 1895–1963', Ph.D. dissertation, University of West Virginia, 1981. They have recently been joined by Thomas Ofcansky's popularized version of his thesis, *Paradise Lost: A History of Game Conservation in East Africa* (Morgantown: West Virginia University Press, 2002).

relationship between hunting and imperialism from which I have benefited immensely. Moreover, his book is 'devoted to establishing the manner in which the African relationship with game was modified or destroyed by the extension of white settlement and imperial conquest'.[15] In addition, his many articles and chapters on hunting and other aspects of imperialism and popular culture set a high standard and blazed numerous trails that appear to me to lead in the direction of a class-based analysis of imperialism. MacKenzie's ideas have played a crucial role in influencing my thinking on the relationship between hunting and empire and my enthusiasm for a class-based study of colonial hunting. *The Empire of Nature* provides a broad canvas, stretching as it does over the British Empire from Bangladesh to Zimbabwe. It is necessarily thin on any one case and its principal African examples, drawn from southern Africa and especially Zimbabwe, where MacKenzie's own studies were focused, gives short shrift to Kenya. I believe that Kenya is the most significant case for the study of the workings of class-consciousness and class conflict in the development of colonial hunting as a result of the attraction of the wealthy and highborn to Kenya's 'sportsmen's paradise'. It also differs in important ways from southern Africa due to the development in Kenya of a corps of professional hunters and guides and in the absence of an independent local dynamic towards conservation.[16]

Stuart Marks's earliest work focused on Zambian hunters and game-keepers and his continuing work on wildlife conservation set a high standard for both social scientists and historians who would venture into African hunting grounds.[17] He also shared with me his insights into the efforts of both foreign white hunters and, later, foreign white conserva-tionists in laying claim to ownership of animals. I believe with him that the proprietary attitudes displayed, particularly by those exemplars of class privilege who dominate these callings, have been a determining factor in the development of both colonial (and postcolonial) hunting and inter-national conservationism. Marks's own primary concern with ecology and conservation are different from my focus on the history of hunting and lead to significant differences in our use of evidence and selection of subjects. Yet I hope that what follows will demonstrate our shared concerns as well as meeting the high standards and ideals exemplified by Stuart Marks's work.

In addition to the studies of hunting that have shaped my thinking, the literature on wildlife conservation has also had a profound effect in moulding this work. Although I began this study with my attention very

---

[15] John M. MacKenzie, *The Empire of Nature: Hunting, Conservation and the British Empire* (Manchester and New York: Manchester University Press, 1988), 81. See also his edited volume, *Imperialism and the Natural World* (Manchester: Manchester University Press, 1990) and refer to the bibliography for some of his relevant articles and chapters.

[16] See below, pp. 131–6, on the importance of 'professional white hunters' and Chapters 8 and 9 on Kenya's impact on the development of international conservation.

[17] See Stuart Marks, *Large Mammals and a Brave People. Subsistence Hunters in Zambia* (Seattle and London: University of Washington Press, 1976); and *The Imperial Lion. Human Dimensions of Wildlife Management in Central Africa* (Boulder: Westview, 1983).

firmly on the history of hunting, I soon realized that it could not be done without consideration of the history of conservation in Africa. Here I owe much to David Anderson, whose pioneering work with Richard Grove on African conservation history helped me to understand something about the place of both hunting and wildlife conservation in the context of colonial environmental history.[18] His professional encouragement of my work and sympathetic hearing of my views have also been an unmitigated advantage to me. In the course of our friendship and scholarly exchanges, I also became aware of how his energy and commitment to scholarship have continually signalled new directions in the study of African history. His intelligence and leadership in the field of African history have reshaped the social, political, environmental, and religious history of Kenya, eastern Africa, and beyond.

On the other hand, it is important to state here that this study is neither an environmental history of Kenya nor a history of wildlife conservation. It attempts to examine efforts at imposing conservation of wildlife and wilderness only to the degree that those efforts constrained and conditioned the hunting of that wildlife by Africans, Europeans, and others in pursuit of Kenyan game. Nevertheless, since this work was begun there have been several important environmental and conservation histories that have caused me to rethink my own researches while contributing supporting evidence for my assertions about the struggle over nature and wildlife that I have placed at the centre of my study. I have in mind the work of Terence Ranger and Roderick Neumann in examining the exclusion of Africans from the process of establishing conservation programmes and, in particular, their expulsion from national parks. Ranger especially shows how the Africans who had lived and worked within the boundaries of what would become the Matobo National Park in Southern Rhodesia (Zimbabwe) were expelled and excluded by the colonial 'reinvention of nature'. Ranger, coming from a decades-long study of African resistance movements, is keenly aware of the social and political struggles over land and conservation that were provoked by the creation and maintenance of the Matobo hills as a national park.[19]

The geographer Roderick Neumann has written by far the best account of the interplay of imperial conservation ideologies and local conservation efforts in his case study of Tanganyika wildlife conservation efforts and national park policy in his book, *Imposing Wilderness*.[20] Once again the role of the colonial and imperial state in excluding Africans from the formulation

---

[18] D. Anderson and R. Grove, eds, *Conservation in Africa: Peoples, Policies and Practice* (Cambridge: Cambridge University Press, 1987). For Anderson's articles on conservation in Kenya, see the bibliography in this volume.

[19] Terence Ranger, *Voices from the Rocks* (Oxford, James Currey, 1999), 4 and 1–5 *passim*. See also his article, 'Whose Heritage? The Case of the Matobo National Park', *Journal of Southern African Studies* 15, 2 (1989), 217–49.

[20] Roderick Neumann, *Imposing Wilderness* (Berkeley: University of California Press, 1998). In addition, the recent book by Dan Brockington, *Fortress Conservation* (Oxford: James Currey, 2002) offers a picture of the contemporary struggle over the Mkomazi Game Reserve in Tanzania with some historical background, of special interest because of Mkomazi's location along Tanzania's border adjacent to Kenya's Tsavo West National Park.

or implementation of conservation policy, both locally and at the metropolitan and international levels, helps underscore the class- and race-biased nature of what was supposedly a scientific and value-free process. His approach differs from mine only in not considering the importance of local white settler and hunter opinion in the formulation of these policies over time. On the other hand, in his essay, 'Dukes, Earls and Ersatz Edens: Aristocratic Nature Preservationists in Colonial Africa', Neumann's caustic examination of the class biases of Britain's leading conservationists gives strong support to my treatment of the Kenyan case I examine in Chapter 9. This research, then, inherits a debt from these and other scholars who have contributed to the convergence of the streams of imperial history, environmental history, and African social and political history. I hope I can ride the wave this work has generated in the pages that follow.

By focusing resolutely on the socially constructed meanings of the hunting of game animals and wildlife preservation among black and white hunters and gamekeepers, I hope to contribute to our understanding of the place of wildlife in the world and our relationship to it. The history of social and political conflict in colonial Kenya has frequently focused exclusively on struggles to answer the question of who owns Kenya's land and its products, including domesticated animals. I would add to this view the idea that it is the ownership of Kenya's wild animals and their contributions to the construction of a good life which are at the root of an equally important struggle to define what it has meant to be Kenyan, what it meant to be male, and what it continues to mean to be 'civilized' in modern Kenya.

Part I

The African Hunters

When a baby boy is born he doesn't go out until after some days. When he is taken out for the first time, a small bow and arrow are made for him and he is carried out and shown a bow and arrow, a jembe [hoe] and a panga [machete]. The mother says: 'a man digs, a man hunts animals'. He is shown what the work of men is.

Nganyawa Mwijo, age 59
of Kinango, Kwale District

One

♦♦♦♦♦♦♦♦♦♦♦♦♦♦♦♦♦♦♦♦♦♦♦

Kenya's People of the Bow

Hunting, along with foraging, is certainly humankind's oldest profession. This being so, Kenya, located in the East African corridor generally agreed to be the earliest home to humans, is the likely candidate for the honour of being the site of the world's first human hunting communities. Moreover, in modern times, Kenya has become a sportsman's paradise, drawing adventurous men and women in search of game that has turned the Kenyan countryside into perhaps the best-known landscape for the pursuit of both humanity's oldest profession and the world's premier sport. In a word, Kenya is among the most ancient and most favoured of 'happy hunting grounds' in the world.

Yet, despite Kenya's primacy as a hunting ground, Kenya's historians and ethnologists have seriously neglected the study of the history of hunting in Kenya. With the partial exception of the study of the small and scattered bands of hunter-foragers variously called Dorobo, Okiek, Boni, and Dahalo, little has been written about the hunting practices, beliefs, and traditions of even the surviving 'Stone Age' hunters. Far less still has been written about those Kenyans who like the great majority of African cultivators and pastoralists have continued to hunt down to very recent times (and, in some cases, still continue clandestinely).[1]

This lacuna seems especially grievous during Kenya's colonial era when the British East African Protectorate of Kenya and neighbouring Uganda

[1] See Michael Kenny, 'A Mirror in the Forest', *Africa* 51, 1 (1981), 477–95; and Corinne Kratz, 'Are the Okiek Really Masai? or Kipsigis? or Kikuyu?' unpublished paper, African Studies Association, Baltimore, MD, November 1978, for ethnological work on the Dorobo and Okiek; for historians, Roger van Zwanenberg, 'Dorobo Hunting and Gathering: A Way of Life or a Mode of Production?' *African Economic History* 2 (1976), 12–24. In contrast, his *Economic History of Kenya and Uganda*, with Ann King (Nairobi: East African Publishing House, 1975), makes no mention of the role of hunting in the economic life of Kenya. Recently, Martin Walsh has postulated the existence of a previously undocumented hunter-gatherer group. See his 'The Degere: Forgotten Hunter-gatherers of the East African Coast', *Cambridge Anthropology* 14, 3 (1990), 68–81.

and Tanganyika emerged as the leading destination for international sportsmen seeking 'big game'. The hunting exploits of European, American, and Kenyan-born whites, such as Joseph Thomson and Teddy Roosevelt, Ernest Hemingway and Robert Ruark, A. Blayney Percival and J. A. Hunter, received international attention as autobiographical accounts and works of fiction made regular appearances on the world's bookshelves.[2] Moreover, hunting by Kenyan Africans as well as by whites became an important element in colonial politics. The struggles over the definition and control of hunting and the products and revenues which it yielded may be key to understanding the contests for power that went on for seven decades between settlers, officials, and Africans. Hunting, second only to the struggle over land, was central to the dynamics of the cultural confrontation of colonial society in Kenya.

The earliest hunters

The first African hunters in Kenya were our prehistoric, Stone Age ancestors. However, the examination of the history and hunting traditions of these earliest of hunters takes us back further than we need to go. We might more properly begin with the emergence of a hunting tradition that is directly ancestral to the tradition of hunting still practised in modern East Africa. Even this will take us back two thousand years when evidence of hunting by Africans can be found in the elephant ivory that was being exported from the coastal regions of East Africa to Asia and the Mediterranean. *The Periplus of the Erythrean Sea* testifies to 'a great quantity of ivory' being the principal export of Rhapta, a coastal emporium, by early in the second century.[3] Moreover, the possibility of an even earlier origin of elephant hunting is suggested by the recent undersea archaeological find of ivory among the cargo of Egyptian vessels plying the eastern Mediterranean fourteen centuries before the evidence of the *Periplus*.[4] The clear implication of this is that the hunting of big game, and there is none bigger than the African elephant, was established behind the Azanian coast well before the arrival of Bantu-speaking, iron-working cultivators.[5] It is my

---

[2] E.g. Joseph Thomson, *Through Masai Land* (London: Frank Cass, 1968 [1885]); Theodore Roosevelt, *African Game Trails: An Account of the African Wanderings of an American Hunter-Naturalist* (New York: Charles Scribner's Sons, 1910); Ernest Hemingway, *Green Hills of Africa* (New York: Charles Scribner's Sons, 1935); and Robert Ruark, *Horn of the Hunter* (Garden City, NY: Doubleday, 1953), and his *Use Enough Gun [On Hunting Big Game]* (London: Corgi Books, 1969 [1967]); A. Blayney Percival, *A Game Ranger's Notebook* (London: Nisbet, 1924), and *A Game Ranger on Safari* (London: Nisbet, 1928); J. A. Hunter, *Hunter* (London: Hamish Hamilton, 1952). The Book of the Month Club selected Hunter's autobiography in 1952, guaranteeing it a large North American readership.

[3] G. Mathew, 'The Coast', in *History of East Africa*, vol. 1, ed. R. Oliver and G. Mathew (Oxford: Clarendon, 1963), 94–5.

[4] George F. Bass, 'Oldest Known Shipwreck Reveals Treasures of the Bronze Age', *National Geographic* 172 (December 1987), 722, 726–7.

[5] Cf. Nora Kelly, 'In Wildest Africa: The Preservation of Game in Kenya, 1895–1933', unpublished Ph.D. dissertation, Simon Fraser University, 1978, 15–16. In recent decades,

contention that the early Kushitic-speaking inhabitants of Azania, the antecedents of the contemporary Dahalo and Waata in Kenya, were the founders of a hunting tradition using iron-tipped and poisoned arrows and long bows, which has come down to the twentieth century in a 'pure' form among coastal hunter-gatherers. Moreover, this tradition would pass from the pre-Bantu Kushitic populations to later-arriving Bantu cultivators and remain the primary technique for the hunting of large game, particularly elephant, until this century.[6]

Ubiquity of hunting

The tradition of bow-and-arrow hunting found in eastern Kenya is not the only one found among East African peoples in modern times, but it appears to me to be distinct from the others. Other methods of hunting were also used as well as other weapons such as catapults, knives, spears, nets, gins, snares, and pits, all of which can be found among the different hunters of the region. The same arsenal can also be found among the Embu and Kikuyu to the west, the Turkana, Samburu, and Boran to the north, the Somali, Pokomo, and Swahili to the northeast. Nonetheless, among the Mijikenda peoples, the Kamba and the Meru, I believe we can see the clearest cases of the development and integration of the early bow-and-arrow hunting tradition into the cultures of modern Kenyan peoples. However, I also believe it would be a mistake to study the hunting traditions of modern Kenyan Africans as a series of synchronic case studies, a catalogue of the hunting practices of each putatively distinct 'ethnic group'. To divide hunting by tribe and speak of Kamba or Giriama hunting as opposed to Nandi or Maasai hunting would blur fundamental distinctions and exaggerate differences which have had only minor significance in the history of hunting and its role in shaping the African societies and their experience of European colonial rule.[7]

---

[5] (contd) the ancient term Azania has come to be used synonymously with the East African or Swahili coast.

[6] The *Periplus* reports the importation of iron into East Africa, which, as it was not used for hoe blades, seems likely to have been used in the crafting of arrowheads and spear blades for use in hunting and warfare. See Mathew, 'Coast', 94–5. It would appear that smaller game, especially dik-dik, was also hunted by early (first millennium AD) peoples, as evidenced by bone collections made by the archaeologist Mark Horton (personal communication, 6 February 1987) in his excavations at Shanga.

[7] The colonial creation of tribal boundaries and the generation of so much of the primary data, both written and oral, within a tribe-based matrix have led many researchers, including this one, to lapse into thinking in these colonially generated and postcolonially perpetuated modes. The very organization of the archives by ethnically based district and provincial files makes the reproduction of the tribal landscape appear natural and logical. The evidence comes to us pre-packaged in units called, for instance, 'Kamba' or 'Kitui District', and it is necessary for the researcher or analyst to unpack these received ideas and images. The perspective I will attempt here is a regional one encompassing a range of ethnic groups in interaction. It is hoped that this will give a more dynamic and a more accurate understanding of the phenomenon of hunting in Kenya. For an excellent example of a regional approach, see Charles Ambler, *Kenyan Communities in the Age of Imperialism* (New

It can be said without fear of contradiction that all of the peoples of Kenya practised some kind of hunting. Although the role that hunting played in the provision of basic food items or in the formation of social values varied enormously from society to society, every one of them hunted to some degree or other prior to the colonial conquest. Until the mid-twentieth century hunting was as ubiquitous among Kenya's African communities as it would become among its European residents and visitors. Despite the universality of African hunting, the view was generally accepted among European observers of Kenyan societies that only the 'pure' hunter-foragers, like the Dorobo, hunted as part of their culture and economy. Europeans were either blinded by their own cultural baggage to hunting by farmers or herders or else came to view it as aberrant, even criminal, behaviour by lazy African men who should have been tending fields or herds.

There appear to be several reasons for the European view that African farmers were not hunters. Chief among these is the European prejudice against peasants. The early colonial administrators and settlers came from a society in which hunting had been a class-biased and exclusively elite preoccupation for centuries. The aristocratic monopoly of legal hunting and the emergence of an illegal poaching culture date back to the Middle Ages, with 'poaching' by peasants prohibited by law and harshly punished since at least the early eighteenth century.[8] As we will see, the prohibition of peasant hunting early in the colonial era forced Africans to hunt in secret and blinded the observers of African life, including colonial ethnographers, to the ubiquity of the practice.

Some African peoples also denied their interest in hunting and game meat for their own ideological reasons. Although some of Kenya's people, such as the Kikuyu of central Kenya, profess a distaste for game meat and claim to prefer the meat of their domesticated animals, hunting remained an important element in the socialization of boys and young men, a central aspect in the definition of self and a motif in the folklore and traditions of many peoples. I believe it also remained a frequent, if clandestine, practice well into the colonial era for rural people.[9]

---

[7] (contd) Haven: Yale University Press, 1988).

[8] For the history of poaching in England, see Charles Chenevix Trench, *The Poacher and the Squire. A History of Poaching and Game Preservation in England* (London: Longman, 1967); and Barbara A. Hanawalt, 'Men's Games, King's Deer: Poaching in Medieval England', *Journal of Medieval and Renaissance Studies* 18, 2 (1988), 175–93. For the suppression of peasant poaching, see E. P. Thompson, *Whigs and Hunters. The Origin of the Black Act* (London: Allen Lane, 1975); and P. B. Munsche, *Gentlemen and Poachers: The English Game Laws, 1671–1831* (Cambridge: Cambridge University Press, 1981).

[9] For the Kikuyu, see W. S. and K. Routledge, *With a Prehistoric People* (London: Frank Cass, 1968 [1910]), 49. For other supposed non-hunting people like the western Kenya Luo, E. S. Atieno Odhiambo, personal communication. In a general way, an examination of colonial ethnographies shows little concern with hunting in the chapters or sections on traditional economy or customs. This negative impression is belied by the regular inclusion of descriptions of hunting weapons and traps, snares, and devices in chapters on material culture and technology. Frequent references to hunting parties and disputes over hunting dogs or division of game in the early migration and settlement accounts are also recorded in the colonial ethnographies.

Among Kenyan farmers, hunting for food was a significant element in their economic activity, providing important protein supplements to the otherwise heavily starchy diet. However, food was only one reason farmers hunted. In defence of crops, property or life, many animals from bush pigs and duiker to lion, leopard, and elephant were frequently chased from the fields and hunted in the bush. In pursuit of wealth and status, large game and small were hunted for skins, horn, teeth, and other trophies. Tusks, teeth, horn, and hides were used in clothing, medicine, and ritual or traded for other items of value. It is rare indeed to find today a mature adult African male who cannot distinguish the taste of various game meats, a food of choice among sophisticated patrons of contemporary Nairobi restaurants.

Even more contentious and clouded by ideological considerations are the treatments of hunting by Kenya's 'pure' pastoralists such as the Maasai. The Maasai, Samburu, and other so-called cattle complex peoples of Kenya are often cited as being averse to eating game meat. They assert that killing and eating wild animals will bring misfortune to themselves and disaster to their herds of domestic stock of cattle and goats, and they believe that only cattleless and hapless people, like the Dorobo, will eat wild animals regularly. The only hunting regularly admitted and incorporated into the central images and representations of pastoral identity is the pursuit of lions that have raided Maasai cattle herds or become man-eaters. They are pursued and killed by young warriors (*moran*) as part of the rites of passage into manhood, requiring the single-handed and courageous confronting of a dangerous enemy. This has done much to contribute to the heroic image and sense of 'being Maasai' among the Maa-speaking herders, as has their contempt for peasant cultivators, which the Maasai and other Kenyan pastoralists share with their European colonialist interpreters.[10]

It is necessary to add a corrective to this overly heroic and ideologically tinged image of the East African 'pure pastoralist', at least as far as his hunting activities go. The persistence of hunting as a food-producing economic activity has been well established among students of East African pastoralism.[11] Even more telling are the comments of observers like the wildlife photographer and naturalist, Hugo van Lawick, which directly challenge the pastoral Maasai ideology: 'The Maasai tribe have traditionally tolerated wild animals. However, contrary to popular belief, they do occasionally eat wild animals and do not survive solely on the milk and blood of their cattle.'[12]

There is little question that historically, during periods of ecological crisis, Maasai and other cattle herders 'took to the bush' and 'became

[10] See Tom Spear and Richard Waller, eds, *Being Maasai* (London: James Currey, 1993), 4–6.
[11] John Lamphear, 'The Persistence of Hunting and Gathering in a "Pastoral" World', *SUGIA* 7, 2 (1986), 227–65. See the papers by Neal Sobania, David Anderson, and Richard Waller presented at the African Studies Association Annual Meeting, Chicago, IL, 27–31 October 1988 for studies of the environmental influences on Kenyan pastoralism, including the role of hunting in pastoral survival strategies.
[12] H. van Lawick, *Among Predators and Prey* (San Francisco: Sierra Club Books, 1986), 142.

Dorobo',[13] as a survival strategy. Hunting as an adaptive mechanism in times of drought-induced famine is widely attested in eastern Kenya among both settled and pastoral communities.[14] Moreover, the cyclical pressures that produce seasonal dispersal of cattle herds under the care and supervision of the young warrior age-sets create a situation among the 'pure' pastoralists in which wild animals must be sought for meat in order to prevent the herdsmen from 'dipping into capital' by killing their livestock during the wet season dispersal.[15] In such situations, the killing of antelope, preferably the cow-like eland, by the young warrior herdsmen must be understood as something more than an occasional, regrettable deviation from high pastoral standards; it becomes a persistent element of the pastoral complex.

In addition to the hunt as a source of food among pastoral peoples, a quick inventory of the material goods of pastoralists will indicate the regular use of objects made from the skins, horns, hair, sinews, and other by-products of the chase in the clothing, housing, and religious and ritual paraphernalia of the herders.[16] This is not to deny the central place in both ideology and practice of cattle and sometimes camels among East African pastoralists. But it will not do to ignore the part played by small stock and wild animals in sustaining the idealized and historically preferred lifestyle of Kenya's warrior herdsmen.

Finally, we may conclude by indicating which individuals and groups among the diverse Kenyan communities engaged in this until recently ubiquitous practice. I am tempted to make what may appear to be a superficial analogy between who hunted in Kenya and who played baseball in the United States or soccer football in Europe and Latin America during the same period. Immediately obvious is the idea that in both places most young boys and a few girls would learn the game and its rules as part of their socialization. Indeed, from infancy, gender was often marked and asserted by the gift of toy bows and arrows and miniature balls, bats, and gloves respectively.[17] At a somewhat deeper level, some adult men, either unmarried or recently settled, would continue to 'play' at hunting or baseball as recreation. Some particularly competent men would make a profession of the game, and one might even find a few old-timers who would go out from time to time to try their hand. For hunters, as for

[13] Richard Waller, '*Emutai*: Crisis and Response in Maasailand, 1883–1902', in *The Ecology of Survival*, ed. D. H. Johnson and D. Anderson (Boulder: Westview, 1988), 73–112.

[14] Ambler, *Kenyan Communities*, 127.

[15] Interview A/11, Richard Wilding, Curator, Ft. Jesus Museum, Mombasa, 11 April 1987, on Boran hunting.

[16] See M. A. Ogutu and C. Kratz, 'Hunting and Gathering', in *Kenya Socio-cultural Profiles: Narok District*, Draft Report (Nairobi: Ministry of Planning and National Development and African Studies Institute, University of Nairobi, 1987), 68–9, for Maasai wild animal-derived products. Also, Interview A/11, Richard Wilding on Boran hunting items.

[17] Among the Luo, infant boys were presented with miniature bows and arrows as crib presents long after wild animals had disappeared from the local landscape and boys would still go hunting with their adult male relatives, despite the absence of game, as a symbolic rite of passage. E. S. Atieno Odhiambo, personal communication. See Interview A/4, Nganyawa Mwijo.

ball players, the equipment and skills once acquired in youth tended to remain available throughout life and pleasure would be taken in recalling youthful exploits and discussing the current status of the 'game'. Finally, football, baseball, and hunting were seen as embodying community values and enhancing community solidarity. Just as it would be hard to find an American or European community in the first half of the twentieth century without a baseball diamond or sandlot, a soccer pitch or open field in an urban park, no African communities lacked the equipment, organization, and locations for the pursuit of game. And, although, for most mature men, hunting was more a matter of nostalgia than activity, there were always some for whom the pursuit of game remained a lifelong calling and meaningful identity.[18]

The universal appeal of the venatic arts among Kenyan Africans was not bound by ethnic, class, or occupational distinctions. Members of predominantly agricultural, pastoral, and foraging communities would engage in hunting for a variety of reasons ranging from subsistence to sport. While our concern in this inquiry will be principally with those hunters who were members of agricultural communities, it will be necessary to examine some of the other hunting traditions and debunk some of the misconceptions about the practice of hunting among Kenyan Africans.

First, we must discard the long-cherished image among both Kenyan whites and many Africans that all hunter-foragers were impoverished and outcast members of other ethnic groups who had fallen from their 'traditional' pursuits to live a life in the bush. We might call this view the Dorobo fallacy. Work among Hadza and San in Tanzania and Botswana has established that hunter-foragers often hunt in preference to the labour-intensive occupation of farmer and prefer the culture of leisure to the accumulation of property.[19] This appears to be the case among Kenyan hunter-foragers as well, where a highly developed hunting ethos, sense of independence, and personal accomplishment seem to have existed. Moreover, studies of Dorobo identity in Kenya have suggested that they tend to act as a mirror to the images of the agricultural and pastoral 'others' whom they live among and who identify themselves in contradistinction to

---

[18] Interview C/4, Kimwere M'tamangara. Kimwere was probably the oldest hunter active in Tharaka in 1987. Circumcised with the *Kyandere* age group, his date of birth would be *c.* 1899.

[19] On the Hadza, see James Woodburn, 'Egalitarian Societies', *Man* 17 (1982), 431–51; and Marshall Sahlins, *Stone Age Economics* (Chicago: Aldine, 1972), 26–7; on the San, Richard B. Lee, *The !Kung San. Men, Women and Work in a Foraging Society* (Cambridge: Cambridge University Press, 1979), 116–19, 188, 440. For the general thesis on forager leisure preference, see Sahlins, *Stone Age Economics*, 1–39; and contrast, Nurit Bird-David, 'Beyond "The Original Affluent Society": A Culturalist Reformulation', *Current Anthropology* 33, 1 (1992), 25–47. The idea of hunting as a preference, at least for the San/Basarwa of southern Africa, has been challenged with great vigour and vitriol. These debates are beyond the scope of my work, but for those interested in either the theoretical or polemical issues, see Edwin Wilmsen, *Land Full of Flies* (Chicago: University of Chicago Press, 1989); and Edwin Wilmsen and James Denbow, 'Paradigmatic History of San-speaking Peoples and Current Attempts at Revision', *Current Anthropology* 31, 5 (1990), 489–524, which includes comments by readers and a rebuttal.

the so-called Dorobo. Paralleling the culture/nature dichotomy familiar to African ethnographic studies, the agricultural and pastoral people project onto the forest-dwelling and 'uncivilized' hunters both the deficiencies and powers of a life in nature.[20]

Although this ethnographic work focuses on the hunters of central and western Kenya, such as the Dorobo of Mt Kenya and the Okiek of the Mau escarpment, it holds as well for the eastern Kenyan hunters variously known as Sanye, Waata, or Waliangulu. Among the Waata especially not only must we abandon the image of the 'other' as forlorn and impoverished, but we must equally discard the fixity of tribal labels and recognize instead a fluid and changeable identity, capable of a number of masks and mergings. In interaction with a malleable and changing identity among the neighbouring settled farmers and herders, the identity of the hunters has shown a remarkable ability to bend and change in chameleon-like fashion. The exchange of goods, services, and ideas has been accompanied by an exchange or borrowing of language, genes, and culture. This is nowhere more true than in the emergence over the centuries of a hunting tradition shared by the 'pure' hunters of the eastern Kenya Nyika area and the hunters among the Bantu-speaking farmers at the centre of this study.

The source of this hunting tradition can best be approached by examining the hunting practices of the scattered remnants of the 'pure' hunter foragers who continued to live a 'Stone Age' economic life well into the twentieth century. The Waata have assumed a variety of names as they adapted to the pressures emerging from their contacts with surrounding people. Called Sanye in the northern coastal region and lower Tana River valley, when living behind the southern coast among the Mijikenda Bantu-speakers such as the Digo and Duruma, they came to be called Waliangulu.

The Waata: people of the bow

During the twentieth century the Waata probably never numbered more than two to three thousand people located immediately behind the Kenya coast from the Tana River district in the north to the arid stretches of territory west of the Shimba hills and north in the Taru desert. Their sparseness and wide distribution added to their capacity to blend in culturally and linguistically with the Bantu-speaking Mijikenda groups and probably account for the fact that they have never been the subject of a full-length ethnographic study, and we must rely on scattered accounts by hunters, administrators, and adventure writers to reconstruct Waata hunting traditions.[21] It would be fruitless to go beyond this scattered evidence in reconstructing Waata life in the colonial era. Even the earliest

---

[20] Kenny, 'A Mirror in the Forest'; C. Kratz, 'Ethnic Interaction, Economic Diversification, and Language Use', *SUGIA* 7, 2 (1986), 189–226.

[21] Brief ethnographic accounts by colonial administrators can be found in A. Sharp, 'The Warungula Elephant Hunters of the Coast Hinterland', Kenya National Archives (hereafter KNA) DC/KWL/3/4; Arthur M. Champion, 'Some Notes on the Wasanye', University of Nairobi Library Africana Collection Offprint (n.p., n.d.), 21–4; C. W.

official account of Waata life in Kwale district reflects the attempts by the administration to settle the hunters and their dependants in villages and the impact this had on kinship and economy.[22] Thanks to the independent research of two observers and their popular accounts of Waata hunting as practised in the 1950s, during the last years of their existence as a hunting community, we are able to reconstruct an image of the kinds of skills and techniques that had sustained these scattered communities over the centuries.[23]

The central feature of Waata hunting was the role of certain individual experts or 'aces' in setting standards of excellence and a code of conduct for the hunting fraternity of perhaps two to three hundred active hunters. Although all adult males might engage in the pursuit of large game animals, certain of them came to be acknowledged as experts whose skill and daring, especially in the pursuit of elephant, made them models among their peers and seem to have established them as paragons of hunting virtue to the Europeans who came to know them. Their methods of elephant hunting described here should not be taken as typical, but rather as exemplary.

Waata 'aces' like Galogalo Kafonde and the Dara brothers, who operated in the 1940s and 1950s, did so in small groups of two or three, often close kin, and less frequently as solitary hunters.[24] While engaged in tracking and pursuing elephants, these hunters would remain in the bush for up to several weeks, sleeping in the open or at temporary enclosures spotted around the hunting territory. With rare exceptions, women did not accompany the men on these expeditions.

Elephants were hunted principally for meat and when killed the rest of the hunter's band would gather at the site of the kill to eat from the carcass on the spot and dry some meat for storage. When the carcass was consumed and all that was useful extracted from it, the carcass and the site would be abandoned to scavengers. The tusks, which had been removed and usually buried for safekeeping in the nearby bush, would be dug up and transported by head porterage to coastal Mijikenda, Swahili, or Arab buyers. Hunters would typically obtain about 10 per cent of the Mombasa market value for the ivory they sold to coastal middlemen. As there was

---

[21] (contd) Hobley, 'The Wa-Langulu or Ariangulu of the Taru Desert', *Man* 8–9 (1912), 18–21, and his 'Notes on the Wa-Sania', *Journal of the Royal Anthropological Institute* 41 (1911), 29–39. Less useful notes, because of their focus on the northern and Oromo-speaking Waata, are found in E. Cerulli, 'The Wátta: A Low Caste of Hunters', *Harvard African Studies* 3 (1922), 200–214; A. Werner, 'A Few Notes on the Wasanye', *Man* 13 (1913), 199–201; and M. Bassi, 'Hunters and Pastoralists in East Africa: The Case of the Waata and the Oromo-Borana', in *Dynamics of Populations, Movements and Responses to Climatic Change in Africa*, ed. B. E. Barich and M. C. Gatto (Rome: Bonsignore Editore, 1997), 164–76.

[22] 'Warungula Elephant Hunters', KNA DC/KWL/3/4: 1–4. Cf. Native Affairs Department Circular #46 of 29/10/25: 7: 'A few ... have been induced to settle and cultivate and one more enlightened, sits on the Digo District Council.' *KNA* DC/Kwale/ 3/4.

[23] Dennis Holman, *The Elephant People* (London: John Murray, 1967); and Ian Parker and Mohammed Amin, *Ivory Crisis* (London: Chatto and Windus, 1983). See Interview D/2, Ian Parker.

[24] Holman, *Elephant People*, 139ff, 166–78; Parker and Amin, *Ivory Crisis*, 41–51.

little call on the Waata for cash outlays, this money was often spent virtually at once, often on a supply of local palm wine. A drunken binge lasting days or weeks would be the frequent result of a successful hunt and ivory sale, to the chagrin of the colonial administration and its vision of 'settling' the Waata down as potential productive cultivators.[25]

The climax of the elephant hunting cycle was the kill itself. It is in this aspect of the hunt that the Waata seem to have maintained their distinctive and dramatic cultural practices, which set them apart from the surrounding Bantu-speaking and Orma hunters, who appear to have adapted their tools and techniques, but not their singular method and spirit. In preparing himself for the chase, the Waata ace would have armed himself with a longbow and a hide quiver of iron-tipped arrows, made by himself or to his specifications with a distinctively shaped, signature motif arrowhead. The arrowhead was otherwise hafted and feathered much as those used by other hunters of the region: a three-piece arrow consisting of a poison-bearing iron tip, a short, poisoned, and detachable fore shaft and a feathered main shaft was standard in elephant hunting. The Waata bow was truly distinctive. The bows were longer and heavier than those of other hunters. They had a draw weight ranging from 120 to as much as 170 pounds. In contrast, the draw weight of a Kamba archer's bow was about 50 pounds and that of an English longbow was 'between 60 and 80 pounds'.[26] Needless to say, this bow was not an easy weapon to use, requiring both great physical strength and dexterity. It also emitted a projectile with great powers of penetration compared to other types of longbow.

The key to Waata hunting success was neither in the powerful longbow nor in the razor sharp arrows but in the poison, which it was the purpose of the bow and arrow to introduce into the elephant's bloodstream. The poison, derived from the *Acocanthera schimperi* tree, is a vegetable-derived cardiac glycoside, similar in its chemical composition and operation to digitalis.[27] Although the poison and the tree from which it is derived was widespread in eastern Kenya and widely used by other hunters, it remained little appreciated and understood by the colonial authorities. Bounded by their own traditions of sportsmanship, the authorities outlawed the use of poison in hunting, except in the killing of 'vermin', from the earliest game legislation promulgated in the colony. Poison was considered cruel and unsporting by the gamekeepers, as it was believed to

[25] 'Warangula Elephant Hunters', KNA DC/KWL/3/4. See H. B. Sharpe, District Station Diary for Shimoni-Vanga District, 27 July–1 August 1924, *KNA* DC/KWL/5/1 for a vivid description of a Waata (Waliagulu) hunting village.

[26] Holman, *Elephant People*, 34. See also Parker and Amin, *Ivory Crisis*, 33–4; and see Champion, 'Some Notes on the Wasanye', 23–4, for an early twentieth-century description of Waata hunting equipment by a colonial official. The draw weight is the pressure or weight produced on a spring scale when the bowstring is drawn to its fullest extent. Modern sport hunting bows have maximum draw weights of approximately 70 or 80 pounds for a composite bow or a recurve bow. Chuck Adams, *The Complete Book of Bowhunting* (New York: Winchester Press, 1978), 17–27.

[27] On acocanthera, see Interview D/2, Ian Parker; Parker and Amin, *Ivory Crisis*, 34ff; Holman, *Elephant People*, 35–42; Interview A/4, Nganyawa Mwijo.

cause its victims to suffer a slow and painful death and to require little skill or courage from its supposed savage users. Those who have become familiar with the Waata and their methods, and experts on the concoction and use of acocanthera poison, such as the Kenyan nature writer and former game warden, Ian Parker,[28] have come to see this form of hunting as far more humane, sporting, and effective a technique than the use of large-bore elephant guns or high-powered sports rifles, typically fired at great distances, even when used by expert marksmen.

The poison was prepared by boiling the bark and roots of a particular tree, called *mutsungu* or *muriju* (*Acocanthera longiflora*), which is found widely in eastern Kenya. My informants were in agreement that the preparation made and distributed by the Mijikenda people of the Coast Province was the most potent and effective.[29] The extract or tincture of the bark and roots would be boiled down to a thick, tarry substance over the course of as much as two or three days. This substance, sometimes enhanced by the admixture of certain animal or insect parts (of more symbolic than chemical efficacy),[30] would be placed in tightly wrapped bark packets for transportation and sale or use. Most Waata made their own poison concoctions on whose potency their success depended.

Only in the hunting area, when the prey had been sighted, would the lethal preparation be applied to the hunter's arrowheads and fore shafts. The poison's potency was known to decrease over time or if exposed to air and light. Waata 'aces', involving a show of courage and bravado, used an extremely dangerous test of the potency of each batch. The hunter used a clean, unpoisoned arrowhead to open a small cut in his forearm or leg. The flow of blood would be allowed to move down his limb until the hunter could apply a small drop of the poison to the end of the trickle of blood. He would then observe how quickly the blood darkened and coagulated, the serum blackening up toward the open cut until, at the last moment, the hunter would wipe away the top of the rivulet of blood and stop the poison from entering his own bloodstream. The rapidity of the blackening and hardening of the exposed blood indicated to the hunter the degree of potency of his batch of acocanthera.[31]

On nearing his prey, the hunter would prepare his poisoned arrows and himself for the kill. He would strip off whatever clothing, skins, or adornment he might be wearing and rub his body in elephant dropping and mud to disguise his own odour and enable him to approach and even mingle with the herd of keen-smelling, but dull-sighted elephants unobserved.

---

[28] Interview D/2, Ian Parker. Contrast Bill Woodley's diary as cited in Holman, *Elephant People*, 41.

[29] Interviews A/4, Nganyawa Mwijo; B/5, Ndambuki Ndeve; B/6, Nzenge Kitoi; and C/1, Kiriamagwa. See Dennis A. Walker, 'Giriama Arrow Poison', *Central African Journal of Medicine* 3, 6 (1957), 226–28.

[30] See M. Walsh, 'Elephant Shrews and Arrow Poison', *East African Natural History Bulletin* 22, 2 (1992), 18–21.

[31] Interview D/2, Ian Parker. Parker also mentions a method of testing using a poisoned thorn and pricking a small animal like a frog. The Waata term for the poison is *hada* (Parker and Amin, *Ivory Crisis*, 36).

Having carefully applied the poison to the arrowhead and fore shaft of his arrows, the hunter would approach from downwind and target the largest animal or the one with the best tusks. For reasons of both effectiveness and the particular bravado of the Waata hunting fraternity, the 'ace' hunter would move amidst the herd to within a few yards of the targeted elephant. Only then would the hunter loose his arrow up at the broad target presented by the elephant's underbelly, hoping to pierce the thick skin with the arrow and have the poisoned head and fore shaft lodge in the animal's intestinal cavity. This would allow the acocanthera to be quickly absorbed into the bloodstream. Carried back to the heart muscles by major veins and arteries, the most potent poisons could cause congestive heart failure and death within minutes, depending upon the size of the prey, the amount of food already in the digestive tract, and the depth of penetration of the arrow into the animal's intestines. But even the largest of elephant, if properly hit, might run just a few hundred yards after the pain of the arrows piercing the skin, before collapsing from the quick onset of the relatively painless 'heart attack'.[32]

These Waata hunting techniques appear to have changed little during the colonial era. Despite the introduction of firearms and their adaptation to hunting uses elsewhere, the Waata seem to have held such methods in contempt. The development of a brisk external market for ivory in the mid-nineteenth century made more of an impact, although, compared to the adaptation to ivory trade made by the neighbouring Kamba peoples,[33] the changes among Waata hunters seem trivial. Occasionally, elephant would be hunted for their ivory exclusively, with the carcasses left to rot after a few select cuts of meat had been taken and eaten on the spot. Even this change represents more of an adaptation to increased anti-poaching activity rather than to the market, as the necessity to leave the sites of what had become illegal kills was as much a part of the abandonment of the elephant meat as the desire to profit from the sale of the ivory.[34]

In most respects, the evasion of detection became the principal adaptation of Waata to the colonial presence. Their success in hunting far from the centres and highways of colonial administration and commerce made them virtually invisible to official eyes for the entire interwar period. They would only come to the attention of the authorities as hunters during the establishment of national parks in the 1940s, with devastating effect. In some ways, it is possible to see the Waata as having collaborated in their own silencing. By hiding their hunting activities, blending in with surrounding peoples, they succeeded for decades in 'flying beneath the radar' of colonial administration and ethnography. This accorded well with the propensity of colonial 'native administration' to work with a limited list of recognized ethnic groups or tribes, collected into districts for administrative convenience and conforming to the colonial idea of what

---

[32] Interview D/2, Ian Parker, and Parker and Amin, *Ivory Crisis*, 39–40. See also Holman, *Elephant People*, 37–8.

[33] See Chapter 2 of this volume, and R. W. Beachey, 'The East African Ivory Trade in the Nineteenth Century', *Journal of African History* 8, 2 (1967), 269–90.

[34] Interview D/2, Ian Parker.

was a tribe. By disguise and obfuscation, the Waata would remain invisible and the presence of these prodigious hunters would be silenced in the colonial record.

The great hunting success of the Waata using 'primitive' weapons and techniques, their commitment to a life of hunting dependent on the great wild elephant herds of eastern Kenya, and the persistent use of elephant-derived meat, hide, and tusks as the basis of their subsistence made them appear to be at least as resistant to changing their core institutions and values as such neighbouring conservative peoples as the pastoral Maasai.[35] Only their conflicts with white hunters and gamekeepers in the mid-twentieth century and the destruction of their relationship with their elephant prey would lead to the sudden collapse of their independent existence as if they were struck by one of their own death-dealing poisoned arrows.[36]

---

[35] See Peter Rigby, *Persistent Pastoralists* (London: Zed, 1985) and his *Cattle, Capitalism, and Class* (Philadelphia: Temple University Press, 1992) on the nature of pastoral conservatism under modern capitalist pressures.

[36] See Chapter 10 below.

Two

▲◆▲◆▲◆▲◆▲◆▲◆▲◆▲◆▲◆▲◆▲◆▲◆▲◆▲◆▲◆▲◆▲◆

Hunters & Farmers
in Kwale & Meru

By the nineteenth century, the Waata hunting tradition using bow and poisoned arrows had diffused to other peoples who had settled in eastern Kenya. Broadly speaking, these peoples were Bantu speakers who lived in an arc of territory stretching from the southern Kenya coast, in what is today Kwale district, northward along the coast and inland across the Taru desert through Kitui district to the slopes of Mt Kenya and the Nyambeni hills in Central and Eastern Provinces. Among these farming and herding people hunting became a secondary economic activity, but retained great cultural and social significance.

The Waata hunting tradition was transformed during the course of centuries as it passed to incoming Bantu-speaking peoples who settled along the coast and the southern interior of Kenya during the second half of the first millennium and the first centuries of the second. Over the course of the past 500 years, the Digo and Duruma of the Mijikenda peoples, the Kamba of Machakos and Kitui districts, and the Igembe and Tharaka people of Meru district differentiated, migrated, and came together as the groups we know today.[1] In the course of the emergence of these groups, bow-and-arrow hunting was adapted and accommodated to the needs of the Bantu-speaking, iron-making, mixed farmers. By the eve of the colonial invasion, these peoples had repopulated and reshaped the region of eastern Kenya.

The entire region of eastern Kenya to be studied is set off at each end by the 'parentheses' of the Shimba hills in the south and the Nyambeni Hills in the north. On and between these hills, for a stretch of almost 600 miles, we can examine the variations in hunting practice produced by a number of crucial factors. The influence of climate and topography, the relative importance of agricultural and pastoral pursuits, the growth of

---

[1] For a general picture of the settlement of Kenya, see B. A. Ogot, ed., *Zamani. A Survey of East African History* (New York: Humanities Press, 1968), 80–92; and R. Oliver and G. Mathew, eds, *History of East Africa*, vol. 1 (Oxford: Clarendon, 1963), 89–96, 198–213.

Islam, and the nineteenth-century expansion of the long-distance trade in ivory and rhinoceros horn would each refine and transform the basic hunting tradition of eastern Kenya's Bantu-speaking hunters.

Hunting in Kwale district

Kwale district lies on the southernmost coast of Kenya and is home to the two southernmost peoples of the Mijikenda or Nyika 'tribe',[2] the Digo and Duruma. Closely related historically and culturally, the Digo are separated geographically by the 1400-foot-high Shimba hills, which dominate the coastal plains to the southeast and form a natural divide between the Digo-inhabited plains and the Duruma areas to the northwest in the rain shadow of the hills. Both groups hunt as a part of their mixed farming activities, although it appears that the Duruma's drier and more difficult environment has made them keener both as pastoralists and in pursuit of game than the agriculturally better-endowed Digo. It may also be that contacts with the Kamba to the north, and the incorporation of Waata and Degere hunters, have further increased Duruma interest in the hunt, especially of elephant, which can still be seen in Duruma country and within the Shimba Hills National Park.[3]

The hunting practices of the Kwale district peoples are very similar and include, in addition to the bow and arrow, numerous complex traps and snares. The use of spring traps (*kwaru*) and nooses (*chipangwa* or *rugwe*), as well as pitfalls (*rwina* or *shimo*), was apparently more common among the Digo, but their use was widespread throughout the region.[4] Hunting with bow and arrow was usually done in small groups of related young men, and all kinds of game was sought, up to and including elephant. When animals were killed, the successful hunters would cook and eat some meat

[2] The basic historical work on the Mijikenda is Thomas Spear, *The Kaya Complex. A History of the Mijikenda Peoples of the Kenya Coast to 1900* (Nairobi: Kenya Literature Bureau, 1978). For an ethnographic description of these people, see A. H. J. Prins, *The Coastal Tribes of the Northeastern Bantu* (London: International African Institute, 1952). Early ethnographic notes can be found in J. B. Griffiths, 'Glimpses of a Nyika Tribe (Waduruma)', *Journal of the Royal Anthropological Institute* 65 (1935), 267–96; C. C. F. Dundas, *The Wadigo*, KNA DC/KWL/ 3/5; and H. M. T. Kayamba, 'Notes on the Wadigo', *Tanganyika Notes and Records* 23 (1947), 80–96.

[3] See Prins, *Coastal Tribes*, 38, 56. For Digo ethnography and history, see L. P. Gerlach, 'The Social Organisation of the Digo of Kenya', unpublished Ph.D. dissertation, University of London, 1961; and David C. Sperling, 'Some Aspects of the Islamization in East Africa with Particular Reference to the Digo of Southern Kenya', unpublished Ph.D. dissertation, University of Nairobi, 1970. William F. McKay, 'A Precolonial History of the Southern Kenya Coast', unpublished Ph.D. dissertation, Boston University, 1975, focuses on the coastal Vumba people, but contains some useful materials relating to Digo history as well.

[4] Interviews A/8, Ali Shehe Rungwa, 5 March 1987; A/10, Rashid Omar Mwakutunza, 10 March 1987; and A/1, Hamisi Ndiyani, 28 February 1987. For the wider use of traps in eastern Kenya, see C. W. Hobley, 'Native Trapping Methods', *Journal of the Society for the Preservation of the Fauna of the Empire* (NS) 23 (1934), 19–24. Unless otherwise indicated in the bibliography, all interviews were conducted in the Digo–Duruma language and all parenthesized terms are from that language, which is closely cognate with Ki-Swahili.

(intestines, heart, and liver) on the spot of the kill, drying some meat and cutting up the remainder for transportation back to the village or homestead. The major food animals were bushbuck (*kulungu*), impala (*mbala*), dik-dik (*kivi*), gazelle (*nause*), eland (*kulo*), zebra (*foro*), warthog (*gwashe*), and wild pig (*nguruwe*).[5] All informants seemed agreed that there was no special portion of a kill set aside for chiefs or headmen, and ownership rights to portions belonged only to the men in the hunting party and their dependants. The Digo and Duruma were also known to hunt lions, generally in defence of livestock, but killing a lion was a sign of exceptional courage and hunting skill.[6]

My own observations indicate that individual hunters make bows and arrows as well as traps, and the techniques are widely known. No secrecy seems to obtain to these techniques, nor do they appear to have been controlled by ritual or ceremonial inhibitions. Indeed, hunting appears to be so open as to be the motif of several rites of passage for male infants and young boys.[7] I was able to observe most of the processes of preparation, except the concoction of poison, during my stay in Kwale district.[8] I was unable to observe hunting in the field due to the total ban on hunting enacted by the Kenyan government in 1977, although a simulated hunt was staged by some of my informants, which led to some interesting observations regarding the influence of Islam on Digo and Duruma Muslim hunters.[9]

In demonstrating the pursuit of a small antelope, Msinda Mahupa[10] loosed a mock arrow at an imaginary target and then, quickly drawing his knife, rushed to the spot of the would-be prey, and enacted the slitting of the animal's throat. This was explained to me in terms of the rules of halal, which require that animals used for food must be slaughtered in a ritually prescribed manner and not die of either natural causes or because of the arrow or its poison. This accounts for the haste in getting to the animal before it dies of its wound or the effects of the arrow poison. I was assured that failure to slaughter the animal would render its flesh useless for the Muslim Digo or Duruma. This was reinforced by the resistance I noted to the use of the Swahili word *sumu* for poison, and the preference for the

---

[5] Interview A/3, Kilute Dalu, 1 March 1987. See also Interview A/2, Harrison Bemwagandi, 1 March 1987.

[6] Interview A/6, Omari Njama, 5 March 1987 and others in the A/ series.

[7] Interviews A/7, Nasoro Njama, 5 March 1987 on bird hunting by boys and the preparation of hunting medicines; A/4, Nganyawa Mwijo, 1 March 1987 on the presentation of a miniature bow and arrow to infants at their first public appearance after birth. See A/5, Juma M. Dzilla, 3 March 1987.

[8] Interview A/9, Nasoro Njama (second interview), 8 March 1987. The subject not only allowed me to observe the making of arrows but offered samples of his work for sale. See A/3, Kilute Dalu, 1 March 1987; and A/6, Omari Njama, 5 March 1987 on bows, arrows, and paraphernalia.

[9] Interview A/3, Kilute Dalu, 1 March 1987. See David Sperling, 'The Coastal Hinterland and Interior of East Africa', in *The History of Islam in Africa*, ed. N. Levtzion and R. Pouwels (Oxford: James Currey, 2000), 281–3.

[10] Nephew of Kilute Dalu; see Interview A/3. A virtually identical description of the role of religious dietary law in the hunting practices of thirteenth-century Jewish poachers in England is contained in B.A. Hanawalt, 'Men's Games, King's Deer: Poaching in Medieval England', *Journal of Medieval and Renaissance Studies*, 18, 2 (1988) 180–81.

vernacular *utsungu*.[11] The rules of halal also forbid the use of poison, and I was given to believe that *utsungu* was not a poison proscribed by Islam, but merely a means of stunning and disabling the prey so that it could be properly, ritually sacrificed in the Muslim manner.

The question of the hunting of wild pig (*nguruwe*) for food was also raised.[12] I was given to understand that pig was hunted for food in the old days (before the coming of Islam), but that now pig was no longer eaten. Yet it continued to be hunted throughout the colonial era. Indeed, the hunting of pig by large groups of men, under the direct supervision of local chiefs and the leadership of recognized expert hunters (with the permission of the district administration), appears to have been the only kind of legally sanctioned hunting in Kwale district.[13] At the height of the growing season, organized groups of hunters with dogs and beaters will pursue and kill bush pig in order to clear them from the fields of standing crops that they threaten. Of course, other animals 'accidentally' caught in this dragnet are 'fair game' for the quick and accurate marksmen. The irony of the only legal hunting being of animals that are forbidden as food was magnified by one answer to my question regarding what became of the meat if the Muslim hunters didn't eat it. I was told that the animals were left where they fell and were collected by the sisters from St. Mary's, a Roman Catholic seminary in Kwale town, who do not share the Muslim prohibition of pork.[14]

Like the symbiotic relationship of Muslim hunters and Catholic sisters, the politically and religiously imposed variations on Kwale district hunting appear to be recent exogenous cultural deviations from the basic hunting complex.[15] The basic equipment, including the use of acocanthera poison, here called *utsungu*, remains the same as that used by the Waata and the other East African hunters. The organization of hunting by small groups of age mates, kin, or local friends seems again to be the standard, as does the nature of the pursuit, the special reverence for elephant hunting, and the individualistic distribution of the products of the hunt, both food and trophy items.

Despite the fact that colonial trade routes and administration had an

---

[11] Interview A/5, Juma M. Dzilla, 3 March 1987.

[12] Interviews A/1, Hamisi Ndiyani, 28 February 1987; A/4, Nganyawa Mwijo, 1 March 1987; and A/5, Juma M. Dzilla, 3 March 1987.

[13] L. P. Gerlach, 'Nutrition in Its Sociocultural Matrix: Food Getting and Using Along the East African Coast', in *Ecology and Economic Development in Tropical Africa*, ed. D. Brokensha (Berkeley: Institute of International Studies, 1965), 254–5. A good deal of killing of baboons, which are a major nuisance as crop raiders, still goes on in the district. If a baboon troop is actively raiding one's fields, their destruction in defence of property is permitted, but no organized hunting of baboon is allowed. Interview A/10, Rashid Omar Mwakutunza, 10 March 1987.

[14] Interview A/5, Juma M. Dzilla. It might also be noted that the use of hunting dogs appears to have been widespread even among Muslim hunters, despite the 'unclean' status of dogs in Islamic culture. See Interview A/10, Rashid Omar Mwakutunza, 10 March 1987.

[15] Information on weapons, techniques and methods, prey, food preparation and distribution, and the role of hunting in the life cycle were part of an informal interview schedule. See Interviews A/1–10, February–March 1987.

impact on the district from early in the twentieth century, this impact seems to have affected only slightly Digo and Duruma hunters. My informants record few changes in their techniques, beyond those caused by the spread of Islam, or in the place that subsistence hunting played in their economy. A decline in hunting by Digo has to be deduced from a contrast of current practices with the idealized images of the past abundance of game and its importance to Digo life. No one seemed to be aware of the imperceptibly gradual effects of increasing population and density of settlement that I would suggest are the primary causes of the reduction of hunting. The only changes recognized by my Digo and Duruma informants were attributed by them to Islamic proscriptions and to the restrictions on hunting imposed by the colonial regime.[16]

Among the Duruma, elephant hunting persisted during the colonial era, but in a far more clandestine manner and at a further remove from the coast, the line of rail, and the censorious eyes of the authorities. The Shimba hills seem to have been avoided in favour of the dry, open plains areas to the north and east. In addition, as the elephant herds declined so did the efforts of Duruma to maintain a position in the international ivory market. By the end of the colonial era, and when the Shimba Hills area was added to the list of national parks and wildlife reserves, only a small number of the smaller forest-dwelling elephants could be found in the area of Digo and Duruma settlement.

Meru district hunting

Just to the east of Mount Kenya lies the colonially delineated Meru district. Built around the congeries of Meru-speaking local communities, the district also contained a community of people speaking the distantly related language of ki-Tharaka or ki-Thagichu.[17] On the spur of foothills called the Nyambeni hills, running northeast from the base of Mount Kenya, a Meru subgroup called the Igembe maintained dialectal and cultural differences from the Meru of the mountain. The Nyambeni hills themselves, like the Shimba hills far to the south, mark off a geo-cultural divide. To the north, the arid steppes of Samburu, Borana, and Orma pastoralists stretch bleakly to the horizon. As you travel north, altitude and moisture drop in a step-like progression until the Ethiopian Highlands, north of Lake Turkana, interrupt the descent. South of the hills, the bush country falls to the banks of the Tana River, which separates Meru district from the vastness of the Kitui district of Ukambani, Kambaland.

The hunters of Igembe and Tharaka represent the northern limit of my study area and, in some ways, the modern hunters of this area represent

---

[16] Interviews A/1, Hamisi Ndiyani, 28 February 1987; and A/4 Nganawa Mwijo, 1 March 1987.

[17] My thanks to Carolyn Harford for information on the Thagichu language and its relations to the surrounding language communities. Informal personal communications, Nairobi and Nkondi, March to September 1987. Ki- is the common Bantu language family prefix for a language.

the most direct descendants of the eastern Kenya bow-and-arrow hunters. The Igembe division of Meru District stretches along the slopes of the Nyambeni hills, allowing Igembe hunters to reproduce in an attenuated form the pattern of hunting land use of their Meru neighbours on the slopes of Mount Kenya.[18] They combine montane forest hunting in the higher reaches of the hills with the pursuit of plains animals at lower altitudes. For the Igembe, the higher slopes have been far less important than the rich array of hunting lands and abundant wildlife on both the northern steppes and the eastern and southern grassland valleys that surround them. To the north, the plains are rich in elephant and antelope, zebra, and giraffe (including the now rare Grevy zebra and reticulated giraffe), and are within easy range of hunters operating from the hills' northern slopes.[19] Inasmuch as the regular hunting of food animals is peripheral to the culture of the northern pastoralists, the only competition for the Igembe and Meru bow-and-arrow hunters in these regions was provided by the scattered groups of so-called Dorobo hunters, cattleless 'outcasts' from the herding societies.[20]

Even more promising hunting lands were those that now comprise Meru National Park and the contiguous game areas along the banks of the Tana River and its northern tributaries. Until recent years, some of Kenya's largest elephant herds occupied this region, and there appears to have been a major concentration of leopard in this area as well. Igembe hunters from the eastern edge of the Nyambenis around Maua location as well as from further afield in Igembe exploited these areas.[21] Further south, beyond the Tana and to the west of its bend, Igembe and Meru hunters would have given way to the more prodigious hunters of Tharaka and eventually to northern Kitui district Kamba bowmen.

---

[18] For the history of Meru settlement and land use, see Jeffrey Fadiman, *Mountain Warriors* (Athens, OH: Ohio University Center for International Studies, 1976); 'Early History of the Meru of Mt. Kenya', *Journal of African History* 14, 1 (1973), 9–27; and 'The Meru People', in *Kenya Before 1900*, ed. B. A. Ogot (Nairobi: East African Publishing House, 1976). For Meru ethnography, see B. Bernardi, *The Mugwe: A Failing Prophet* (London: Oxford University Press, 1959); and see C. W. Hobley, *Bantu Beliefs and Magic* (New York: Barnes and Noble, 1967).

[19] Interviews C/11, Isaac Kabura, 25 September 1987; and C/16, Stefano Mwenda, 29 September 1987 on hunting from Kangeta location towards the northern plains, called *ruanda*, the desert.

[20] Roger van Zwanenberg, 'Dorobo Hunting and Gathering: A Way of Life or a Mode of Production?', *African Economic History* 2 (1976). The fluidity of the line between pastoralists-turned-hunters as a survival strategy and the 'pure' hunters makes it difficult to distinguish the two, although Maasai pastoral ideology would have all hunters condemned as would-be herders who lost their cattle or their capacity to keep cattle. See Richard Waller, '*Emutai*: Crisis and Response in Maasailand, 1883–1902', in *The Ecology of Survival*, ed. D. H. Johnson and D. Anderson (Boulder: Westview, 1988), 73–112; and John Lamphear, 'The Persistence of Hunting and Gathering in a "Pastoral" World', *SUGIA* 7, 2 (1986), 227–65.

[21] Interviews C/12, Francis Kibunja, 26 September 1987; and C/14, Kinjuki M'mbuiria, 28 September 1987. In general, Meru hunters appear to have moved their hunting, either further up the slopes of Mt. Kenya, or to the Igembe, further north into the dry, plains area known as *ruanda* in response to increasing colonial (and post-colonial) pressures, both administrative and demographic.

In terms of hunting method, technique, and organization, the Igembe were clearly part of the bow and arrow tradition derived from the Waata. Their equipment, including acocanthera arrow poison, was indistinguishable from their southern counterparts as far away as Kwale district and northern Tanzania. The same kinds of traps were used and the same kinds of animals sought.[22] In some respects, such as the persistence of individual and small hunting groups and the relative unimportance of ivory, Igembe hunters appear to have been less influenced by the commercial impact of the caravan trade and ivory buyers than those within easier reach of the coast. Whether this was a function of lack of opportunity or of cultural conservatism among the Igembe – for whom hunting was a lower priority to begin with – is unanswerable from the materials I was able to collect.[23]

The Tharaka hunters

In the Tigania subdivision of southern Meru District, and lapping over the Tana River into Kitui district, live the people known as the Tharaka.[24] Hunting among these Bantu speakers retained its cultural centrality and economic importance to a degree unmatched by any but the 'pure' hunter-foragers of eastern Kenya. Two factors, environmental and cultural, would appear to explain this phenomenon and to offer further insight into the position of hunting among the people of the region.

Environmental factors that favoured hunting and militated against successful adaptation to either farming or stock raising constitute the defining or limiting feature. According to Frank Bernard, the restricted development of Tharaka agriculture 'with a much more hostile environment ... in the eastern lowlands' accounts for the divergence of 'their entire economy'.[25] My own research supports this observation. The Tharaka environment north of the Tana, where I studied and interviewed informants, was the most challenging and difficult one in which I worked. Remote from the road system and poorly served by administrative services, it remains a pocket of rural poverty despite agricultural development and settlement schemes undertaken since Kenyan independence. Even in the precolonial period, intense isolation and poverty appear to have characterized life in Tharaka. Despite the Tana River's dissection of Tharaka territory, the kind of agriculture that flourished along the lower Tana among the Pokomo or the upper Tana among the Embu and Mbeere seems not to have been practised by the Tharaka. Away from the river, the arid, dusty, or rocky soils made the Tharaka 'homeland' the least desirable

---

[22] Interview C/14, Kinjuki M'mbuiria, 28 September 1987.

[23] See Interviews C/11, C/12, C/13, C/14, and C/16 on Igembe hunting practices.

[24] There is little published ethnographic work on the Tharaka, but see Arthur Champion, 'The Atharaka', *Journal of the Royal Anthropological Institute* 42 (1912), 68–90; and Richard Lowenthal, 'Tharaka Age-Organization and the Theory of Age-Set Systems', unpublished Ph.D. dissertation, University of Illinois, 1973.

[25] Frank E. Bernard, *East of Mount Kenya: Meru Agriculture in Transition*, Afrika Studies no. 75 (Munich: Weltform Verlag, 1972), 37.

agricultural land in Meru district.[26] In a word, the Tharaka environment would appear to provide little encouragement for a people to adopt agricultural pursuits and many inducements to persist in the pursuit of game as their main economic activity.

Cultural factors involving ethnic identity and institutional persistence gave substance to the ecological determinants. Tharaka and Meru traditions agree that the Tharaka are descendants of aboriginal hunter-foragers, pushed from the better-watered and more fertile uplands to the west on the slopes of Mt. Kenya.[27] In the poor lands bordering the Tana, they were forced to preserve and expand their hunting culture. Folk explanation of the changes undergone in modern times focus on the introduction of goats as a source of meat that would gradually replace the meat of game animals in the Tharaka diet.[28] This explanation may reveal, as well, the role played by new colonially introduced crops and small stock both in reducing game animals in the region and in soil and natural vegetation degradation. Certainly by the 1940s, Tharaka had suffered not just economic stagnation resulting from the district's isolation, but real economic decline. Hunting, then, would have played an important role in Tharaka survival strategies and their growing reputation for being truculent and difficult to administer.[29]

Hunting practice among the Tharaka (as opposed to frequency or success in hunting) has been little changed by new crops and domesticated animals. The bow and arrow with acocanthera poison remained the weapon of choice, although both traps (*tiringi*) and pitfalls (*erinya*) were widely used, and unpoisoned broad-bladed arrows (*kirunda*), wooden-pointed arrows (*iguti*), and others with wooden points and iron barbs (*ithati*) were used for small animals and birds.[30] Small hunting parties of kinsmen and neighbours were the preferred method of hunting organization and small ungulates like dik-dik and bushbuck the preferred prey.[31]

One hunting institution of which I could find no evidence in Igembe or

---

[26] Conducting my research during the dry season may have influenced my own impressions. This was necessitated by the impassability of Tharaka's lowland roads and the difficulty of making the steep descent from the west in the rainy season. Nevertheless, I found nothing in the literature or oral evidence I collected to suggest that anyone thought of Tharaka as a potential garden-land or anything but a dismal, barren, and thoroughly undesirable region. Tharaka even lacked the occasional oasis-like green spots provided by arable highlands such as those found on the Nyambeni, Shimba, and Kitui hills in the Igembe, Digo, and Kitui Kamba regions.

[27] On Meru migration from the coast (Mbwa) and early settlement, see Fadiman, 'Early History of the Meru', 11–25; for the pressure on hunters, see J. Fadiman, 'Traditional Warfare among the Meru of Mt. Kenya', unpublished Ph.D. dissertation, University of Wisconsin, 1973, 70–75; and Interview C/7, John Livingstone Mate, 11 September 1987.

[28] Interview C/7, John Livingstone Mate, 11 September 1987; and Meru District Annual Report (henceforth MDAR) 1940: 3–4 KNA DC/MRU/1/4.

[29] MDAR 1934: 3–4 *KNA* DC/MRU/1/2; and MDAR 1940: 3–4 *KNA* DC/MRU/1/4. See Bernard, *East of Mount Kenya*, 45 for initial conflicts *c*.1908.

[30] Interviews C/1, Kiriamagwa, 6 September 1987; and C/4, Kimwere M'tamangara, 9 September 1987.

[31] Interviews C/1, Kiriamagwa, 6 September 1987; and C/4, Kimwere M'tamangara, 9 September 1987.

Kwale was still operating among the Tharaka. Despite persecution during the colonial era and the secrecy that continues to surround it today, the Waathi society, which has been described among the Kamba of Kitui, was still carrying on a tenuous existence among the Tharaka.[32] Waathi organizations appear to have been introduced among the Tharaka from Ukambani in the nineteenth century.[33] They involve at least two levels of initiation into ranked membership, and all hunters had to be initiated for their protection from the spirits of slain animals and the hazards of the pursuit of wild animals in remote precincts.[34]

In September 1987, Mr Joseph Kibunjia, a local primary school headmaster, arranged a gathering of Waathi members from the vicinity of Nkondi market.[35] I was privileged to interview the hunting society members and to participate in my own initiation ceremony. This consisted of the singing of esoteric hunting songs, a rite of initiation, the application of protective medicine, and finally a mock hunt and display of hunting weapons and methods. An initiation fee of Kenya shillings 500/- (equal to approximately US$20 or one large he-goat) was paid by the candidate and honey beer (*uki*) worth 120/- was supplied for the company of initiators.

The ceremonies began at about 1 pm, following the arrival of Mr John Mate, a retired civil servant and knowledgeable former hunter, who would provide an English commentary as well as participate in the singing and dancing. A hunting song, lasting somewhat over 15 minutes, was sung in unison by the group, interspersed with solos sung over a background chant and a call and response between soloist and chorus. The soloists appeared to select their own themes and lyrics in ki-Tharaka, frequently involving praise of the singers' hunting prowess. A recording was made of the song and played back to the company at their request.

Following this, the chief initiator, Mr M'kirebu Mukangau, began the initiation proper, by spreading the following objects on the ground in front of the candidate: a hunting bow, an arrow shaft, fire sticks, a hunting knife, and a needle. He marked each of these objects with seven stripes using a red powder (*ndondo*), and added contrasting white stripes in alternation using a white powder (*era*) that was wrapped in a banana leaf packet. Both powders appeared to be made from mineral matter, produced by pulverizing and grinding rocks to a fine consistency.

After marking and replacing the ceremonial objects, the initiator marked his own right arm and leg with alternating red and white stripes. The initiator then reproduced the same pattern on the right arm and leg

---

[32] MDAR 1940: 46–48 KNA DC/MRU/1/4 on anti-witchcraft campaign against 'Athi Witchcraft Society'. See Hitoshi Ueda, 'Wathi Ritual Among the Kamba', working paper, 115, Institute of African Studies, University of Nairobi, 1979.

[33] Charles Dundas, 'History of Kitui', *Journal of the Royal Anthropological Institute* 43 (1913), 541–49; and Chapter 3 of this volume.

[34] Although only men were regularly initiated into the hunting society, women who killed animals in their fields in protection of their crops or small stock would undergo initiation after the fact to extend the society's protection retroactively. Interview C/7, John Livingstone Mate, 11 September 1987.

[35] The following section is documented as Interview C/2, M'kirebu Mukangau et al., 7 September 1987.

of the initiate and a white circle was traced around the right eye of both initiator and initiate, followed by a red semicircle around the white. I could elicit no direct explanation of the purpose or meaning of the red and white materials or the pattern or number of designs from Mr Mate or my sponsor, Mr Kibunjia.[36] However, there is little doubt that these rites invoked spiritual powers to strengthen the physical powers of arms and legs and the power of vision essential to the pursuit of wild animals.

The initiator then proceeded to gather up the ceremonial objects in both his hands, being sure that they were properly marked and the red and white stripes were aligned. He then applied millet bread (*guero*) to the exposed ends of the bundled objects. *Guero* has been largely supplanted by maize meal as the staple grain in Meru district, but the Tharaka have maintained its primacy as a ritual food and symbol of health and well-being. Millet bread or cakes are prepared by boiling a mixture of water and pounded millet flour until a thick porridge is produced, which will harden to a sandy-textured loaf from which pieces can be pulled off, balled up in one's fingers, dipped in a relish, and eaten. In this ceremony, it would appear that the *guero* was applied as a protective coating to ensure the well-being of the symbolic objects of the hunt. Holding these objects, the initiator began to rhythmically stamp his right foot (clad in a sandal), while pointing with the bundle and calling out the names of the objects at which he was pointing. The other Waathi celebrants echoed each word or phrase called by the initiator. Pointing first at the initiate's right foot, ankle, knee, wrist, elbow, and forehead, the initiator chanted a formulaic phrase over each body part. This chanting, stamping, and pointing was repeated seven times. The bowl of *guero* was then passed among the initiate and celebrants, with each breaking off and eating a small piece. The entire company of initiators then lined up facing the initiate, and each approached and spat a mixture of *guero* and water from their mouths in the direction of the initiate. *Guero* was applied to each of the designated body parts of the initiate from foot to forehead, and a mixture of *guero* and water was used to 'erase' the seven red and white stripes marking his arms and legs. Again no explanation was offered, but the cleansing, healing, and protective (symbolic closing) attributes of the *guero* were apparent at the centre of the ritual actions. The ceremony was declared concluded by the initiator, and a gratuity of 7 shillings each was given to the initiator, Mr Mokena, the sponsor, Mr Kibunjia, and the builder of the ceremonial house, Mr M'takwenda N'takarichi.[37]

[36] A candidate for initiation into the Waathi requires the sponsorship of a member. Usually the father of the initiate would assume this role. In this case, Mr Kibunjia, whose son was, at the time, a doctoral student in archaeology in Nairobi and was thus an age mate of the candidate, stood in as my sponsor. On colour and number symbols among east Kenya hunters, see H. Ueda, 'Wathi Ritual Among the Kamba', and 'The Power of Hunting Leaders among the Kamba', unpublished paper No. 116, 3–7 (Institute of African Studies, University of Nairobi, 1979).

[37] The construction of an initiation house in the bush was formerly a key element of the ceremony. Along with the initiation fee (a he-goat) and the supply of *uki* for the celebrants, the construction of the house was an additional expense of initiation formerly borne by the candidate. As this ceremony was hastily arranged and took place over the course of a few

Following the initiation, six *athi* led the new initiate on a mock hunt. The five singers of the opening chorus were the members of the hunting party and the initiator now became the hunt leader (*athiani*). The party proceeded to the edge of the cultivated field (*shamba*) bordering Mr Kibunjia's homestead. There they drew themselves up in a row facing the bush they were about to enter. The *athiani* recited a brief prayer, pointing to and naming each area of bush to be entered by the hunters and climaxed by a chilling sound onomatopoeically representing the piercing of the prey that would be sought, flushed, and killed by the arrows of the hunters. The hunters then deployed—three with bows and arrows at the ready stood or crouched at the edge of the bush, while three others proceeded in an arc around the edge of the overgrown bush area. The sounds of these men could be heard as they shouted and 'beat the bush' with sticks to drive the prey in the direction of the waiting 'shooters'. When they came into sight, in this case without any animals before them, the mock hunt was at an end.[38]

Among the ten men gathered to celebrate and assist in my initiation, several were men of standing in the modern economy of the district. Although none were active hunters, all continued to value the traditions of Tharaka hunting as basic to their cultural identity. This was expressed in both the seriousness of even this mock exercise and the oft-repeated concern of my sponsor and others than these rituals and traditions, songs, and ceremonies be properly recorded and transmitted so that they would not be lost to the wider world or to their own children. Hunting particularly was regarded as essential to Tharaka identity and worthy of preservation. This cultural emphasis, in addition to the economic constraints and advantages of the Tharaka environment, has made Tharaka a key area in the preservation and continuity of the traditions of bow-and-arrow hunting in eastern Kenya. It was indeed the only area in which informants boasted proudly that they continued to hunt to this day, avoiding only hunting in or near the closely patrolled areas of national parks.[39]

I present this detailed picture of Waathi initiation as it existed among the Tharaka in the 1980s for several reasons. Partly, it is to indicate the centrality of ritual to the maintenance of a hunting ideal among a people who have by and large abandoned the field due to economic and political pressures. But, in addition, it is due to my desire to convey something of the immediacy of the idea of a hunting fellowship, a community or congregation of devotees, that animated the ceremony and its participants. In many ways, my presence in the community and in the ceremony was

---

[37] (contd) hours at midday, no house was built, but the designated house builder still required symbolic compensation.

[38] The demonstration was followed by a collective or group interview in which Mr Mate and Mr Kibunjia in particular provided useful material on the origins of hunting, social differentiation, and colonial impact on the Tharaka. Interview C/2, M'kirebu Makangau, 7 September 1987.

[39] I will not identify these informants for obvious reasons, but note that they asserted their right and desire to hunt animals excepting only those animals held within the parks as part of the efforts to increase national wealth through wildlife tourism.

merely the occasion on which these now elderly men could assert the continuity of their commitment to their Tharaka heritage. Mr Mate and Mr Kibunjia seemed especially keen to have the ceremony documented and despite their having gone on to establish careers and make contributions in the colonial and post-colonial service of their district, they seemed intent on conveying to me how important the Waathi society and its ceremonies were to their sense of history and identity.[40]

[40] Interview C/2, M'kirebu Mukangau, 7 September 1987.

Three

▲▼▲▼▲▼▲▼▲▼▲▼▲▼▲▼▲▼▲▼▲▼▲▼▲▼▲▼▲

Hunting Transformations in Kitui
1860–1939

The last few decades before the beginning of the colonial era in Kenya witnessed a period of rapid social and political change as Kenyan peoples were drawn into the web of international commerce culminating in the 'Scramble for Africa'. Behind the coast, where the convergence of African and alien was most intense, the Kamba peoples of Kitui and Machakos districts appear to have been decisively influenced by long-distance trade and the opportunities and challenges that it presented.[1] The Kamba emerged as major participants in the caravan trade, which increased with the tempo and extent of the northern coastal trade. They operated at every level of this commerce, as porters, caravan leaders, and organizers, reshaping their social and political institutions according to the dictates of profit and commercial advantage.[2] At the base of this economic transformation of Kamba society were the production, transportation, and sale of elephant ivory. It is all the more remarkable, then, that the chief method for the procurement of ivory for sale by Kamba local merchants and caravan traders has been so frequently ignored: Kamba elephant hunting.

In this chapter we will look at the adaptations made by the Kamba hunters of Kitui district to the changing environmental, economic, and political conditions in Kitui district and the Kenya colony. The opportunities and challenges opened up by the caravan trade from Zanzibar and the coast will be re-examined from the perspective of the stimulus they

---

[1] J. Lamphear, 'The Kamba and the Northern Mrima Coast', in *Precolonial African Trade*, ed. R. Gray and D. Birmingham (Oxford: Clarendon, 1970), 75–102; and I. Kimambo, 'The Economic History of the Kamba', *Hadith* 2 (1969), 79–103.

[2] R. J. Cummings, 'Aspects of Human Porterage with Special Reference to the Akamba of Kenya: Toward an Economic History, 1820–1920', unpublished Ph.D. dissertation, University of California, Los Angeles, 1975. See also Stephen Rockel, '"A Nation of Porters": The Nyamwezi and the Labour Market in Nineteenth-Century Tanzania', *Journal of African History* 41 (2000), 173–95, and his 'Wage Labor and the Culture of Porterage in Nineteenth-Century Tanzania: The Central Caravan Routes', *Comparative Studies of South Asia, Africa, and the Middle East* 15, 2 (1995), 14–24.

gave to elephant hunting.[3] Similarly, the imposition of colonial rule would present the widely travelled and highly skilled elephant hunters of Kitui with new prospects, possibilities, and limitations.

To understand the place of elephant hunting among the Kamba of Kitui district, we must first examine the elements of Kitui experience that placed the Kamba, geographically and culturally, in a position to engage in this enterprise. Kitui district is a secondary area of Kamba settlement. The original 'homeland' of the Kamba is in the hilly region of Machakos district called Mbooni. From there, beginning in the late eighteenth century, Kamba settlers struck out to the south and east driven by famine, itself the result of increasing population and decreasing productivity in the Mbooni region. Thus, Kitui begins its existence as a Kamba frontier area and retains its rough and remote pioneer reputation throughout its history.[4]

The key element of this pioneer character was a high degree of individual social and geographical mobility. Partly this was a function of famine survival strategies such as mobility of residence, the willingness to relocate a considerable distance from home in times of ecological stress. The economic survival strategies of hunting, blood brotherhood, pawnage, and cattle culling during drought and famine periods also form part of this frontier tradition that shapes Kamba history.[5] However, the key to Kamba success on the nineteenth-century frontier was the adaptation of their local and inter-regional trade practices – which had served both to diversify and ensure their agro-pastoral base – to the opportunities presented by merchant capitalist penetration. The local *kuthuua* system of family-organized local exchange was expanded in the early 1800s to accommodate a wider range of goods and a regional pattern of distribution that extended ultimately to the coast, where it linked up with Arab–Swahili long-distance trade.[6] In this process of trade expansion, the emergence of commercial specialists, who derived legitimacy and experience from their roles as hunting leaders, would be crucial. Their hunting backgrounds allowed

[3] R. W. Beachey, 'The East African Ivory Trade in the Nineteenth Century', *Journal of African History* 8, 2 (1967), 269–90; R. Bridges, 'Elephants, Ivory and the History of the Ivory Trade in East Africa', in *The Exploitation of Animals in Africa*, ed. J. C. Stone (Aberdeen: Aberdeen University, African Studies Group, 1988). See E. A. Alpers, 'The Ivory Trade in Africa: An Historical Overview', in *Elephant: The Animal and Its Ivory in African Culture* (catalogue) (Los Angeles: Fowler Museum, 1993), and his *Ivory and Slaves in Eastern Africa* (London: Oxford University Press, 1975); also A. A. Sheriff, *Slaves, Spices and Ivory in Zanzibar* (London: James Currey, 1987).

[4] K. A. Jackson, Jr., 'An Ethnohistorical Study of the Oral Traditions of the Akamba of Kenya', unpublished Ph.D. dissertation, University of California, Los Angeles, 1972, is a complete if not fully convincing study of Kamba origins and migration traditions. On Kitui migrations, see M. F. O'Leary, *The Kitui Akamba* (Nairobi: Heinemann Educational Books, 1984), 17–19.

[5] C. H. Ambler, *Kenyan Communities in the Age of Imperialism* (New Haven: Yale University Press, 1988), 9–43, 143–4. See P. Mbithi and P. Wisner, 'Drought and Famine in Kenya', *Journal of East African Research and Development* 3 (1973), 113–43.

[6] R. Cummings, 'The Early Development of Akamba Local Trade History, c. 1780–1820', *Kenya Historical Review* 4 (1976), 85–110. See also Cummings, 'Aspects of Human Porterage', 46–93.

them to capitalize on these skills and contacts needed to develop the extensive travel and commercial skills that would characterize Kamba long-distance trade. It is this capacity for innovation, adaptation, and market response that has been so frequently studied and admired by modern historians of the region.[7]

Of special interest has been the development of Kamba entrepreneurs utilizing the wage labour of porters in creating by mid-century a network carrying imports of cloth and other western industrial and oriental craft goods and exports of ivory.[8] The linchpin of this network was the ability of the Kamba entrepreneurs to produce a regular and growing supply of ivory. Here again the need for innovation and responsiveness to demand proved essential to the transformation of ivory hunting in Kitui during the last half of the nineteenth century.

Kamba small-scale hunting

Like their neighbours to the north and south, examined in the previous chapter, but unlike the hunters of central Kenya,[9] the Kamba were bearers of a tradition of hunting that we traced back to the Waata. Although their bows were noticeably smaller and less powerful, the adoption of acocanthera arrow poison as part of the hunting kit had made the early Kamba pioneers effective predators on the grasslands game of both the Machakos and Kitui regions. Elephant were certainly a part of the communities of prey animals recognized by the Kamba, but they were not specifically hunted for their ivory prior to the late eighteenth-century growth of long-distance trade. As with the growth of trade, the Kamba hunters would build and expand their hunting repertory in response to new opportunities.

Kamba migration stories assert that the original Kamba settlers were hunters and beekeepers rather than the agro-pastoralists they have come to think of themselves as being. Both traditions explicitly state that the first settlers were without cattle.[10] This may be another way of saying that they were poor in contrast to the people of today. It may also show admiration for the skills and courage of their ancestors, as hunting and beekeeping are

---

[7] See Kimambo, 'The Economic History'; and Lamphear, 'The Kamba'.

[8] Cummings, 'Aspects of Human Porterage', 145–72. See also his 'Wage Labour in Kenya in the Nineteenth Century', in *The Workers of African Trade*, ed. C. Coquery-Vidrovitch and P. Lovejoy (Beverly Hills: Sage Publications, 1985), 193–207; see Beachey, 'The East African Ivory Trade'. For general background on the nineteenth-century East African ivory trade in the context of precolonial underdevelopment, cf. Alpers, *Ivory and Slaves*; and Sheriff, *Slaves, Spices and Ivory*.

[9] Although bows and arrows are used among the Kikuyu and Mt. Kenya peoples, they tend to be associated with Asumba, the legendary original inhabitants and symbolic 'others' of Kikuyuland. The Kikuyu in general prefer spears, which are markedly less effective in elephant hunting. G. St. J. Orde-Brown, *The Vanishing Tribes of Kenya* (Westport, CT: Negro Universities Press, 1970), 20–21, 63. Also Interview B/10, Kathukya Kikwai, 28 April 1987.

[10] Jackson, 'Ethnohistorical Study', 157–8; Lamphear, 'The Kamba', 75ff. Also Interview B/9, King'oku Kaluku, 24 April 1987.

dangerous professions requiring both great ability and exceptional bravery. It might also be noted that, conceptually, beekeeping among the Kamba is still spoken of as a form of 'hunting' or pursuing honey. It requires either setting 'traps' – honey-collecting barrels made of hollowed logs – high up in trees to attract the bees, or locating naturally-occurring hives in dead trees in the forests. Both techniques involved the dangers of climbing to considerable heights and smoking out the bees.[11]

Paralleling the development of long-distance trade, we can discern a growth in the organization, the purposes, and, most significantly, the evaluation of the role of hunting among the Kitui Kamba. The last emerged clearly from the number of informants who made a distinction between hunting for food and hunting for elephant ivory – which they referred to as 'real hunting'.[12] Subsistence hunting was clearly less prized than the hunting of elephant, which produced wealth in the form of ivory, convertible to cattle and wives. Moreover, subsistence hunting did not distinguish the Kamba from their neighbours, who also hunted the same animals with the same or very similar techniques. In contrast, the methods and organization, the rituals and beliefs that came, in the late nineteenth century, to characterize Kamba elephant hunting became a central element in Kamba cultural identity. The Kamba hunters raised the venatic arts from a part-time, subsistence, and supplemental activity to the motor force of their social and economic system.

The base from which the transformation would arise was the set of local hunting practices in the Kitui district. The pattern of small groups of five or six young men hunting for game animals locally, which we have observed in Kwale and Meru districts, seems to have prevailed in Kitui and persisted into the colonial era. No elaborate hunting or ritual leadership seems to have been involved in this type of hunting, which appears to have been ubiquitous throughout the broad Kitui area.[13] The favoured prey and even the favourite portions of meat seem to be consistent across the map and similar to those of other Kenya hunters. Somewhat surprising

---

[11] Interviews B/8, Musembi Mulaki, 24 April 1987; and B/9, King'oku Kaluku, 24 April 1987, for the early history of beekeeping. See C. Dundas, 'History of Kitui', *Journal of the Royal Anthropological Institute* 43 (1913), 502–3; and J. Akong'a, ed., *Kenya District Socio-cultural Profiles, Kitui District*, draft report, Institute of African Studies, University of Nairobi, 1986, 53–56 on the persistence of beekeeping and honey making in the colonial era.

[12] In general, informants appeared to categorize hunting into three types: elephant hunting involving commercial objectives, long-distance travel, and a high level of organisation; subsistence hunting of food animals individually or more often in small groups; and juvenile hunting, especially of birds, by boys and young men (*anake*) as a practical training for adult or warrior age grade (*nzele*) hunting activities. Interviews B/7, Mwaniki Vila and Kilungu Musyoka, 24 April 1987; and B/10, Kathukya Kikwai, 28 April 1987 on 'real hunting'. See Interviews B/3, Julius Nduilu Kimau, 15 April 1987; B/5, Ndambuki Ndeve, 23 April 1987; B/6, Nzenge Kitoi, 23 April 1987.

[13] For the broad similarities of small-scale hunting, see Interviews B/1, J. M. Munyoki Kieti, 13 April 1987; and B/4, Kioko Mulanga, 16 April 1987, for the central Kitui hills area; Interviews B/7, Mwaniki Vila and Kilungu Musyoka, 24 April 1987 for the southern Mutomo region; B/10, Kathukya Kikwai, 28 April 1987; and B/11, Petero Kitheng'e, Paulo Ngutu Ngutha, and Musila Muli, 28 April 1987, for Migwani location in north central Kitui.

was the frequently stated preference for the liver (*itema*) of the various ungulate prey items. The liver was generally roasted at the kill site and shared by the hunting party, with the less favoured portions air-dried and brought back for distribution in the village of the hunters.[14] The declining status of organ meat in western culture had prejudiced me against this preference. Nonetheless, the practice seems consistent with both the nutritional value and difficulties in preservation of the innards. I might also postulate a possible link to the observation by hunters of the behaviour of large predators like lions, who also consume the innards first.[15]

One element in the local hunting tradition among the Kitui Kamba that diverges slightly from the general regional practice is an extended range and duration in subsistence hunting. Small, village-based groups, at least from the central areas of settlement around the Kitui hills (site of modern Kitui Town), seem to have travelled longer distances in pursuit of game than the truly localized hunters, whose pursuits seldom took them more than a day's walk from their base. In particular, hunters in pursuit of meat organized longer trips to either the Yatta plateau on the eastern edge of the district or to the Tana River to the north. The special features of both these areas, particularly the park-like grasslands found on top of the Yatta plateau, made them excellent game areas. The uplifted Yatta plateau resulted from an ancient lava flow that ran south-southeast from the foot of Mount Kenya for over a hundred miles to just north of the confluence of the Athi and Tsavo rivers. The long narrow plateau and the valley of the Athi River, flowing just to the east of it, mark the modern boundary between the Kitui and Machakos districts of Ukambani (Kambaland). The plateau, with its steep slopes on both east and west and its higher altitude, provided a naturally protected area with good rainfall, a haven for both wildlife and predators, not unlike the isolated plains within the Ngorongoro crater in northern Tanzania.

Elephants were found on the Yatta plateau and were hunted there even by the smaller hunting parties. By the middle years of the nineteenth century, however, increasing demand for ivory at the coast had led not only to a revolution in Kamba commerce, but to a transformation of Kamba ivory production methods as well. This transformation would have a profound impact on the subsequent hunting of elephants by Europeans, and eventually on the practices of game preservation in colonial Kenya.

Elephant hunting in Kitui

The growth of elephant hunting specifically for ivory export paralleled the emergence of large-scale caravan commerce in Ukambani. This parallelism was more than coincidental. Indeed, the same individuals who would

---

[14] Interviews B/2, Kitonga Kusewa, 14 April 1987; and B/10, Kathukya Kikwai, 28 April 1987, on prey and food preferences.

[15] Even more speculative would be the symbolic identification of the liver as the seat of courage among some Bantu speakers, comparable to the symbolic valuation of the heart in western culture.

emerge as leading long-distance traders were also the principal organizers of large-scale hunting expeditions. Both as individual entrepreneurs and as leaders of the merchant societies called *mwethia*, these individuals were crucially placed to tap the labour needed to operate both the production of ivory by hunting and the transportation of the tusks to coastal markets. They were also key figures in the process of linking together the smaller-scale, family-based trading organizations into wider networks at the heart of the Kamba commercial empire.[16]

The expansion of hunting was able to follow a path of development that was beaten by the early nineteenth-century expansion of trade examined by Robert Cummings.[17] Just as the *kuthuua* networks of local barter evolved into the large-scale trading organizations, sanctioned by the local councils (*nzama*) and led by outstanding war and hunting leaders (*athiani*), the local work groups (*mwethia*) would be tapped for both wage labour on trading caravans and volunteers on large-scale hunting expeditions. The integration of large-scale hunting into the pre-existing social institutions of work groups and the continuity of leadership by recognized hunting and warrior leaders made it possible for the Kamba to adapt the new economic practices of large-scale hunting and trading expeditions without 'undermining their historical society or making far reaching societal changes'.[18]

The new authority assumed by the *athiani* as hunting leaders was rooted in the oldest traditions of Kamba society, the traditions of migration and settlement, which were similarly led by *athiani*. These early population movements often originated in a response to drought or famine crises and the search for new opportunities. They were initiated by small groups of hunters and warriors led by their 'spies' or advance men. These men also exercised control of hunting and war magic, administered binding oaths to ensure group coherence, and enjoyed the blessings and official sanction of the senior elders on the *nzama*. By the mid-nineteenth century, a similar structure of leadership, labour recruitment, and official sanction had been adapted to the search for elephant herds and the new opportunities they represented to create wealth for the successful entrepreneurs.

The transformation to ivory harvesting

Between the early decades of the nineteenth century and the colonial era, elephant hunting in eastern Kenya underwent an economic and cultural transformation. The organizational changes that allowed for the emergence of long-distance trading enterprise were adapted to the needs of elephant hunting. By the 1840s, entrepreneurs and local leaders were organizing expeditions to travel beyond the local boundaries of Kitui

---

[16] Cummings, 'Aspects of Human Porterage', 56–61. See also his 'Wage Labor in Kenya'; and Kimambo, 'Economic History', 80–81.

[17] The following section relies heavily on Cummings's unpublished thesis, 'Aspects of Human Porterage', esp. 46–90.

[18] Cummings, 'Aspects of Human Porterage', 169.

district to purchase, find, or harvest ivory from the large herds of elephant that could be found across the region. The proceeds of these expeditions would be used to supply the coastal caravans of Kamba porters and merchants. Any means for obtaining ivory was permitted, and one should not overlook the efforts of Kamba 'hunters' to scavenge for the tusks of elephants that had died of natural causes, disease, and injury. Such 'found ivory' may have initially made up a considerable proportion of the supplies reaching the coastal trading network. Similarly, the exchange of cattle, small stock, cloth, and other imported goods for ivory with the Kamba's neighbours to the north and west remained an important and growing part of the overall supply throughout the pre-colonial period.

However, it was only the collection of ivory by means of finding and killing tusk-bearing elephants which made possible the rapid expansion in supply to satisfy the growth in demand created by the expanding coastal market. It was in the development and control of the procurement by hunting, transportation by caravan, and sale of ivory to Arab and Swahili merchants that led to the emergence of a new entrepreneurial elite among the Kitui Akamba during the mid-nineteenth century.

Far and away the most successful of these entrepreneurs in the 1830s and 1840s was Kivoi Mwenda. Born in the last decade of the eighteenth century, Kivoi had by the 1830s established a position as the premier ivory trader in Kitui, with headquarters near the modern Kitui Town, and an ivory-gathering network reaching across the Tana River to Mount Kenya and beyond. He was well known on the coast and regularly sent caravans of porters to Mariakani and Mombasa to sell ivory and obtain trade goods and cattle. His wealth and power, generated by commercial profits and his organizational skill demonstrated in both elephant-hunting expeditions and the caravan trade, earned him a considerable reputation outside Ukambani. We owe much of what we know of this reputation to the attention Kivoi received in the missionary researches of Johannes L. Krapf.[19] However, far more remarkable and interesting to us, is Kivoi's reputation within the Kamba community, which he dominated until his death during a hunting expedition in *c.* 1851.[20]

In most accounts of the Kamba ivory trade, the relationship between wealth derived from commerce and political leadership has been assumed. The ability to control new forms of revenue outside the constraints of village or community-based authority seemed sufficient explanation for the 'retinue' of followers and dependants, both family and non-kin, who surrounded Kivoi at the height of his power. The tendency was to attribute to Kivoi the powers associated with the kind of chieftaincy only instituted a half-century later by the colonial administration.[21] The connections between new forms of wealth and the increasing centralization of power by 'new men' is at the heart of this positivist view of the transition

---

[19] J. L. Krapf and J. Rebmann, *Travels, Researches and Missionary Labours During an Eighteen Years' Residence in Eastern Africa*, 2nd edn (London: Frank Cass, 1968 [1860]), 283–321.

[20] Ibid., 321 on Kivoi's death. See also Jackson, 'Ethnohistorical Study', 251–64.

[21] Krapf and Rebmann, *Travels, Researches and Missionary Labours*, 23–4 on Kivoi as a 'chief'.

from village or kinship-based, traditional society to a modern society of commodity production, occupational specialization, and commercial exchange. Kivoi in this paradigm becomes the entrepreneur who directly translates commercial profits into political power.

However, among the Akamba, for whom Kivoi has become an almost legendary culture hero, his wealth and power are both understood in less historicist or positivist terms and are more culturally grounded in the values and ideals of the non-commercial Kamba social order. Rather than a dichotomy of traditional and modern, Kivoi can best be understood as accommodating new sources of power within old paradigms of authority. I would also suggest that the central paradigm that Kivoi (and, to a lesser extent, other ivory caravan leaders) manipulated was that of the hunting leader.

In popular memory, Kivoi's place is described as that of a big man (*munene, wanene,* pl., from fat person). His authority as such was not a matter of the village or kinship-based structures, but rather was a product of the trading networks he had developed in the early nineteenth century, and the accumulation of wealth they had provided. It would be a mistake, however, to assume that the status of *munene* was merely a recognition or reflection of the accumulation of wealth. Indeed, 'Akamba informants state for as long as they can remember, the words *mundu munene* have been used descriptively to designate a special type of person within their society.'[22] At the core of this designation are two elements: first, the control of great wealth; and second, the use of that wealth in culturally approved patronage and social expenditure. The translation of the new sources of wealth into cattle, wives, and clients, rather than the accumulation of wealth *per se,* is what provided Kivoi with social approval and increasing status. At this, Kivoi proved himself as masterful as he was at hunting and trade organization, surrounding himself with clients and kin who were equated by the western visitor, Rev. Johannes Krapf, with the retainers or retinue of a major chief or prince.[23] I would suggest that the loyalty expressed by these followers more closely resembled not the political support due to a chief, but the respect and awe that attached to successful hunting leaders among the Kamba. The Kamba regarded highly those who travelled widely, endured hardship and danger, demonstrated power over the forces of nature through the manipulation of hunting magic, and generously shared the rewards of successful hunts by directly distributing meat to kinsmen and indirectly converting the proceeds of ivory sales into the social goods which build a cohesive community – cattle, wives, and dependants.

Within a decade of Kivoi's death while on an ivory-hunting expedition to the Tana River, the Kitui Kamba commercial empire of which he was an important, but not unique figure, had been successful challenged and undermined by the growth of the Arab–Swahili caravan trade.[24] This

---

[22] Jackson, 'Ethnohistorical Study', 252.

[23] Krapf and Rebmann, *Travels, Researches and Missionary Labours,* 310–16. See Jackson, 'Ethnohistorical Study', 253–4.

[24] See Alpers, *Ivory*; and Ambler, *Kenyan Communities,* 74–121.

trade has been the subject of numerous studies, principally from the perspective of the coastal merchants and international capital.[25] Even when the internal aspects of the trade have been examined, the focus has been on the commercial and political effects of the penetration of foreign capital and influence. Little attention has been paid to transformations wrought in the productive systems attached to the extractive trade in ivory, the hunting of elephants. Two aspects of this precolonial transformation are important for our study of colonial hunting: the decline in elephant numbers in Ukambani, and the growth in the hunters' secret society, Waathi, in the late nineteenth century.

The arrival of Arab–Swahili traders from the coast in increasing numbers after mid-century ought to have brought about an increase in elephant hunting to meet the increased demand for ivory. However, the opposite seems to have been the case in Kitui. This is probably due to the fact that, for the Kitui Akamba, the hunting of elephant and the sale and transportation of ivory were an integrated operation controlled and organized by *anene*, who combined the skills of hunting leader and merchant prince. With their displacement from the caravan trade, there appears to have been a decline in the ability to organize large-scale hunting expeditions. Other factors contributed to this decline. The elephant-hunting frontier seems to have passed beyond Kitui and, increasingly, Kamba and coastal purchasers of ivory had to seek hunter-sellers farther to the north and west, where the elephant herds were not depleted by persistent hunting or grown shy and defensive. The ability of Kitui hunters to exploit these distant territories was limited by what had become the large size of the Kamba hunting expedition, necessitated in part by the need for large numbers of porters to carry supplies out and ivory back, and in part by the wide spread in hunting participation among the Kamba male population. By the last half of the century, instead of small groups of from three to perhaps a dozen experienced hunters travelling together in pursuit of elephant herds, expeditions of several score, often upwards of a hundred and more hunters, had become common.[26] Organizing and sustaining such an expedition across difficult, sometimes hostile, territory, became more and more problematic as the herds retreated and opposition grew. Even Kivoi Mwenda's unparalleled skills seem ultimately to have foundered in this way.

Another effect of the growth of the size, scale, and broad participation in elephant hunting seems to have been the transformation and growing importance of the Waathi society. Because of its role in controlling the forces of nature, the Waathi society was frequently treated as a witches' coven by the colonial authorities and suppressed under anti-witchcraft legislation. This has made it difficult, especially in Ukambani, to directly

---

[25] In addition to Alpers, *Ivory*, and Sheriff, *Slaves*, cited above, from a dependency school perspective, see also C. S. Nicholls, *The Swahili Coast* (London: Oxford University Press, 1971) from a more classical economic theory of economic development and trade.

[26] Interview B/13, Kitema Ngumbi, 30 April 1987 for a vivid description of such an expedition.

study its organisation and practices. The major fieldwork conducted on the *waathi* society, that of the Japanese ethnologist, Hitoshi Ueda, has viewed it principally as a cult of affliction, in which the powers of the hunting leaders was seen as deriving from the nature and severity of the afflictions which they were empowered to heal.[27] However, Robert Cummings, in his essay on 'Akamba Local Trade History', provides an insightful account of the role of magic and its control in the early development of leadership and the accumulation of wealth by locally reputed expert hunters (and warriors).[28] Respect for the personal skills and courage of hunters was enhanced by the belief that such skills were 'god-given', in recognition of the spiritual powers inhering in such gifted individuals. Control of this spiritual power, organized through the hunters' cult or Waathi society, would become a crucial element in the later transformation of hunting practices on the eve of colonization.

The crisis of the 1890s

My own research among former hunters in Kitui district unearthed a graphic description of what appears to have become the prevailing pattern of organization and control of large-scale hunting expeditions in the late nineteenth and early twentieth centuries. The profound effects of the great famine of 1898–9, called 'Yua ya Ngomanisye',[29] and other environmental, economic, and political stresses may have exaggerated the ruthlessness of the hunt and distorted the control by the Waathi leadership. On the other hand, European travellers reported large hunting parties, often in excess of 100 hunters, several years before the Ngomanisye.[30] Let us examine the changes in the methods and organization of the hunt, and then try to explore the causes, which are rooted in the complex crisis years of the late 1890s.

According to Kikuli Mutulya of Bondoni in Mwingi location, northern Kitui District, in answer to my question about hunting elephants:

[27] H. Ueda, 'The Power of Hunting Leaders Among the Kamba', unpublished paper No. 116, University of Nairobi, Institute of African Studies, 1979. See also his 'The Wathi Ritual Among the Kamba', working paper No. 116, University of Nairobi, Institute of African Studies, 1979. My own field research was on the Waathi society, as it existed among the Tharaka of southeastern Meru district (see Chapter 2 of this volume). In contrast, Ueda's work was conducted in nearby Kyuso Division in the extreme north of Kitui district. I did not find any evidence of the Waathi still functioning in Kitui.

[28] Cummings, 'Early Development', 98–101.

[29] See Jackson, 'An Ethnohistorical Study', 30–31, for the names of famines in Ukambani and their uses in dating. Also see C. H. Ambler, 'The Great Famine in East Central Kenya, 1897–1900: A Regional View', unpublished paper, Kenya Historical Association Annual Conference, Nairobi, August 1977, 1–21, for a description of the regional effects of the famine and especially Kamba strategies for coping.

[30] W. A. Chanler, *Through Jungle and Desert: Travels in Eastern Africa* (New York: Macmillan, 1896), 284, reports on the activities of a large Kamba hunting party of 'about 100' encountered by von Hohnel in 1892. See H. Tate, 'Notes on the Kikuyu and Kamba Tribes of British East Africa', *Journal of the Royal Anthropological Society* 34 (1904), 36, for famine and increased hunting in this period.

[*Q: Did you ever hunt elephants?*] No, but my father did and I know how they hunted.

[*Q: Where did they hunt?*] Near Meru on the other side of the Tana River starting at Ng'iru and then travelling along the Tana for 4 days up to Garissa looking for herds of elephant.... I don't know exactly how many [days] but they would await the new moon and then prepare and go and leave on the third day of the new moon. There were about 100 men who went together.

[*Q: Were they all from Bondoni?*] No, they were in three groups: one from Bondoni, Ngomeni, and Kamuyoni. They were divided into three by age: the Mavisi, young boys; the Anake, they were married men with 5 [sic] children, and the Athiani or leaders. The athiani were old men and considered as the 'generals'.

[*Q: Would each man bring his own bow and arrow?*] And he would have a quiver the size of your thigh [indicating by circling his fingers around his upper leg] and 150 arrows with poison (*iwal*). Now you must listen carefully because I am going to tell you the whole story. The anake would go ahead followed by the athiani.... Two anake called *anake ma ngila* (fierce anake) carrying *kithiku* and *nzevu* (medicine for witches) and look for the footprints of the animals and report back to the athiani. The athiani would come and at least four of them would gather around the footprints and perform rituals that would make the animals or enemies stupid so they could not attack and would just stand still.

[*Q: The athiani were in charge of the medicine?*] Yes, yes, they would use the ritual to bring luck and make the enemies stupid.

[*Q: What happened when they met elephants?*] They had to bewitch them first, the fierce ones like elephants and lions, before they could be approached. First the *anake ma ngila* would go and test the wind by dropping dirt to see which way the wind was coming and then they would encircle [gesturing] upwind and approach as close as from here to the house [c. 20 metres] and then shoot [demonstrating with sound effects]. But first the athiani would bewitch them so that at least ten would just stand in a straight line and when they were close enough the athiani would give the word to shoot. They would shoot them all, everyone they could!

[*Q: Did they shoot the ones with big tusks first?*] They would shoot everyone regardless of size. Even a small tusk like this [indicating the length of his forearm] would fetch at least 3 cows, and bolts of cloth. They wanted the tusks to sell at Usuini to get cattle.[31]

The strict control of the hunt by the leaders, and hence by members of the Waathi society, emerges clearly from this text. Decisions as to when and where to hunt, and the control of medicine and ritual, gave the *athiani* a strong grip on hunting practice and technique. However, their control of rewards was even greater. Mr Mutulya continued:

After killing the elephants, the athiani would chase away the anake and in secret checked the marked arrowheads to see to whom they belonged. There were one or two *anake ma ngila* who would be allowed to stay. They

[31] Interview B/12, Kikuli Mutulya, 30 April 1987. The interviewer's questions appear in brackets and italics.

would hide the arrowheads of those they hate, who had been disobedient, and substitute the arrowheads, by dipping them in blood of those they liked. The athiani would also remove the genitals of the elephants. [Pause] Now in the forests they would take the tusks to a good spot and the athiani would declare whose arrows had killed and whose had not. They would give the tusks to those who had killed and they would carry them home.... If you didn't kill anything, you wouldn't get anything.

[*Q: If you had killed the elephant, you would get both tusks?*] It wasn't easy to kill an elephant with one arrow, so the owners of the different arrows that had been found would each share in the tusks, even if there were ten.[32]

Afterwards the tusks would be carried home and frequently buried until traders visited the area or, at the next new moon, a caravan could be organized to transport the tusks to buyers at the coast (Usuini). The difficulties of transport, especially as the colonial administration increased its effort to monopolize the ivory trade during the century, would become a key factor in limiting the returns of ivory to local hunters and increasing the take for local big men, middlemen, and ivory buyers in the lucrative ivory export business. The possibilities for corruption in this trade would not go unnoticed by the members of the Game Department and Customs officials, creating what would become one of Kenya's most persistent conservation problems of the twentieth century.

By these methods the elders of the Waathi society, both as *athiani* and as caravan organizers, maintained control over their juniors and could direct the proceeds from these large group hunts to those they favoured.[33] It is clear from the evidence that the most proficient hunters assured their success by being among those who dared to approach the animals at the closest range before shooting. Those with less skill, courage, or confidence would hang back and at the signal let fly with their arrows. This 'browning the herd' would have a very low likelihood of success and must be seen as justified only by the high gains to be had from a lucky shot.[34] Moreover, it explains why no regard seems to have been paid by these hunters to the size of tusks or the age and sex of the animals attacked. If even a small share in the ivory might be obtained by the fortunate amateur, it was worth loosing an arrow in the general direction of the herd.

There are two further implications of this description of *fin de siecle* hunting methods in Ukambani. One is the apparent absence of a conservation policy among these hunters. Their efforts to kill entire herds, regardless of age and sex, shows a complete lack of a sense of conserving animals for

---

[32] Ibid. See also Ueda, 'Power of Hunting Leaders'.

[33] This may be the explanation of the excision of the genitalia and especially the 'dugs' of the female elephants killed in this way. The resemblance to human genitals and breasts, often cited as the reason for hiding them from the younger men, may well be a rationale which served to keep the young and inexperienced hunters at a distance while the crucial negotiations over whose arrows were to be credited with the kill were taking place. See G. Lindblom, *The Akamba in British East Africa*, 2nd edn (Uppsala: Archives D'Études Orientales, 1920 [1916]), 333.

[34] See Lindblom, *Akamba*, 465–9; Dundas, 'History of Kitui', 505; and C. W. Hobley, *The Ethnology of A-Kamba and Other East African Tribes* (London: Frank Cass, 1971 [1910]), 45. All tend to confirm this view.

future exploitation or for a more general aesthetic or moral purpose. Does this say something about deeply held African ideas about the abundance of nature's bounty? Or is it the result of a half-century or more of increasing commercialization of ivory and elephant hunting, and the late nineteenth-century economic and ecological crisis that threw any such ideas of limiting the bag to the winds? Or, is it likely to be a combination of ideas of unlimited abundance, restricted technology, and increasing pressure that created such scenes of wanton slaughter as Mr Mutulya's father related to him?

The second consideration is the high value placed on the hunting of elephant, and the considerable fortunes that were accumulated by selling ivory for cattle. More than one prominent family in Kitui in the late twentieth century could trace its fortune to the profits of successful elephant hunting in the late nineteenth century. Although the wealth continued to be expressed and enjoyed in the form of large herds of cattle and large followings of men and women,[35] the commercialization of hunting through the coastal (Usuini) markets – opened first by Arab and Swahili merchants and later by Somali and Indian traders – transformed both the hunt itself and its place within Kenyan African society.[36]

There can be little question that the forms of elephant hunting adapted by Kamba hunters by the end of the last century are extreme versions of the traditional methods. There seem to me to be several possible explanations of the roots of this transformation. First and most significant are the growth of the coastal trade and especially the penetration of the interior by coastal merchants looking for ivory. The increase in demand for ivory and the simultaneous suppression of the long-established Kamba caravan trade pushed many ambitious men into the production end of the ivory trade. Instead of using their organizational and leadership skills to develop commercial enterprises, the *athiani* would use those same skills to increase the size, scale, and scope of the elephant-hunting safari. By 1900, larger and larger expeditions that were gone for longer periods and travelled longer distances in search of elephant herds became the rule rather than the exception. In part, the disappearance of elephant herds from Ukambani and the pursuit of big tuskers further to the north and west had been factors gradually shifting the duration and distance of the hunt during the last half of the century. To this must be added the effects of the devastating drought of 1897–9. Hunting had long been one of several famine strategies used by the people of Ukambani.[37] What is strange about the events of the post-Ngomanisye famine is that it was ivory

[35] E.g. interviews B/9, King'oku Kaluku, 24 April 1987; and B/11, Petero Kitheng'e, Paulo Ngutu Ngutha, and Musila Muli, 28 April 1987. See K. Ndoo, *The Life Story of a Kenya Chief as told to J. B. Carson* (London: Evans Bros., 1958).

[36] M. Stone, 'Organized Poaching in Kitui District: A Failure of District Authority, 1900 to 1960', *International Journal of African Historical Studies* 5, 3 (1972), 436–52.

[37] Ambler, 'The Great Famine', and B. E. Conn, 'Ecology in Historical Perspective', unpublished paper, Historical Association of Kenya Conference, 1972. See also W. E. H. Stanner, 'The Kitui Kamba: A Study of British Colonial Administration', unpublished ms. in KNA DC/KTI/6/2/1, 52–8.

hunting in an effort to obtain cattle rather than hunting for food directly that seems to have increased dramatically until its suppression by the colonial authorities.[38]

Colonial era adaptations

The direct suppression of elephant hunting by colonial law and adminis-tration is only part of the story. During the first half of the twentieth century, Kamba hunters would first conceal their hunting from the gaze of Europeans and their agents, and then increasingly attach and subordinate themselves to the hunting of the Europeans, in the process redefining the meaning and altering the practice of both African and white hunting. The Kamba would emerge as important actors in the rise of colonial hunting as gun bearers, trackers, skinners, camp organizers, and other hunting auxiliaries and so-called subordinate staff. They would also bring to bear their profound knowledge of the prey, the terrain, and the skills required to exploit them. And they would go on hunting in numbers and in secret until the last decades of colonial rule.[39]

Much of the colonial transformation of hunting in Ukambani took place beneath the radar of the colonial authorities. In the early stages of colonial rule in Kitui district, this simply meant that hunters tried to steer clear of the eyes of the administration, especially the colonial headquarters in the Kitui hills. For local hunters, this led to reducing the scale of operations and frequenting the game areas like the Yatta plateau instead of areas close to the government station (*boma*) or to those areas under closer administration.[40] As colonial administration extended out from the *boma* at Kitui Town, more caution had to be exercised, even by the small-scale hunters, to conceal their periodic hunting parties.

As the colonial presence expanded and intensified, the process of occultation of small-scale hunting would become more difficult. Locally, the killing of elephant and other *shamba*-raiding animals might be disguised as defence of the life and property of the hunter-farmer and his crops and fields. Even if the kill took place at some distance from the fields, it might still be represented as following up a rogue elephant or a known field raider. As often as not, the local African authorities, the chiefs and head-men who were charged with the enforcement of the game laws, were often themselves members of the hunting fraternity and in sympathy with their aims. They would either collude in the offence or turn a blind eye to the colonial crime that had often been responsible for their own elevation to positions of power.[41]

Deception was another tactic. The carrying of bow and poison arrows would be presented to the colonial agents as a matter of personal protection

---

[38] See Akong'a, *Kenya District Socio-Cultural Profiles*, 45–50.

[39] H. Seaton, *Lion in the Morning* (London: John Murray, 1963), 70–90.

[40] Interviews B/3, Julius Ndiulu Kimau; and B/1, J. M. Munyoki Kieti.

[41] See Ndoo, *Life Story of a Kenya Chief*.

against human enemies and predatory animals. Yet these weapons were always in readiness to seize opportunities to hunt. Small-scale hunting for food would seemingly disappear from under the eyes of the administration, but would continue its role both as a means of obtaining food and of acculturating young men to Kamba values of manliness and achievement.

For the larger elephant-hunting safari, the problems posed by the extension of colonial authority were more complex. Large groups of armed men could hardly be represented as having a legitimate purpose, given the colonial prohibition on both military and hunting expeditions. As colonial scrutiny increased, it became harder to explain the absence of large numbers of young men from the villages and fields. The result was that the areas of large-scale elephant hunts withdrew as the colonial purview expanded. By the time of the Second World War, elephant hunting had become largely restricted and relocated to the distant margins of the vast Kitui district. In the northern reaches along the bend of the Tana River, both Tharaka and Kamba hunters continued to hunt elephants, bury their tusks, and move them to markets in Somalia and the coast beyond and beneath the gaze of the colonial officers and the game rangers. In the south, towns like Mutha, Kanziko, and Mutomo would become poachers' havens, bases for hunting expeditions which extended deep into the wildlife-rich areas that would shortly after the war be gazetted as Tsavo National Park, Kenya's premier elephant reserve.[42]

The process of obfuscation, occultation, and relocation of the pre-colonial heritage of hunting in Kitui district was a gradual one that must be reconstructed from bits and pieces of testimony, gathered by inter-viewing individual informants still residing in the neighbourhoods in which they had hunted as young men and boys. This is a difficult task, but far easier than the task that remains to be done: documenting the activities of those young men who were forced to abandon the 'traditional' hunting field and find other ways to earn their livelihoods, maintain their skills, and steer clear of the lengthening arm of colonial law.

Prior to the colonial era, Kamba men had earned a well-deserved reputation as travellers, as a result of their recruitment and employment as caravan porters and organizers, their commercial travels as procurers of ivory and distributors of imported goods, and their participation in far-flung hunting expeditions.[43] By the end of the Great War, they had added to their reputation for travel an equally well-deserved reputation as loyal and effective soldiers and police. The timing of this emergence of Kamba men as suitable for recruitment to the uniformed services lends weight to the supposition that young, able-bodied men, who had previously sought employment for wages in the caravan trade or pursued careers as elephant hunters and ivory merchants and porters, now turned up in numbers as military and police recruits. This was no doubt largely a result of the prejudices and attitudes of British recruitment officers in looking for

---

[42] Interviews B/10, 11, 12 and 13 on the northern region and B/5, 6, 7, 8, 9, and 15 on the southern areas bordering Tsavo Park.

[43] See above, pp. 42–4.

Photo 3.1 *Philip Percival and Kamba Trackers, c.* 1915   (*Kenya National Archives*)

members of 'warlike tribes'.[44] However, we should not ignore the fact that this kind of outdoor life, involving travel, discipline, and a sense of adventure, was very much consonant with Kamba cultural expectations of what was a suitable vocation for young men.

It should be even less surprising to discover that opportunities opened up – especially after the Great War – for employment in the rapidly expanding safari industry as porters and camp assistants, and for those with hunting experience as trackers, skinners, and the most exalted of the subordinate positions, gun bearers. Our supposition is borne out by the myriad testimonies to the faithful and 'stout-hearted gun bearer', dedicated trackers, and efficient guides who were the silent 'dark companions' of the great safaris of the 1920s and 1930s.[45] With the introduction of safari cars and lorries, Kamba men would also develop the skills that would enable them to work as drivers and mechanics. The anecdotal evidence for this is widespread in the many safari accounts written by visiting and professional hunters, and can be supplemented by the evidence of the histories and biographies of the pioneer safari companies.[46] And there is

[44] Timothy Parsons, '"Wakamba Warriors Are Soldiers of the Queen": The Evolution of the Kamba as a Martial Race, 1890–1970,' *Ethnohistory* 46, 4 (1999), 671–701. See his *The African Rank and File* (Portsmouth, NH: Heinemann, 1999); and below, pp. 344–5 on Kamba recruitment to the game and park service.

[45] S. E. White, *The Land of Footprints* (Garden City, NY: Doubleday, Page, 1913), 196–209 for a particularly glowing example of this kind of tribute. See also Chapter 4 below, pp. 82–4).

[46] E.g., works by safari hunters such as C. Akeley, S. E. White, T. Roosevelt, G. Eastman, P. H. Percival, and J. A. Hunter attest in passing to the presence of Kamba staff in various positions. For histories of the safari industry, see K. M. Cameron, *Into Africa. The Story of the East African Safari* (London: Constable, 1990); A. Cullen, *Downey's Africa* (London: Cassell, 1959); J. Hemsing, *Ker and Downey Safaris. The Inside Story* (Nairobi: Ker and Downey Safaris, 1989); and D. Holman, *Inside Safari Hunting with Eric Rundgren* (New York: Putnam, 1970). For photographic evidence, see Fig. 3.1 above, and the many safari and museum

ample if mute testimony from the many photographs of Kamba safari staff from the earliest days of the safari industry (Photo 3.1). This is one case in which a picture is not worth so much as even a few paragraphs might be in documenting the lives and work experience of the young men and old who served as guides and trackers to the white hunters.

The African voice attesting to the importance and omnipresence of Africans on safari has been silent – or perhaps silenced. The lack of literacy (and numeracy) among African subordinate staff means that for the contemporary observer, the Kamba and other African companions of the safari hunters have been made largely invisible by both the white hunters and their historians.[47] The fact that employment in the safari industry led to the urbanization and deracination of the Kamba, their separation – from the life of the village and the ways of those who continued to hunt elephant and smaller game in Machakos and Kitui – has made it difficult, if not impossible, for the contemporary historian to record the African voice on safari. We must read their histories between the lines of the white hunters who employed them, learned from them, and created the Kenyan safari together with them as a transcultural production.[48]

[46] (contd) expedition photographs in the collections of the Museum of Natural History, New York.

[47] Steven Feierman, 'Colonizers, Scholars, and the Creation of Invisible Histories', in *Beyond the Cultural Turn*, ed. V. Bonnell and L. Hunt (Berkeley: University of California Press, 1999), 182–216. See Chapter 6 on safari hunting for a discussion of the impact of African inaudibility on our understanding of this hunting subculture.

[48] For the concept of transcultural construction, see M. L. Pratt, *Imperial Eyes* (London: Routledge, 1992), 1–11.

Part II

★★★★★★★★★★★★★★★★★★★★★★★★

The White Hunters

Hunting was a favorite sport of rulers in both Moghul and Rajput courts. Quite apart from its pleasures, hunting demonstrated the king's valor and prowess. The royal hunt was also a symbolic battle between civilization and wilderness, in which the king vanquished threatening beasts of the woods. The king could not afford to lose this contest, and the royal hunt was often an elaborate campaign with advance preparations that ensured success.

From the exhibition of South Asian Paintings at
Hong Kong Museum of Art, December 2001

Four

◆◆◆◆◆◆◆◆◆◆◆◆◆◆◆◆◆◆◆◆◆◆◆◆◆

Class & Tradition
in the Making of the Hunt

The Europeans who began in the last half of the nineteenth century to hunt 'big game' in what would become Kenya were the inheritors and carriers of an ancient tradition of hunting. Since the Middle Ages, this tradition had become a highly charged symbolic activity, steeped in ritual and social meaning beyond the simple pursuit of animals for food and hides. 'The hunt', as this tradition has been called,[1] would clash in crucial ways with the traditions of hunting practised in Kenya by the diverse hunting and farming communities that Europeans would encounter from the late nineteenth century. In the following pages, I will examine the most salient elements of the European tradition as it developed and manifested itself among East Africa's invaders, so that we can better understand the transformation of hunting that the colonial situation would produce.

Unlike the African traditions examined in the previous chapters, the European hunting heritage had become, since the late Middle Ages, a class-divided and contested arena for the symbolic expression of mastery over both nature and the lower orders of society.[2] Three elements of the tradition would directly affect the relations between African and European hunters in Kenya: the view of hunting as the exclusive prerogative of gentlemen and the exclusion of peasants from the legal pursuit of game; the understanding of wildlife as a form of property whose ownership and use were controlled and determined by law; and finally, the symbolic uses of the hunt as reaffirmation and demonstration of the social hierarchy that

---

[1] See J. M. MacKenzie, 'Chivalry, Social Darwinism, and Ritualised Killing', in *Conservation in Africa*, ed. D. Anderson and R. Grove (Cambridge: Cambridge University Press, 1987), 41–61.

[2] For the place of animals and hunting in general within the Western tradition, see Keith Thomas, *Man and the Natural World* (New York: Pantheon, 1983); Harriet Ritvo, *The Animal Estate* (Cambridge, MA: Harvard University Press, 1987); and Matt Cartmill, *A View to a Death in the Morning* (Cambridge MA: Harvard University Press, 1993).

gave meaning to the lives of the gentleman hunters or sportsmen of the European tradition.[3]

Since classical antiquity, the significance of hunting within the cradle areas of Western culture has been on hunting as a manly exercise for princes, its virtues connected to the development of leadership skills and martial ability among the rulers and warriors of ancient societies.[4] This is not to say that hunting was in any way restricted to the ruling classes of antiquity, merely that among the elite of warriors and princes it was those skills honed by hunting that were seen as giving value and meaning to the pursuit of game and that elevated it from the common practices of hunting for the pot.

During the Middle Ages, hunting in northern and western Europe would begin its transformation from a practical skill and subsistence-oriented, economic activity to the ritualized sport of gentlemen and nobles, the Hunt. This can best be understood as part of a dialectical process by which the hunting of common folk was demeaned and eventually forbidden by the growing power of the landed classes and the warrior nobility and their expropriation of hunting resources (animals, forests, and technology) for their own exclusive use. Thus, hunting by peasants and commoners was transformed into an illegal act against the king and his privileged nobles.

Poaching, the illegal taking of game, especially the king's deer, can be seen as the defining crime of the medieval social order. Poachers from the lower orders of society who took only small game for the pot might be tolerated or ignored by the king's gamekeepers and foresters. Those men of means, gentlemen without the private estates or access to the privileges extended to the nobility by royal assent, who would hunt the king's deer enjoyed no such tolerance. The gentleman poacher would become a figure of legend and folklore, with Robin Hood being only the best remembered of the breed. Poaching by gentlemen signified an act of defiance of the social order, a ritual of rebellion and declaration of independence.[5] A popular culture based on 'poaching fraternities' of gentleman hunters was being created by the dialectic of medieval hunting.[6]

On the other hand, as legal hunting became a more exclusive privilege of the landed elite, it 'took on an opposite significance among the aristocracy [to the notions of freedom and defiance among the poachers].

---

[3] For an extreme example of the aristocratic view of hunting, see J. Ortega y Gasset, *Meditations on Hunting* (New York: Charles Scribner's Sons, 1972). Paul Shepard's *The Tender Carnivore and the Sacred Game* (New York: Charles Scribner's Sons, 1973) offers an equally romantic view of the universality of the hunting ethos. In contrast, Simon Schama's *Landscape and Memory* (New York: Vintage, 1995), 43ff offers a view of the forest hunting practices of the eighteenth-century Polish nobility that stresses the variations and divergences from a single European hunting ethos.

[4] J. K. Anderson, *Hunting in the Ancient World* (Berkeley: University of California Press, 1985), offers the best overall view of ancient hunting available. For a study that illuminates the social and political context of ancient hunting, see Judith Barringer, *The Hunt in Ancient Greece* (Baltimore: The Johns Hopkins University Press, 2002).

[5] Cartmill, *A View to a Death*, 60ff.

[6] R. B. Manning, *Hunters and Poachers* (Oxford: Clarendon Press, 1993), 135–70.

In those circles, hunting became associated with upper-class status, and hunting practices became encrusted with courtly ceremony.'[7] Thus, the creation of a class of commoner and gentleman poachers, who 'associated [hunting] with freedom, feasting, and rebellion against authority',[8] was the obverse of the emergence of an aristocracy of the chase, for whom the symbolic significance of hunting, as much as that of the nobleman's sword, was to designate high status as members of Europe's (and especially England's) warrior elite.

The association of hunting with military skills and leadership among the feudal rulers of Europe made noble hunting a sign of superiority as it changed all other hunting into poaching. In late medieval England, 'Hunting was a preparation for war and was regarded as the best means, short of actual combat, for testing valour and developing the skills necessary for mounted combat. Hunting was less dangerous than duelling, which in any case, was forbidden by the laws of England.'[9]

The old connection between hunting and combat became, under medieval conditions of a ruling class of mounted warriors, an outward sign of nobility, proclaimed in custom and law.

During the early modern era from 1485 to the English Civil War (1640), 'English game legislation became more and more socially restrictive.'[10] Parliamentary game laws severely curtailed legal hunting by imposing high property qualifications, leaving many who had previously enjoyed the right to hunt to turn their resentments against aristocratic privilege. These laws 'can also be viewed as part of the seignorial assault upon commons and wastes',[11] and thus as part of the destruction of the independence of smallholders and peasants by the landed aristocracy.

The laws of hospitality supported what the parliamentary laws proclaimed. Only the wealthiest of individuals could afford to entertain in the royal manner, which normally 'included opportunities for hunting'[12] in the private parks and estates of the nobility and in royal game parks. By 1600, only the great lords could offer such accommodation and 'hunting was for great men only, not peasants'.[13] The drama of the struggle over the control of wildlife and the suppression of poaching was being moved onto the same stage where the central struggle for class hegemony within English society was being enacted.

The response of the peasantry and gentry to the aristocratic assault on their access to wildlife resources was to make 'poaching ... a national pastime in Tudor and Stuart England'.[14] A century-long conflict replaced

---

[7] Cartmill, *A View to a Death*, 61.

[8] Ibid.

[9] Manning, *Hunters and Poachers*, 4, and 35–56 on medieval hunting and warfare. The connection between military prowess and hunting skill is made in an African imperial context by R. S. S. Baden-Powell, *Sport and War* (London: Heinemann, 1900), 17–40.

[10] Baden-Powell, *Sport and War*, 5, and 57–82 on the role of socially restrictive game laws.

[11] Ibid., 58.

[12] Ibid., 9.

[13] Ibid., 11.

[14] Ibid., 183.

the medieval game of gentlemanly poaching during the seventeenth century. This 'long affray' of the poaching wars would continue with mounting intensity in the eighteenth century and last until the Great War brought English rural society into the twentieth century.[15]

Prior to this time, the authorities and the poachers had treated 'illegal hunting … [as] a manly game … a game that reinforces male gender identity'.[16] For the poachers, deer stealing in particular was 'an assertion of independence and an act of private rebellion'.[17] For the gamekeepers and foresters 'among the "poaching fraternity", the game [of controlling poaching] was an opportunity to display male virtuosity'.[18] This sense of poaching as 'a boy's game played by men', which developed in the Middle Ages, would never completely die off and would influence many of the attitudes to poaching among gamekeepers and settlers we encounter in colonial Kenya. But changes in English society would bring about new, more severe attitudes that would, in the modern era, come to overshadow these more playful views.

A new seriousness seems to have entered the long affray when the turmoil of civil war and revolution brought the landed gentry to a new social and political prominence in England in the eighteenth century.[19] The squirearchy, less secure in its new status and privileges than the old nobility, and perhaps recognizing new economic values in their land and its animal resources, would approach hunting as an attack on their property rights. Along with a host of other crimes against property such as smuggling, arson, and even the blacking of faces to hide one's identity, poaching would be subject to a draconian code imposing capital punishment on those who continued to play the game. Not only would royal game – the king's deer – be protected by the game laws, but even the snaring of hares on private land would, after 1723, be subject to the harshest of penalties.[20] This change in the legal treatment of poaching reflected a social transformation within English rural society from aristocracy to squirearchy that would run up to the industrial transformation in the second half of the eighteenth century. Hunting would all but cease to be a manly game and a contest among gentlemen: 'In the early eighteenth century, … deer-stealing …

[15] Harry Hopkins, *The Long Affray: The Poaching Wars, 1760–1914* (London: Secker and Warburg, 1985). Although Hopkins restricts the poaching wars to the period after 1760, it appears to me that its first skirmishes and the drawing of battle lines took place in the aftermath of the English Civil Wars, almost a century earlier.

[16] B. A. Hanawalt, 'Men's Games, King's Deer: Poaching in Medieval England', *Journal of Medieval and Renaissance Studies* 18, 2 (1988), 175.

[17] Ibid., 192.

[18] Ibid., 193.

[19] This passage draws heavily on the work of E. P. Thompson, *Whigs and Hunters. The Origin of the Black Act* (London: Allen Lane, 1975), on the social history of English poaching. Also, see Douglas Hay, 'Poaching and the Game Laws on Cannock Chase', in *Albion's Fatal Tree*, ed. D. Hay, P. Linebaugh, and E. P. Thompson (London: Allen Lane, 1975), 189–253. See also P. B. Munsche, *Gentlemen and Poachers: The English Game Laws, 1671–1831* (Cambridge: Cambridge University Press, 1981).

[20] Thompson, *Whigs and Hunters*. See also Schama, *Landscape and Memory*, 165, who suggests of the Whig hunters of the early eighteenth century that 'their mastery of the country hunts [were a way of] symbolizing their political and social supremacy'.

was no longer "a brave diversion" for persons of quality. The gentleman poacher, apart from an occasional eccentric, passed into history.'[21]

A new, rougher element of society would engage in illegal hunting, while the gentry would come to see poaching as a form of class warfare, to be opposed with ruthless determination. Allied now with the declining nobility in what had become their common attachment to hunting privilege, the gentry would shift the face of battle down the social scale. It would be the rural poor who would now bear the brunt of the assault on their access to hunting opportunities and resources that accompanied the assault on the commonage and forests that had in the past supported peasant independence. Enclosures and game law restrictions were the two fronts of the same advance of the new propertied classes in rural England against the lower orders or rural workers, peasants, and cottagers. The campaign against poaching was the symbolic standard beneath which marched the advancing power of the squirearchy.

Nowhere are the power and the values of the landed gentry more evident than in the emergence of fox-hunting, or 'riding to hounds', as the preferred form of sport among the upper classes. During the late eighteenth century, fox-hunting 'came to be looked upon as one of the chief promoters ... of unity, stability, harmony, and devotion to traditional deferential values' in English country districts.[22] Fox-hunting would bring together in the field of sport all the classes of rural society in a visible ritual re-enactment of the privileges and deference required by the rural elite: a dramatization of the mastery over the natural world and the subordination of the social world to the local lords of the countryside. According to David Itzkowitz, fox-hunting 'meetings were, in fact, one of the major sources of contact among the various classes, but the relative differences in social station were never forgotten.... While hunting people boasted of the openness of the hunting field, there was no question that the values the field fostered were conservative and aristocratic.'[23]

In the ritualized fox-hunt, as in the less formal and stagy, but still symbolically loaded, shooting party, a profoundly antidemocratic and hierarchical impulse among 'hunting people' was periodically reinforced by the ritual slaughter of a wild animal by sportsmen and their ladies, riding horses and aided by hunting dogs and the assembled lower orders of rural society. Combining the symbolic elements of medieval military authority with the very real economic powers of the landed classes, fox-'hunting alone developed a mystique that raised it to the level of a national institution that, to the minds of more than just hunting men, could be trifled with only at the risk of wide ranging social consequences'.[24]

It might be noted here that such an important institution of English rural life in the nineteenth century was a natural candidate for introduction into

---

[21] C. Chevenix Trench, *The Poacher and the Squire. A History of Poaching and Game Preservation in England* (London: Longman, 1967), 114.

[22] D. C. Itzkowitz, *Peculiar Privilege: A Social History of English Foxhunting 1753–1885* (Hassocks: Harvester Press, 1977), 1.

[23] Ibid., 26–7.

[24] Ibid., 16.

Kenya in the early twentieth century. Such efforts were made in the vicinity of Nairobi, where English settlers bred the horses and dogs, and where silver-backed jackals substituted for foxes, and African servants and peasants for their English counterparts. However, fox-hunting was already *passé* in England and never really took root among the transplanted English gentlemen of rural Kenya. Nonetheless, the breeding of both horses and dogs remained a popular and profitable business in Kenya for many years.[25]

The decline of English fox-hunting came in the period of the 1870s and 1880s, largely because of the agricultural depression of that period, the chorus of complaints by the non-hunting farmers against the damage hunting caused to their profits, and the demand for the payment of compensation.[26] An increase in the poisoning of foxes and the growing use of wire fences were further evidence of the efforts of non-hunting landholders to spoil the game for hunters. This was only one aspect of a broader opposition to fox-hunting that had emerged in English society among those branches of the middle class who saw fox-hunting in particular (but also hunting privilege in general) as a waste of time and valuable resources, as a neglect of duty, and, in what would become a key part of the modern anti-hunting sentiment, as a particularly obnoxious form of cruelty to animals.[27]

Behind the attack on fox-hunting as England's 'national institution', ensuring the social order and the stability of traditional rural society, lay the profound transformation of English society and values engendered by industrialism and the rise to prominence of a new middle class. New attitudes towards nature were 'linked to the growth of towns and the emergence of an industrial order in which animals became increasingly marginal to the processes of production'.[28]

Hunting of all kinds was significantly affected by the industrial and urban transformation and the commercialization of agriculture that led to the decline in fox-hunting. From the early 1800s, especially after the railways linked town to country, an increasing intrusion into the countryside by members of the new urban middle classes – including many women – meant a gradual displacement of the landed gentry from their exclusive seats of privilege.[29] By the early twentieth century, the figure of the fox-hunter or country gentleman as a weekend sportsman was becoming one of ridicule and contempt. The general decline of the aristocratic classes, which was sealed by the First World War, left the sportsman within

---

[25] The background to Kenyan horse breeding and training can be found in B. Markham, *West with the Night* (Boston: Houghton Mifflin, 1942); and M. Lovell, *Straight on Till Morning. The Biography of Beryl Markham* (London: Hutchinson, 1987).

[26] Itzkowitz, *Peculiar Privilege*, 152–79.

[27] Ibid., 139–46.

[28] Thomas, *Man and the Natural World*, 181, 243–54.

[29] The argument for a general or single trend toward more humane treatment of animals in nineteenth-century Britain has been contested in recent work by Harriet Ritvo, 'Animals in Nineteenth-century Britain: Complicated Attitudes and Competing Categories', in *Animals and Human Society*, ed. A. Manning and J. Serpell (London: Routledge, 1994), 106–26, esp. 112–14 where this relates to English hunting and empire.

European culture as a symbol of the now decadent old order of rural life. Nowhere does this become more evident than in the use, by film-makers, of hunting and gentlemen hunters as symbols for the decadence and moral bankruptcy of the rural elite. Jean Renoir's classic, *La Règle du Jeu*, 1939, is a poignant and humorous eulogy to the dying order as seen through the weekend hunting party in rural France.[30] A more recent and stinging account of the anachronistic violence and moral decay of the upper classes is Alan Bridges' *The Shooting Party*, which is merciless in its caricatures of hunters as symbols of social decadence.[31]

The embourgeoisement of European culture not only drove the gentleman hunters from their perches atop the rural social hierarchy, it also began to drive them out of Europe. Moreover, the decline of animal and bird populations in England that accompanied the enclosure and systematic agricultural exploitation of the countryside sent would-be hunters who could afford to pay for their sport in pursuit of game elsewhere – first to the continent of Europe, especially Switzerland, and to the Indian subcontinent in pursuit of tigers and the hunting of wild pigs from horseback (*shikar*).[32] Frequently, European sportsmen came to figure in the saga of the North American wilderness, as the trans-Mississippi West became a happy hunting ground for those seeking bison, bear, moose, and elk. By the mid-nineteenth century, European gentleman hunters had discovered – and by the early twentieth century would virtually eliminate – the wild game of South Africa, aided in good measure by the 'Boer' farmers and settlers, who were not considered gentlemen.[33]

By the 1880s, African game trails were leading European sportsmen and professional hunters north of the Limpopo and Zambezi, into the yet unexploited hunting grounds of East Africa. They would carry with them not just the desire to hunt 'big game', but the banner of imperial conquest.[34] Most importantly, they would display in East Africa a very distinctive idea about what hunting meant. Its associations over centuries with military skill and virtue, with robust athleticism and manliness, with chivalry and honour, differed markedly from the understanding of hunting by the

---

[30] *La Règle du Jeu* (*The Rules of the Game*) (1939), dir. Jean Renoir; cast: Marcel Dallo, Nora Gregor.

[31] *The Shooting Party* (1985), dir. Alan Bridges; cast: James Mason, Edward Fox, Dorothy Tutin, and Sir John Gielgud.

[32] W. K. Storey, 'Big Cats and Imperialism: Lion and Tiger Hunting in Kenya and Northern India, 1898–1930', *Journal of World History* 2, 2 (1991), 135–73 for the imperial implications and ritual elements of Indian as well as African big-game hunting. See J. M. MacKenzie, *The Empire of Nature. Hunting, Conservation and the British Empire* (Manchester: Manchester University Press, 1988), 167–96 on hunting in British Imperial India.

[33] M. Brander, *Hunting and Shooting* (New York: G. P. Putnam's Sons, 1971), 204–20 in particular, on the pattern of hunting in nineteenth-century Africa. Also see Stanley Trapido, 'Poachers, Proletarians and Gentry in the Early Twentieth Century Transvaal', unpublished seminar paper, Institute of Commonwealth Studies, University of London, 18 October 1983; and Lance van Sittert, '"Keeping the Enemy at Bay": The Extermination of Wild Carnivora in the Cape Colony, 1889–1910', *Environmental History* 3, 3 (1998), 333–56.

[34] See B. Stoddart, 'Sport, Cultural Imperialism, and the Colonial Response in the British Empire', *Comparative Studies in Society and History* 30, 4 (1988), 649–73.

Africans these European hunters would encounter. Moreover, the idea that hunting was the exclusive privilege of an upper class, that it betokened wealth and status denied to common folk, and that it conferred on the hunter membership in an aristocracy of blood and wealth would set them directly at odds with their African hunting counterparts.[35] Now, let us turn to the application of these ideas by early European hunters in what would become Kenya.

Big game hunters: 1895–1914

Just as it can be said that virtually all African men in Kenya hunted at some time or other, it could also be said with some justification that every European man and quite a few women who came to Kenya from the late nineteenth to the mid-twentieth century also hunted. The prevalence of white hunters in Kenya would have a profound effect on the lives and livelihoods of African hunters. 'Big game hunting' would profoundly alter the ways in which Africans hunted big and small game, how they thought about this age-old activity, how they conceived of wildlife, and the relationship between themselves and the world of nature. From a post-modern perspective, an age-old European discourse on hunting and a philosophy of humanity's place in nature would attempt to impose itself on Africans, interacting with equally old and established African views of the relationship between culture and nature, especially as it focused on the pursuit of animals for food and material goods as well as for 'sport', recreation, and as an assertion of manhood.[36]

The careers and initial influence of the principal carriers of the imperial hunting tradition, who reached Kenya between the late nineteenth century and the outbreak of the First World War, will be examined here in a reading of the attitudes and hunting practices they recorded in a range of hunting adventure accounts.[37] This will be largely an exercise in taxonomy, establishing the different categories of white hunters, great and otherwise, whose influence on African hunting would be significant for one of two reasons. These were white hunters who either directly influenced the new hunting practice through the exchange of ideas, techniques, and the negotiation and invention of a new and distinctly Kenyan or East African hunting tradition, or indirectly influenced the new tradition through their efforts to control nature and its wild resources – such as

---

[35] For a discussion of these attitudes among white hunters and their connection with European imperialism, see MacKenzie, *The Empire of Nature*, 7–53, and his 'Chivalry, Social Darwinism'.

[36] See my paper entitled 'White Hunters in Kenya: 1895–1909, The Ivory Harvesters and Pioneers', African Studies Association Annual Meeting, Toronto, Ontario, 2–6 November 1994.

[37] It is impossible to say if the examples selected here are in any way representative of the many hunters who left no written record of their exploits. Their interest in recording their stories argues against their being representative, but suggests instead that they are the most self-conscious exemplars of a hunting practice that they championed 'in word and deed'.

game animals – and to regulate hunting and the access to wildlife by Africans within the colonial encounter.

The pioneer hunters

In the first phase of Kenya's white hunting history, the hunting of big game was an activity of both those who came to Kenya exclusively to hunt for sport and profit and those who came for other purposes, but for whom hunting was an economically crucial and in many ways an ideologically fundamental activity. Explorers, colonial administrators, missionaries, scientists and technicians, and a handful of pioneer settlers, including a number of titled aristocrats and gentlemen of high repute as sportsmen, would set the tone of privilege and luxury that became the hallmark of the imperial hunting tradition in Kenya. Kenya would also become a happy hunting ground, in those early days, for what have been termed the 'ivory hunters'.[38] Often rogues and adventurers, these men of means came to Kenya in pursuit of game, trophies, and the thrill of the chase, but also for the high profit that a haul of elephant ivory or rhinoceros horn could bring on the international trophy market. In the pioneer days of imperialism, before the beginnings of hunting regulation that included limits on the number of animals permitted to be shot and their trophies exported, this form of hunting would have an equally profound impact, both on the representations of white hunting to an international public and on the reputation and impact of white hunters among Kenya Africans who came to see or know of the work of slaughter done by these professing sportsmen.

The earliest phase of Kenyan big game hunting was that in which the pursuit of trophies and of sport was contaminated by what, even in their own terms, could only be characterized as 'butchery', the wanton killing of game animals for profit.[39] Yet, because the elephant was considered a noble animal, difficult and dangerous to pursue and worthy of the most expert of sportsman, the hunting of elephants for their tusks, which might produce enormous revenue, was masked behind the façade and ritual of the hunt. Although these ivory harvesters did not display the full range of aristocratic hunting ideals (such as were held by the Kenya settlers described in Chapter 5), they did the important transitional work in laying the foundations for new relationships between the tradition derived from aristocratic Europe and Kenyan hunting praxies.

As with other white hunters in Kenya, it is important to establish a distinction between those ivory hunters who came exclusively to hunt and

---

[38] Dennis Holman, *Inside Safari Hunting with Eric Rundgren* (New York: Putnam, 1970), 26–36, presents both a definition and a description of this type of hunter in his four-part typology of white hunters.

[39] Although frequently justified by appeals to a sporting ethos, the evidence of the concern with turning a profit, or at least covering the expenses of travel, equipment, porterage, etc., belies the non-commercial principles of sport hunting among the ivory hunters we will be examining. For an early defence of sport hunting in these terms, see James Greenwood, *Wild Sports of the World* (London: S. O. Beaton, n.d. [1862?]), 250.

those who did so as an adjunct to their other activities and purposes: to explore, soldier, administer, missionize, police, and pioneer in a new land. It is among the first group of 'pure' hunters with no other agenda that we will find the clearest examples of the ivory harvesting type. I want to examine briefly a few representatives of this group who, having recorded their experiences in adventure or travel accounts, are those from whom we can best abstract the outlines of ivory harvesting as a hunting practice in Kenya and East Africa. The best known of these early hunters who will compose our sample are W. D. M. 'Karamoja' Bell, Arthur H. Neumann, A. Arkell-Hardwick, and Captain Charles H. Stigand.[40]

Before we examine their exploits and influence, let us identify a few preconditions to the emergence of ivory hunting in the late nineteenth century. First, the practice of elephant hunting by trophy-seeking specialists is neither original nor unique to East Africa or Kenya. Its origins lay far to the south in the Cape Colony, the Transvaal, and the interior of southern Africa during the first half of the nineteenth century. The hunting grounds on and beyond the frontier of European expansion in Boer and British South Africa would see the first flourishing of this pursuit of elephants by such famous hunters as R. G. G. Cumming, William C. Harris, and later Frederick Selous.[41] By the late nineteenth century, two changes had caused a shift in the hunting frontier from southern to East and Central Africa. First was the exhaustion of the game in the south through over-hunting and continual disruption of the hunting grounds in the absence of any regulation of the relatively dense resident population of white hunter-farmers. The growth of commercial hunting and poaching in South Africa and Mozambique also contributed to this shift, as did the eventual efforts to develop a conservation policy in the Transvaal and a vermin extermination policy in the Cape Colony.[42]

Matching the decline of elephant hunting opportunities in the far south was the opening of East Africa, through the surge of exploration and intensification of contacts with the coast that accompanied and constituted the Scramble for Africa in the region. Even a cursory reading of the

---

[40] The books by Bell, Neumann, Arkell-Hardwick, and Stigand, as well as other related hunting accounts, will be cited in full below as they are discussed in the text.

[41] See MacKenzie, *The Empire of Nature*, 85–117. Frederick Selous would extend his hunting range to East Africa as well; see his *A Hunter's Wanderings in Africa* (London: Richard Bentley and Son, 1890), and *African Nature Notes and Reminiscences* (London: Macmillan, 1908). For Selous's influence on imperial ideas about hunting and character, see Kathryn Tidrick, *Empire and the English Character* (London: Tauris, 1990), 52–87; and E. Mandiringana and T. J. Stapleton, 'The Literary Legacy of Frederick Courtney Selous', *History in Africa* 25 (1998), 199–218.

[42] MacKenzie, *The Empire of Nature*, 107–16. On early conservation efforts, see Jane Carruthers, 'Game Protectionism in the Transvaal, 1900–1910', *South African Historical Journal* 20 (1988), 33–56, and her 'Creating a National Park, 1910 to 1926', *Journal of Southern African Studies* 15, 2 (1989), 188–216. Also, see Jane Carruthers, *Wildlife and Warfare: The Life of James Stevenson-Hamilton* (Pietermaritzburg: University of Natal Press, 2001). On southern African poaching during the early twentieth century, see her '"Police Boys" and Poachers: Africans, Wildlife Protection and National Parks, the Transvaal 1902 to 1950', *Koedoe* 36, 2 (1993), 11–22. See also Trapido, 'Poachers, Proletarians and Gentry'; and van Sittert, '"Keeping the Enemy at Bay"'.

exploration accounts of Sir Richard Burton, and most especially Joseph Thomson, who travelled across Kenya in the 1880s, gives ample evidence of both the extensive possibilities of big game hunting that their accounts revealed to a large metropolitan readership, and the significance of hunting to their own ability to explore and advance from the East African coast to the unexplored areas of the savannah and forest lands of the interior with their as yet unnamed lakes and mountains.[43]

Among the first rank of hunter-adventurers to exploit the elephant herds of East Africa, and Kenya in particular, was Walter D. M. 'Karamoja' Bell, who, the dust-jacket of his autobiography tells us, was 'the greatest elephant hunter of all times'.[44] Born in 1880, too late for the precolonial heyday of hunting in East Africa, Bell nevertheless displayed an unreserved enthusiasm for, and an unapologetic belief in, the naturalness of killing as many elephants as he desired. His first trip to Africa at age 17 took him to Mombasa, but, because of his youth, he was unable to get a safari to take him up-country. After adventures in the Yukon gold rush and the Boer War, he returned to East Africa, where he was able to travel across Kenya to Uganda in pursuit of elephant and 'to learn how to kill them'.[45] His indiscriminate taking of whatever elephant killing opportunities presented themselves was qualified only by the fact that he considered hunting the solitary bull elephant the 'most interesting and exciting form of elephant hunting', to the extent that he made it the subject of the very first chapter of his book.[46] To reinforce the notions of both his daring and his total absorption in the pursuit of elephant with the biggest ivory, the second chapter offers the reader a detailed discussion of his preference for small-bore rifles of .275 or .256 to the heavier and more powerful elephant guns of the day, as well as his preference for the 'brain shot' to the heart shot, a frequently debated subject among *cognoscenti* of elephant killing at the time.[47] All in all, Bell reveals little introspection about the nature of his

---

[43] Richard Burton, *Zanzibar: City, Island, and Coast* (2 vols.) (London: Tinsley Brothers, 1872); Joseph Thomson, *Through Masai Land* (London: Frank Cass, 1968 [1885; 2nd ed. 1887]). Equally impressive for the descriptions of hunting prospects, but less influential, was the earlier account by the pioneer missionary-explorer, J. L. Krapf (with J. Rebmann). See his *Travels, Researches, and Missionary Labours During an Eighteen Years' Residence in Eastern Africa*, 2nd ed. (London: Frank Cass, 1968 [1860]). On the general character and influence of these East African explorers, see N. Pavitt, *Kenya. The First Explorers* (New York: St. Martins, 1989); R. Rotberg, ed., *Africa and Its Explorers* (Cambridge, MA: Harvard University Press, 1970); J. Casada, 'The Imperialism of Exploration: British Explorers and East Africa, 1856–1890', unpublished Ph.D. dissertation, Vanderbilt University, 1972; and P. J. Imperato, *Quest for the Jade Sea* (Boulder: Westview, 1998), 127–41.

[44] W. D. M. Bell, *The Wanderings of an Elephant Hunter* (London: Country Life, 1923) provides an unabashed introduction to the braggadocio and blood-lust of the ivory harvester. A second edition under the title *Bell of Africa* (London: N. Spearman, 1960) includes a useful biographical sketch and additional materials compiled by Col. Townsend Whelan.

[45] Whelan in Bell, 'Introduction', *Bell of Africa*, i.

[46] Bell, *The Wanderings of an Elephant Hunter*, 1. In addition to the chapters on elephant hunting at the beginning, there are additional chapters on buffalo, lions, etc., as well as one devoted to the choice of rifles.

[47] Ibid., 5–11. See also Denis D. Lyell, *Memories of an African Hunter* (London: T. Fisher Unwin, 1923), 98–123, 247–64.

chosen path, which he says claimed him from childhood for the life of adventure. In his defence, I would say that he does offer respectful and considered opinions on African beliefs, termed 'medicine', and 'its Bearing on Sport', which included a careful and accurate description of the 'Wa-Boni' or 'M'Sanye' bow-and-poisoned-arrow hunters and the remarkable facility with such weapons demonstrated by these coastal hunters, akin to the Waata.[48] As we will see, such willingness to offer respect to African hunters was by no means common.

A similar lack of introspection can be found in the writings of Abel Chapman, who hunted in East Africa, especially the western districts of Kenya, the Rift Valley, and the Athi River plains in 1904 and 1906.[49] Chapman considered that 'British East Africa affords today probably the most glorious hunting-field extant, certainly the most accessible', contrasting it sharply with South Africa, where the butchery of game has left 'devastated herds'. This he blames mostly on settler hunters and the over-hunting of the region by sportsmen.[50] Although Chapman's interest in other game besides elephant, his observations on animal behaviour and bird life, and his seeming lack of monetary motives may distinguish him from the group of 'pure' ivory hunters, he does offer the reader an informative aside on the attitudes and motives of many of the early ivory hunters. Regarding the uses of Empire as an escape from 'sordid "Trades Unions" and such like' debasements of the life of privilege at home, Chapman issues an exhortation to 'Wake Up, England', in which he rails against the growing working-class movement at home, which speaks loudly to the underlying class motives in the construction of an imperial hunting ethos.[51]

Arthur H. Neumann ranks with 'Karamoja' Bell among the most prolific killers of elephant and harvesters of their ivory. Unlike Bell, he appears to have been sharply aware of the moral questions raised by such profligacy and its possible inhumanity. At least he was introspective and concerned enough to offer an elaborate apologia and defence of sport hunting in his account of his hunting travels.[52]

Neumann entered the Kenyan hunting field in 1894, an earlier date than Bell, but as a more mature man. Using Dorobo guides in the Meru area of the Nyambeni hills and north to the Uaso Nyiro River, he seemed driven to kill almost continually by three factors. First, he 'shot something every day to keep up a supply of beef [*sic*] for all hands, generally oryx'. The need to supply porters, African auxiliaries and camp followers with meat is a recurrent theme in the hunting practices of virtually all the early travellers in East Africa. Neumann is no exception, but rather an exemplar

---

[48] Bell, *The Wanderings of an Elephant Hunter*, 16–19.

[49] See Abel Chapman, *On Safari. Big Game Hunting in British East Africa* (London: Edward Arnold, 1908), 201–57 in particular for his hunting in eastern Kenya.

[50] Ibid., 'Preface', 5, 295–302. See Lyell, *Memories*, 261.

[51] Chapman, *On Safari*, 188.

[52] Arthur H. Neumann, *Elephant Hunting in East Equatorial Africa* (London: Rowland Ward, 1898), viii–ix.

as he appears in his account to be almost continually shooting animals as if unwilling to let pass any prospect of a shot.[53]

Second, Neumann is motivated to collect as much ivory and rhinoceros horn as he can 'for paying the expenses of my rather large caravan'.[54] Both by providing meat – thereby saving on the purchase of provisions – and by harvesting as much ivory as he could, regardless of age, sex, or condition of the elephants he targeted, Neumann displayed the same attitude toward hunting as I have described for Kamba hunters in the same era: shoot anything in case it is valuable. He knowingly pursued 'a troop of cows' near the Tana River and on several occasions shot rhino, which he had little chance of following up, or hippo, which he regularly lost to the river currents.[55] To the sensibilities of later generations of white hunters and poachers, this was criminal behaviour, not the deeds of either a gentleman or a sportsman.[56]

Finally, Neumann seems to be willing to kill continually and without limit because he shares with his African cohort the belief that the animals he hunts are provided by nature in an infinite supply. Although he expresses contempt for certain African hunting methods, such as the spear drops used by the Nyambeni,[57] this appears to be a matter of aesthetics and sportsmanship, not of reaction to the randomness, wantonness, or excesses of such methods. No expressions of the need to curtail either African or white hunting in the interests of conservation of the elephant herds which, it would appear, he considered virtually limitless, can be found in Neumann's 435-page account.[58]

The account of the ivory hunting and trading expeditions of the British trader A. Arkell-Hardwick is a curious combination of unselfconscious greed and blood-lust on the one hand, and a keen awareness of the author's place within a historical tradition of big game hunting on the other.[59] In the opening pages of the account, he offers the reader a brief historical account of his predecessors in the hunting field in Kenya, beginning in 1885 with Joseph Thomson, the explorer whom we will meet below, and ending in 1893 with A. H. Neumann and Dr Kolb. This is less to establish his pedigree than to inform the reader of the basis on which the hunting field in general, and the Lorian swamp area of northeast

---

[53] Ibid., 83, and 33–93 *passim* for evidence of continual hunting.

[54] Ibid., 93.

[55] Ibid., 150, 102–3 on pursuit of cow elephant; 33–34, 148 on the loss of rhino and hippos killed or wounded.

[56] See J. A. Jordan, *Mongaso: Man Who is Always Moving* (London: Nicholas Kaye, 1956), 18–19, for an expression of these values by a self-confessed poacher.

[57] Ibid., 33. 'They are no hunters and the only way they ever kill elephants is by setting traps consisting of javelins (poisoned) in heavy shafts suspended over their paths, … so that when a large animal passes along it falls on its head or back after the manner of a school "booby-trap".' These Nyambeni we have already met as the hunters of Meru district's Nyambeni hills.

[58] Where he does note a scarcity of game, it is attributed to natural limits ('Of game there is little, as might be expected in so water-less a district.') or the effects of diseases like rinderpest on the buffalo herds. See Neumann, *Elephant Hunting*, 141, and 84 on rinderpest.

[59] A. Arkell-Hardwick, *An Ivory Trader in Northern Kenia* (London: Longmans, Green, 1903).

Kenya in particular, was selected by him as 'practically unexplored'.[60] On his expedition in 1900, Arkell-Hardwick was accompanied by a mysterious English adventurer referred to only as El-Hakim (The Doctor),[61] who was, if anything, an even more profligate elephant hunter than the author. Speaking of El-Hakim, Arkell-Hardwick wrote:

> He had shot elephants persistently for the previous four years in Somaliland, Galla-land and the country around Lake Rudolph, having killed over 150, on one occasion shooting twenty-one elephants in twenty-one days – a fairly good record. Commenting on the size of the tusks available in the districts north of the Uaso Nyiro River, he mentioned that his largest pair weighed just over 218 lbs. and measured nine feet in length.[62]

On this safari, the two hunters also shoot a considerable number of rhino, including five in a two-day period – perhaps not a record, but done with such casualness as to deserve comment:

> On the plains to the eastward of the camp [on the Uaso Nyiro] roam vast herds of game – zebra, oryx, water-buck, and grantei [Grant's gazelle]. Rhinoceros were disgustingly frequent, El-Hakim shooting two more that had evinced an impertinent curiosity regarding his movements, when he was walking abroad one afternoon.[63]

Perhaps what makes the story of this expedition most intriguing is that its main purpose was the accumulation of elephant ivory by trade as well as hunting. Although relatively little attention is paid in the pages of the book to the commercial aspects of the expedition, the purchase of ivory from Africans, with payment made in sheep and cows, is not hidden or treated as a violation of the hunter's code.[64] Hardwick's self-identification as an 'ivory trader' is clearly not ironic. However, he just as clearly knows that his readership is interested in the romance of the chase. His frequent detailed descriptions of elephant and rhino hunts and his occasional paeans to the sporting life amply testify to his own appreciation of the sporting life in northern Kenya.[65] On this, he addresses his audience directly and in rapturous terms:

> Game was more than plentiful, the climate glorious, and we were free as the pure air we breathed. Only those who have been placed in similar circumstances can appreciate the full value of that word 'free'. We did precisely what seemed good to us in our own eyes. We rose early, bathed in the warm spring, ate our breakfast, and then went shooting, or, if

---

[60] Ibid., 5.
[61] El-Hakim is misidentified by Kenneth Cameron, *Into Africa. The Story of the East African Safari* (London: Constable, 1990), 61 as a Dr Rainsford. However, a more contemporary and reliable source named Arkell-Hardwick's companion as Dr Donaldson Smith. See George Fitzhugh Whitehouse, 'To Lake Rudolph and Beyond', in *Hunting and Conservation*, ed. George B. Grinnell and Charles Sheldon (New York: Arno, 1970 [1925]), 261.
[62] Arkell-Hardwick, *An Ivory Trader*, 142.
[63] Ibid., 191.
[64] Ibid., 123–31.
[65] Ibid., 142–7, 182–8, 303–9.

disinclined for that, we sat in a folding-chair in the shade of the trees and read ... ever and anon raising our eyes to watch the herds of game walking steadily past our camp on the way down to the river to drink.... It was a perfect Arcadian existence, which we left with real regret ... to resume our weary march over the sun-scorched desert country down river.[66]

Arkell-Hardwick, despite his commercial purposes and unrestrained pursuit of elephant ivory, is clearly not one to short-change the aesthetic and sporting side of his own endeavours or the sheer pleasures of the outdoor life. Yet the absence of any indication of the part played by his 'dark companions', his African guides, gun bearers, porters, skinners, and cooks, except to mention their appetite for fresh meat, would indicate that he failed to recognize any such aesthetic or sporting sensibility among the Africans who accompanied him or those who, like the Dorobo, hunted in their own right, but also acted as guides on occasion.[67] But his disregard for the talents and contributions of African hunters is nothing compared to the contempt and vilification expressed by my last example of the ivory harvesting hunter, Captain Charles H. Stigand.

In many ways, Stigand's three books on African hunting are unexceptional. The first, *Central African Game and Its Spoor*, was written as a 'handbook ... intended as a help or guide to the young or inexperienced sportsman who intends making a hunting trip to Central Africa'.[68] As such it is replete with advice on techniques, especially regarding animal behaviour and ethology useful in tracking, shooting, and following up dangerous game. His other books contain much of this naturalist interest, which may account for their popularity as well as for the fact that he was able to persuade the then ex-President Theodore Roosevelt to offer a foreword to his account of *Hunting the Elephant in Africa*.[69] But most important for understanding the impact on the relations between white and black hunters is the fact that all his works contain disparaging remarks about African character, intelligence, and capacity for hunting. Drawing on his experiences with the Chewa, Yao, and Ngoni hunters of central Africa, Stigand declares 'The native is a keen hunter, but we are inclined to think that his hunting instinct is derived from a love of meat and a lust of killing than from any sporting feeling.' In defence of imposing restrictions on African hunting, which 'some people think [indicates] that the native is ill used', Stigand argues that if 'the native ... [is] allowed a free hand to shoot in his own country ... it would only be for a few years ... as with the weapons of precision the traders would at once bring him, ... and the indiscriminate slaughter of the young and females he would indulge in, he would soon denude the country of game'.[70]

[66] Ibid., 191–2.

[67] E.g. ibid., 23–4, 201. On Dorobo guides, see ibid., 194.

[68] Captain C. H. Stigand, *Central African Game and Its Spoor* (London: Harper Cox, 1906), iii.

[69] T. Roosevelt, 'Foreword', in Captain C. H. Stigand, *Hunting the Elephant in Africa* (New York: Macmillan, 1913), v, in which Roosevelt states: 'More and more of late years the best type of big game hunter has tended to lay stress on the natural history of the regions into which they have penetrated, and to make his book less and less a catalogue of mere slaughter.'

[70] Stigand, *Central African Game*, 34–9.

Besides their lack of a true 'sporting feeling', Stigand attacks Africans for lacking the basic skills and physical and intellectual equipment for being hunters. He asserts that they lack skills of bush craft once taken from their familiar environs. They are poor stalkers and trackers of game, lacking acuity of eyesight and other physical attributes. Moreover, they are incapable of judging distances properly and have no sense of time. As a group, Africans, he believes, are wanting not only in hunting skills, but also in a sense of profession and the division of labour, as well as in the capacity for the accurate description of the naturalist and true lover of hunting. Nonetheless, after completing a thoroughly demeaning portrait of the African hunter, Stigand assures his readers, 'but I am none the less very fond of him'.[71]

This derogation of African skill can be understood only as the consequence of the racist stereotyping of Africans that Stigand seems to exemplify. His acceptance and propagation of an image of 'the good-humoured, happy go lucky Bantu savage' is classical in its disregard for any real evidence drawn from particular individuals.[72] 'The improvidence of the savage is wonderful', he tells us, and seems to be the counterpart of his 'irresponsible' attitudes to the preservation of game that threatens to 'irreparably upset the balance of nature'.[73] Improvidence, matched with modern weapons in the hands of the African, Stigand warns the reader, can lead to the denuding of the country as quickly as the threat posed by 'advancing civilisation', the settlement of the African wilderness by white farmers and ranchers.[74] Only the true sportsman, a trophy hunter who will shoot 'a few selected heads (generally of males only) of each of certain animals', can assure the preservation of game in the interests of future generations of sportsmen.[75]

Similarly, the lack of true 'sporting feeling' attributed to Africans by Stigand is simply the application to hunting of his racially stereotypical demeaning of African emotional capacities. If Africans do not love animals and their pursuit, it is because they lack true human affections. 'Affection between husband and wife, parent and offspring, as we know it, is practically nonexistent in many of the savage peoples, whilst the mother's love for the child is much the same as that of an animal.'[76] In a chapter on the subject of punitive expeditions against African peoples, significantly entitled 'Stalking the African', Stigand tells us 'the Native is so innocuous and appears so brainless that one is apt to grow careless with him'.[77]

Despite these dehumanizing and prejudiced attitudes, it is important to recognize that when Stigand went to the Kenyan Kinangop forest on the slopes of the Aberdare mountains in pursuit of the shy and elusive bongo, the second largest of the world's antelope, he sought and obtained the aid

[71] Stigand, *Hunting the Elephant*, 225, and 209–24 *passim*.

[72] Ibid., 205, 207.

[73] Captain C. H. Stigand, *The Game of British East Africa* (London: Harper Cox, 1913), Preface.

[74] Ibid., 224–5.

[75] Ibid., 225, and 217–36 passim.

[76] Stigand, *Hunting the Elephant*, 208.

[77] Ibid., 315.

of Dorobo hunters as guides and trackers.[78] And his expeditions in Central and East Africa were no different from others in using Africans in a wide range of capacities, from unskilled porters and carriers of loads to trackers, skinners, cooks, and gun bearers recruited through local African, Swahili, and Arab agents, and who would be the prototypes of the 'dark companions' accompanying virtually every Kenyan safari of the colonial era. This mixture of contempt with the need for the skills, expertise, and labour of African hunters would be central to the process of transforming the ivory hunting expedition into the champagne safaris of the heyday of Kenyan white hunting.

Individual ivory harvesters would continue to pursue elephants for profit into the 1930s, first to the Lado enclave in the Sudan, then to remote areas of Portuguese East Africa, where the enforcement of game regulations was weak or non-existent. But it was increasingly hard to describe oneself as a sportsman, and, in British East Africa, non-sport hunting would meet with increasing vigilance by game departments. Some ivory hunters tried to romanticize their mercenary pursuits as 'poaching' in an effort to draw on the images of defiance and rebelliousness of the European tradition,[79] but they were a dying breed. The end of the era came with the outbreak of war in Europe and the steep drop in ivory prices to below 10 shillings a pound. After a last swansong of ivory hunting in Ubangi Shari, now the Central African Republic, 'one by one these poachers became game wardens or white hunters', and the ivory hunters among whites in East Africa disappeared from the scene.[80]

Explorers and administrators

The pioneer hunters were not alone in the Kenyan hunting field. Others, who, although they had purposes for being in Kenya beyond stalking and shooting big game, were prodigious hunters in their own right joined them. I speak of the pioneer explorers, soldiers, and civil administrators who came on behalf of the Imperial British East Africa Company and the Foreign and Colonial Offices. While passing through Kenya *en route* to some treaty-making rendezvous or enforcing a previous agreement as soldiers, or simply from their stations, which spread across the Kenya landscape as depots, strong points, or governmental outposts, these men found it central to their routines to pursue wildlife. Whether hunting for the pot, or to supplement their salaries with trophies, or for sport, these early colonial officials and their mission and merchant counterparts would make an important, indelible contribution to the emergence of Kenya's hunting culture.

The literature on the exploration of East Africa is considerable and illuminates the careers of several figures who, in pursuit of their quests of discovery and conquest, managed to pursue large numbers of animals. John

[78] Ibid., 325ff.
[79] See Jordan, *Mongaso*, 13.
[80] Holman, *Inside Safari Hunting*, 36, and 26–36 for his account of the ivory hunting era.

MacKenzie has even argued that, without being successful in the pursuit of game, it is unlikely that these men could have been successful in the recruitment and control of the African labour and the supply of food for their caravans necessary for meeting their objectives. What he terms a meat subsidy was an essential element in successful African exploration, along with the financial subsidy provided by the ivory, horn, and hides which the explorers accumulated.[81]

Kenya's most famous nineteenth-century explorer was no doubt Joseph Thomson, whose book, *Through Masailand*, drew attention to the wealth of ivory and game available in Kenya and amply demonstrated MacKenzie's thesis.[82] Thomson's Kenyan experiences, repeating in many ways his own earlier experiences in Central Africa and those of V. L. Cameron in Tanganyika a decade earlier, confirm the importance of hunting as part of both the 'Day's Routine' and the 'Dangerous Moments' of exploration.[83] Hunting for the pot – to feed the numerous porters and labourers attached to the caravans of traders and explorers (often difficult to distinguish) – formed a central part of the daily routine of African exploration and travel. Alongside confrontations with 'hostile' native peoples, life-threatening encounters with wild animals lay at the heart of both the adventure of travel and the art of retailing that experience to the reading public. As early as Thomson's Kenyan expedition of the mid-1880s, the dramatic scene of a charging rhino or elephant and the hastily loaded gun and 'cool and collected' marksman had become the standard fare of the African travel account.[84]

By the late 1880s, the penetration of Kenya's interior by representatives of the Imperial British East Africa Company was adding to the explorer's adventures, the excitement of travel, and shooting in the name of the conquest of empire. Frederick Lugard's meticulously documented travels make clear the importance of hunting, especially of ivory, for the financing of Britain's imperial mission, but also the emotional importance of hunting to the sense of accomplishment and purpose of the pioneer soldier-administrator.[85] However, it is the work and writings of Frederick Jackson, Lugard's contemporary and successor as both a Company and colonial official, that best exemplify the centrality of hunting to early colonial administration.

Jackson came out in the 1880s to hunt, but quickly entered the employ of the British East Africa Company, and in the course of over twenty years' residence in East Africa (1883–1911) he eventually rose to become governor of Uganda. He would write and reflect on these experiences in

---

[81] MacKenzie, *The Empire of Nature*, 130–31, 148–64. See his 'Hunting in East and Central Africa in the Late Nineteenth Century, with Special Reference to Zimbabwe', draft essay, July 1993.

[82] Thomson, *Through Masai Land*.

[83] Ibid., 171–6, 137–41. See also V. L. Cameron, *Across Africa* (New York: Negro Universities Press, 1969 [1877]); and MacKenzie, *The Empire of Nature*, 150–51.

[84] Thomson, *Through Masai Land*, 139, and 131–2.

[85] F. Lugard, *The Diaries of Lord Lugard*, 2 vols (Evanston: Northwestern University Press, 1959), and his *The Rise of Our East African Empire*, 2 vols. (Edinburgh: Blackwood and Sons, 1893).

the 1920s, displaying his veritable obsession with hunting and his role as a model of the hunter-administrator, which was conveyed to those who worked with and under him.[86] His first visit to Kenya in 1885 included a hunting trip in the company of the novelist Rider Haggard, in the country behind the Lamu area of the north coast and in the Tana River valley, where he added sixteen new species to his bag while killing at the rate of three animals a day.[87] Extensive hunting followed during his Company days in 1885–6, when Sir Harry Johnston was his travelling companion and where, in addition to giraffe, he added impala, hartebeest, sable antelope, and greater kudu, 'all new antelopes to me (103)', to his list of newly shot species.[88] A two-month 'shooting trip round about Kilimanjaro' in 1886 is followed by a three-week trip 'devoted to elephants'.[89] His employment by the Company in 1888 barely slows his hunting pace, but it adds new purposes. In 1889, Jackson finds it necessary to feed his caravan travelling in western Kenya with the carcasses of three elephants when the 'gift' of cattle provided by a local chief, Mumia, all die. He also comments that the people of this region, called Kavirondo, 'were out and away the greatest gluttons for meat I have ever met with'.[90] It was clearly among his purposes to sweeten his administration's reception by providing the local 'gluttons' with what they wanted, and, in doing so, to be able to do what he most wanted – to hunt.[91]

Why did Jackson become such an exemplar of the hunter-administrator? It is difficult to answer this question with any assurance, but perhaps we can see Jackson as a 'happy' hunter. In the foreword to Jackson's reflections, Lord Cranworth, one of Kenya's leading, or perhaps ranking, aristocratic settlers, wrote:

> The sportsman will find it hard to lay down the chapters that tell of the *safaris* over the plains teeming with herds of game, or through the vast elephant-haunted forests … happiness was a characteristic of the man. He was happy … in his domestic life … in his work … in his natural history…. Happy in his sport.[92]

Untroubled by the destruction of animals and humans, which were part of his work and his sport, Jackson would set an example to others later in the field and lower in the colonial pecking order. It was with apparent clear conscience and no hint of irony that he could relate 'big game hunting yarns' about himself or stories of Count Teleki, the Hungarian hunter-traveller, who killed '35 elephants and 300 "niggers"' on his Kenya safari.[93]

Ultimately, the fact that Jackson saw himself as a hunter before everything else sets him apart as a singular figure. It was not the sheer quantity

---

[86] F. Jackson, *Early Days in East Africa* (London: Dawsons, 1969).
[87] Ibid., 27–43, 44–59, 49.
[88] Ibid., 103.
[89] Ibid., 104, 123.
[90] Ibid., 224, 225.
[91] Ibid., 27–225 passim.
[92] 'Foreword', in F. Jackson, *Early Days*, ix.
[93] Ibid., 225–7.

of game, but his passion and devotion to sport hunting that attracted him to the African field and kept him there through his long administrative career. Perhaps this is best exemplified by the final chapter of his book, devoted to 'Hunters, Professional and Otherwise'.[94] Here, as a coda to a memoir filled with hunting exploits, he finds it important to provide his readership with a series of moral admonitions and anecdotal examples of what it means to be a sportsman, gentleman, and hunter in colonial Africa.

The high regard for sport hunting that Jackson exemplified became a pervasive value in the Kenyan administrative service. Clearly this was a result of more than Jackson's example or the influence of the gentleman hunters who pioneered and dominated the establishment of colonial rule in Kenya. Indeed, the values and culture of the English countryside and leisure class, which became proverbial among Kenya's white settlers, were as deeply ingrained in the Kenyan civil service. In the words of Bruce Berman: 'The Colonial Office looked for modest intellectual achievement, athletic prowess, a taste for the outdoor life, and, implicitly, unquestioned acceptance of the "aristocratic" ethos of rule and the ideals of imperialism.'[95]

At the local level of Kenya administration, no one better exemplified this than S. L. Hinde, a district collector in Ukambani and Fort Hall districts at the turn of the century. Hinde was, among his other attributes, an amateur ethnographer and naturalist, and a prodigious hunter.[96] Having served in military capacities in West Africa and the Congo Free State, he came to Kenya in the 1890s somewhat older than most junior officers, and married. Nonetheless, Hinde found ample time in addition to his official duties to hunt regularly. Like the Meru district administrators of a slightly later period, Messrs. Horne and Hopkins, Hinde was known for his regular weekly expeditions away from the collectorate offices in pursuit of his avocation. Ample evidence of his proficiency and preoccupation as a hunter is provided by the photographs that accompany his ethnographic account of Maasai life, a third of which is devoted to 'Field Notes on the Game of East Africa', a guide to would-be visiting hunters.[97]

Despite this evidence of proficiency as a hunter, in 1903, no less a hunting stalwart than Captain Richard Meinertzhagen would impugn Hinde's hunting prowess, accusing him of being 'a humbug', for stretching the skin of a lion which he had been given, allegedly so as to later claim that he had shot the posthumously oversized lion himself. Hinde would also stand accused in Meinertzhagen's book of 'a breach of the game regulations' in stalking and shooting rhino while accompanying a traveller on a hunting expedition. This 'unsportsmanlike action' was an act of 'pure

[94] Ibid., 368–88.

[95] B. Berman, *Control and Crisis in Colonial Kenya* (London: James Currey, 1990), 100.

[96] S. L. and H. Hinde, *The Last of the Masai* (London: W. Heinemann, 1901). See also Mrs S. L. Hinde, 'Man-hunting by Lions', *Blackwood's Magazine* 178 (1905), 192–8.

[97] Hinde and Hinde, *The Last of the Masai*, 113–76. For the Meru administrators, see Interviews C/7, John Livingstone Mate, 11 September 1987; and C/8, Joseph Mugao Kibunjia, 11 September 1987.

slaughter', a far more serious breach of hunting etiquette and ideology than merely overshooting the limit.[98]

The question of violation of the game laws by those colonial officers empowered to enforce them would become a serious problem for game-keepers and conservationists later in the century. Often these incidents would be both laughable and provocative. One case from Meru district deserves note, as it illustrates very clearly the conflict between the hunting activities and the official responsibilities of civilian officials. J. G. Hopkins, a Meru district officer in the 1930s, according to Charles Chenevix Trench, 'was a small sharp eyed man who looked as though he was planning to sell you something'. Chenevix Trench goes on to write:

> He was the only DC [District Commissioner] to educate his children entirely from the profits of elephant-hunting. He hunted both inside his own district on control and outside it on licence. The tusks of elephants shot on control, however large, had to be handed in to the government. The tusks of elephants shot on licence belonged to the shooter. As DC, Meru, Hopkins shot a huge tusker on control in his district. But it was within yards of a cairn marking the district boundary, so he wrote himself a cheque, issued himself with a licence and moved the cairn, thus starting a dispute between Meru and Isiolo districts which was still unresolved thirty years later.[99]

The boundary dispute initiated by this incident is exceptional, but the practice of colonial officers who had both local authority to issue hunting licences and their own private hunting purposes, whether economic or sporting, frequently led to technical violations of the game regulations by colonial officials. Officials could abuse their power by issuing licences to themselves or their friends after the fact of the shooting of game animals. No doubt they considered themselves to be sportsmen and gentlemen, and therefore inherently deserving of a variance in the law or a blind eye. Only the separation of administration from game preservation and regulation would obviate this problem later in the century.

Not only the general administrative officials, but also many of the technical staff of the colonial establishment, proved to be hunters of great ardour and proficiency. Perhaps the best known single – or I should say double – hunting exploit to capture the imagination of the reading public, one that shaped the legend of white hunting in Kenya, was that of an engineering officer attached to the construction of the Uganda Railway by the British East Africa Company. Colonel J. H. Patterson had served in India building bridges, and was called on to design and oversee the 1898 construction of a railway bridge across the channel of the flood-prone Tsavo River. The company had employed thousands of Indian labourers, or 'coolies', to undertake the actual construction. But shortly after Patterson's arrival at Tsavo station, a pair of marauding male lions began

---

[98] R. Meinertzhagen, *Kenya Diary 1902–1906* (Edinburgh: Oliver and Boyd, 1957), 99 and 110. My thanks to Dr Nigel Rothfels for bringing this to my attention.

[99] Charles Chenevix Trench, *The Men Who Ruled Kenya. The Kenya Administration, 1892–1963* (London: Radcliffe, 1993), 83–4.

persistently and mysteriously to attack the workers' compound, carrying off the hapless and soon terrified 'coolies'. Patterson, a keen hunter who had already shot lion, undertook, with the aid of other local administrators, to calm the fears of his workmen by shooting the rogue pair. It would take him fully nine months and over 100 fatalities before the lions were killed and work could be resumed. The mysterious behaviour of the man-eaters of Tsavo, attacking entrenched positions by day and night, and evading the many traps, snares, and baited traps set for them, made this one of the most adventurous of Kenya's early hunting narratives. It also made the lions themselves items of intense scientific curiosity. Their stuffed carcasses are now at the Field Museum in Chicago and the study of their behaviour is an ongoing scientific enterprise.[100]

Police and soldiers

In addition to the provincial and district administrative officers and technicians, Kenya's civilian police force also included among their numbers, from early in the century, hunters of ability and distinction. Although they were less likely to write about their experiences than the more upper-class officials and soldiers, there was at least one individual who would record his experiences as both policeman and big game hunter. Major W. Robert Foran was the author of no fewer than fifteen works of fiction, history, biography, travel, and reminiscences. He joined the Kenyan police force in 1904, and would serve as a senior police officer for many years. He wrote the first published history of the Kenyan police based on this long experience begun during the early days of colonial rule.[101] It is his writings on hunting and wildlife, however, which make him exceptional.

The interface between police work and hunting would involve Foran in several hunting and game preservation activities early in his police career. He would be called on during his first years as a Kenyan policeman to do game control work on behalf of an understaffed Game Department that included only three Europeans. This meant that Foran was called upon to kill rogue animals, field raiders, and other dangerous game – especially lions – that interfered with the work of settlement and cultivation. He would also be involved, as early as 1906, in police operations against ivory poachers, which would involve him in hunting as well. In his official capacity as a police officer, as well as because of his reputation as a sportsman, Foran was attached to visiting dignitaries such as Theodore and Kermit Roosevelt, and the Duke and Duchess of York, on their highly publicized hunting safaris.[102]

---

[100] J. H. Patterson, *The Man-eaters of Tsavo* (New York: St. Martins, 1986); and J. K. Peterhans et al., 'Man-Eaters of Tsavo', *Natural History* (November 1998), 12–14.

[101] W. Robert Foran, *The Kenya Police, 1887–1960* (London: Robert Hale, 1962), v–viii. On the wide-ranging duties of the police in early colonial and frontier situations, see *Policing the Empire*, ed. D. M. Anderson and D. Killingray (Manchester: Manchester University Press, 1991), esp. 5–13, 183–200, and 106–23.

[102] Foran, *The Kenya Police*, 32–3, 60, and his *With Roosevelt in Africa* (London, Robert Hale, 1924).

Foran's first major work on hunting is thinly disguised as a work of natural history, 'a study of wildlife in its natural environment … [for] those about to take up big game shooting or to others who have already done so'.[103] Published in 1958, *A Breath of the Wilds* makes a spirited defence of sport hunting, blaming 'confirmed game-butchers' for the modern extermination of wildlife and describing sportsmen as 'the trustees of wild life for future generations'.[104] However sharp the distinction, he makes an exception to his objection to 'heartless profit seeking' for those sportsmen who kill elephants and sell the ivory to cover the costs of their safaris, an excusable form of shooting for profit when done by proper sportsmen. Of course, his own use of the significant proceeds of his elephant tusks for supporting the sporting life would require such an exemption.[105] After the excuses and apologies for sport hunting given at length in spite of the fact that he says they are unnecessary,[106] the remaining chapters of his natural history are given over to the recounting of hunting exploits and nostalgic tales for the armchair hunter-naturalist of the mid-twentieth century.

Foran's account of his hunting exploits, *A Hunter's Saga*, was written near the end of his long career. By that time the genre of hunting account was well established and he deviated little from the successful formula. He recorded his hunting experiences before coming to Kenya in chapters on *shikar* (pigsticking from horseback) in India and big game hunting in the western United States and Mexico. He described his ivory harvesting phase when the proceeds of the sale of bull elephant ivory paid for his hunting safaris in Kenya.[107] He recounted exciting encounters with elephant (pp. 115–24), buffalo (pp. 146–54), and rhino (pp. 169–78). He even gives a rough count of the number of elephant – 400 – killed by him in a six-year period (p. 98).

Of particular interest to us, he includes a paean to his faithful and 'stouthearted gun-bearer, Hamisi, and my 'Ndorobo tracker, Juma' (p. 125). Indeed, Hamisi's death as a result of an encounter with a rogue elephant while on safari with the author in Uganda leads to his renunciation of elephant hunting (pp. 184–8). Like many long-term African hunters, he is generous in his praise of 'an efficient gunbearer … the unsung heroes of countless shooting safaris'. This fulsome, if patronizing, tribute, especially its posthumous element, is a regular motif in the hunting sagas of many big game hunters. It serves not only to pay an often unacknowledged debt to the so-called 'dark companions' of the hunting safari, but should open our eyes to the innumerable intersections of African

---

[103] W. Robert Foran, *A Breath of the Wilds* (London: Robert Hale, 1958), 15.

[104] Ibid., 18. There is a certain anachronistic quality to these descriptions, with 'game-butchers' very much a term of the early twentieth century, and 'trustees of wild life for future generations' coming straight from the language of postwar international conservationism.

[105] Ibid., 18–23. See also Foran's *A Hunter's Saga* (London: Robert Hale, 1961), 98.

[106] Foran, *A Hunter's Saga*, 20–22.

[107] Foran, *A Breath of the Wilds*, 18–23.

[108] The career of Fundi, a porter who rises to gun bearer, is typical of this motif. See S. E. White, *The Land of Footprints* (Garden City, NY: Doubleday, Page, 1913), 196–209.

and European hunting traditions, stories, and practices. The relationship of white hunter to African gun bearers, trackers, and skilled skinners, as well as safari porters, cooks, and labourers, is the active interface on which the combined tradition of Kenya hunting is created.[108] I introduce it here because it is in the work of the Kenya policeman, Foran, that this intimate connection is so vividly expressed.[109]

Robert Foran is unique among Kenya's policeman-hunters for having written extensively about his experiences and attitudes toward both his roles. In the same way, Colonel Richard Meinertzhagen, whom we encountered earlier as a critic of the hunting practices of the administrator Hinde, will serve as our exemplar of the soldier-hunter. He was at once the colonial soldier, an officer and gentleman *par excellence*, and the most ruthless and proficient of Kenya's pioneer hunters. Although far from the first or only person to combine the roles of hunter and soldier in East Africa, his own character, marked by the extremity of his opinions, the brashness of his expression, his remorseless self-righteousness, and his contradictory and contentious attitudes to Africans, to officialdom, and, most strikingly, to animals make him a thoroughly engrossing figure.

The connection between soldiering and hunting has been frequently noticed and commented on in terms of the mutually reinforcing skills and values they inculcate.[110] However, seldom have they been as closely entwined as in East Africa. Most frequently, it has been a matter of soldiers on active duty, like Meinertzhagen or Major. R. MacDonald, who have combined military duty with their passion for the pursuit of game. Occasionally, those who came to East Africa for sport, such as the soldier-adventurer Sir Claude Champion de Crespigny, a companion of Meinertzhagen in hunting and comrade in arms on the Nandi expedition in 1904–5, would find themselves recruited or volunteering for active duty in what has been termed a 'chasse de nègres'. As their accounts indicate, there is a close functional and symbolic relationship between the two activities.[111] But it is in the controversial career and contentious character of Meinertzhagen that this amalgam of hunting and soldiering can be closely contrasted and deconstructed.

The first thing to note about Meinertzhagen was the sheer magnitude of blood that flowed in Kenya as a result of his hunting and soldiering activities. In the preface to his published diaries, he states: 'Two criticisms may occur to the reader: one, the excessive taking of human life; the other, the slaughter of game.' However flimsy the justifications in terms of war and 'pacification' offered for the first, he is unabashed in his defence of the latter.

> As regards the second criticism, the fighting and hunting activities of man require an outlet; if suppressed hatred and malice occur. There are outlets which are not harmful. Active sport and competitive games are substitutes;

---

[109] Foran, *A Hunter's Saga*, 188–90.

[110] The classic statement of this functional connection is found in Baden-Powell, *Sport and War*.

[111] Major J. R. L. MacDonald, *Soldiering and Surveying in British East Africa 1891–1894* (Folkestone: Dawsons of Pall Mall, 1973 [1897]); Sir C. Champion de Crespigny, *Forty Years of a Sportsman's Life* (London: Mills and Boon, 1925).

hunting, the joy of adventure and facing danger, discovery and creation [sic] are other outlets. We should neither ignore nor regret them.[112]

There follows an account of his exploits in which he expresses no regrets for the lives of people or of animals, which he takes by his own hand. If anything, he sometimes expresses regret that insufficient numbers of people have been killed or their livestock confiscated to allow for their easy control.[113] Paradoxically, he does express regret at the killing of elephant by Africans, which he considers to be a regrettable loss of intelligent and sensitive life. He does not himself list elephants among the list of animals killed and weighed 'by me personally' presented in an appendix. But that list runs to some 448 individuals of 57 species, including 19 lion, 5 cheetah, 16 rhinoceros, 7 hippopotamus, 6 hyena, 2 giraffe, 5 eland, 3 oryx and 2 waterbuck among the larger animals that he killed in Kenya. No such listing is given of the people who were killed 'by me personally'.[114]

There are two even more curious paradoxes. First is Meinertzhagen's awareness of the need for game preservation in the face of his own wantonness in the destruction of wildlife. In conversation with the early game warden and hunter, Blayney Percival, he recommends the creation of a large game reserve where hunting would be strictly controlled and limited. He sees (correctly) the threat to wildlife as coming principally from newly arriving white settlers, rather than sport hunters like himself. He believes (wrongly) that he is the first person to suggest such measures, and sees it as a precursor of the policy of game reserves, sanctuaries, and eventually national parks that became the keystone of Kenya's wildlife conservation policies.[115]

The second paradox stems from Meinertzhagen's uncanny ability to recognize the wrongs being done to Africans by conquest, colonization, and the expropriation of their property while engaged in the very campaigns of conquest that make colonization possible, and in the self-same practices of expropriation of land and livestock. In November 1905, at the conclusion of the first phase of the Nandi Expedition, during which he estimates that 500 Nandi young men are killed and 10,000 head of their cattle and 70,000 sheep and goats are confiscated, Meinertzhagen states:

[112] Meinertzhagen, *Kenya Diary*, vi.

[113] In March 1904, he records: 'To my mind the people of Embu have not been sufficiently hammered, and I should like to go back at once and have another go at them. During the first phase of the expedition … we killed about 796 niggers, and during the second phase … we killed about 250.' Ibid., 152.

[114] Ibid., 337–46. On the insufficiency of punishment of the Nandi, see ibid., 265. For a sympathetic treatment of Meinertzhagen in Kenya, see N. West, *Happy Valley: The Story of the English in Kenya* (London: Secker and Warburg, 1979), 49–57.

[115] Meinertzhagen, *Kenya Diary*, 156–7. Meinertzhagen also claims that he advocated game conservation in a meeting with his uncle, Sir Charles Eliot, the governor of Kenya, in 1904. However, the claim to priority in advancing the idea of game reserves must go to Sir Harry Johnston, who had earlier recommended their creation in East Africa. These inconsistencies and the seeming ability of Meinertzhagen to foretell the future may benefit from hindsight, as the original manuscript diary at Rhodes House, Oxford and the edited and published *Kenya Diary* are separated by a half century. My thanks to D. Anderson (personal communication, 1 June 1997) for this point.

The reserve they [the colonial authorities] contemplate is much too small and does not allow for expansion; I fear it is all based on requirements for white settlement and not on the welfare of the Nandi. This is a very shortsighted policy and must lead to grievances; after all, it is African land, not ours to dispose of.[116]

Moreover, he recognizes that the Nandi have legitimate grievances against a corrupt administrative official and weak, ineffectual government. Yet he believes he is entirely justified in meting out brutal punishments for the hostility that the Nandi leadership and young men display towards the same colonial authorities who would dispossess and despoil them.[117]

How can we reconcile these contradictory attitudes and behaviours? It appears to me to be resolvable by an examination of the symbolic congruence of Meinertzhagen's dual identities as soldier and hunter. Two incidents that bear a striking structural similarity illustrate this congruence.

On 17 July 1904, while on leave near Nairobi, Meinertzhagen went for a walk with his pet dog, Baby. Uncharacteristically, he went unarmed. On the route to the Athi River, the soldier and his 'companion' chanced upon a troop of baboon. Meinertzhagen recorded:

On approaching the Athi River ... I saw a large mob of baboon close to the river, and Baby and I decided to stalk them and give them a good fright. We did it most successfully, and getting to within about 60 yards of them we jumped up with a shout and chased them into the river, when I called to her. Normally she would have returned, but there was a strong head wind and I suppose she did not hear me. On she went, for she feared nothing. Suddenly the whole mob turned on her. Undismayed she went straight for the nearest baboon, but the contest was hopeless from the first.[118]

The dog was quickly killed and dismembered by the baboons in clear view of her master and his expressions of grief are immediately suffused with a desire for revenge. 'I saw the disgusting creatures making off with her limbs. Never did I long so much for a rifle.'

If the story ended there it would be remarkable. The author's anthropomorphizing of his animal friends and enemies was, if somewhat excessive, certainly not unusual. Baby is not only a 'companion', but had been one for so long that 'we ... thoroughly understood each other'. The decision to attack and frighten the baboons was a mutual decision between dog and man. The dog's behaviour, its seeming disobedience, lack of fear, and absence of dismay when she is faced with a counterattack, is described as if Baby were a thoroughly human actor. Moreover, the 'mob' of baboon is similarly portrayed in human terms: alternately fearful, panic-stricken, and vengeful. But they are 'disgusting creatures', showing none of the

---

[116] Meinertzhagen, *Kenya Diary*, 266. His estimates of Nandi dead and stock losses appear on p. 249. See G. H. Mungeam, *British Rule in Kenya, 1895–1912* (Oxford: Clarendon, 1966), 156 for the official estimates, which are not vastly different except in terms of small stock losses.

[117] Meinertzhagen, *Kenya Diary*, 184–5, 215–17, on colonial corruption and maladministration.

[118] Ibid., 171–2.

loyalty of the dog or appreciation of the good joke and sport that Meinertzhagen's sudden assault represented. But it does not end there.

> When my first horror was over I sat down and contemplated how I could teach those baboon a lesson. [Having identified 'a rocky cliff' that served the baboons as a roost,] if I could get out to their roosting place before light, surround it with men and then open fire from the front, I should most certainly stampede them and kill the bulk of the brutes. As I returned sadly that evening I had murder in my heart.[119]

Quickly, Meinertzhagen organized a patrol of 30 men and a sergeant-major, who departed for the roosting place at 3 am 'with rifles, bayonets and 100 rounds each.... The baboon were to be shot down without mercy.' In a military operation that went from first light to before noon, the baboons were attacked with rifle fire and driven down a gauntlet of Meinertzhagen's troops, forced to retreat to the cliff face where two senior male baboons were pursued, surrounded, and killed. 'We collected altogether 25 baboon, only some 15 or so escaping. We killed every full-grown male, and I was pleased,' remarked the commander of this operation. As a reward, Meinertzhagen 'shot an impala and a haartebeest [sic] for the men who had assisted ... in avenging Baby'.[120]

The close association and mutually supportive skills involved between hunting and soldiering could not have been lost on as keen a sportsman and soldier as Meinertzhagen. He is as unapologetic about the one as the other:

> The hunting of big game gave me good healthy exercise when many of my brother officers were drinking rot-gut or running about with somebody else's wife; it taught me bushcraft and how to shoot straight. After all, the hunting of men – war – is but a form of hunting wild animals, and on many occasions during the First World War I thanked my God that I had learned several tricks of my trade when hunting wild and dangerous game.[121]

Nonetheless, Meinertzhagen seems to be unaware of the more deeply rooted psychological and symbolic connections between his vocation and his avocation.

His account of the death of the Nandi Laibon (properly *orkoiyot* or priest) reads, as does the account of the revenge of Baby, like the report of a well-prepared and executed military operation. Moreover, the elements of provocation, vengeance, and blood-lust that they share are more than suggestive of the psychological and symbolic elements of the hunting–soldiering nexus. On 18 October 1905, Meinertzhagen entered in his diary

---

[119] Ibid., 172.

[120] Ibid., 173.

[121] Ibid., 179. A training manual for British forces engaged in the suppression of Mau Mau in the 1950s makes this same point, graphically comparing the skills needed to pursue Mau Mau fighters to those required 'to track down and shoot shy game'. Government of Kenya, *A Handbook on Anti-Mau Mau Operations* (Nairobi: Government Printing Office, n.d. [1954?]), 11. My thanks to Dr John Lonsdale of Trinity College, Cambridge, for bringing this to my attention and allowing me to read his copy of the manual.

his plans 'for the undoing of the Laibon'.[122] Koitalel, as the chief politico-religious leader of the Nandi people on the Mau escarpment in western Kenya, had long been a hindrance to British occupation and the distribution of land to settlers. Orders to remove the Nandi to a native reserve had fallen to Meinertzhagen to enforce. In an effort to locate Koitalel's residence so that he might attack and arrest him at night, Meinertzhagen arranged for a meeting with him on the morning of 19 October. Koitalel asked that Meinertzhagen come accompanied by only five men. For his part, Meinertzhagen prepared an escort detachment of 80 men and a machine gun, as he was convinced that the interpreter and messenger who arranged the meeting was 'a spy of the Laibon's, for [my agents] have heard him conspiring to destroy us when we meet tomorrow'. He continued in his diary: 'If he attacks me at our meeting I know how to defend myself. However, come what will, I will meet him tomorrow, and during the next 24 hours I suspect that either he or I will have said goodbye to this world; I do not really very much care which of us it is.'[123]

The following day, Meinertzhagen entered an account of the meeting, in which he stated that the Laibon, true to his suspicions, attempted to ambush him under a flag of truce as they stood facing each other after shaking hands. He continues: '...but, we were ready, and he [Koitalel], the interpreter and several others, some 23 in all, were left dead. I had my clothes torn by a spear and arrow and one of my men was slightly scratched by a spear.'[124]

How could he have escaped from this face-to-face confrontation so unscathed? 'Before going down to meet the Laibon I had warned Butler [his second in command] to open fire at once if he saw us being overwhelmed. He mounted the machine gun and covered the place of meeting,' along with 75 men left in reserve. In addition, after withdrawing from the scene of the ambush, harried by the Nandi, the column of 80 men is rescued by 'a welcome patrol that had been sent out on my instructions to cover our retreat'.[125]

The inherent unlikelihood of such a complete reversal of the ambush, and Meinertzhagen's clear preparation for a confrontation with the Nandi leader, along with his admitted intentions of seeing the Laibon 'undone' on that day, would lead to questions being raised about his conduct of the meeting with Koitalel. Meinertzhagen would be forced to defend himself against rumours of foul play amounting to the murder of the Laibon, charges levelled by members of the civil administration. A series of three

[122] Meinertzhagen, *Kenya Diary*, 232. The background to the situation is given from Meinertzhagen's perspective on pp. 224–32. Unfortunately, the standard work on Nandi resistance by A. T. Matson, *Nandi Resistance to British Rule, 1890–1906* (Nairobi: East African Publishing House, 1970), fails to include anything on the incident. Instead, the best critical account of the background and encounter is D. M. Anderson, 'Visions of the Vanquished', in *Revealing Prophets*, ed. D. M. Anderson and D. Johnson (London: James Currey, 1995), 168–78. See Mungeam, *British Rule*, 145–6, 156–61 for an administrative perspective on the expedition.

[123] Meinertzhagen, *Kenya Diary*, 233.

[124] Ibid.

[125] Ibid.

courts of inquiry were held between 1 December 1905 and 11 January 1906, during which Meinertzhagen was officially exonerated, but in the wake of which the rumours persisted that his was 'an unconscionable act of treachery'.[126] It is this stain on his honour as a gentlemen, even more than the threat to his military career, which seems to have concerned him most directly and, without exaggeration, would haunt him for the rest of his life.

Clearly, we will never know with certainty the exact events that transpired between the two leaders which left the Laibon and his retinue dead and Nandi–British relations shattered for the next several years. But elements of Meinertzhagen's mind-set do emerge clearly from the evidence of his own pen, elements that bear directly on his dual identity as a hunter-soldier. First, it is clear that Meinertzhagen viewed the confrontation as involving the same kind of 'risk and excitement' as the pursuit of dangerous game. Moreover, he was so convinced that his prey was wily and treacherous, and that it was in his very nature as an African and a Nandi to be so, that he was justified in setting a trap for him. In many ways, we might describe the act of killing the Laibon and what Meinertzhagen believed to be his entire entourage and immediate male family members, as an act of 'pre-revenge' justified by the inherent lack of honour of these 'disgusting creatures'. Once again, Meinertzhagen had left the field of battle strewn with the corpses of all the males upon whom he sought revenge for prior wrongs. 'So may all the King's enemies perish.' He expressed regret only for the wives of Koitalel, who he believed would be killed and buried with him, and some sadness at the idea that the dynasty of Laibon was ended (or so he also mistakenly believes) on that October morning. True, he believed that the Laibon deserved burial and 'some obituary notice', an honour he would not have accorded the unlucky baboons he had chosen to frighten with Baby and then to attack and destroy with military force.[127]

One other aspect of Meinertzhagen's soldier-hunter character deserves mention: his relationship to civilian administrative and police authorities, which reveals his class bias against those he considers are not gentlemen. These attitudes clearly predate his confrontation with civil officials over the death of Koitalel and his departure from Kenya under a cloud of suspicion raised by the civil administrators in Nandi country. He attributes the hostility of civil officials to soldiers like himself 'to the low class of man who is appointed to administrative appointments. Few of them have any education and many do not pretend to be members of the educated class.... When such men are given unlimited power over uneducated and

---

[126] Ibid., 334; 234–8 contain Meinertzhagen's official report of the incident entered in his diary at the time. Rumours of his conspiring to murder the Laibon first reached him in November and he would insist on defending his honour in military court. Ibid., 249, 257, 275. See J. Lord, *Duty, Honor, Empire* (New York: Random House, 1970), 230–53, on both the Nandi expedition and Meinertzhagen's removal from Kenya.

[127] Meinertzhagen, *Kenya Diary*, 234. The identification of Africans with 'vermin' by 'settlers, military officers and colonial officials' in South Africa at this time is also noted by van Sittert, 'Keeping the Enemy at Bay', 352.

simple-minded natives it is not extraordinary that they should abuse their powers, suffer from megalomania and regard themselves as little tin gods.'[128]

Nor did he reserve such blatant class-biased attacks to the privacy of his diary. Even after his affray with the civil administration, he would brashly and directly criticize the civil administration and its police in the person of the Nandi Collector, Stephen Bagge, a respected and experienced official, for the violence and failure of the Nandi Expedition, necessitating the misuse of soldiers like himself to do the work of civilian police who lacked proper training.[129]

Although Meinertzhagen expressed his hostility to civil administrators and police in terms of inadequate education or training, it seems clear to me that beneath these criticisms lie the deep-rooted prejudices against those who lack the attributes of gentlemen, attributes that diminish as one moves down the social scale and rank within the administration and civilian police. Chief among the traits of gentlemen that Meinertzhagen valued and idealized were those of the hunter and sportsman, which he assimilated to the qualities of a good soldier. It was the love of nature and the outdoors and of the chase and conquest of animal and human enemies which led him and men like him to 'the slaughter of my fellow men and wild animals' to an extent that left him 'shocked at the cost', if only after half a century.[130]

Meinertzhagen was not typical of the soldier-hunters I am characterizing here; he was too exceptionally ruthless as a soldier and too determined as a hunter to be typical. He is instead an exemplar of the kind of symbiotic association of hunting and soldiering, of sport and war, that makes one a powerful metaphor for the other, and allows us to justify the taking of lives, both human and animal, as part of what Meinertzhagen and others saw as a deep-rooted psychological inheritance of modern men.

By the time of the outbreak of war in Europe in 1914 and the extension of hostilities to East Africa the following year, the pioneer days of big game hunting in Africa were over. The elephant harvesters were already rapidly disappearing and the end of the period of 'pacification' and the establishment of colonial rule would shortly bring to an end the era of the soldier and the administrator as dominant figures on the hunting landscape. But hunting and trophy collection and display by imperial officials played an important role in the ideological support of empire. '[The] rows of horns and hides, mounted heads and stuffed bodies clearly alluded to the violent, heroic underside of imperialism.'[131] The new figures who would emerge as bearers of an imperial tradition were to have no less of an impact on the formation of the Kenyan hunting image and on the displacement and destruction of an indigenous African hunting tradition.

[128] Meinertzhagen, *Kenya Diary*, 132.
[129] Ibid., 300.
[130] Ibid., 333–4.
[131] H. Ritvo, *The Animal Estate*, 248, as quoted in Molly H. Mullin, 'Mirrors and Windows', *Annual Review of Anthropology* (1999), 205.

Five

The Settler Hunters
1903–39

In the first decades of the twentieth century, the pioneer period of wanton and unlimited slaughter of big game was brought to an end by increasing settlement and the effective enforcement of colonial game legislation. This sea change, ushering in a grand, new era in white hunting, reflected both a shift in attitudes and popular imagination in Europe and America, and the altered realities of Kenya's white hunting scene. The principal factor was the introduction of large-scale European settlement begun under the aegis of the colonial governor, Sir Charles Eliot (1900–04), which would in a few years transform the Kenyan landscape, increasingly occupied by the fenced and carefully cultivated settler farms and decreasingly by wildlife habitats.

Secondly, even before Theodore Roosevelt's highly publicized safari of 1909 brought Kenya to the centre of the international hunting culture, a new breed of visiting hunter was beginning to emerge on the Kenyan scene. The distinctive culture of the big game hunting safari would soon become a romantic ideal in literature and imagination, rivalling the frontier epic of the American West. This romantic image would remain the dominant representation of Kenyan life for a decade and longer after the 'champagne safaris' of the Prince of Wales and Dukes of York and Gloucester signalled the high-water mark of the Kenyan big game safari. We shall examine the hunting safari as Kenya's most distinctive contribution to the venatic tradition in the following chapter. For now we turn to the transformation of Kenyan hunting initiated by permanently resident hunters, the settler farmers, and other lifelong residents. As we shall see, they would profoundly alter the relations between black and white hunting, and pave the way for cataclysmic conflicts to come at the climax of the colonial era.

The aristocrats

The Kenya settlers, although diverse in origins in terms of nationality and class, would be moulded into a self-conscious elite that emerged by the 1920s as a dominant force in the political and cultural life of the Colony. They would enjoy the championship of talented writers such as Elspeth Huxley and, to a lesser degree, Errol Trzebinski.[1] But they have not enjoyed a good reputation among scholars of Africa. Their reputation for arrogance, overbearing disdain for Africans, and decadent 'lifestyle' has come to characterize the postcolonial portrayal of the settler community of Kenya. Individually they are seen to have exhibited strong personality, but little character.[2]

The settler reputation as big game hunters would suffer a similar sea change. At first they were admired for their prowess and sporting spirit; later they would be vilified as a major factor in 'The End of the Game'. We can seek the roots of both images in the collective biography of the early leaders of the Kenya settler community. The dominant figures of the Kenya settler community from before the Great War until the post-Second World War era were extremely wealthy, landed, and often titled aristocrats and gentlemen. In sharp contrast to other British African colonies such as Rhodesia, Kenya attracted settlers of high social and economic status in their countries of birth, especially Britain. Indeed, men and women of modest means were generally discouraged from settling, with the exception of the immediate post-Great War period of the Soldier Settlement Scheme. Not surprisingly, then, we will find Kenyan settler society, like the top ranks of the colonial service, to show a marked tendency to a monopoly by those of aristocratic and privileged backgrounds.

One clear mark of this background was the prodigious number of active hunters who came to settle in Kenya because of the hunting opportunities it provided, or who would come to develop a passion for hunting once the attractions of land ownership proved less than fully satisfactory. Indeed, hunting in particular and sporting activity in general would come to be the chief feature of self-identification of the Kenya settler elite. To be a leader of society, one must be a gentleman and a Kenya gentleman was synonymous with being a hunter and sportsman.

In order to demonstrate the social bias exhibited by settler hunters, and to trace the effects of settler influence on the imperial hunting tradition leading to what I shall argue is the emergence of a Kenya big game hunting culture, I propose to examine several key figures in the early period of Kenya settler history. These men (and one woman) would set the tone for what it meant to be a Kenya settler and hunter; they would become the leading lights of Kenya's version of high society for the first

---

[1] E. Huxley, *Out in the Midday Sun* (Harmondsworth: Penguin Books, 1987), and *Settlers of Kenya* (Westport, CT: Greenwood, 1948); E. Trzebinski, *The Kenya Pioneers* (New York: Norton, 1985). In a similar romantic vein, see E. Huxley and A. Curtis, *Pioneer's Scrapbook: Reminiscence of Kenya 1890 to 1968* (London: Evans Brothers, 1980); and A. Curtis, *Memories of Kenya. Stories from the Pioneers* (London: Evans Brothers, 1986).

[2] D. Kennedy, *Islands of White: Settler Society and Culture in Kenya and Southern Rhodesia, 1890–1939* (Durham: Duke University Press, 1987), esp. 44–7. See also the popular portrait of settler society in J. Fox, *White Mischief. The Murder of Lord Erroll* (New York: Random House, 1982).

three decades of the century. Additionally, they would individually and collectively oversee the slaughter of wildlife on a vast scale in pursuit of sport and in defence of their investment in Kenya's land and wealth.[3]

The first point to be made relates to the settlers as the agents for the transfer of the traditions of the aristocratic hunt, from Europe to Kenya. The pioneer hunters examined earlier, with their disregard for the ritualized, symbol-laden, and formal aspects of the hunt, were clearly not the carriers of this tradition. Their concern with the quantity and commercial value of the prey, and their recruitment of Kenyan Africans into the hunting enterprise, had important effects on local adaptations of the sport-hunting creed and may have set the terms of the synthesis that would emerge. However, they could hardly have brought the culture of the hunt with them. For that we should look to the aristocrats and their comrades-in-arms, who were both adherents of the tradition in Europe and interested in transplanting European ideals to Kenyan soil. We will not have to look far.

The leading members of Kenya's settler elite in the period before the Great War were indisputably the aristocratic sportsmen Hugh Cholmondeley – better known by his title of Lord Delamere – and Lord Cranworth.[4] They were also, and not coincidentally, among the highest-ranking members of the peerage. Both would display the curious contradiction of being at times the leading settler defenders of animals and game conservation and the leading destroyers of wildlife and habitat in the name of progress. Their careers, if not typical, should be illustrative of this paradox.

As a young man, Delamere had enjoyed the pleasures of the hunt to excess. Indeed, 'he had no interests but shooting and hunting' until just prior to his first expedition to Kenya in 1896–7. Having just returned from shooting tiger in India and elk in Scandinavia, he suffered a riding accident on a local hunt, and during his recuperation began to develop an interest in ethology and science under the tutelage of his physician and companion, Dr Atkinson. Until this time, the focus of his life was the chase. It may still be said of Delamere, as Elspeth Huxley put it: 'The English seasons were marked off for him, as for others of his tradition, by the species of animals it was appropriate to kill. Success was largely measured in terms of destructive ability.'[5] I would add that the rest of the world was divided, for him, in terms of the species of animals available for destruction in each region. Prior to his settlement in Kenya, Delamere had hunted on virtually every continent, including five hunting trips to Somalia in East Africa. And his decision to settle in

---

[3] Again, no attempt is made here to create a representative sample. On the contrary, individual settler hunters are selected for their distinction in both those categories and because they have recorded their own versions of their hunting exploits or been the subject of biographical accounts by others (or both).

[4] For Delamere, see E. Huxley's two-volume, laudatory biography, *White Man's Country* (London: Chatto and Windus, 1980 [1935]); for Cranworth, see his autobiographical, *Kenya Chronicles* (London: Macmillan, 1939). A less prominent member of the aristocracy who recorded his views on settling and hunting in Kenya is Lord Hindlip, *British East Africa: Past, Present and Future* (London: T. Fisher Unwin, 1905).

[5] Huxley, *White Man's Country*, 1: 25.

Figure 5.1 *Uganda Railway's advertising poster in the style of a* Punch *cartoon*

Kenya had far more to do with his hunting avocation than with his interest in farming.

Delamere returned to Kenya in 1899 with his new wife, Florence Cole, on a second hunting safari to the highlands, when the prospect of settling in the district was discussed for the first time.[6] Paradoxically, it would be the encouragement of white settlement by Sir Charles Eliot that would lead to the Delameres' relocation to Kenya in January 1903. This is curious because, unlike so many of the early Kenyan officials, Eliot was distinctly hostile to the hunting culture and feudal attitudes Delamere exhibited, favouring more economically minded, export-oriented working farmers. However, it would be the gentlemen hunters, anxious to a fault to shoot big game, such as those caricatured in the famous Uganda Railway's advertising poster in the style of a *Punch* cartoon (Figure 5.1), who would travel up-country on the newly built railway, firing rifles at cartoon animals from the observation car on their way to claim vast acres of what became the 'White Highlands'.[7]

Delamere's biographer would claim for him that his interest in game preservation began as early as 1900, when his concern over the decimation of elephants would lead him to recommend to the Foreign Office's representative in East Africa, Sir Harry Johnston, the creation of a game reserve in the Baringo district of the Rift Valley.[8] In fact, by the end of his career, Delamere's reputation as a conservationist was so solid that the 1949 official draft history of the Kenya National Parks would begin its history section with the following tribute regarding his role: 'Due entirely to the foresight of Lord Delamere, two Game Reserves were established in British East Africa in 1900.'[9] As further evidence of his lifelong conservationist principles, it was asserted years later, when Delamere had hung up his hunting guns, he would convert his farm at Soysambu in the Rift Valley to a game preserve.[10]

Unfortunately for Delamere's well-burnished reputation as sportsman and conservationist, contemporary evidence of his behaviour over a lifetime of hunting suggests otherwise. Most glaringly, in regard to the decision to establish a game reserve in 1900, Sir Harry Johnston, the High Commissioner stated:

> The fact is Lord Delamere, who secured 14,000 on ivory in the Baringo District by shooting elephant *with a maxim gun*, was exceedingly annoyed on returning to his old hunting ground to find that I had created Baringo Game Reserve which was intended to preserve elephants ... until such time as we were able to establish a station to control so-called sportsmen.[11] [Emphasis added]

[6] On this and his early hunting trips, prior to settling in Kenya, see ibid., 1: 23 and 26–85.
[7] Ibid. 1: 76; C. Eliot, *The East African Protectorate* (New York: Barnes and Noble, 1905), 276–9; and Hindlip, *British East Africa*, 130, 131–2, who shares the concern about shooting too near the railway line.
[8] Huxley, *White Man's Country*, 1: 85.
[9] 'Royal National Parks of Kenya', *Kenya National Archives* (*KNA*) KW/1/76 #224, 6.
[10] Huxley, *White Man's Country*, 1: 22.
[11] Johnston to Sclater, 6 March 1900, F.O. A7/6 quoted in Trzebinski, *Kenya Pioneers*, 28.

Whether Delamere himself was the source of the story of his positive contributions to the creation of Kenya's first game reserve, or whether that invention was entirely the work of Elspeth Huxley, his biographer, is moot.[12] In terms of sources, there can be little doubt that Johnston's account must be relied on in judging Delamere's role. This version of his behaviour would indicate that when the interests of animals clashed with his sporting impulse, his economic interests or his view of progress, Delamere could be totally ruthless in suppressing and destroying wildlife. And, the use of a Maxim-gun (an early machine-gun) in pursuit of sport or game control on his estate would not have gone down well with conservationists in his or any age.

Delamere's pursuit of his interests as a hunter and as a representative of the settlers is unintentionally supported by his aristocratic compatriot, Lord Hindlip, who recorded Delamere's role in gaining administrative approval of a cheap settler's hunting licence by intentionally overshooting the legal limit of a more stringent licence and inviting a court case. Not surprisingly, Hindlip sees this as being in the interest of fairness to the wealthy settlers. He also believes that the 'good ones' among the settlers 'will assist greatly in … [game] preservation'.[13]

This same disregard for the wildlife in his path can be seen in Delamere's campaign to reduce the lion population of Soysambu in 1912 when these animals, then considered as vermin and open to any means of destruction, posed a threat to his farming operations. He would import a professional hunter, Paul Rainey, and hunting dogs for this operation. Later, in 1912 and 1913, when he began to develop Soysambu as a major dairy farm, the extermination rather than the reduction of other animals, including giraffe, zebra, and antelope, on his rangeland would lead to their total elimination.[14]

The importance of Delamere as a 'role model' for settler society can hardly be overstated. He would be a model hunter, landowner, political figure, and socialite, *primus inter pares* of that dazzling set that would make up Kenya's 'Happy Valley' social in-crowd by the 1920s. 'The feudal system was in his bones and blood,' as Elspeth Huxley observed, 'and he believed all his life in its fundamental rightness.'[15] Those who shared both his ideas on deference and leadership and his commitment to hunting would shape Kenyan traditions very much in the image of this lordly and lusty hunter.

What Delamere did by example, Lord Cranworth furthered by his pen. Cranworth settled in East Africa in 1906, for reasons that he frankly acknowledged in his 1939 autobiography as: 'Love of sport, more

---

[12] Along with other Kenya notables, Delamere is treated 'with a discretion amounting to deception' throughout the account, in Huxley's efforts to establish the moral quality of the Kenya settler elite. K. Tidrick, *Empire and the English Character* (London: Tauris, 1990), 144, and 130–45 *passim*.

[13] Hindlip, *British East Africa*, 122 and 119–21 for his report of Delamere's leadership on behalf of settler hunting rights.

[14] E. Huxley, *White Man's Country*, 1: 306–11.

[15] Ibid. 1: 6.

especially of big-game shooting, and shortage of cash.'[16] The ability to create a landed estate at low cost, and run it with cheap labour, was an important motive to many of Kenya's high-born settlers, but for Cranworth – as for Delamere and his two brothers-in-law, Berkeley and Galbraith Cole – the game was the thing. Recognizing this, Cranworth soon set his pen to encouraging English settlement and immigration. Within a year of his arrival, he had published an essay in the *National Review* on 'Game Preservation in East Africa', in which he strongly supported the role of sports hunting in the preservation of wildlife. He asserted that neither visiting sportsmen nor settler hunters were responsible for the deplorable decline in game animal numbers. Indeed, 'far from wishing for the extermination of the game, a majority of settlers were among those most indignant at the ravages being made in it'.[17]

Cranworth so believed in the importance of sportsmen in the settlement of Kenya that he made their immigration a central burden of his 1912 efforts to encourage settlement. Of the several reasons he offered in support of settlement in Kenya, he stated, 'Last, but to the Englishman by no means least, the sport of all kinds is not to be surpassed.'[18] Indeed, the very title of his pro-settlement tract, *A Colony in the Making, or Sport and Profit in British East Africa*, gives pride of place to the sporting motive. His encouragement of settlement, however, is restricted to British settlers of the right class, and he launches a scathing condemnation of South African Boers, 'a crowd of indigent Dutch who don't farm the land they occupy but ... have supported themselves by the unlicensed slaughter of the once numerous game' of the Uasin Gishu plateau. This low opinion of Boer settlers was shared by the Acting Game Warden, A. Blayney Percival, who complained, in the department's annual report for 1909–10, of widespread destruction of game in the same region.[19] Moreover, reports 'of promiscuous shooting by Boers in different parts of the Protectorate' had already been a source of concern to the Foreign Office in 1906, as the Boers earned a reputation for being 'no respecters of game regulations'.[20]

Even British colonial officials who hunted were exempt from blame by Cranworth. Their 'paltry salaries' were such that he would recommend 'an entertainment allowance' to permit them to live at a more suitable level for gentlemen, as well as 'a free shooting license, not to include elephants', to 'keep up the supply of sportsmen which is so eminently desirable'. If sportsmen were not responsible for the ravages to game, and were to be encouraged to come to Kenya to hunt, who did Cranworth

[16] Cranworth, *Kenya Chronicles*, 1.

[17] Lord Cranworth, 'Game Preservation in East Africa', *National Review* (May 1907), 413.

[18] Lord Cranworth, *A Colony in the Making, or Sport and Profit in British East Africa* (London: Macmillan, 1912), 5. For his plea for settler immigration see ibid., 1–19, and for the role of sport in settler life see 231–40 and the following chapters and appendices on animals, hunting equipment, and advice.

[19] Ibid., 81–3, and draft copy, Game Department Annual Report, 1909–10, KNA KW/23/ 170, 30.

[20] J. H. Sadler, Commissioner to the Earl of Elgin, 28 September 1906, PRO Cd 4472 (1909), Africa Further Correspondence Relating to the Preservation of Wild Animals in Africa.

believe were to blame? He can be 'credited' for avoiding the easy target of African subsistence hunters, whom he thought lacked the destructive technology to do the kind of damage he perceived to be under way. Several historical factors were indicated: the 1890s rinderpest epidemic led to years of decline in certain animals such as buffalo, but he recognized that elephant were exempt from this scourge. Some responsibility was laid at the door of the Uganda Railways and the influx of 'rapacious ivory hunters' armed with guns. 'The result was deplorable', but temporary, as the Colonial Office imposed licensing changes and weight limits on ivory exports in response to pressures from the newly formed Society for the Preservation of the Fauna of the Empire.[21] The bulk of the blame Cranworth attributed to '"poaching" or the illicit slaughter of game without licence, such poaching being of two kinds, by natives and the meaner class of white men, the latter being at present by far the worst'.[22]

Although his judgement about the long-term impact of sports hunting was probably justified,[23] and his views about the depredations of the meaner classes, especially Boers, were both prejudicial and exaggerated, his efforts to exonerate the settlers were both self-serving and misleading.[24] In the words of another early and lifelong resident of the Colony, 'Every settler and farmer depended on the game for his meat supply.'[25]

His own autobiography, in which he inadvertently reveals his biased underestimation of the impact of settlers on game preservation, belies Cranworth's view of the benign impact of the settler. While paying lip-service to game preservation through licensed and controlled hunting, he graphically describes the destructive impact of large-scale settlement, even by well-meaning gentlemen like himself. In 1907, Cranworth established a large farm in the Thika district to the north of Nairobi at Makuyu, where he cleared and fenced the land for farming and grazing. The animals would be eliminated: 'It was years before we were troubled at Makuyu with a butcher's bill. There were buck in variety and abundance, indeed, at the roughest of estimates, I put the number on our estate in the region of 14,000.'[26]

Moreover, justified by the supposed requirements of his own domesticated animals, and unrestricted by licensing requirements or limits on his own land, the landscape was completely transformed in a short period, making it uninhabitable by wildlife in any number. He wrote that 'Today [1939] the house is surrounded by tens of thousands of acres of blue-green

[21] Cranworth, 'Game Preservation', 411–12.

[22] Ibid., 413.

[23] See J. Alladay, 'Elephants and Their Interactions with People in the Tana River Region of Kenya', Ph.D. dissertation, Cornell University, 1979.

[24] For a vivid description of the role of shooting in settler life, see Cranworth, *Kenya Chronicles*, 95–125; and L. Powys, *Black Laughter* (New York: Harcourt, Brace, 1924). Cranworth's apologetics for settler depredation of game are similarly expressed by Hindlip, *British East Africa*, 119–32.

[25] J. A. S. Watt, 'Recollections of Kenya, 1895–1963', Mss.Afr s.391, Rhodes House, Oxford.

[26] Cranworth, *Kenya Chronicles*, 21.

sisal and dark green coffee, not a buck or zebra is left upon the remnant of the plain.'[27]

In my judgement, settler destruction of wildlife habitat through fencing, clearing, and burning, as well as intense predation, constituted white settlement as the single most important factor in the decline of game numbers during the first half of the twentieth century. This is also in keeping with the view of many contemporary ecologists, who regard habitat destruction as the most important factor in species extinction today.

Cranworth also tips us off to another settler impact on wildlife that both influenced African hunting and devastated game populations in the early colonial era: the role of settlers as merchants and traders in game products. Being short of the cash needed to establish a working farm, Cranworth, like many other early settlers, entered into trade. Even gentlemen like himself and the redoubtable Denys Finch Hatton found it expedient to find partners and engage in commerce, especially in elephant ivory. 'Here there were at that time not only an incredible number of live elephants but also large stores of tusks, buried and otherwise.... Ivory was fetching somewhere about twenty five shillings a pound.'[28]

And so Cranworth purchased ivory from Africans who might well claim it as 'found' or buried ivory, killed before game restrictions were imposed. In exchange he offered the proverbial 'beads and trinkets', including opera glasses and hats. 'I am afraid', he confessed, 'that in this instance I might with justice be accused of exploiting the native.'[29] That he may also have contributed to the destruction of East African elephant is not so readily admitted, even by so punctilious a gentleman.

The gentlemen

By the 1920s, Lords Delamere and Cranworth had been joined by a few hundred other settlers, many of good breeding and high status, who joined in the sporting life. Many would make signal contributions to the life of the colony in politics, agriculture, and sport. Some, like Baron Bror Blixen and his illustrious and accomplished wife, Karen – best known as the writer and storyteller, Isak Dinesen – would bring continental pedigrees and genteel breeding the equal of the English lords.[30] The Cole brothers, if not so feudal in their attitudes – even stooping to fraternize with Africans – were as well born as their noble brother-in-law, Delamere. Similarly, the class credentials and educational attainments of Denys Finch Hatton were second to none in the Kenyan firmament.[31]

Others only slightly less well born would become full members of the aristocratic set by association, marriage, and dalliance. Northrup

[27] Ibid., 20.

[28] Ibid., 22–3.

[29] Ibid., 23.

[30] U. Aschan, *The Man Whom Women Loved: The Life of Bror Blixen* (New York: St. Martins, 1987), 3–13.

[31] E. Trzebinski, *Silence Will Speak* (Chicago: University of Chicago Press, 1977), 10–61.

MacMillan and Ewart Grogan would bring their personal fortunes and sporting obsessions to the young Kenyan elite.[32] Even those of humble middle-class background and no fortune might find a place among the Kenya pioneers. Beryl Markham nee Clutterbuck would translate her good looks and Kenyan social network into world fame, first as an aviatrix and adventuress, and eventually as a writer and autobiographer.[33] Elspeth Huxley, cousin to the scientist and conservationist, Julian Huxley, would represent white Kenya to the world of letters by her writings and her life.[34] Many of these settler hunters would make important contributions to the development and popularization of Kenya as a hunter's paradise, a cavalier's Garden of Eden without the puritanical banishment of carnal knowledge.

Two of the most interesting of the elite settlers were the American-born millionaire William Northrup MacMillan and the English adventurer Ewart Grogan. Neither wrote of their experiences as settlers, but both became well-known figures in the settler community for their wealth, hospitality, and eccentricity. Both also settled in Kenya having first travelled to East Africa for other purposes, hunting prominent among them.[35]

Sir Northrup MacMillan, a devoted Anglophile, led the life of an itinerant big game hunter in Africa – including Ethiopia and the Sudan – before he decided to settle in Kenya in 1904. With his wife Lucie, he purchased a large estate of 20,000 acres just northeast of Nairobi, called 'The Juja Farm', which was overlooked by the dramatic humpbacked mountain Ol Doinyo Sabuk.[36] The MacMillan estate and their handsome stone town house, called Chiromo, on the Nairobi River, became places of pilgrimage for visiting hunters and a place of refreshment for the sporting set among the settlers. Chiromo would also serve as a nursing station for wounded soldiers during the Great War, for which service MacMillan would be knighted.[37]

Today MacMillan is best remembered for the subscription library in Nairobi built by his widow, which bears his name,[38] and a romantic story about his burial. On his death, MacMillan's desire to be buried on top of Ol Doinyo Sabuk was frustrated by his great weight. The porters from his farm, unable to carry him to the top of the mountain, were allowed to bury him on the slopes. This kind of romantic legend, as it quickly became in the settler clubs and watering-places, enhanced MacMillan's reputation for devotion to the land. It seems to have served as a trope indicating the commitment of the white settlers to turn Kenya into a 'White Man's

---

[32] B. H. Jessen, *W. N. MacMillan's Expeditions and Big Game Hunting in Southern Sudan, Abyssinia, and East Africa* (London: Marchant Singer, 1906); E. S. Grogan and A. H. Sharp, *From the Cape to Cairo* (London: Hurst and Blacklett, 1902).

[33] B. Markham, *West with the Night* (Boston: Houghton, Mifflin, 1942); and H. K. Binks, *African Rainbow* (London: Sidgwick and Jackson, 1959).

[34] E. Huxley, *The Flame Trees of Thika* (New York: Weidenfeld and Nicolson, 1987 [1959]).

[35] Grogan did co-author a book about his Cape to Cairo trek, which passed through western Uganda. Grogan and Sharp, *From the Cape to Cairo*, 145–249.

[36] Jessen, *MacMillan's Expeditions*, 383–404.

[37] Trzebinski, *Kenya Pioneers*, 58, 95, 182–3, and 187–8.

[38] Ibid., 12n.

Country', a place in which they hoped to live and eventually to be buried amidst the beautiful sights and loyal African servants who had surrounded and served them in life.

Ewart Grogan's first visit to East Africa was part of his successful attempt to walk from South Africa to Egypt in 1898–1900, and included a two-week stint of elephant hunting in Uganda.[39] By this remarkable feat of endurance and skill as a hunter – feeding himself with his rifle for the better part of two years – Grogan established a reputation for extreme behaviour that would follow him to Kenya when he settled there in 1903. A Kenya original, Grogan would become famous as a politician and orator by 1906, as well as the developer of properties, including the creation of a sisal estate at Taveta and an important Nairobi hotel in 1928. He and Delamere would be extolled as progressive farmers, and along with the Cole brothers, MacMillan, and others would become mainstays of both the Turf Club and the hunting fraternity among the wealthy settlers.[40]

Grogan alone would become infamous for his abuse of Africans and his opposition to Indian immigration, which he saw as a threat to civilization and white dominance. But it was his act of publicly whipping an African that would enshrine Grogan in memory as a particularly brutal representative of settler attitudes. In March 1907, Grogan administered a severe and very public flogging to his own servants over an incident in which his niece was frightened by his rickshaw driver's erratic behaviour. The incident, in which 25 lashes were administered by Grogan and two other white settler leaders to each of three of Grogan's servants on the steps of the Nairobi courthouse, was done without benefit of formal charges, trial, or conviction in the colonial courts. This would result in Grogan's arrest and imprisonment for taking the law into his own hands. Coming in the wake of settler complaints about the threat to white women represented by unruly and disrespectful town-dwelling 'natives', Grogan's own culpability was intensified by the fact that he held the conspicuous and responsible position of President of the Colonists' Association, and had been their forceful spokesman in demanding stricter enforcement of controls on Africans in town, especially with regard to real and imagined threats to white womanhood. Fined and sentenced to a month in jail, Grogan would become the darling of the settlers and the bane of the administration, and the incident and its punishment would become a *cause célèbre*, poisoning settler-administration relations and Grogan's personal reputation for many years.[41]

Ewart Grogan had been a dedicated hunter and that was among his chief reasons for coming to Kenya. But after his arrival and settlement in Kenya with his wife he would abandon the hunting field, except to be a host and companion to visiting hunters on his estates. Today he is better

[39] Grogan and Sharp, *From the Cape to Cairo*, 202.

[40] Trzebinski, *Kenya Pioneers*, 156–8, 170, 178–85. On Grogan's early retirement from hunting, see Edward Paice, *Lost Lion of Empire* (London: Harper Collins, 2001), 181–2.

[41] Trzebinski, *Kenya Pioneers*, 126–30, and Paice, *Lost Lion of Empire*, 211–23, on the 'Nairobi Incident'. See L. Farrant, *The Legendary Grogan* (London: H. Hamilton, 1981), 134–56, 165–85, and 216–27 on Grogan's public life spanning six decades.

known for his career as a settler politician and businessman. His less famous younger brother, Quentin, who came to Kenya in 1905 to assist Ewart in the development of a timber concession, would devote himself to hunting far more assiduously than to his business career. He would hunt widely in Kenya, Uganda, and the Belgian Congo, including ivory poaching in the Lado enclave. He would also accompany Theodore Roosevelt's hunting safari in 1909. He would settle on his own farm at Turi in the White Highlands in 1915 and remain there until 1933, when he would sell his farm and move to South Africa. His papers, including diaries and a memoir, give a vivid picture of the hunting life of resident gentlemen during the first three decades of the century.[42]

The contributions by these men of wealth and vision to Kenya's hunting history extend far beyond their own early hunting exploits and the tone they set in making hunting a cornerstone of white settler life. Both men would play an important role as hosts to visiting hunters during the period in which the safari was becoming the distinctive hunting form. Moreover, they played a crucial role in using other local hunters as paid guides and safari organizers for themselves and their guests in the first examples of the creation of the 'Professional White Hunter'.[43]

The ladies

The aristocratic ideal that animated Kenya's aristocratic and gentlemen hunters had little place for the refinements of literature or the arts. That was left to the settler women, whose achievements and reputations as writers have given Kenya an international reputation far out of proportion to the small number of Kenyan white authors. They have also made signal contributions to popularizing Kenyan hunting internationally. The doyenne of Kenya settler authors, until her death in 1997, was Elspeth Huxley.[44] Briefly in the 1980s, her reputation as Kenya's literary lioness was eclipsed by the revival of interest in the works of two other settler women: Baroness Karen Blixen – who wrote under the pen-name of Isak Dinesen – and Beryl Markham, the supposed author of a captivating autobiography, *West with the Night*, and several short stories set in Kenya.[45] All three writers used their talents to describe and romanticize Kenyan big game hunting; Beryl Markham would also contribute directly to the development of the safari hunting praxis.[46]

---

[42] Papers of Quentin O. Grogan, Mss.Afr s. 1949, Rhodes House, Oxford.

[43] Trzebinski, *Kenya Pioneers*, 137–8; and Chapter 6 below.

[44] S. Lyall, 'Elspeth Huxley, 89, Chronicler of Colonial Kenya, Dies', obituary, *New York Times*, 17 January 1997, 13. Her major work was her autobiographical memoir of Kenya, *The Flame Trees of Thika*, originally published in 1959.

[45] Isak Dinesen's most influential work was a memoir, *Out of Africa* (New York: Vintage, 1985), originally published in 1938. Due to its wartime appearance, Markham's autobiography, *West with the Night*, remained obscure until it was reissued in the 1980s.

[46] The remarkable revival of both women's reputations lies outside the scope of this history. However, it should be noted that the filming of Blixen's *Out of Africa* by Sydney Pollack in the early 1980s, and the publication of two literary biographies, not only had a dramatic

Huxley's account of her childhood in Kenya focused principally on harmonious domestic relations on the family farm, including those with Africans, who appear often in the role of servants and victims of accidents requiring the benevolent intervention of sympathetic white people. She came to Kenya in 1913 as a child of six, and left it for England when she married at age 21. Her memories, not surprisingly, are painted in the pastels of youthful exuberance and nostalgia, contributing no doubt to their popularity among Western readers in the wake of the Mau Mau revolt in the 1950s. Hunting is only important in her memories in two ways: as a marker of childhood adventure and as an element of hospitality.[47] It is these two points that I hope to explore using the writings of the three women writers.

Beryl Markham came to Kenya as a two-year-old in 1904 with her father, who worked as a horse trainer for Lord Delamere, buying a parcel of land from him at Njoro. For the young Beryl, hunting and horses made up a juvenile idyll conveyed with intense excitement in her autobiography and reflected in the few works of fiction she wrote while living in the United States in the 1940s.[48] In fact, both horse training and hunting would remain central to her life and work until her death in 1986. It would be as a young tomboy that Beryl would learn to hunt: 'You couldn't live in Africa and not hunt. Kibii [a young Nandi companion] taught me how to shoot with a bow and arrow, and when we found we could shoot wood pigeons and blue starlings and waxbills, by way of practice, we decided on bigger things.'[49]

The 'bigger things' she hunted with her Nandi teachers and guides using spears included reedbuck, warthog, and 'wild boar', and the occasional unplanned encounter with a lion. Her account of her childhood hunting adventures are remarkable for the respectful treatment of her Nandi friends as equals or betters from whom she could learn, not just the techniques of hunting and bushcraft, but the spirit of adventure in the 'sport' of the chase, which was a key part of their hunting ethos.[50]

The crux of her autobiography was the lifelong spirit of adventure that she learned on these childhood safaris and expanded as a young woman in

---

[46] (contd) effect on the reputations of Blixen and Markham, it also had a profound, if temporary, impact on Kenya tourism.

[47] E. Huxley, *The Flame Trees*, 232–40, on her relations with Dorobo hunters in the Molo area of the Mau Escarpment. Also her 'Memoir' in Nellie Grant, *Nellie* (London: Weidenfeld and Nicholson, 1984), 47–9, and her *Out in the Midday Sun*, 45–58.

[48] There is a dispute as to the authorship of all of Markham's works done when she was married to the Hollywood screenwriter, Raoul Schumacher. Regardless of the actual authorship or ghost writing of her autobiography and stories, there can be no doubt that her personal experiences formed the factual basis of these creative efforts. See E. Trzebinski, *The Lives of Beryl Markham* (New York: Norton, 1993); J. Fox, 'Not Quite the Only Begetter', *The Spectator*, 1 August 1987, 30–31; D. Ackerman, 'A High Life and a Wild One', *New York Times Book Review*, 23 August 1987, 1ff.; and K. A. Appiah, 'White Mischief', *Transition* 62 (1993), 122–9.

[49] Markham, *West with the Night*, 103–4.

[50] Ibid., 75–98. See also M. Lovell, *Straight on Till Morning. The Biography of Beryl Markham* (London: Hutchinson, 1987), 28–33.

the hunting exploits she shared with her friends and lovers. Among these men, she had clandestine affairs with the Kenyan settler hunters Bror Blixen and Denys Finch Hatton, and had a romantic tryst with H. R. H. Prince Henry, Duke of Gloucester, and Tom Delamere, the son and heir to Lord Delamere. Her marriages to Mansfield Markham and Raoul Schumacher would be unquiet interludes between the exciting episodes in a life of adventure.

The centre-piece of that life, and her claim to fame, would be her supreme or extreme adventure as a pioneer aviator. Tom Black, a pioneer Kenyan pilot and one of the young Beryl's lovers, would teach her to fly and introduce her to the third passion of her life after horses and hunting. He would support and encourage her in the exploit that would land her in the record books and the feminist pantheon: her solo flight across the Atlantic from east to west, the first person to accomplish this feat of daring and skill.[51]

Beryl Markham's direct contribution to the Kenya safari hunting tradition came in the mid-1930s. She combined her love of flying with her connections to the hunting fraternity by offering to spot elephant herds from the air and report their location to the professional safari guides, greatly improving their ability to locate animals for their clients. Begun as a favour to Bror Blixen, she would eventually offer aerial reconnaissance as a commercial service.[52]

Elspeth Huxley's youthful hunting adventures (as well as her far less turbulent romantic life) would pale in comparison to Markham's. Perhaps this is because her parents were peripheral to the aristocratic hunting milieu in which Markham would thrive. Huxley's father 'never really cared for it', and her mother gave up hunting fairly early in her long life in Kenya.[53] For Elspeth, hunting formed an important element in the social life of the colony in which both men and women could participate, albeit on an unequal footing. Sunday mornings were generally spent riding and hunting – in the English sense, riding to hounds. A neighbour near the Huxleys' place in Thika, Mervyn Ridley, had imported English foxhounds, and the young Elspeth would ride over to his place at Makuyu to chase jackals and steenbok. Similarly, James Elkington, an important horseman and member of the elite Turf Club of Nairobi, kept foxhounds imported from India by the Game Ranger, S. H. Goldfinch, for the pleasure of his fox-hunting friends.[54]

Margaret Elkington asserted, moreover, 'When guests arrived from England they expected to be taken on safari.'[55] In fact, I would argue that the old English tradition of aristocratic hospitality was crucial to the early

[51] Markham, *West with the Night*, 277–91; and Lovell, *Straight on Till Morning*, 76–93, 106–9, 113–33, and 156–90.

[52] Trzebinski, *The Lives of Beryl Markham*, 190–91; Lovell, *Straight on Till Morning*, 135–6, 150–51; and below Chapter 5, pp. 000–00. Also see Aschan, *The Man Whom Women Loved*, 166; and Trzebinski, *Silence Will Speak*, 210–11.

[53] Huxley, 'Memoir', 69.

[54] M. Elkington, 'Recollections', Mss.Afr s.1558: 23, Rhodes House, Oxford.

[55] Ibid., 47, 48–9.

development of the Kenyan safari. Not only did the wealthy visitors from England and the United Sates expect to be taken hunting by their hosts, but they also expected those hunting adventures to be organized and catered for, complete with fine dining, ample alcohol, and fireside entertainment. Included in the entertainment were no doubt the conversational attentions of young women like Beryl Markham, who would be in attendance not only on the royal safaris of Prince Henry, but on those of Ernest Hemingway, Alfred Vanderbilt, and other visiting sport seekers.[56] But, most importantly, young settlers who knew the territory and were accomplished hunters were often invited along and were sometimes paid for their services as hunting guides, companions, and raconteurs. But we shall have more to say on this later.

Karen Blixen was a grown woman when she first came to Kenya in 1913 to settle and join her fiancé, Bror Blixen. Unlike the other women writers, her hunting experiences were forged in the continental aristocratic tradition shared by the *haute bourgeoisie* of her native Denmark. Her marriage to Bror Blixen brought her the title of Baroness; her family fortune would buy her famous farm in Africa.[57] Bror would introduce Karen (or Tanne as she was known) to African big game hunting, for which she showed both an aptitude and passion. While Bror quickly tired of domestic life on the coffee farm at Ngong, west of Nairobi (in what is now the suburb known as Karen), and took to hunting and safari work full-time, Karen would also take to hunting in Kenya with a real passion that bordered on blood-lust.[58] She was often able to combine this passion with her romance with Denys Finch Hatton. What emerges clearly from a reading of Karen Blixen's letters and memoirs is the conflation of her love of hunting and her aristocratic pretensions. The freedom to cross a gender line between helping in the hunt and actively hunting in one's own right was facilitated by Blixen's upper-class exemption from gender taboos, her transgressive behaviour across class lines, and her translocation to Africa, where she could escape the constraints of conformity to 'the fearful living death of the English middle-class mediocrity'.[59] Hunting would free and even ennoble her in ways her marriage into a titled family could not. By writing about her hunting experiences as a Kenya settler, she would contribute indelibly to the romanticization of that tradition.

The men whom women loved

The Kenya settlers Bror Blixen-Finecke and Denys Finch Hatton shared a great many things in common, not least of which were the affections of Karen Blixen and brief affairs with Beryl Markham. But they also shared

56 See Lovell, *Straight on Till Morning*, 71–137 *passim*, and Chapter 5 in this volume.
57 I. Dinesen, *Out of Africa and Shadows on the Grass* (New York: Vintage, 1985 [1938, 1960]); J. Thurman, *Isak Dinesen: The Life of a Storyteller* (New York: St. Martins, 1982).
58 Thurman, *Isak Dinesen*, 142–3. Also Isak Dinesen, *Letters from Africa, 1914–1931* (London: Picador, 1983), 27 and *passim*.
59 Dinesen, *Letters from Africa*, 49.

a great fondness for each other, which was forged in the pursuit of wild animals rather than women. Both came out to farm, or, rather, to be gentlemen farmers, but both found the work too demanding of their time. Blixen in particular found the sedentary life too confining for his exuberant spirits. 'For Blix, Africa spelled adventure.'[60] Long before he would take up hunting professionally, he was consumed by it emotionally. He would describe his birthplace, the family seat of the Blixens, 'Nasbyholm at Skane', as the place: 'where the best shooting in Sweden is to be found....
The atmosphere is charged with sporting observations and experiences which cannot fail to stir a boy's imagination, and if the boy is a sportsman by instinct to begin with, his outlook on life is pretty quickly determined.'[61]

Indeed, his boy's imagination and his aristocratic upbringing seem to have stayed with him throughout his life, along with the impatience and insouciance of childhood. His autobiography treats the sum of his experience as a planter (and husband) as follows:

> The soil was cleared. The coffee fields were marked out. The cultivator's hopes swelled in my breast.
> Summer went and autumn came – the autumn of 1914.
> The war. The price market was chaotic, communications were chaotic. Difficulty upon difficulty arose. The plantation had to be sold – my home was broken up.
> I stood there in the forest empty-handed. But I still had my sporting rifle.[62]

The remaining 250 pages of his autobiography, written in 1936 and appropriately entitled *African Hunter*, is devoted to his hunting adventures. After an initial chapter on game laws and regulations in the interests of conservation, the book is organized, as was typical of an earlier generation of hunting adventure writers, around the different species of prey he had pursued.[63] In a word, Blixen's was a life viewed through cross hairs.

In contrast, Denys Finch Hatton was a man of parts.[64] Born to 'a long line of aristocrats, noble soldiers, seafarers, politicians and scholarly predecessors', he attended Eton and Oxford University.[65] The kind of boy to whom learning, leadership, and admiration came easily, he would excel as an athlete. Restless and in search of escape from the confinements of English country life, he would settle in Kenya in 1910 at age 23. When his farming attempts fell on bad times, he would try his hand at trade, but eventually he would find his calling, like Bror Blixen, in hunting for pleasure and profit. Going on safari would become the focal point of his

---

[60] Aschan, *The Man Whom Women Loved*, 18. See Baron Bror von Blixen-Finecke, *African Hunter* (New York: St. Martins, 1986 [1938]), 3–25, for the primacy of adventure and sport over other considerations in the decision to settle in Kenya.

[61] von Blixen-Finecke, *African Hunter*, 3–4.

[62] Ibid., 26.

[63] Ibid., 27–8.

[64] This section is based largely on the biography of Finch Hatton by Trzebinski, *Silence Will Speak*.

[65] Ibid., 10, 30–61.

calendar; time spent at his house in the Parklands suburb near Nairobi or at Karen Blixen's farm was for him an interlude of ease and renewal between the hunting trips for which he lived.[66] By the late 1920s, he had made hunting his profession as well as his passion.[67]

I do not mean to suggest that either Blixen or Finch Hatton became market hunters, something beneath the dignity and outside the ethical mind-set of either man. Rather they would turn their own hunting prowess into profitable employment by serving as hunting guides and safari organizers for rich visitors. They would thus be crucial players in the transformation of sport hunting from Kenya's leading pastime to its leading service industry. Their role as professional white hunters belongs to the next chapter. Here I want simply to point out their backgrounds and the beginnings of the careers that enabled them to meld their knowledge of local hunting with their aristocratic positions as cultural icons of the settler elite of Kenya. Their high birth and personal grace not only made them leaders and trend-setters, but would also lend professional hunting the curious combination of respectability and glamour.

Hunting, science and religion

Before turning to the visiting safari hunters, there is another category of resident hunters that requires some discussion. Among those who came to Kenya and settled were some who came not to farm, but rather to harvest souls and knowledge. Missionaries and ethnologists shared with settlers a long-term, often permanent, commitment to living out their lives in East Africa. As such, their hunting activities form a piece with those of other resident hunters, requiring the same licensing and involving similar if not identical practices, technologies, and ideals. But, in some crucial ways, these resident hunters differed from their settler counterparts, especially in the degree and nature of their interactions with local African hunters. The results were a qualitatively different impact on African hunting and the development of a minor tradition of white hunting practice in the colonial period.

Missionary enterprise in Africa, like that of other early travellers and settlers, was greatly assisted by the ability of the missionaries to use their weapons to feed their flocks. From the German missionary, Johann Ludwig Krapf, early in the nineteenth century, to the Anglican Bishop, Alfred Tucker, at the end of the century, missionaries regularly used their hunting abilities to shoot for the pot, feeding themselves and their entourages while travelling, and hunting for recreation when settled.[68]

---

[66] His biographer chooses to introduce the story of his life with a highly charged romantic anecdote of a hunting trip with his lover, Karen Blixen, in an attempt to underscore the intensity of passion aroused in both of them by their love of the hunt as of each other. Ibid., 1–9.

[67] Ibid., 233–85.

[68] J. Lewis Krapf and J. Rebmann, *Travels, Researches, and Missionary Labours*, 2nd ed. (London: Frank Cass, 1968 [1860]), and Chapter 3 of this volume on Krapf's hunting; J. H.

But it would be the resident missionaries, and the rare anthropologist who had long-term and intimate interactions with African hunters, whose impact would be most pronounced. We can illustrate this from the experiences of two individuals who worked for extended periods in Ukambani: Reverend Stuart Watt, an Anglican missionary, and Gerhard Lindblom, a Swedish ethnographer.

Originally, Watt worked as a missionary among Kamba-speaking residents of Usagara in northern Tanganyika, but in the mid-1890s he transferred to Ngelani near Machakos in Kenya. As early as 1885 in Usagara, Watt recognized the importance of hunting to Akamba men. He notes: 'The greater part of their time seemed to be given to the chase ... [and they were] very expert with the bow and arrow.'[69] But for the early converts among the Kamba hunters the pickings were not so good. Reverend Watt's wife, Rachel, recorded:

> We often pitied the few natives who lived with us on the Station, as they had far less variety of food than the savages of the surrounding tribe did. They begged of my husband to go and shoot some meat for them, which he promised to do.
>
> The larger antelopes do not make their way far into the thick bush, but confine themselves to open grassy plains and the forest contiguous to these feeding places. It was ten hours march through thick jungle to the nearest place where these animals were to be found in numbers. My husband and his men started one morning and arrived at the rendezvous of the game in the evening and there pitched their tents.
>
> The following day, an eland and a zebra fell to the shot of the rifle and my husband dispatched two men with a leg of meat and a message for me.[70]

Two points need be made about this episode. The first relates to the importance of hunting by missionaries in the maintenance of their communities of settled converts in and around their mission stations. The fact is that, by getting the local missionary to use his rifle to procure meat for them, Africans who might otherwise have hunted for themselves would begin to abandon the field to better-armed hunters as part of the process of religious conversion. Conversely, the missionary used his ability to hunt as a means to sedentarize and convert his mission adherents. Secondly, because of their long residence and close interaction with their adherents and the missionary focus on learning local languages and customs, a two-way exchange of ideas about hunting, meat, and nature could take place between the African and European hunters. Even in Ukambani, where game was abundant in the immediate vicinity of the station (on land adjacent to Ol Doinyo Sabuk later sold to Northrup MacMillan in 1908),

---

[68] (contd) Patterson, 'Diary', Mss.Afr r.93, Rhodes House, Oxford, 26 March 1898; and A. Tucker, *Eighteen Years in Uganda and East Africa* (2 vols.) (London: Edward Arnold, 1908), on Tucker's hunting.

[69] R. Watt, *In the Heart of Savagedom* (London: Marshall Bros., n.d. [1922?]), 52, 259–78, for descriptions of the effectiveness and ability of Kamba hunters in Kenya.

[70] Ibid., 87.

Kamba hunters would be discouraged from hunting for themselves and encouraged instead to accompany the missionary on his own hunting safaris.[71] In addition, Reverend Watt would never hunt for sport but only 'for food or in defence', perhaps reflecting both his own humble origins and his adoption of Kamba attitudes towards the killing of game other than elephant.[72]

Those who came to collect secular knowledge, like those who came to spread the gospel, shared a special relationship with their African hosts. The extensive period of field research conducted by Gerhard Lindblom not only enabled him to give the first thorough and 'scientific' treatment of Akamba hunting, but afforded him an opportunity to hunt with the Akamba for guinea-fowl and other small animals.[73] He was able not only to observe and learn from his companions, but also to provide them with useful knowledge about weapons and techniques of hunting as well as meat. By the time of his researches, hunting by Akamba had been severely restricted, and the attendant skills such as arrow making were 'rapidly disappearing'.[74] In addition, he noted that 'in former times, when they were able to steal cattle and hunt big game without hindrance, they ate considerably more meat than now'. Lindblom also noted, like so many observers of Africans on safari, the voraciousness of Akamba appetites for meat, and their frequent demands on his time for hunting on their behalf.[75]

The ability of Europeans to observe African hunting at close quarters, and the reciprocal ability of Africans to watch and learn from Europeans about weapons, techniques, and attitudes, led to the beginnings of a synthesis. The emerging professional safari hunters among the settlers, and their visiting big game enthusiasts, were the main beneficiaries of this exchange of knowledge and of the local experience and expertise of these Kamba hunters and others like them across newly colonized Kenya.

---

[71] Ibid., 108, 150–51, 163–4, and esp. 292–6, on hunting for meat for porters and mission workers while on safari. On the abundance of game near the stations, see ibid., 177–8; and J. A. S. Watt, 'Recollections of Kenya, 1895–1963', Mss.Afr. s.391, Rhodes House, Oxford. J. A. S. Watt was born to Stuart and Rachel Watt in 1895.

[72] Watt, *In the Heart of Savagedom*, 329–30.

[73] G. Lindblom, *The Akamba in British East Africa*, 2nd ed. (Uppsala: Archives d'Études Orientale, 1920 [1916]), 120, and 449–64 on weapons and poison, 465–74 on hunting methods; and Chapter 3 of this volume.

[74] Lindblom, *The Akamba in British East Africa*, 135.

[75] Ibid., 511. See also K. Cameron, *Into Africa: The Story of the East African Safari* (London: Constable, 1990), 22–3.

Part III

▼◆◆◆◆◆◆◆◆◆◆◆◆◆◆◆◆◆◆◆◆◆◆▼

Black & White Together

In hunting, the finding and killing of game is after all but a part of the whole. The free, self-reliant, adventurous life, with its rugged and stalwart democracy, the wild surroundings, the grand beauty of the scenery, the chance to study the ways and habits of woodland creatures – all these unite to give to the career of the wilderness hunter its peculiar charm. The chase is among the best of the national pastimes; it cultivates that vigorous manliness for the lack of which in a nation, as in an individual, the possession of no other qualities can possibly atone.

Theodore Roosevelt, US President and hunter
(*The Works of Theodore Roosevelt*, Vol. II, ed. Hermann Hagedorn.
New York: Charles Scribner's Sons, 1927: xxix)

Six

Safari Hunting

1909–39

The word 'safari' seems to have entered English common usage as a result
of the publicity that attended President Theodore Roosevelt's 1909
expedition to East Africa.[1] However, we should be mindful of the fact that
the trade safari, the direct predecessor of the big game safari with which we
are concerned, has a long history in East Africa. The word itself is of Arabic
origin via Swahili, the coastal Bantu language of Kenya and Tanzania. It is
derived from the verb *kusafiri*, meaning to travel, and the cognate term,
msafiri, a traveller. The trading caravan was developed by the Arab and
Swahili merchants of Zanzibar and the coast in the course of the nineteenth
century from the Kamba, Yako, and others who had for centuries carried
goods for sale at the coast. These same peoples continued to work as porters
in large numbers as the organization and financing of the safari passed into
coastal hands. And they would also form the backbone of the safari's labour
force as it metamorphosed into the 'big game safari'. Thus it should not
surprise us to learn that many elements of the hunting safari, in terms of
organization, methods, and leadership, as well as vocabulary and cultural
practices, were also rooted in African ideas and beliefs. The efforts to
'whiten' the safari, to see its inventors and developers as the European
pioneers of African exploration and settlement, were begun early in the
history of the transition from trade to hunting, as colonial officials, white
settlers, and local resident hunters replaced the coastal caravan leadership
and organization with their own. This image still persists in the popular
literature, which remains blinded by prejudice and popular mythology to
African initiatives and contributions.[2]

[1] D. Holman, *Inside Safari Hunting with Eric Rundgren* (New York: Putnam, 1970), 42 credits
Theodore Roosevelt's *African Game Trails: An Account of the African Wanderings of an American
Hunter-Naturalist* (New York: Charles Scribner's Sons, 1910) with spreading the word
'safari', with the meaning of a hunting expedition, to most European languages.

[2] A recent and substantial such popular account is K. M. Cameron's *Into Africa: The Story of
the East African Safari* (London: Constable, 1990), 16–23, which duly notes the Arab
contribution, but seems to equally credit the missionary-explorer David Livingstone, while

Although only a few of the 'great white hunters' have acknowledged their debt to their African teachers and models, there is reason to believe that the success of all of them must be shared with African hunters. Not surprisingly, when hunters like George Adamson or J. A. Hunter do give credit, it is often to their Kamba hunting companions, whom we have already met as the most prolific and successful of Kenya's precolonial hunters. Kamba knowledge of bushcraft and tracking is most frequently cited with respect and admiration. 'They were in great demand for the police force; and in the field of sport they were unrivalled. They poached a certain amount of game, but not inordinately, and to go hunting with them was a liberal education.'[3] It is not too much to say that the vast majority of white hunters, professionals and sportsmen, took their degrees in bushcraft, tracking, and stalking from their Kamba companions. And they continued to depend on their skills and loyalty throughout the era of the big game safari. The tragedy is the scarcity of this recognition in both the contemporary and historical accounts of the big game safari. This is a silence in the sources that, when combined with the silencing of any African voices from among the safari workers, amounts to a significant distortion of an understanding and appreciation of the place of hunting in the colonial encounter.

The safari, I will contend, was the central arena in which European and African ideas about hunting met and merged to create a truly Euro-African synthesis by the 1930s. We can see clearly, in the various meanings with which the idea of safari has been inscribed, the workings of what Mary Louise Pratt has described as transculturation 'in the contact zone' between Western imperialism and indigenous ideas.[4] This chapter will look at the development and climax in the 1930s of the big game safari, this peculiarly Kenyan hunting synthesis, and the exploits of its leading practitioners and popularizers, as an example of transcultural production.

Inventing the big game safari

Three elements mark the continuity from the commercial safaris of the nineteenth century to the hunting safaris of the twentieth: the size of the entourage, the military demeanour of the caravan, and the central role of hunting in the daily operation. The large size, often numbering in the hundreds of porters, was necessitated by the absence of any means of transportation other than by foot. Lacking in carts, wagons, and beasts of burden, the requirement of carrying the food, trade goods, and ammuni-

---

[2] (contd) ignoring African contributions beyond porterage. See Brian Herne, *White Hunters* (New York: Henry Holt, 1999), for a popular and romantic account by a professional hunter.

[3] This praise was offered by the first warden of the National Parks of Kenya, Henry Seaton, in his *Lion in the Morning* (London: John Murray, 1963), 70–90. See also G. Adamson, *Bwana Game* (London: Collins and Harvill, 1968), 20–21, 163–73; J. A. Hunter, *Hunter* (London: Hamish Hamilton, 1952), 180–81.

[4] M. L. Pratt, *Imperial Eyes* (London: Routledge, 1992), 1–11.

tion to be consumed over the course of several weeks to several months on the trail meant that the majority of the caravan participants in the early days were simple bearers of loads, carried on heads. Only the wealthiest and most extravagant of caravans would carry food. Although Lord Delamere's 1896 hunting safari carried food for the porters, so as not to have to carry trade goods and therefore stay near populated areas where food could be obtained, it was made possible only by his purchase of 200 transport camels, requiring an enormous outlay of cash.[5]

The big game safari also maintained the military appearance and organization it had acquired during the age of imperial exploration and conquest when, in addition to porters and leaders, a contingent of soldiers frequently accompanied the safari, swelling its size and its meat require-ments. Even when a military escort ceased to be needed, the practice of the safari leader shooting meat on a daily basis for his own table and to satisfy the meat hunger of the African staff was maintained as a regular feature, shaping the routing and tempo of the safari's progress. In other words, even when hunting of big game trophies was limited by law and custom to a small number of prized animals, the daily killing of animals to provision the caravan made the daily and mundane activity of hunting for food the overwhelming trademark of the sport safari.

It has been said that 'the *annus mirabilis* of East African hunting was 1909'.[6] In that year, the East African safari of recently retired President Theodore Roosevelt of the United States marked what we might call the official beginning of Kenya's sport hunting era, popularizing the image of the big game safari far beyond its Kenyan locale.[7] Roosevelt's much publicized expedition to Kenya and down the Nile, which he undertook almost immediately after stepping down from the American chief executive's office, was not the first safari by a political celebrity to be devoted virtually exclusively to sport shooting. Several years before, Winston Churchill enjoyed an almost equally celebrated hunting trip, although his role as a leading colonial policy-maker gave the visit added overtones of high politics.[8] Nor was Roosevelt the first American millionaire to indulge in 'an expensive luxury'. He was preceded by Philadelphia's Percy Madeira and his wife, and followed by the Californian Stewart White and his wife 'Billy', as well as the New York-born A. Barton Heyburn and a party of his Yale classmates. They would write accounts of their adventures in the tradition of travel adventures, offering highly romantic and frequently grossly biased images of Kenyan life and wildlife.[9] In some ways these were more representative of the early big game safaris.

---

[5] Ibid., 29.

[6] V. Pakenham, *Out in the Noonday Sun: Edwardians in the Tropics* (New York: Random House, 1985), 157.

[7] The semi-official account is Roosevelt, *African Game Trails*.

[8] W. Churchill, *My African Journey* (London: Hodder and Staughton, 1908; New York: Doubleday, Doran, 1909).

[9] P. Madeira, *Hunting in British East Africa* (Philadelphia: J. B. Lippincott, 1909), esp. chaps. 5 and 7; S. White, *The Land of Footprints* (Garden City, NY: Doubleday, Page, 1913); and A. B. Hepburn, *The Story of an Outing* (New York: Harper and Bros., 1913).

These men were sometimes accompanied by their wives, making the presence of women on safari a common, if somewhat controversial, aspect of East African hunting expeditions. In contrast, Roosevelt was accompanied by his son, Kermit, and an entirely male entourage of scientists. 'Teddy' and Kermit would enjoy the hospitality of the colony's settler elites and the services of over 100 porters, bearers, and subordinate staff of African workers. These were still foot safaris, although the use of horses by the safari leaders and clients, along with some hunting from horseback, was an important part of the foot safari at this time.

What then did Roosevelt's safari signal? I would suggest that Roosevelt's contribution was to introduce and sanctify by celebrity example what would become three key elements in the evolving ritual and drama of the African hunt. First, he would canonize the extravagance of death and the luxury living with which even foot safaris would be pursued. Secondly, the rituals of hospitality and local organization that would distinguish the pursuit of African game from other hunting were vested in the person of an official local guide and expert entitled 'professional white hunter'. Thirdly, Roosevelt added the thin veneer of scientific and naturalist rationale, even of conservationist respectability, that would clothe the safari for decades to come.

Roosevelt's administration had contributed to his reputation for both bellicosity and a passion for nature. It was altogether fitting, therefore, that as his second term of office drew to a close he decided to reward himself with a major sporting holiday: a Kenyan big game safari such as had become popular among the wealthy of both Britain and the United States in the previous decade. Although conceived of in terms of recreation and sport, as his plans began to gel he sought and received the scientific sponsorship of the Smithsonian Institution in Washington, DC, and the financing of the publishing house of Charles Scribner's Sons, who were interested in a travel memoir by the soon-to-be-former president.[10]

Roosevelt's attraction to African hunting dated back more than a decade, when he had discussed his hopes with Frederick Selous. It was Selous who would advise him on the organization and equipping of his expedition during 1908, and who would eventually accompany Roosevelt from the Mombasa dock to his Nairobi Hotel. There, the overall leadership of the safari proper would be handed over to R. J. Cuninghame, with the newly organized safari firm of Newland and Tarleton as local agents. The safari was also joined by Philip Percival, who would become the doyen of white hunters, and several other notable local hunters (Photo 6.1).[11]

It can be said that no expense was spared in outfitting the former president, although firms interested in securing Roosevelt's endorsement and goodwill donated much of the scientific and hunting equipment. Roosevelt would be accompanied by bona fide biological scientists

---

[10] P. Cutright, *Theodore Roosevelt, the Naturalist* (New York: Harper Bros., 1956), 186–9.
[11] Philip H. Percival, *Hunting, Settling and Remembering* (Agoura, CA: Trophy Room Books, 1997), 29–33.

Photo 6.1 *Vivien Percival and Colonel Roosevelt, 1909* (Kenya National Archives)

arranged by the Smithsonian, and by his son, the 19-year-old Kermit, who would almost match his father's noteworthy tally of 'Game Shot with the Rifle during the Trip'.[12]

The total of 512 animals bagged by the Roosevelts, *père et fils*, only begins to hint at the scale of blood-letting involved in this safari. Although the large number of different species killed by them (76) may be an indication of their devotion to science, the haunting suspicion remains that, like so many hunter-naturalists, when it came down to it 'hunting achievement' was Roosevelt's first and foremost motivation and objective, 'the lodestone that originally attracted him to Africa, and continued to attract him'.[13] Despite his desire, expressed in a letter to Selous, 'to make this trip essentially a naturalist trip ... a scientific one with a real object rather than merely a holiday after big game', his sporting motives were always paramount. This meant that the sheer numbers and size of the animals he bagged, their trophy quality rather than their scientific value as specimens, were always central to Roosevelt's safari. The Roosevelt family hunters

[12] Roosevelt, *African Game Trails*, 466–8, lists 296 game animals shot by TR and 216 by his son. In all there were 76 different species represented among the specimens shot by the two Roosevelts. In addition, the scientific personnel also shot animals, bringing the total to '5,013 mammals, 4,453 birds, 2,322 reptiles and amphibians ... [plus] fish, insects, shells, plants and a quantity of anthropological material'. This made the 'collection, especially of large mammals, ... the largest that had ever been brought out of Africa by a single party'. Cutright, *Theodore Roosevelt*, 209–10. For Kermit's recollections, see K. Roosevelt, *A Sentimental Safari* (New York: Alfred A. Knopf, 1963).

[13] Cutright, *Theodore Roosevelt*, 189. See G. Bederman, *Manliness and Civilization* (Chicago: University of Chicago Press, 1995), 207–13, for the place of the safari in the construction of Roosevelt's ideas about race, gender, and 'civilisation'.

would keep only 'about a dozen trophies', the rest being shot as specimens or food.[14] But even the large size of the entourage, befitting such a high-ranking dignitary, could not account for the prodigious amount of death. 'Sport hunting' was the reason. Why else kill 15 common zebra or 18 of the diminutive antelope, the oribi, for instance?

Similarly, Roosevelt's protestations of his desire to keep the costs and opulence of the expedition to a minimum ring hollow in the face of the remarkable extravagance of this trend-setting safari. I do not refer merely to the scores of African porters and staff employed, or the large number of European personnel hired by Cuninghame or Newland and Tarleton, or seconded to the expedition by the colonial government. The true extravagance was in the notion of what constituted a good and sufficient supply of comforts. That Roosevelt sought advice on what kind of evening wear might be appropriate is not surprising, given the understanding about gentlemen 'dressing for dinner' even in the bush. But his 'wish to take only the minimum amount of whiskey and champagne which would be necessary in the event of sickness', expressed in a letter to Selous, strikes me as being extraordinarily revealing about the shifting boundary between necessity and luxury. In the event, three flasks of whisky and a case of champagne were deemed to be sufficient for the President's medicinal requirements.[15] I do not point out Roosevelt's extravagance in a spirit of puritanical abstemiousness. Its significance is that here, as in so many matters, Roosevelt set a standard and institutionalized a practice that would influence the Kenyan hunting safari for decades to come. By the end of the 1930s, no less an authority on Kenyan life than Elspeth Huxley could offer a fictional monologue that named liquor and luxury as the two most important elements of a successful safari, far outstripping successful shooting in providing customer or, in this case, client satisfaction.[16]

The provision of comforts on Roosevelt's safari principally fell to two groups of men: the hired African guides and workers employed by Newland and Tarleton, and the wealthy and prominent settlers who offered hospitality. Before we examine the history of the professional white hunters and safari organizers, we should point out that hospitality such as that enjoyed by Roosevelt was an important element of the safari tradition that can be traced directly back to its European sources. Although Roosevelt brought his own champagne (hardly, however, enough to last a year), much of the luxury enjoyed by Roosevelt and his party was provided gratis by a series of hosts among the leading settler hunters of 1909 Kenya. Two weeks of hunting on the Kapiti plain southeast of Nairobi were conducted from the ranch of Sir Alfred Pease.[17] Sir Northrup MacMillan's Juja Farm and Lord Delamere's Rift Valley ranch at Njoro would also provide bases of operations for Roosevelt for a week

---

[14] Roosevelt, *African Game Trails*, 268. Here and elsewhere Roosevelt goes to great lengths to excuse himself and to defend himself against anticipated charges of being a 'game butcher'. See Cameron, *Into Africa*, 51.

[15] Cutright, *Theodore Roosevelt*, 191–2.

[16] E. Huxley, *Murder on Safari* (New York: Viking, 1989 [1938]), 17–18.

[17] Roosevelt, *African Game Trails*, 37–66.

and ten days, respectively.[18] Hospitality on such a grand scale was expensive, but was also clearly an obligation of the nobility for whom the tradition of the weekend shooting party had to be suitably expanded to accommodate the needs of prominent visitors and the big game hunting itinerary. Eventually, Delamere would finance a hotel (Torr's) in Nairobi, while such elegant establishments as the New Stanley and Norfolk Hotel would try to match the splendour and opulence of the lordly estates for those somewhat less distinguished visitors than former presidents and future kings and queens. However in 1909, Roosevelt had fixed the idea that an African safari need not be an experience of hardship. On the contrary, it became the boast of safari companies that their clients would not only get to shoot the animals that they desired, but would have all the luxuries and comforts that could be provided for a fee. Indeed, for late twentieth-century camera-toting clients from America, Europe, and Japan, I believe it is the unique combination of the reality of coddled comfort with the exciting illusion of the romance of outdoor adventure, and the dubious dangers of the proximity to wild animals, that account for the continued popularity of the Kenyan safari.[19]

Roosevelt would spend a full year on his great safari – fully eight months of it hunting in Kenya – before he would return home via Uganda, the Lado Enclave of the then Congo Free State, and the hunting-grounds of the southern Sudan, eventually sailing down the Nile to Egypt and home in 1910.[20] The length of the stay, like virtually everything else about Roosevelt's safari, was extravagant. But it is important to realize that the conditions of travel by sea to and from East Africa, added to the length of time it took to travel about on foot, horseback, or even in motorcars and lorries, made the Kenyan safari a holiday only for those with vast resources of money and the kind of leisure time that only great wealth could purchase. It was simply not feasible to plan a safari of less than three to four months and expect to achieve very much in the way of hunting. This would remain true until after the Second World War, when the conditions of international travel and the clientele of the big game safari would change dramatically. By 1910, when Roosevelt made his way home and published his safari journals, the champagne safari had entered its heyday.

The champagne safaris

During the last three months of 1907, the *Official Gazette of the East Africa and Uganda Protectorate* for that year listed among those who came to Kenya and purchased licences to hunt big game 'a total of four counts, three lords,

---

[18] Ibid., 123–48, 415.

[19] On the appeal to luxury see the print brochure or website for Abercrombie and Kent's 2003 advertising brochure, *Africa*, especially the 'Kenya Hemingway Safari' section, 76–83.

[20] The party would depart from New York on 23 March 1909, arriving in Mombasa on 21 April. Departure from Kenya was on 18 December and from Nimule in southern Sudan on 17 February 1910. Roosevelt, *African Game Trails*, 3, 7, 425, 506.

two marquis, two barons, two princes and one duke'.[21] The numbers of titled noblemen and crowned heads who would gather in East Africa for recreation starting in the first decade of the century, although extraordinary and comparable only to the great watering-places of Europe, were not preponderant. Off-duty army officers and wealthy commoners from Britain, Europe, and America would remain a majority. Nonetheless, as with the cultural dominance of aristocrats among Kenya's settler hunters, the aristocratic impact on the Kenyan safari was out of proportion to its numbers. These noblemen and their ladies were the pillars of society and arbiters of style wherever they went. They would set the standard for both expenditure and sportsmanship, creating a distinctive hunting culture from the mix of aristocratic ideals forged and tempered in the lordly hunt and gentlemanly shooting party, and adapted to the conditions of the African savannah and its big game, that would last for decades to come. Joined and reinforced by the trickle of American millionaires and *haut bourgeois* that itself would grow to a stream by the 1930s, the popular image of luxury and even decadence was firmly established by the outbreak of war in Europe in August 1914 and in East Africa in the months that followed.

The impact of the war, and the influx of soldiers and later more modest settlers, would bring a brief crisis to Kenyan wildlife and to the safari hunting tradition. But, as we shall see, the big game safari had recovered and reached new heights by the mid-1920s. There are two aspects of the war-engendered crisis that concern the history of hunting. First was the direct and devastating impact it appears to have had on animal numbers, due to unregulated human predation using firearms. Secondly, and indirectly, by putting the settler elite under arms for the duration, and suspending both their own safari hunting and their function as hosts to visiting hunters, the war would disrupt and briefly interrupt the safari tradition.

The large number of animals killed for meat probably led to only a temporary decline in game numbers, but the short-term effect was exaggerated by the concentration of predation in the southern game reserve along the border with German territory, where the forces and hostilities were concentrated.[22] According to one observer, 'During the 1914/1918 war the Army Supply Department kept some hundreds of men in camps on the plains shooting game and making "biltong" (sun-dried meat) for the army operating in German East Africa.'[23] Kenya's chief game ranger estimated that '40,000 head had been killed for meat for the army' during two years of war, five times the number that might have been killed legally in the period.[24] In addition, it proved impossible to

[21] Cited in Dane Kennedy, *Islands of White: Settler Society and Culture in Kenya and Southern Rhodesia, 1890–1939* (Durham, NC: Duke University Press, 1987), 215n.

[22] H. Frost, Asst. Game Warden, 'Report', Appendix II, 1, *Game Department Annual Report (GDAR)* 1919–20, Kenya National Archives (KNA) KW/23/173.

[23] J. A. S. Watt, 'Recollections of Kenya, 1895–1963', unpublished ms. diary, Rhodes House, Oxford (unnumbered pages).

[24] Cameron, *Into Africa*, 79.

restrain the large numbers of armed men from hunting for sport during their leaves or whenever they could slip away from duties. Moreover, even African hunters gave themselves over to hunting for the wartime profit to be made by dealing in contraband. In one melodramatic account, 'Organised corruption by traders and others ... seduces the lazy natural bowmen from comparatively harmless hunting for food into killers and handlers of contraband.'[25] With the Game Department and local administration understaffed and ill-prepared for disciplining British soldiers or African poachers, little could be done until after the end of the war to limit the hunting and allow the herds to recover.

At the outset of the war, many of the settlers rallied around the flag, volunteering to do service against the German enemy so close at hand. Swedish nobleman Baron Bror von Blixen's behaviour was typical of the response of the hunting fraternity among the settlers. Despite the suspicions that attached to him as a Scandinavian who might harbour pro-German sympathies, he was quick to volunteer along with other non-British settlers. In the wake of the war, Blixen would grow even more restless with farm life and turn to hunting as a full-time occupation. He would seek to earn a living or, more precisely in Blixen's case, to maintain an extravagant lifestyle by becoming a professional hunter. In this he would be joined, as we shall see, by other well-born and erstwhile well-off settlers. But, for the course of the war, the hunting they did would be strictly for the pot as the absence of foreign visitors to be led on safari, and the call to arms, kept them occupied in the other honourable pursuit of men of their class, warfare.[26]

The end of war and of the brief, postwar economic recession led to a sharp increase in visiting hunters and a great flourishing of the Kenyan safari in the decade of the 1920s. But it was more than economic recovery and the economic and cultural boom times that underlay the safari recrudescence. The safari had become a symbol of elite life in Kenya, and Kenya itself had become the beacon for those seeking the return to the lost era of aristocracy and opulence. The flourishing of safari hunting in the Kenya of the 1920s was, like the decade of the roaring twenties itself, a false dawn to be followed by the grim days of depression and decline that ensued in Africa as in Europe and North America, a worldwide depression of trade, production, and spirit. But in Kenya, at least for a time, the golden age of the champagne safari was at hand.

The ageing old guard of Delamere, Grogan, and MacMillan was being supplanted by the glittering and glamorous age of the Blixens and Denys Finch Hatton, Lord Erroll, and Beryl Markham. These were not to be pioneers, suffering hardship and building for the future of empire. Rather they were to be remembered, as a generation, for their sybaritic self-indulgences, sexual excesses, and extravagant weekend shooting parties,

---

[25] H. Frost, 'Report', Appendix II, 1, *GDAR* 1919–20, *KNA* KW/23/173.

[26] B. von Blixen-Finecke, *African Hunter* (New York: St. Martins, 1986 [1938]), 174–9. See E. Trzebinski, *The Kenya Pioneers* (New York: Norton, 1985), 177–94, for the responses of the Kenya elite to wartime pressures.

becoming caricatured as 'Happy Valley'.[27] The combination of Happy Valley hunters and revellers, the postwar influx of wealthy and prominent visitors in search of sport and adventure, and the new technology of the automobile would transform the Rooseveltian safari into the symbol of romance and glamour it has remained to the present.

Three particular safaris of international importance will allow us to characterize the champagne safari of the late 1920s and early 1930s. They are the Eastman-Pomeroy–Akeley safari of 1926–7, the royal safaris of the Prince of Wales in 1928 and 1930, and the literary safari of Ernest Hemingway in 1933–4. Each would add something of importance to the tradition and romance of the safari, building on the foundations established by Teddy Roosevelt.

Science on safari

The Eastman–Pomeroy–Akeley expedition of 1926–7 manages to embody three of the principles of the champagne safari in the names of its illustrious leaders. Seventy-two-year-old George Eastman, the founder of the important pioneer photographic company that bears his name, was the financial backer and moving spirit behind the expedition. He would privately publish a journal of his journey, from which it is easy to glean his own sporting and prestige-seeking motives in supporting and accompanying this trip.[28] His own account and those of his companions amply testify that Eastman's principal interest was in hunting.[29] Moreover, the failure of Eastman to find and kill an elephant on this expedition is the probable motive for his return to East Africa, particularly to the Lado area, the following year to complete his bag.[30]

In addition, the photographic record of this trip is especially rich, attesting to the importance of Eastman's professional interest in photography among his motives. It may also account for the presence of Martin and Osa Johnson, the noted nature and wildlife photographers, among Eastman's companions on his expeditions.[31] Many of the photographs

---

[27] By far the most entertaining introduction to the Happy Valley set is James Fox's real-life murder mystery, *White Mischief: The Murder of Lord Erroll* (New York: Random House, 1982). For the politics of colonial Kenya in the interwar period, see B. Berman and J. Lonsdale, *Unhappy Valley* (London: James Currey, 1992).

[28] G. Eastman, *Chronicle of an African Trip* (Rochester: Priv. pub. for the author, 1927). Unfortunately, this volume was not well introduced or annotated, unlike the journal of his second safari. See G. Eastman, *Chronicles of a Second African Trip* (Rochester, NY: Friends of the University of Rochester Libraries, 1987), which contains a brief foreword by Dr Elias Mandala and an introduction by Kenneth Cameron.

[29] See G. Eastman, 'A Safari in Africa', *Natural History* 27, 6 (1927), 533–8; M. L. J. Akeley, *Carl Akeley's Africa* (New York: Dodd, Mead, 1930), 55.

[30] Eastman, *Chronicles of a Second African Trip*, xvii–xviii.

[31] In addition to those published in the Eastman volumes, the American Museum of Natural History [AMNH] Photography Collections contains a large number of photographs attributed to both the Johnsons and Carl Akeley. My thanks to the American Museum Library staff for their assistance in using these materials.

would be deposited with the American Museum of Natural History in New York, the official sponsors of the scientific expedition.

Official sponsorship of the expedition by the American Museum of Natural History was personally attested to by the presence of Daniel E. Pomeroy, a trustee of the Museum, who was charged with fund-raising for a planned African exhibit hall. This sponsorship continued the Rooseveltian concern to provide the safari with clear scientific objectives. Whether this was merely 'protective coloration' or camouflage for the hunting or represented a sincere effort to advance science is arguable. However, the pairing of scientific and venatic pursuits in this expedition was more artfully and profitably done than in Roosevelt's cruder effort. Although Pomeroy was perhaps a figurehead representing scientific concerns, the presence and efforts of Carl Akeley would give real substance to the claims made on behalf of science by the Natural History Museum's sponsorship of the expedition.

Carl Akeley was on his fifth and, it would turn out, his final safari to Africa. He is perhaps one of the most romantic and confusing figures to hunt on safari in Kenya in the early twentieth century.[32] A man of science with a limited formal education and the temperament and pretensions of an artist, his romantic identification with the continent and its wildlife could well serve as a model for the generations of conservationists who would follow him throughout the century. And yet he was an avid hunter who shared with that fraternity the idea of a spiritual union with nature embodied in the pursuit and destruction of individual animals. For Akeley, the spiritual and physical union were made manifest in his pioneering and signal efforts to create by taxidermy a visual, artistic, and scientifically educational record of his hunting. The result would be the famous dioramas of the American Museum's African Hall, which now bears Akeley's name.[33]

Akeley's work as a taxidermist and creator of the Museum's African dioramas would advance, indirectly through public education, the cause of African wildlife among generations of youth inspired by the lifelike representations of African animals and habitats that were Akeley's triumph. His technological contributions to photography, including the invention of a lightweight camera, would also contribute to the popularizing of natural history and wildlife conservation. His five African trips, beginning with a Field Museum of Chicago expedition in 1896 and culminating in his gorilla-collecting expedition to Kava in 1921, established him as the most important collector of African specimen animals of

---

[32] The biography by P. Bodry-Sanders, *Carl Akeley: Africa's Collector, Africa's Savior* (New York: Paragon House, 1991), 227–57, offers a concise, if somewhat overblown, description of Akeley's last expedition and his death.

[33] Perhaps because of his death and burial in Africa on this expedition, a great deal of hagiographic literature was generated by his wife and others associated with his museum work. See M. L. J. Akeley, *Carl Akeley's Africa*; her 'In the Land of His Dreams', *Natural History* 27, 6 (1927), 525–32; and other memorials in the same issue, especially the tribute of the museum's president and Akeley's champion, H. F. Osborn, 'Vanishing Wild Life of Africa', *Natural History* 27, 6 (1927), 515–24.

the century. Indeed, it has been argued that his work was directly responsible for saving the African gorilla from extinction.[34]

These significant achievements only heighten the contradictions at the heart of modern conservation. In the words of his biographer, '"Collecting" is a scientific euphemism for killing,' and each successfully mounted exhibition of scientifically stuffed and realistically displayed family groups of African mammals was achieved only by the killing of large numbers of 'specimens'. It is at best a difficult calculus to know how much killing is needed to save species, but it became standard practice in Kenya from the turn of the century for the game department to grant collectors an exemption from game limits such as that enjoyed by the Roosevelt party 'in the interests of scientific research'.[35] We must add to this the irony that the very popularity of the animals, created by conservationists in their efforts to increase awareness of the plight of wildlife such as the mountain gorilla can lead to increasing pressures by tourists and governments to exploit wildlife resources, often at great cost to the animals themselves in terms of destruction of their habitats and disruption of their lives.

But the central contradiction was embodied in Akeley himself. Akeley, the collector, was the other side of Akeley, the hunter. They make each other possible, and yet they could not both be easily acknowledged. From early on, Akeley was not above exaggerating or falsifying his own achievements in his museum work or his collecting efforts.[36] And deception was an important feature in the dissolution of his first marriage and his relationship to his second wife and hagiographer, Mary Jobe Akeley.[37] Indeed, a key feature of his legend was based on the falsification of the record of his first marriage by his second wife. An essay by Donna Haraway brilliantly explores the entire complex relationship between Akeley and his legacy.[38] Truth was a frequent sacrificial victim to the creation of the legend of Akeley as Africa's saviour by both husband and wife. Part of that sacrifice was the blurring of the role of hunting in Akeley's achievements.

Efforts to hide the discomfiting relationship between collecting and hunting go back to Akeley himself and to his second wife, both of whom tried to disguise and obfuscate the death that existed at the root of Akeley's *métier*.[39] The contradictions appear to have been less troublesome for Akeley than for his wife. 'Akeley genuinely enjoyed a good hunt, revelling

[34] Bodry-Sanders, *Carl Akeley*, for his contributions in general and xiii–xviii on his 'saving' the gorilla. For his own more modest account of his gorilla work, see C. Akeley, 'Gorillas – Real and Mythical', *Natural History* 23, 5 (1923), 428–47.

[35] P. H. G. Powell-Cotton, *In Unknown Africa* (Nendeln: Kraus Reprint, 1973 [1904]), 12.

[36] See Bodry-Sanders, *Carl Akeley*, 35, where he claims originality for display techniques he developed in Milwaukee as a young taxidermist.

[37] Ibid., 204–8.

[38] D. Haraway, 'Teddy Bear Patriarchy', in D. Haraway, *Primate Visions* (New York: Routledge, 1989), 26–58.

[39] In examining the Akeley collection of photographs at the American Museum, I discovered that certain photographs were embargoed and could not be reproduced. They included a number of pictures that showed Carl Akeley in the classic hunter's pose atop his fallen prey. In creating the legend of man of science and art, the image of Akeley as 'white hunter' could be disillusioning.

in his prowess like any white hunter.' But not all his hunting was good sport, and he suffered pangs of guilt in the killing of some animals in ways he could not conceive of as sporting.[40]

Ambiguities in the relationship between the animals he admired and killed were paralleled by the complexity of his friendships with his African companions and workers, and the racism that undergirded their subordination. In particular, Akeley's collaborative relationship with a young Kikuyu gun bearer demonstrates the deeply transcultural nature of safari work, and the fundamental denial of equality and African initiative at the root of the white hunter's ethos.[41] But it should be acknowledged to Akeley's credit that he is among the few safari hunters who even acknowledge their African companions beyond the level of the literary stereotype of faithfulness and devotion.

Royal safaris

If the Eastman/Akeley safari of 1926–7 would become the standard of the mixed hunting/scientific expedition,[42] the grand tours conducted by the Prince of Wales and his brother, the Duke of Gloucester, performed a similar exemplary role for the elite safari, establishing in the popular mind the image of the safari as a form of outdoor recreation for the upper classes.[43]

Royal safaris were nothing new when in 1928 the Prince of Wales, the future Edward VIII, visited East Africa for the first time. The first visit by British royalty to Kenya came as early as 1906 when the Duke and Duchess of Connaught and their daughter visited Nairobi. They would return to Kenya in 1910 along with their son, to go on safari with over 400 African staff consisting of headmen, gun bearers, porters, porters' 'boys', grooms, police, runners, valets, and cooks. However, it was the visit in 1924–5 by the Duke and Duchess of York, later King George VI and Queen Elizabeth, which would set a new standard for regal processions and hunting grandeur.[44] The imperial hunting safari would reach a glamorous crescendo in 1935 with the safaris of the Duke of Norfolk and

---

[40] Bodry-Sanders, *Carl Akeley*, 56ff.

[41] Haraway, 'Teddy Bear', 53–4. Akeley's relationship with Gitungu, called Bill, could serve as a paradigm for the collaborative and asymmetrical relationships created by the safari between Africans and their white student-masters. See C. Akeley, *In Brightest Africa* (Garden City, NY: Garden City Publishing, 1925), 131–47.

[42] That the Akeley expedition was representative can be seen by even a cursory examination of some of the other collecting safaris. See K. Kittenberger, *Big Game Hunting and Collecting in East Africa 1903–1926* (London: Longmans, Green, 1929); Powell-Cotton, *In Unknown Africa*; and, for the Maytag expedition of the mid-1950s, see Dr Oscar T. Owre, Department of Biology, University of Miami, personal communication, 2 December 1987.

[43] Edward VIII, King of Great Britain, *Sport and Travel in East Africa: An Account of Two Visits 1928 and 1930*, compiled by P. R. Chalmers (New York: E. P. Dutton, n.d.) is the official if, somewhat tame, account of these royal safaris.

[44] Meru District Annual Report, 1924, 14–15; KNA DC/MRU/1/1, and *Game Department Annual Report* for 1925, 8–12, for an official account of the Duke of York's safari and his

the Maharajah of Jodhpur.[45] For the full royal treatment, the two safaris in 1927 and 1930 by the Prince of Wales mark the apex of the champagne safari tradition. This is due in part to the remarkable visibility and publicity that attended the royal visits. But there was something intrinsic in the princely style that not only heightened international perceptions, but also made an indelible impression on the Kenyan safari mentality.

One important change evident in the royal safaris was the downplaying of hunting pure and simple. Although plenty of animals would fall to the Prince's gun, 'Yet H.R.H. had not come to collect heads. His main concern was to observe, to photograph and to film big game ... [with a movie camera].'[46] Certainly he expressed disdain for shooting in favour of the more sporting use of a camera, but his own considerable total of animals killed, especially on his second safari, belies the idea that big game shooting was not of major significance.[47] Although the Prince's favouring of the camera over the gun may have fitted in with and perhaps accelerated the broader trend towards camera safaris, that is not the new element that can be discerned in his daily diary entries. Rather, the innovation lay in the large number of social occasions, garden parties, '*fantasia*', official meetings or Baraza, dinners, and dances that filled the days and evenings between the actual hunting excursions. When one adds the receptions with governors, commissioners, and civil officers, the gatherings and visits to the settler elite, such as Lord Delamere, the royal social schedule was a true buzz of activity.[48] Indeed, the title of the published account based on the royal diaries, *Sport and Travel in East Africa*, takes on additional meaning when one considers that travel for the sake of travel seems to have been what this safari was all about, and the Prince of Wales was not so much a hunter seeking fresh fields as a tourist seeking fresh experiences. Even the term hunting must be expanded beyond its conventional meaning of hunting wild animals, as we find the Prince riding in horse races, playing golf, watching the annual cricket match between officials and settlers, and awarding the trophy to the winners.[49] The Prince's brother Henry, Duke of Gloucester, added to the outdoor sports a royal dalliance with the not-yet-divorced Beryl Markham, which, rather than shaking society, seems to have been viewed as the bestowal of royal recognition on the social and sexual folkways of 'Happy Valley'.[50] Although their royal status meant that they

---

44 (contd) reception. For Connaught's visit, see N. Frankland, *Witness of a Century: The Life and Times of Prince Arthur, Duke of Connaught, 1850–1942* (London: Shepheard-Walvyn, 1993), 259–61, and the photograph below, p. 135.

45 See *East African Standard*, 14 March and 8 March 1935, respectively, for the Norfolk and Jodhpur visits. KNA KW/20/3.

46 Edward VIII, *Sport and Travel in East Africa*, 24.

47 Ibid., 62–4 and 180–213; for a partial list of the game shot in Tanganyika, see 195.

48 Ibid., 24–35 *passim*. For the history of camera safaris, see below 239ff.

49 Ibid., 32–5. See M. Lovell, *Straight on Till Morning. The Biography of Beryl Markham* (London: Hutchinson, 1987), 79–82.

50 Lovell, *Straight on Till Morning*, 78–93.

would be entertained and received as few others in the world might be, the Prince of Wales and Duke of Gloucester were in many ways merely modern tourists out for holiday fun in the tropical sun.

Perhaps the fact that the holiday was cut short after only three months, when a cable from home brought news of a family emergency, explains the Prince's decision to return to East Africa in 1930. In late November 1928, a telegram informing the royal entourage of the illness of the King led to the Prince's rapid return from a hunting trip with Baron Bror and Baroness Tanne von Blixen, and HRH's quick departure from Kenya on 2 December 1928.[51] But it was his desire to continue the hunting adventure that led him to return to East Africa, reaching Mombasa in January 1930 via southern Africa. The Prince was met there by Baron von Blixen and Denys Finch Hatton, the aristocratic and romantic gentlemen who had turned their love of sport to good purpose by earning money as professional safari hunters. This is the second element underscored by the royal safari: the new commercial role of the professional white hunter in Kenyan safari hunting.

In his memoir of the 1930 safari, the Prince of Wales would devote much attention to extolling the sportsmanship and hospitality of the two professional hunters who accompanied His Royal Highness. It becomes apparent that it was far more than their local knowledge of the territory or their minimal skills with the Swahili language that made them attractive travelling companions. Blixen is praised for his geniality and storytelling ability. His *bon vivant* client clearly appreciated Blixen's own dapper manner and ability to organize a 'sundowner', the late afternoon drinking and socializing that is antecedent to the 'cocktail party' of later years.[52] As for Denys Finch Hatton, the schoolboy athlete and perpetually promising young man, the Prince seems most taken with his homilies about safari leadership and organization offered as the core of a separate chapter entitled 'Some Maxims of Finch-Hatton [sic]'.[53] In sum, the Prince's royal seal of approval gave legitimacy and a certain glamorous cachet to the role of the professional white hunter as a key ingredient of the truly luxurious champagne safari.[54] It would be but a short time before the professional white hunter was enshrined as the model of the modern hunting gentleman, *bon vivant*, and man of courage in the decade ahead.

---

[51] Ibid., 136–48.

[52] Ibid., 100–119, especially 105–7, on sundowners. See von Blixen-Finecke, *African Hunter*, 178–204.

[53] Von Blixen-Finecke, *African Hunter*, 169–75. See E. Trzebinski, *Silence Will Speak* (Chicago: University of Chicago Press, 1977), 233–71, for Finch Hatton's perspective.

[54] It is perhaps not surprising that the Prince was later asked to become the patron of the newly organized East African Professional Hunters' Association. He declined until it was more firmly organized. Minutes, East African Professional Hunters' Association [EAPHA], 27 April 1935. KNA KW/5/48.

Literary safaris

Ernest Hemingway had become in the 1920s one of America's great writers of fiction, despite his own pronouncement that America did not produce great writers.[55] During a fallow period in his writing career in the early 1930s, Hemingway would announce himself as one of the great authors of hunting literature, with two stories and a book-length account of his 1934 Big Game hunting safari, thinly disguised by changing the names of the other participants, leaving only his own persona uncamouflaged. Hemingway's safari memoir, *Green Hills of Africa*, would romanticize and popularize the big game safari to a vastly wider audience and change the face of safari hunting. His romantic ideas about hunting and writing were expressed in the opening pages:

> The way to hunt is for as long as you live against as long as there is such and such an animal; just as the way to paint is as long as there is you and colours and canvas, and to write as long as you can live and there is pencil and paper or ink or any machine to do it with, or anything you care to write about, and you feel a fool, and you are a fool, to do it any other way.[56]

The glowing descriptions of landscapes and fauna, of hunting success and failure, and mostly of the sense of mastery and manliness that emerge from the pages of Hemingway's clear and unembellished writing would popularize the romantic tourist possibilities of East Africa in the 1930s, as did the film version of Isak Dinesen's *Out of Africa* in the 1980s.[57]

Hemingway discusses other writers who have described their hunting exploits, and offers occasional asides on the art of writing, as well as hunting, in the pages of *Green Hills of Africa*. His recognition that a first visit to a country can result only in the production of a work of superficial description – 'it would just be landscape painting' – may help explain the success of his work of description.[58] In terms of deeper readings, Hemingway reveals far more of himself than he does of Kenya or Tanganyika, and more of his own obsessions and fears than of his companions and fellow-travellers. Moreover, he reveals virtually nothing about the Africans who work for him and his white hunters as trackers, gun bearers, porters, and cooks. The Africans, like the terrain, are the backdrop for his exploits, valued only in terms of how they add to or detract from his hunting

[55] E. Hemingway, *Green Hills of Africa* (New York: Charles Scribner's Sons, 1935), 19.

[56] Ibid., 12. For an account of the place of the African safari in Hemingway's literary development, see C. Baker, *Hemingway: The Writer as Artist* (Princeton: Princeton University Press, 1963), 162–96.

[57] This is especially true of the story and film version of his 'The Snows of Kilimanjaro', in Hemingway's *Fifth Column and the First Forty-Nine Stories* (New York: Scribner, 1938).

[58] Baker, *Hemingway*, 193ff. Popular safari hunting accounts to which Hemingway refers positively include D. Streeter's *Denatured Africa* (New York and London: G. P. Putnam's Sons, 1926); C. Curtis's *Hunting in Africa East and West* (Boston: Houghton Mifflin, 1925); and White's *The Land of Footprints*, although White is generally dismissive of other hunting writers.

experience. Nonetheless, their presence is noted; they speak and are heeded to the degree they contribute to the success of the chase. Occasionally they register, in their own attitudes and expressions, Hemingway's view of the universality of the manly code of honour among hunters.[59] However, we should not look to Hemingway's green hills for a psychological or social portrait of African hunters.[60] Although visible like the landscape, they remain silent.

What Hemingway does explore and ultimately establish in the popular image of the safari hunter are two related ideas: the morally ambiguous position of women on safari, and the romantic ideal of the professional white hunter as sexually charged master of the beasts – both the inner beasts of cowardice and fear and the outer beasts of nature. In *Green Hills* and the short story 'The Snows of Kilimanjaro', women are present to comfort and support in times of failure and to bear witness in moments of triumph for their men.[61] The greatest praise offered to P.O.M. (a.k.a. Pauline, Hemingway's wife) by the white hunter in *Green Hills*, Pops or J.P. (a.k.a. Philip Percival, the same who had accompanied Roosevelt in 1909 and was the doyen of professional white hunters by 1934) was to call her a 'terrier', feisty and loyal. She bears up under both the physical hardships of ill-fitting shoes and mean-spirited competitiveness from the hero, Hemingway. But if P.O.M. is the model female companion, long-suffering and loyal, Margaret Macomber is Hemingway's idea of Jezebel.[62]

'The Short Happy Life of Francis Macomber' uses the setting of an East African safari to explore Hemingway's recurrent theme of the quest for mastery in life and the ultimate frustration of desire once its object is achieved. The story artfully reveals the conflict between Francis Macomber, a wealthy 35-year-old American businessman, and his wife of 11 years, when the young man shows cowardice in the face of a wounded lion. The penalty for this lapse is the withering ridicule of his wife and the contempt of the white hunter, Robert Wilson (a.k.a. Bror Blixen).[63] When

[59] This is especially true for the silent expression of the African staff in E. Hemingway, 'The Short Happy Life of Francis Macomber', *Fifth Column and the First Forty-Nine Stories*, 115, 134.

[60] Africans appear to play a larger role in the recently posthumously published novel-cum-memoir with an African setting by E. Hemingway, *True at First Light* (New York: Scribner, 1999). But here it is Hemingway's sexual exploits and exploitation of African 'brides' that has drawn attention, rather than the hunting exploits of his 1954 safari. See 'A New Book by Hemingway: Blend of Life and Fiction Tells of African Bride', *New York Times*, 24 August 1998, B1, B3; and J. Wood, 'The Lion King', *New York Times Book Review*, 11 July 1999, 15.

[61] Hemingway, 'The Snows of Kilimanjaro', 150–75. On women on safari, see Cameron, *Into Africa*, 63–77, although Cameron focuses on the atypical situation of women on safari without men. Also see the accounts of the 1920s safaris of Vivienne de Watteville, *Speak to the Earth* (New York: Penguin, 1988 [1935]).

[62] For Hemingway's troubled relationships with women and their psychological basis, see K. Lynn, *Hemingway* (New York: Simon and Schuster, 1987), esp. 15–48, 53–65, on his childhood.

[63] Although most people have recognized the real Blixen as the basis for the fictional Wilson, some have seen in him a composite that includes Percival. See N. West, *Happy Valley: The Story of the English in Kenya* (London: Secker and Warburg, 1979), 130–31. My own view that it is Blixen stems from both the description of Wilson's sexual availability and Blixen's established penchant for the sexual exploitation of his clients.

Margaret openly flirts with Wilson and 'sneaks away' to his bed at night, Macomber begins a process of recovery that has him out the next day in pursuit of buffalo, reputed to be the most dangerous game in Africa. In the course of the buffalo hunt, Francis regains his courage and the respect of Wilson, who 'had seen men come of age before and it always moved him'. When once again a dangerous, wounded animal has to be pursued into dense bush, Macomber is game, 'a ruddy fire eater'. But his pursuit will be the tragic frustration that comes with the achievement of mastery. Francis is 'accidentally' killed by his wife's bullet.[64]

The moral ambiguity of the ending establishes two things: the dangerousness of women to manly virtue in Hemingway's lifelong 'drama of sexual confusion',[65] and the complete professionalism and mastery of Robert Wilson, the professional white hunter. Indeed, it appears that, from Hemingway's first meetings in Nairobi with Philip Percival and Bror Blixen, he was greatly taken with their professionalism, which for Hemingway was the highest virtue of any man. Their dedication to the lifelong pursuit of animals, like his own romantic view of a writer's calling, elevated the real-life 'white hunter' of Kenya to the status of hero. The fictional heroes Pops and Wilson – the old man of grace and consummate ability, and the younger man of daring and mastery – both hard-drinking and fast-living, would become the models against which future generations of professional white hunters would measure themselves.[66]

I need not point out that neither Hemingway's women nor his 'white hunters' were in any way representative of their real-life safari counterparts. Many women would be as active and effective as shooters of big game as their usually more renowned male companions. The case of Osa Johnson, wife of Martin, the wildlife film-maker of the 1920s, is one such prominent case, to which we could add a host of settler and visiting women who may have travelled with male companions and white hunters but did their own shooting.[67] In addition, the professional white hunters had among their number a fair share of worthless adventurers and cads. But there can be little argument that the romantic image of the big game hunter and the professional white hunter was enormously enhanced and enriched by Hemingway's effortless prose, which created a fictionalized safari reality that became its own truth and contributed to the international popularity of Kenya as a hunting paradise.

---

[64] Ibid., 130–35.

[65] Lynn, *Hemingway*, 58.

[66] Percival, *Hunting, Settling and Remembering*, 119–20. In the 1950s, Robert Ruark would become the leading example of this macho tradition of safari writers. See R. Ruark, *Horn of the Hunter* (Garden City, NY: Doubleday, 1953) and his *Use Enough Gun [On Hunting Big Game]* (London: Corgi Books, 1969 [1967]).

[67] On Martin and Osa Johnson, see below Chapter 7. See Cameron, *Into Africa*, 63–77; U. Aschan, *The Man Whom Women Loved: The Life of Bror Blixen* (New York: St. Martins, 1987), 157–98.

The professional white hunters

The idea of a professional corps of big game hunters available to visiting hunters as guides, companions, and semi-official hosts emerged gradually over the decades from small beginnings before the Great War. The first appearance of what would become the professional white hunter (PWH) of Hemingway's imagination was the ad hoc request from Carl Akeley in 1905 that someone be engaged to accompany him on his second safari. The request was made of the Nairobi-based firm of Newland and Tarleton, which had been set up principally as a real estate and auction business. 'Unquestionably, Newland and Tarleton was the first successful non-Indian safari firm in Nairobi … the first to advertise in London, the first to grasp that complete safari outfitting was what the new breed of customers wanted.'[68]

Complete safari outfitting had to be built around two key elements: the provision of transport and equipment, and the supply of experienced and competent hunters as safari leaders – the white hunters. The term 'white hunter' itself seems to have been used officially for the first time in *The Handbook of British East Africa* for 1912–13. His expertise was supposed to include an acquaintance with 'the districts his employer desires to shoot …, previous experience with the game of the country', and the ability to arrange the preservation of trophies, interpret for, and advise his visiting hunter client.[69] If necessary, he had to be able to use his guns to protect his client, to follow up wounded animals, and to advise him on licence limits, acceptably sporting hunting methods, and the best methods of pursuit and shooting the animals his client required. In the early days, it was only those settlers who took an active interest in hunting who had the requisite language skills and local knowledge to accomplish this. So it would be local men with reputations as sportsmen, like R. J. Cuninghame and Philip Percival, who would be sought out by the early safari firms or be recommended by individuals as capable and available to accompany hunting safaris. It was a combination of employment by Newland and Tarleton and the recommendations of Frederick Selous, that would eventually lead to the employment of these two settler hunters to accompany Teddy Roosevelt on his 1909 safari.[70] And it would be this safari's fame and success that would establish the white hunter as Kenya's unique contribution to the white hunting tradition. Government would take official notice and, from 1911, official efforts were made to organize 'an Association of White Hunters or Guides, with the double object of safeguarding their own interests and preventing abuses of the Game Regulations'.[71]

However, beyond the description of the white hunter's qualifications

[68] Cameron, *Into Africa*, 47.
[69] Holman, *Inside Safari Hunting*, 41.
[70] Cameron, *Into Africa*, 51–3.
[71] Game Department Annual Report, 1909–10, KNA KW/23/171: 58.

131

and responsibilities, the symbolic significance of the white hunter requires some examination. Beside the denotation of 'white' to simply differentiate it from black-skinned African hunters,[72] whose activities had by and large been outlawed and denigrated by the 1920s, the term 'great white hunter' has important connotative overtones. '"Great White Hunter" seems to represent a form of white supremacy over blacks, who are usually portrayed as either ruthless barbarians or – very occasionally – as loyal but inherently limited, servants.'[73]

It was necessary as well to distinguish the Kenyan white hunter from other professional hunters, who hunted for the market, either in meat, skins, or trophies. Such commercial hunting was beneath the dignity of the kind of sports hunters required to accompany lords and ladies, presidents and princes, in pursuit of sporting adventure. White-ness among these Kenyan professionals came to symbolize their virtues of honesty, probity, and courage befitting sportsmen. As in the common expression of the 1920s, 'that's white of you', whiteness would also convey the 'racist overtones of "decent" and trustworthy personal attitudes and behaviour'.[74] Whiteness would be worn as a badge of honour, distinguishing sporting gentlemen from the lesser breeds outside the law and custom of the hunt.

The Roosevelt safari consolidated the nexus of hunter and client, establishing a pattern and practice of mutual responsibility and participation in the chase that would become the ideal for the next half-century. But the romanticization, even sexualization, of the white hunter would only develop after the Great War and the emergence of Bror Blixen and Denys Finch Hatton as leading PWHs. Once again, it is the symbolic overtones of the hunter–client relationship and the mediation that the hunter provided between the civilized world and the world of savage nature that he bridged. If the visiting hunter on safari was to maintain his status and class position as a gentleman (or woman), then the relationship to the white hunter had to be something other than a straight commercial transaction. The white hunter, in the interests of his client's stature, had to be as much the gentleman and sportsman as his employer. He masked the cash nexus by investing it with an almost mystical bond of protection based on the white hunter's esoteric and exotic knowledge, for which he could be rewarded without reducing him to a mere tradesman or servant. He was not a guide in the conventional sense, but a person whose virtue and skills enabled him to cross from the world of culture to nature and thereby mediate with the fantastical forces to be confronted and conquered. The mystical oxymoron of 'safe danger', still at the heart of the lure of wildlife tourism, was the core of the hunter–client nexus.

The savage world through which the white hunter would lead his fellow adventure seeker/sportsman was not just the world of wild animals, but

---

[72] E. Host, 'The Professional Hunters of East Africa', *East African Annual* (1951–2), 70–71.

[73] E. Mandiringana and T. J. Stapleton, 'The Literary Legacy of Frederick Courtney Selous', *History in Africa* 25 (1998), 218.

[74] See J. Middleton, 'Tourism in Kenya: Fantasies of the Other', unpublished draft essay, May, 1997, 12n.

also the savage world of African 'natives'. Africans may have been employed by the white hunters principally to perform the necessary tasks of porterage, skinning and preserving trophies, making camp, cooking, and driving. However, they were also required to behave with deference, accepting their class subordination and playing the roles of 'dark companions', whose language and bearing always carried the stigma of savagery against which the hunter's whiteness was protection. The white hunter was thus a guarantee of the class and race superiority of the tourist hunter, who stood between the civilized values of the sportsman and the savage Africa of the colonial imagination.[75]

In men like Blixen and Finch Hatton, these qualities of class superiority and the social skills of gentlemen, even aristocrats, were combined with the skills at hunting, tracking, local knowledge, and familiarity with African language and custom that made them model white hunters. The ability to drink and eat with their gentleman and lady clients, to make intelligent, witty, and sometimes even literary conversation would provide a major advantage to men of high birth and education. Blixen was reputed to be as engaging a storyteller as his more famous ex-wife, Isak Dinesen, even by her own account. She told a friend, 'If I should wish anything back of my life, it would be to go on safari once again with Bror Blixen.'[76] His capacity for liquor was unmatched, and he was at ease in the homes of his rich and aristocratic clients, whom he visited and by whom he was entertained as a social equal in Europe and the United States.[77]

Following the death of Finch Hatton in an aeroplane crash in 1931, Blixen emerged as the most glamorous of the white hunter breed. He could command enormous fees for his services, becoming 'the highest paid and most sought after professional in the Colony'.[78] But he would never be a mercenary, gaining a reputation for spending the considerable fortunes he earned with the profligacy of a drunken lord.[79]

If Blixen represented the acme of white hunter professionalism and competence, as Hemingway and others seem to have agreed, and if Philip Percival, the 'Dean of White Hunters',[80] came to represent the solidity and probity for which the professional hunting fraternity wished to be known, there were plenty of lesser lights who came to Kenya seeking fame and fortune as big game hunters and who would become professionals. As well, there was a fair share of rogues.

It is difficult to know how many white hunters were not gentlemen but

[75] Ibid., 15ff.

[76] Quoted in J. Thurman, *Isak Dinesen: The Life of a Storyteller* (New York: St. Martins, 1982), 132.

[77] Aschan, *The Man Whom Women Loved*, 144, 192. See Thurman, *Isak Dinesen*, 162–4, on his drinking and dissolute lifestyle.

[78] Holman, *Inside Safari Hunting*, 44.

[79] See Aschan, *The Man Whom Women Loved*, 210; and Trzebinski, *Silence Will Speak*, 126, on Blixen's fecklessness, constant indebtedness, and casual attitude to financial matters.

[80] Host, 'The Professional Hunters', 73. Percival and Blixen had formed a safari firm called Tanganyika Guides, Ltd in the late 1920s. See Aschan, *The Man Whom Women Loved*, 132–3.

simply brash young men, who took to hunting and guiding others as part of a life of outdoor adventure, during the boom years of the 1920s. At least one such hunter has left a record. Roger Courtney came to Kenya in 1922 at age 19 to hunt and would return to become a professional after a brief stint as an ivory harvester. There is little indication that he developed any familiarity with the languages or customs of the Africans he employed or any sense of responsibility to his adopted environment by the time he wrote of his adventures at age 31.[81]

Occasionally, cases of malfeasance would come to the attention of the Game Department. In 1934, the young American millionaire George Vanderbilt was in Kenya, and would become embroiled in a controversy that threatened his status as a sportsman. The use of a baited hook to drag a wounded zebra behind a safari car, to attract lions to within range, may have reflected more on the professional ethics of the PWH rather than on Mr Vanderbilt. But unsportsmanlike practices indicate just how important client satisfaction had become to the success of the safari and its operators.[82]

There were enough cases of professional misconduct for some observers to call the entire enterprise of professional white hunters into question. In 1931, a letter to the Game Department recommended to A. T. Ritchie, the Game Warden: 'Get rid at any cost of the professional white hunter. It would not be tolerated by public opinion anywhere else.' Nonetheless, professional hunters would soon be established as integral to 'the present scheme of things'.[83]

By the 1930s, safari organizing had become a major source of revenue for the colony, and many new companies had emerged that combined the hunting reputations of some of the white hunters with business and organizational skills needed to run a sizeable business. Ker and Downey, formed in the early 1930s, would be one such company that continues to operate camera safaris in East Africa today. These two uneasy partners were also exceptional in giving credit to their African staff for what the Kamba and Kikuyu hunters and trackers had contributed to the business's success.[84]

The danger that competition between professional hunters for clients might lead to abuses seems to have surfaced in 1937 when a leading safari company, Cottar's Safari Service, fell foul of the Game Department for its advertisement of services whose performance would put them in violation of the game regulations. Night hunting, hunting from cars, and the use of set guns were clear violations, and the guarantee of success in finding and

---

[81] R. Courtney, *Claws of Africa: Experiences of a Professional Big-Game Hunter* (London: George G. Harrap, 1934), 38ff. See, the more sober, if sentimental, account of a German hunter and safari guide in Tanganyika in the 1930s and 1940s, in Oskar Koenig, *Pori Tupu* (New York: McGraw-Hill, 1954).

[82] 'Catching Lions with Baited Hooks', KNA KW/17/3.

[83] A. Mathews to Game Warden, 27 January 1931, KNA KW/18/13, and reply by A. T. Ritchie on 4 February 1931 in ibid.

[84] A. Cullen, *Downey's Africa* (London: Cassell, 1959), 1–5. For a history of the firm, see J. Hemsing, *Ker and Downey Safaris: The Inside Story* (Nairobi: Ker and Downey Safaris, 1989).

Photo 6.2 *Philip Percival on the Duke of Connaught's Safari,* 1906
(Kenya National Archives)

bagging certain animals was an equally clear violation of the spirit of the regulations. The result was the public condemnation and criminal conviction of the professional hunter, Mr C. W. (Budd) Cottar, a second-generation Kenyan safari operator, for seven violations of the game law.[85]

Incidents like these, plus the growing suspicion that pleasing the client might bring pressures on PWHs to cut corners, would lead to increasing regulation by the Kenya Game Department despite the creation of a professional association to set and maintain standards and police themselves. The first head of the EAPHA was none other than Philip Percival, the dean of Kenyan professional hunters (Photo 6.2).[86]

Despite regulation and public praise, privately the Kenya gamekeepers expressed grave doubts about the integrity and trustworthy qualities of the members of the hunters' guild. In 1938, the acting game warden would write to Kenya's Colonial Secretary: 'Both Capt. Ritchie and myself say nice things about the East African Professional Hunters' Association, but, to be perfectly truthful, with the exception of perhaps two.... I would not trust the members of the Association for an instant unless I was right on the spot watching them.'[87]

By the mid-1930s, the adventure of guiding safaris of rich Americans[88] and titled Europeans had become an industry, closely regulated by both the Game Department on behalf of government and by its own trade association. By the outbreak of the Second World War, the romance was gone, but the heroic image of the 'great white hunter' of legend would cling to the occupation for many years. Robert Ruark, the novelist and safari hunter, could write without embarrassment in 1953: 'In some respects, the white or professional big game hunter, African variety, is the toughest man in the world, and in others he is as gentle as a dead dove and as innocent as Huck Finn.... The function of a professional hunter on safari is almost godlike.'[89]

---

[85] 'Sports Without Tears', *Society for the Preservation of the Fauna of the Empire* [SPFE] *Journal* 32 (1937), 36–8. Also see 'Cottar's Safari Service Again', SPFE *Journal* 34 (1938), 90–92. East African Professional Hunters Assn. 'Minutes of the Meeting of 31 December 1937', KNA KW/5/48 condemns Cottar and mentions that he is not a member of the association. See Interview D/1, Glen Cottar, 16 July 1987, and J. A. Hunter, *Hunter's Tracks* (New York: Appleton-Century-Crofts, 1957), 25–30.

[86] Hunter, *Hunter's Tracks*, 38–9; and A. Dyer, *The East African Hunters* (Clinton, NJ: Amwell, 1979), 1–29, on the founding of the association. The official correspondence of the association in its efforts to secure government recognition, and minutes of monthly meetings can be found in KNA KW/5/48 Professional Hunters (1934–38). In addition, a draft article by Chief Game Warden Archie Ritchie on the Association, written for the British sporting magazine, *The Field,* and various press clippings are also contained in this file. I have been unable to obtain a copy of Philip Percival's autobiography, *Hunting, Settling and Remembering* (Agoura, CA: Trophy Room Press, 1997) to compare his reminiscence of this occasion or of the various safaris in which he participated.

[87] F. Clarke to Col. Secretary, 3 May 1938, KNA KW/27/2.

[88] A 'far from comprehensive' list of 57 such Americans who visited 'during the last few years', which contains the names of prominent businessmen representing companies from Boston's First National Bank to Los Angeles' May Company and Union Oil, is included in A. T. Ritchie to Secretary, SPFE, 12 April 1930, KNA KW/27/1.

[89] Ruark, *Horn of the Hunter*, 70, 72.

Perhaps this would be a good time to remind the reader that despite the Olympian perspective assumed by the great white hunters, from Roosevelt to Hemingway to Ruark, they were in fact standing on the shoulders of the thousands of Africans who had gone before them historically, as well as literally, as guides and trackers. They would seldom acknowledge their debt to their 'dark companions' and predecessors, preferring to cast themselves as the active agents and their Africans as both subordinate and without initiative. Even when they praise their loyalty and courage, they deny to their African colleagues any capacity for independence of thought or purposes and agendas of their own. Only occasionally can we see the veil slip in the travel, hunting, and safari literature to allow an African to take an initiative. For instance, Philip Percival offers us a glimpse of a 'strike' by his safari workers on the Rothschild safari of 1911 and Ewart Grogan presents an instance of the self-selection of his Tonga companion as headman and gun bearer from 'the Cape to Cairo'.[90]

The safari hunters of the twentieth century had found the safari a vital commercial and organizational enterprise in the late nineteenth century, and had adapted it to their sometimes grandiose purposes. Much as the white hunter might draw our attention to the head of the column, where he stood with his faithful gun bearer, the real organization and leadership of the column of porters, skinners, trackers, and cooks was in the invisible hands and feet, minds, and hearts (or livers as the Kamba might put the same notion), of Africans. The big game safari was all about adaptation and compromise, or, perhaps, about synthesis, the negotiation of a truly transcultural production.

---

[90] Percival, *Hunting, Settling, and Remembering*, 65ff, also offers a glimpse of the role of threat and intimidation in maintaining 'discipline'. For Grogan's 'Watonga' porter, Makanjira, who asserted his leadership and 'assumed the role of Grogan's gun-bearer, lieutenant and principal advisor', see Edward Paice, *Lost Lion of Empire* (London: Harper Collins, 2001), 72. Makanjira would remain with Grogan for two years, travelling all the way to Alexandria with him. These are among the few instances I have found in which we can see the process of recruitment of 'subordinate staff' and it comes before the full protocols of the white hunter–African staff relationship were developed with the tropes of unquestioned loyalty and subordination.

Seven

New Technologies, Changing Values

Between the wars, the big game safari underwent a sea change. Although it remained beyond the means of most middle-class Americans and Europeans, safari hunting enjoyed a growing clientele of the super-rich and aristocratic who could afford not only the cash outlay involved in international travel in the days before jet air transport, but also the time to spend travelling by sea, rail, and foot to get to the remote locations where lions, elephants, and rhinoceros roamed.[1] However, even before jet planes would rewrite the history of the safari in the 1940s and 1950s, other technologies were working profound changes on the experience of hunting by whites in Kenya. We shall focus on three seminal technological changes: cameras, motor cars, and aeroplanes.

Cameras on safari

Cameras were present on safari from very early in the history of the hunting safari. But their role in the beginning was simply to document the hunting achievements of the white hunters, and occasionally to record the curiosities of nature and of people they encountered *en route* to the kill, which remained the central object of the safari. Contrary to the idea that 'From the 1890s to the 1920s, cameras and guns jostled one another in wildlife books,'[2] I believe that during that period in particular they forged

---

[1] Clippings from the *East African Standard* on the 1935 visits of the Duke of Norfolk (2 February and 14 March 1935) and the Maharajah of Jodhpur (8 March 1935) give colourful accounts of these dignitaries and the travel arrangements for their safaris.

[2] P. S. Landau, 'With Camera and Gun in Southern Africa: Inventing the Image of the Bushman, c.1880 to 1935', in *Miscast: Negotiating the Presence of the Bushman*, ed. P. Skotnes (Cape Town: University of Cape Town Press, 1996), 135. Landau makes a similar argument regarding the 'essential shift in the Western apprehension of the wild' (135ff) during the 1920s that I am trying to make, without tying the shift to the change in the class character of the Western shooters of guns and cameras. See also J. R. Ryan, *Picturing Empire*

a working alliance. First, the hunter shot the wildlife with a gun and then posed over the carcass with his or her boot on the shoulder or rump of the dead animal; then a photograph was taken to record the triumph.[3] Thus did the hunters display their mastery and claim their trophies. Only after the Great War, and during the reaction against the carnage and brutality of that conflict, did the camera and the gun fall to jostling for pride of place. The 1920s and 1930s would see a metamorphosis of the role of the camera from auxiliary to centre stage in the hunting safari.

Symbolically, this was achieved by reversing the order in which one shot. The camera was used first to shoot the wildlife and capture its living image for posterity. Only then would the animal be shot with a gun to capture it for its trophies to hang on the den wall, alongside the picture of the living but framed object of desire. This double shooting is represented in the numerous books from this period that speak of 'hunting' with camera and gun linked in their titles.[4] This linking of the two methods of 'possessing' prey has become commonplace, frequently expressed by noting the similarity of terminology of 'aiming' and 'shooting' both the camera and the gun. But this masks an important distinction expressed by many who engaged in the transition from rifle to camera. They came to see camera hunting as ultimately more civilized, and hence more worthy, than killing game. Eventually this perception would lead to a de-linking of the two kinds of 'shooting' so that, by the end of the colonial era, the camera safari would become the standard and the hunting safari would appear more and more as a vestige of times past. No one expressed this transformation more succinctly than C. T. Stoneham, early in the history of the transition:

> Of late years the camera has superseded the rifle as a means of forming closer contact with wild animals. Sportsmen have come to recognize that destruction is senseless; that the 'hunting instinct', far from being admirable, is a brutal attribute to be found most fully developed in the lower forms of creation.... It is time we exercised our overlordship more rationally; abandoning the methods of the feudal baron, and adopting those of the amiable squire. In the future, then, the true sportsman will be the friend and champion of the beasts; he will secure his trophies with the film and shutter, instead of the rifle and trap.[5]

It would be easy to dismiss this as metahistorical musings but, stripped of the evolutionist language, I believe Stoneham expresses important insights into the perceived historical changes in the idea of hunting.

[2] (contd) (Chicago: University of Chicago Press, 1997), 99–139, for a convincing exposition of the role of photography in safari hunting from an imperial perspective.

[3] These images are too well known to require extensive documentation. Let me merely point to one of the latest images to appear, in this case as a frontispiece entitled 'Two lions shot by the author', in M. Daly, *Big Game Hunting and Adventure 1897–1936* (London: Macmillan, 1937).

[4] E.g. E. Bennet, *Shots and Snapshots in British East Africa* (London: Longmans, Green, 1914); and C. T. Stoneham, *Hunting Wild Beasts with Rifle and Camera* (London: Thomas Nelson and Sons, n.d. [1932?]). Bennet especially represents a photographer who killed first and then pictured himself posed above the fallen prey.

[5] Stoneham, *Hunting Wild Beasts*, 47, 48.

First, he advances the idea, expressed by many advocates of camera 'hunting', that somehow or other, for technical or emotional reasons, shooting with the camera brings you into 'closer contact' with nature and wildlife. It is not clear whether this is because getting a 'good shot' with a camera in the days before high-powered telephoto lenses required even more skill and daring in stalking to within close range of the target, or because the process of observation created a deeper sense of knowledge of the behaviour of the prey. However, it has been argued that 'It will be found with absolute certainty that one learns more about animals in one year's photography than in ten years' shooting.'[6] Most importantly, camera safaris came to be thought of as less destructive of nature, more humane, and, rightly or wrongly, as an adjunct of modern conservation efforts.

The humane image of camera hunting survived several incidents in which cruelty to animals and various unsportsman-like practices were brought to light.[7] As safari guides and professional white hunters sought to satisfy their camera-carrying clients through the use of baited traps and hooks and the photographing of wounded and mauled animals, the camera safari came in for a share of the criticism before the East African Society for the Prevention of Cruelty to Animals and the Game Department, for using what were considered unethical and unsportsmanlike methods to attract animals before the camera's lens.[8] Ironically, in 1940, Charles Cottar, the subject of one of these accusations of lion baiting for the camera and a member of a safari-operating family with its roots in the pioneer period of Kenyan big game hunting, would fall victim to a charging rhinoceros while a client was shooting a motion picture.[9]

Finally, in a book published in 1947 devoted to the promotion of camera safaris and subtitled *The Reformation of a Big Game Hunter*, James Sleeman wrote an impassioned appeal for the substitution of cameras for rifles in the name of conservation. Sleeman cited a long pedigree of wildlife authorities who shared and promoted this view.[10] Although he frequently lays blame where it does not belong, his views seem to clearly reflect the passage from feudal brutality to the bourgeois sensibility that focused on

---

[6] Lt.-Col. C. H. Stockley, *African Camera Hunts* (London: Country Life, 1948), 1. See also his 'Camera Stalking', *SPFE Journal* 33 (1938), 20–25.

[7] Colonial Secretary to Game Warden, 7 November 1934, and reply of 8 December 1934, *KNA* KW/27/1 on British Board of Film Censors complaints about the depiction of death and cruelty to animals on film.

[8] E.g. C. H. Cottar to A. T. Ritchie, 9 January 1939, KNA KW/5/46. By the late 1930s, the Kenya Game Department was regularly overseeing camera safaris as part of its licensing procedures. A. Ritchie, 'Game Photography in East Africa', draft, KNA KW/18/17, as well as correspondence regarding photographic permits, for which a printed permit form was created after the Second World War.

[9] Hunter, *Hunter's Tracks*, 30–31; and Interview D/1, Glen Cottar, 16 July 1987. Charles Cottar, the son of J. L. Cottar of Texas, came to Kenya with his father to hunt, and settled near Nairobi, starting the safari firm that was still operating a safari camp in the Maasai Mara in the 1990s. Charles's son Glen operated the camp as a photo safari base, while his son led bow-and-arrow safaris in Tanzania.

[10] J. L. Sleeman, *From Rifle to Camera: The Reformation of a Big Game Hunter* (London: Jarrolds, n.d. [1947?]), 187–96. Sleeman's expertise is based on 40 years of hunting experience, including 13 African safaris.

possession of the image of the animal, rather than its sacrifice. A. W. Redfern, another long-time hunter turned camera buff, put the sentiment pithily: 'It took me sixty years to realize that a loaded rifle was a peculiar token of "love".'[11]

To the reformation of big game hunters and the growth of humane attitudes we must add the important sanction that science gave to wildlife photography. Beginning with Carl Akeley's use of photography as an adjunct to his taxidermy and his development of lightweight camera equipment to facilitate the use of photography in the field, the camera became standard equipment on the many scientific safaris that also frequently served as a cover, as it did for Akeley, for the desire to hunt.[12] The cachet of modernity and humane values that science lent to the camera safari also contributed to the de-emphasis on blood sport in favour of the civilized pursuit of animals and their capture on film.

However, it would be the work of the American couple Martin and Osa Johnson that probably tipped the scales in favour of the camera as the preferred instrument of big game hunting in the 1920s and 1930s. There is a certain irony in this benign influence exercised by the Johnsons' popularity with movie-goers, who saw them very much in the tradition of Frank Buck's 'Bring Them Back Alive' propaganda.

In the Johnsons' many books and films, it is the capturing of animals on film that is dramatized.[13] Yet it is also clear that, while Martin was stalking and shooting with his cameras, Osa was by his side with a hunting rifle, prepared to shoot to kill if the animal attacked, and to shoot anyway once the camera had stopped rolling.[14] So, although the express purpose of the safaris is 'to film … a record of Africa's fast vanishing wild life', their own contribution to the process of destruction is evidenced by the possession of an arsenal of eight guns to go along with their twenty-one cameras, and a 'general license to shoot all the common game … [of which] lions, zebras leopards and hyena are unlimited. Special licences are issued for elephant, rhino, giraffe and ostrich.'[15]

The Johnsons' films and books not only popularized the idea of photographic safaris, but, by working on behalf of the American Museum of Natural History (which houses a large collection of their original photographs) and by joining forces with George Eastman of Eastman Kodak on his second hunting safari in 1928, they established photography as a scientifically valuable and commercially viable form of 'hunting'.[16]

[11] A. W. Redfern, 'Camera in Place of Rifle', *SPFE Journal* 37 (1939), 22.

[12] D. Haraway, *Primate Visions* (New York: Routledge, 1989), 42–6.

[13] See Martin Johnson, *Camera Trails in Africa* (New York: Grosset and Dunlop, 1924), and *Safari* (New York: G. P. Putnam's Sons, 1928) on his 1923 safari, and *Over African Jungles* (New York: Harcourt, Brace, 1935) on his five African safaris. In addition, a popular biography of Martin Johnson can be found in F. Green's *Martin Johnson, Lion Hunter* (New York: G. P. Putnam's Sons, 1928).

[14] Johnson, *Safari*, 208–34.

[15] Ibid., 4, 9, 16.

[16] M. Johnson/C. H. Cole, 1933–5, and Martin Johnson Expedition, 1921, American Museum of National History (AMNH), Photography Collection; G. Eastman, *Chronicles of a Second African Trip* (Rochester, NY: Friends of the University of Rochester Libraries, 1987).

Although at this time the 'double shooting' of wildlife was still the norm, the growth and popularity of non-hunting safaris dedicated exclusively to photographic capture was not far in the future.[17]

Among the subtler changes the camera would bring was a transformation in the image of the African, who also became increasingly the subject or, rather, the object of the camera, either as a member of the hunting safari or as the object of the photographs in his or her own right. Just as 'Photographs tamed the animals they touched and made the unknown familiar,' they also tamed and familiarized the image of the African, though always holding him at a distance, captured and framed by the camera's eye. Landau makes this argument regarding 'an essential shift in the Western apprehension of "the wild" in the case of the Bushman during the 1920s'[18] that I am trying to make for Kenyan Africans of the same period. However, he does so without relating the shift to the change in the class character of the Western shooters of guns and cameras that I see as central to understanding the changing nature of the hunt.

Motor cars in the bush

Between 1914 and the beginning of the Second World War, a transportation revolution, comparable in its impact on East Africa to that of the opening of the railway, transformed not only the economy but also the newly developing safari tradition of hunting. Like most such rapid changes, the effects were at first feared and resisted, but would eventually transform the hunting safari into what we would now recognize as the modern tourist safari. The technological means for this transformation was the adaptation of both the motor car and the aeroplane to the hunting safari and to reducing the time and expense required to 'go on safari'.

First, the use of motorized transport during the Great War made Kenya settlers familiar with the motor car – and especially the lorry – as something more than a plaything of the rich. It was not long before the tour organizers and professional hunters were providing lorries and drivers, instead of an army of head porters, to carry the safari equipment to the field. In addition, the use of saloon cars and specially adapted safari cars, the precursors of the Land-rover and Range-rover, were soon obviating the key element of the pioneer safari: the need to walk vast distances to locate prey and to stalk them within range of gunshot.[19] By the late 1920s,

---

[17] P. J. Fetner's *The African Safari* (New York: St. Martins, 1987) is meant to serve as a handbook for exclusively photographic safaris and a coffee-table book of animal pictures. For those who have a desire for hunting books *per se*, I recommend the writings of Peter Capstick such as *Death in the Long Grass* (London: Cassell, 1977) and *Safari: The Last Adventure* (New York: St. Martins, 1984).

[18] P. Landau, 'With Camera and Gun', 135. See Ryan, *Picturing Empire*, 140–82, for the role of photographing 'natives' in the construction of racial stereotypes and the objectification of native subjects.

[19] Martin Johnson claims to have organized the 'First Motor Car Expedition' in 1921. 'Outside of Meru' shows Johnson with two safari vehicles on the road. Photo no.128724, AMNH Library, Photography Collection.

the Akeley–Eastman–Pomeroy expedition for the American Museum of Natural History included five vehicles. As Mary Akeley explained, 'motor transport has supplanted the native carrier, destroying the romance of the days of primitive travel and making possible ... the completion of an expedition in a very short time'.[20]

The use of motor transport on safari would lead to a transformation in both the hunting party's size and the nature of the staff, as the camp cook and lorry driver's skills (particularly the skills of a mechanic) replaced those of the gun bearer and porter. Although the 'faithful' gun bearer-companion to the white hunter would remain a picturesque part of safari companies and of hunting lore, the actual need for men carrying heavy weapons along with hunting and camera equipment was supplanted by more efficient, if less reliable, mechanical surrogates.[21] The safari vehicles were in some ways no less picturesque than the gun bearers, and many safaris would leave a photographic record of the vehicles along with pictures of the clients, white hunters, and the reduced staff of African safari specialists.[22]

The advent of the motor car on safari was not without its critics. Beyond the purist nostalgia for the 'romance of the days of primitive travel', serious concerns began to appear that the ubiquity of motor vehicles might lead to 'motor poaching'.[23] But, as long as the hunter did not actually shoot without getting down from the vehicle, the requirements of sportsmanship seem to have been fulfilled.[24] Nonetheless, the increased ease and safety of being able to drive right up to within a few yards of one's prey – even lions – without disturbing them led to severe criticism of both the ethics and the impact on the disappearance of the game caused by the motor safari. Eventually, it would be made illegal to shoot either from cars or from within a 100-yard radius of a motor vehicle.[25] More drastic proposals, such as closing certain game areas to motor traffic, would not receive serious consideration because of the 'great hardship' this would inflict on the resident hunters of Kenya.[26]

[20] M. L. J. Akeley, *Carl Akeley's Africa* (New York: Dodd, Mead, 1930), photograph caption facing p. 88.

[21] K. M. Cameron, *Into Africa. The Story of the East African Safari* (London: Constable, 1990), p. 83–5.

[22] See J. Hemsing, *Ker and Downey Safaris. The Inside Story* (Nairobi: Ker and Downey Safari, 1989), cover photograph. The Ker and Downey vehicles themselves became familiar sights around Nairobi and a symbol of the modern motor safari used in advertising the company and its services. Also, see the photograph of Straus Central Africa Expedition 281719–281722 of Denys Finch Hatton's motorized safari vehicles and staff in 1929. AMNH Library Photography Collection.

[23] The East African Professional Hunters Association denounced the use of cars in lion hunting in 'The Problem of Motor Poaching', *East African Standard*, 31 January 1936, *KNA* KW/5/48.

[24] A local ordinance regulating the use of motor transport on safari was passed on 8 May 1931. Colony and Protectorate of Kenya, *Game Department Annual Report* for 1931, KNA KW/1. This was reinforced by the 1933 International Convention on the preservation of African wildlife, Article 10, see *Cmd* 4453, Africa (Flora and Fauna) for full text.

[25] Cameron, *Into Africa*, 84–5.

[26] F. H. Clarke, quoted in *East African Standard*, 6 February 1936, KNA KW/5/48.

By the mid-1930s, Frederick T. Davidson, president of the American Museum of Natural History, which had done so much to promote the use of motor vehicles on safari, could report that 'Methods of hunting have changed considerably as a result of the advent of motor trucks and planes'.[27] Also, as early as 1925, the Chief Game Warden of Kenya had already observed, 'No aspect of civilization has more increased the complexity of game conservation problems than the advent into general use of motor-cars.'[28]

The romance of the aeroplane

If the impact of air transport was initially less devastating and dramatic than that of motor cars and trucks, its direct application to hunting and its indirect influence on reducing the time and expense needed to engage in safari hunting would ultimately be even more transformative. The earliest use of aeroplanes for hunting purposes is attributed to the initiative of Bror Blixen and Denys Finch Hatton as professional white hunters (PWHs) and Beryl Markham as pilot. Although neither of the men would rely on this small contribution to establish his fame, their collaboration in using Beryl Markham's skills as a bush pilot – to spot elephant herds from the air and to direct the PWH and his paying clients to the location – did a great deal to ensure the success of these safaris and reduced the time and risk involved in locating and reaching large prey.[29] Martin Johnson would also pioneer the use of aircraft in transporting his equipment and spotting animals from the air by bringing out two Sikorsky amphibian planes from New York for his 1933 photo safari.[30] Air reconnaissance, however, would prove an expensive and dangerous technique for the safari business and was never fully developed.

Still, aircraft would become an important adjunct to the safari business, by providing quick and reliable transport from Nairobi's Wilson Field to various game reserves, and later to national parks around the country and into Tanganyika and Uganda. Kenya had its own locally owned airline, Wilson Airways, from as early as 1929.[31] Ultimately, the use of small planes would find a regular place in the tourist industry's efforts to save time by delivering tourists, including hunters, to the various game-rich

---

[27] F. T. Davidson, 'Elephants, Lions and Airplanes', *Natural History* 34, 2 (1934), 108–9.

[28] Colony and Protectorate of Kenya, *Game Department Annual Report* for 1925, 13, KNA KW/1. The doyen of Kenya's wildlife conservation educators made similar comments on the impact of motor vehicles. See N. Simon, *Between the Sunlight and the Thunder: The Wild Life of Kenya* (Boston: Houghton Mifflin, 1962), 52, 151.

[29] U. T. Aschan, *The Man Whom Women Loved. The Life of Bror Blixen* (New York: St Martins, 1987), 166; M. S. Lovell, *Straight on Till Morning. The Biography of Beryl Markham* (London: Hutchinson, 1987), 150–51; Trzebinski, *Silence Will Speak*, 210–11.

[30] Johnson, *Over African Jungles*, 3 and *passim*. See also Davidson, 'Elephants, Lions', 106.

[31] Robert L. McCormack, 'Imperialism, Air Transport and Colonial Development: Kenya, 1920–46', *Journal of Imperial and Commonwealth History* 17, 3 (1989), 381–8. My thanks to Prof. Bruce Daniels for bringing this and other works by his former colleague, Prof. McCormack, to my attention.

regions of the country, avoiding the tiresome and often bone-jarring overland hauls in safari cars and later 'kombis', the now ubiquitous, brightly painted safari minivans used for the transportation of tourists.[32]

However, the central contribution of the aeroplane to the transformation of the hunting safari was the result of the indirect influence of the development of intercontinental air routes in the late 1930s. In 1936, the East African Professional Hunters' Association's *Handbook of Information* was advising prospective clients of the twice-weekly passenger service to Nairobi, available on Imperial Airways and taking a mere six days each way.[33] Although strategic reasons may have predominated in the development of these imperial air routes,[34] for East and southern Africa the burgeoning tourist trade clearly played a significant, if not a determining, role. According to Robert McCormack, 'the full exploitation of Africa's air transport potential had to await the years following 1945'.[35] By 1948, after the 'Second World War resulted in a six-year hiatus in air transport development',[36] British Overseas Airways Corporation, the successor to Imperial Airways Company, initiated a weekly flying boat service between Southampton and Johannesburg, with stops at Port Bell on Lake Victoria and Victoria Falls in the Rhodesias, to serve tourist and business travels.[37] The increasing use after the war of new American-built passenger aircraft and American carriers in African air transport also worked a sea change in East African tourist travel and safari hunting.[38]

The convenience and speed of intercontinental air travel would increasingly change the complexion of the Kenyan safari clientele, from blue-blooded aristocrats and multimillionaires to the merely rich and not necessarily famous. This change in class background or the *embourgeoisement* of the safari clientele was accompanied by a change in the national origins of the hunter/tourist, from British and European nobility to American leisure and upper middle classes. The British press in 1950 noted this change with some irony:

> A new dollar industry is in the making – big game hunting. [There is] … a craze for the sport among Americans who can spare time and money for it. [But] … Americans do not want the traditional safari. They want motor caravans with hot and cold running water, instead of tents and lorries instead of native bearers.… And so the cost for just one American big game hunter is nearly £2000 a week. They want the sport. But even more

---

[32] See Hunter, *Hunter's Tracks*, 81–6.

[33] KNA KW/5/48, 13.

[34] Robert L. McCormack, 'Airlines and Empires: Great Britain and the "Scramble for Africa": 1919–1932', *Canadian Journal of African Studies* 10, 1 (1976), 87–105, and his 'Imperialism, Air Transport', 374–89.

[35] McCormack, 'Airlines and Empires', 89 and his 'Imperialism, Air Transport', 386–8.

[36] N. Cockerell, 'Air Transport in Sub-Saharan Africa', *Interavia* 4/5 (1978), 339. See also R.L. McCormack, 'War and Change: Air Transport in British Africa, 1939–1946', *Canadian Journal of History* 24 (1989), 341–59; R. Higham, *Britain's Imperial Air Routes 1918 to 1939* (Hamden, CT: Shoe String Press, 1961), 147–64, 203–12, 289–309.

[37] See the mural inscription at Victoria Falls Hotel, Victoria Falls, Zimbabwe. A photographic reproduction is in the possession of the author.

[38] McCormack, 'War and Change', 359.

than that they want the trophies … a game room is not a good game room until there is one of everything mounted and hanging from the wall.[39]

Most importantly, the changes in nationality and class seem to have been accompanied by a change in sensibility, as more and more hunters would come to see rather than to kill. Even within the Game Department, which, as we shall see, took the promotion of hunting as one of its major projects, a growing sense of the anachronism of killing animals for sport was beginning to emerge. The levelling effect of motor transport was also seen as a factor in promoting camera safaris as early as 1928.[40] By 1934, no less a champion of hunting than the Chief Game Warden of Kenya, Captain Archie Ritchie, was reported as saying to the Rotary Club of Nairobi:

'The justification for shooting at all is becoming among thinking people more difficult day to day,' Captain Ritchie declared. It was not defensible in Captain Ritchie's mind to kill a magnificent beast like an eland merely because of the length of its horns. Increasingly Captain Ritchie found it more difficult to pull the trigger on anything at all.[41]

In place of the hunting ethos, a new attitude that saw the conservation of wildlife, rather than the destruction of game, as the proper role for the Kenya Game Department would come to predominate. Eventually, this attitude among Kenya's gamekeepers and settlers would spawn a new Kenya-based movement that, together with the international movement of which it was an integral part, would take as its objective the preservation of Kenya's wildlife for posterity.

[39] 'On Safari', *Daily Express*, 8 April 1950, KNA KW/20/20. For the influence of air transport on American tourism after 1945 more generally, see Douglas Karsner, ' "Now Hawaii is only hours away!" The Airlines Alter Tourism', *Essays in Economic and Business History* 18, 1 (1999), 181–94.

[40] Colony and Protectorate of Kenya, *Game Department Annual Report* for 1928, 18–19, KNA KW/1.

[41] *East African Standard*, 29 January 1934, *KNA* KW/27/1.

Part IV

◆◆◆◆◆◆◆◆◆◆◆◆◆◆◆◆◆◆◆◆◆◆◆◆◆◆◆

Gamekeepers & Poachers

THE WILDLIFE OF TODAY IS NOT OURS TO DISPOSE OF AS WE PLEASE. WE HAVE IT ON TRUST. WE MUST ACCOUNT FOR IT TO THOSE WHO COME AFTER.

> Inscription at Main Entrance, Nairobi National Park (1946)

THE NATURAL RESOURCES OF THIS COUNTRY — ITS WILDLIFE WHICH OFFERS SUCH AN ATTRACTION TO BEAUTIFUL PLACES IN WHICH THESE ANIMALS LIVE, THE MIGHTY FORESTS WHICH GUARD THE WATER CATCHMENT AREAS SO VITAL TO THE SURVIVAL OF MAN AND BEAST — ARE A PRICELESS HERITAGE FOR THE FUTURE.

THE GOVERNMENT OF KENYA, FULLY REALIZING THE VALUE OF ITS NATURAL RESOURCES PLEDGES ITSELF TO CONSERVE THEM FOR POSTERITY WITH ALL THE MEANS AT ITS DISPOSAL.

MZEE JOMO KENYATTA , THE 1ST PRESIDENT

> Inscription at Main Gate, Nairobi National Park (1964)

Eight

◆◆◆◆◆◆◆◆◆◆◆◆◆◆◆◆◆◆◆◆◆◆◆◆

The Kenya Gamekeepers
& Conservation

1895–1925

The most prolific and successful hunters in the history of colonial Kenya were those men who were appointed as keepers of the game and conservators of the country's wildlife resources. From the late nineteenth century to the Great War, a rudimentary Game Department and a corps of volunteer honorary game wardens and rangers would set the tone that established Kenya's reputation as a 'sportsman's paradise'. By the late 1920s, an increasingly professional and disciplined department would begin to take more seriously its mandate to conserve and protect Kenya's wildlife resources. Finally, in the 1930s and 1940s, a local movement inspired by a growing international conservation movement would lead to the emergence of a full-blown preservationist ethos among Kenya's white hunters and naturalists. This new consciousness would find expression in the creation of the National Parks of Kenya, one of Africa's most extensive programmes of set asides of land as habitat and refuge for wildlife. Ironically, in the decades between the Second World War and Kenyan independence, the development of increasing awareness and dedication to the preservation of Kenya's wildlife heritage would also lead directly to a confrontation with African hunters and the ultimate destruction of the African hunting tradition in Kenya.

Percival, Woosnam, and the pioneer period

Although the Kenya Game Department was formally created in 1899, it can hardly merit that name until a full decade later. And, although its creation can be traced to growing concern expressed by imperial officials, such as Sir Harry Johnston, about the destruction of large animals, especially elephant, it can hardly be said to have been an important force for the preservation of wildlife in these early years.[1] Only one (white) game

---

[1] N.T. Simon, *Between the Sunlight and the Thunder: The Wild Life of Kenya* (Boston: Houghton

warden was named, with no administrative support and an indeterminate number of African subordinate staff to maintain the department's writ. On top of that, the appointment of A. Blayney Percival as the first Game Ranger (the first title for Kenya's chief gamekeeper and head of the department) was hardly calculated to discourage hunting or underscore the government's commitment to conservation. Percival was a well-known sportsman, who was himself rather adept at pushing the limits of acceptable hunting methods in the name of good sport. In his own accounts of his life as a game ranger, his official duties weigh very lightly compared to his hunting exploits, to the point where it is difficult to see any significant difference in his personal reminiscences and those of any number of elephant harvesters, 'big game' hunters, or, for that matter, poachers. His signal contribution to East African hunting seems to have been his pioneering efforts at developing the sport of hunting lion from horseback. In an effort to protect the lives and the domestic livestock of the pioneer settlers, lions were classified as vermin by early game law. This meant that there was no licence required to shoot lions and no limit on the number of lions killed, which hardly exhibits the kind of conservation agenda the Game Department was supposed to promote.[2]

It seems that from the very outset the efforts of conservationists and hunters would create contradictions. It was a growing awareness of the devastating effects on Kenya's elephant herds by the ivory harvesters that prompted the colonial government to move towards establishing a game department as an instrument for saving the elephants.[3] Unfortunately, the colonial policy of encouraging white settlement, adopted by Sir Charles Eliot in the first decade of the twentieth century, ran counter to the efforts to restrict hunting and preserve elephants. Even more importantly, until the development of agriculture was advanced and could be relied upon as a source of revenue by the colonial treasury, the government and its fledgling Game Department would find themselves in a financial squeeze. Revenues from ivory exports alone often represented as much as half of the government's tax revenues annually and amounted to as much as 75 per

---

[1] (contd) Mifflin, 1962), 33–4. For the earliest game regulations and its rationale, see East African Wildlife Protection Regulations, 1897, Inclosure 36 in E. Wingfield to Foreign Office, 11 January 1897, PRO FO 881/6951; and F. Bertie to Colonial Office, 8 September 1897, PRO FO 881/7018.

[2] A. B. Percival, *A Game Ranger's Notebook* (London: Nisbet, 1924; reprint, Camden, NC, 1987), ix–xxii, contains an introductory appreciation of the author by John MacKenzie. See also A. B. Percival's *A Game Ranger on Safari* (London: Nisbet, 1928), and J. MacKenzie, 'Poachers and Preservers: Game Law in British Colonial Africa', unpublished ms. For South African parallels involving predator extinctions at the hand and behest of white farmers, see L. van Sittert, '"Keeping the Enemy at Bay": The Extermination of Wild Carnivora in the Cape Colony, 1889–1910', *Environmental History* 3, 3 (1998): 333–41.

[3] Two unpublished works that focus on the administrative history of the colonial Game Department have informed those aspects of this chapter. They are Nora Kelly, 'In Wildest Africa: The Preservation of Game in Kenya, 1895–1933', Ph.D. dissertation, Simon Fraser University, 1978; and Thomas P. Ofcansky, 'A History of Game Preservation in British East Africa, 1895–1963', Ph.D. dissertation, University of West Virginia, 1981. See also Ofcansky's recently published revision of his dissertation entitled *Paradise Lost: A History of Game Conservation in East Africa* (Morganton: West Virginia University Press, 2002).

cent of the East African Protectorate revenues in 1902.[4] Additional ivory revenues were derived from the sale of confiscated and 'found' ivory, the sale of hunting and special elephant licences, gun permits, and fines. These funds are reflected in the financial reportage from the district level up through the overall colonial accounts.[5] Given the extraordinary value of ivory to colonial revenues, the contradictory nature of the ivory question would predictably wreak havoc on efforts to develop a consistent and effective policy of game preservation to the end of the colonial era and beyond.

Blayney Percival did a creditable job, given the manpower and ideological constraints under which he operated as the sole Game Ranger in the earliest years. However, the prospects for the Game Department's development as an instrument of wildlife conservation took a turn for the worse with the 1907 appointment of Col. J. H. Patterson (of *Man-eaters of Tsavo* fame). Although three European rangers would assist Patterson, his tenure would last only one year with no notable growth in the department's effectiveness. R. B. Woosnam was named as his replacement in 1908, but would only assume effective control of the department in late 1910.[6]

Woosnam as a man of science – an entomologist – brought a different mind-set to the job of Kenya's chief gamekeeper from that of the sportsman-hunter Percival or the soldier-engineer Patterson. Woosnam would officially serve as warden until the outbreak of the Great War, when he was recruited for military service (along with the four other European Game Department wardens). Woosnam was killed in action in 1915, ending the only period in the colonial history of Kenya that a scientist rather than a sportsman would head the Game Department.[7]

Woosnam's main contribution to Kenya's Game Department would come in the initial years of his tenure. His recruitment of the first Africans to serve as Game Scouts[8] was probably his most enduring contribution to Kenya game keeping, as it provided a continual input of local intelligence about hunting, along with a ready and inexpensive supply of manpower in the field. By and large, Woosnam's contribution to the department's staffing problems, along with the contributions made by the African subordinate staff and the methods or principles on which they were recruited, would go largely unrecognized. Recognition for Woosnam came instead with regard to his delineation of the thorny problem of creating a consistent ivory policy for the colony.

[4] Kelly, 'In Wildest Africa', 136–7. Kelly also provides figures for annual ivory export duty receipts for the Protectorate period in a table on p. 136, showing a high of 67,592 rupees in 1899–1900.

[5] Ibid., and 152–4. See also draft *Game Department Annual Report [GDAR]*, 1909–10, 52ff, Kenya National Archives [KNA] KW/23/171 and *GDAR*, 1918–19 and *GDAR*, 1919–20, KNA KW/23/172-173.

[6] Kelly, 'In Wildest Africa', 150–51, and Ofcansky, 'A History of Game Preservation', 32–4. Contrast the dismissive treatment of Woosnam in Ofcansky, *Paradise Lost*, 21–2.

[7] Ibid.

[8] Within the Game Department, the white senior staff were styled 'Game Rangers' and the African junior staff, 'Game Scouts'. The national parks would use a different nomenclature, calling the African junior staff 'Park Rangers', creating both confusion and jealousy.

In 1911, Woosnam's report on the ivory problem would become the clearest statement of the dilemma facing sportsmen and conservationists and its possible solutions until the policy of creating national parks as refuges was articulated in the 1930s.[9] In outlining the history of the 'Ivory Question', Woosnam detailed the establishment by the first Game Ordinance of the policy of paying what amounted to a bounty, fixed in 1909 at rupees 4/– per pound, on ivory that was required to be brought into government bomas or district headquarters. This policy of paying for 'female and old ivory' had two direct consequences. First, the banning of the private sale of ivory 'gave birth to the ivory smuggling trade'[10] and, secondly, 'the purchase of ivory from natives at Rs.4/– per lb. by Government … resulted in large quantities of ivory being brought in to Government'.[11] To this point, Woosnam suggests that there had developed three distinct positions or points of view on the ivory question, leaving out an official Game Department position:

(i) *The Customs Officers*, who necessarily look at it from the immediate revenue point of view.

(ii) *The Trader*, who thinks solely of the money he can make out of it.

(iii) *The Sportsman*, and advocate of game preservation who of course looks at it from that point of view.[12]

Although, as 'an advocate of game preservation', Woosnam would like to have weighed in on the side of conservation, not surprisingly the combined interests in profit and revenue of traders and customs officials would tip the scales in the direction of a continued policy of ivory purchase.

In his recommendations, Woosnam first recognized that at the heart of the government's ivory purchase policy was a real dilemma. Africans were being told, on the one hand, that it was right and proper for them to bring in 'found' ivory or ivory from elephants that had been killed before the passage of the game ordinance, but, on the other hand, that if they brought in ivory that showed signs of having been recently killed, those tusks would be confiscated and the bearers would be subject to penalties. Inasmuch as traders had been actively purchasing ivory for many years both before and after the passage of these restrictions, it was reasonable to assume that no significant stocks of ivory were still stored and that most ivory being presented for purchase by government at fixed rates was in fact the result of the recent hunting of elephants. Government was thus tacitly encouraging the slaughter of elephants while denying responsibility for it by making the claim that only legally obtained ivory was being purchased.[13] As late as 1925, the Assistant District Commissioner for Kipini wrote: 'Elephants are snared, shot and

---

[9] The report constitutes 13 pages of the draft *Game Department Annual Report* for 1909–10, KNA KW/23/171, 46–58.

[10] Ibid., 46.

[11] Ibid., 50.

[12] Ibid., 46.

[13] Ibid., 53–4.

hunted at every waterhole and the tusks solemnly brought as "found" to Government and the amount of reward claimed.'[14]

On the other hand, it was argued that to close down the purchase of ivory by government or traders would not save the elephants, but would merely create an opportunity for illegal buyers and smugglers. 'The slaughter of elephants will go on as before, with the exception that the ivory will all be smuggled out of the Protectorate, and be lost to the revenue.'[15] After considering and dismissing the idea of licensing a limited number of 'respectable residents to trade in ivory',[16] Woosnam puts forth two stark alternative prospects:

(i) Any form of trade in ivory, whether disguised under a system of government purchase or allowing a limited number of licensed traders, must inevitably encourage the slaughter of Elephants and lead to their eventual extermination in the not very distant future.

(ii) The absolute protection of Elephants, comprising the abolition of all trading, i.e., purchase of ivory, whether privately or by government. When ivory can only be legally possessed under a Sportsman's or Residents license.[17]

Accepting the assumption that the continuation of the ivory trade will lead to extermination, Woosnam argues that the considerable revenue that will be lost to government from the ivory purchase programme would in any case be a dwindling resource and with its disappearance would take the additional revenues generated by hunting licences to sportsmen and other trophy seekers. On the other hand, a permanent ban on the ivory trade, although it would reduce revenues considerably in the short term, would preserve the elephant as a resource, attracting sportsmen and naturalists, who share 'the very legitimate and laudable desire … to prevent the extermination of the Elephant as a species'. This, he suggested, is akin to a choice between 'spending capital or living on the interest'.[18] With hunting licence revenues in the short run supplemented by export licences and fines from confiscated ivory payable by those who violated the law, Woosnam believed that even short-term revenue losses could be minimized. More-over, he boldly suggested that an ivory ban, which might be expected to 'increase the smuggling trade … on the contrary will probably reduce it owing to the greater attention which will be given to the subject'.[19] Woosnam then recommends that, in the interest of preserving elephants as an economic asset, a total ban on the ivory trade except by government for export be proclaimed. The policy suggestion was stillborn.[20]

I have paid what may seem an inordinate amount of attention to explaining a policy discussion that came to nothing. After all, the decision to ban trade in elephant ivory as a perceived endangered species would

[14] A. D. C. Kipini, Annual Report, 1925, KNA KW/23/174.

[15] Ibid., 57.

[16] Ibid., 54.   [17] Ibid., 55–6.

[18] Ibid., 56.   [19] Ibid., 57a.

[20] R. Woosnam to Colonial Secretary, 8 May 1911; R. Woosnam to Chief of Customs, 15 and 29 October 1910, KNA KW/14/6.

not be proclaimed until more than a decade after independence, as a response to the worst poaching crisis in the history of the Kenya Colony or the Republic of Kenya. Woosnam's premature suggestions would fall prey to the continuing importance of ivory to the revenues of the colony and the inability of a weak colonial government to enforce laws against hunting or trading in this highly valued good. However, ivory and elephants would remain the central issue in Kenya's conservation debates until the last years of the colonial era. Meanwhile, the outbreak of the Great War, with its siphoning of manpower from the Game Department and the heightening of demand for game meat to feed the troops and provide sport for the officers, would lay to rest the ivory question until a new ivory crisis arose between the wars. The death of Woosnam in October 1915, while serving as an intelligence officer in the Dardanelles, would leave the conservationist perspective without a spokesman and the Game Department without real leadership for the next decade.

The interwar ivory crisis

The end of the Great War found the Kenya Game Department in a shambles. Not only was it leaderless since the departure and death of Woosnam, its day-to-day functioning had virtually ceased during the war years. Even the publication of the minimally informative annual reports did not resume until 1924, and both skilled and unskilled staffs were either missing or unsupervised.[21] Even the department's transport mules had been commandeered for war service.[22] Moreover, as noted earlier, the war had created a hunting epidemic, by introducing large numbers of armed men who were encouraged to seek diversion and supplemental income by shooting both for the pot and for trophies. The absence of Game Department officials and the laxity of district administration in regulating hunting meant that much of this soldierly exercise was conducted outside the law and was technically poaching.[23]

The first efforts to remedy this situation were in some ways worse than feeble. The appointment of Blayney Percival for a second term as Game Ranger in 1919 could hardly be considered a discouragement to hunting. Although Percival might be a different man from the brash young hunter of a decade earlier,[24] he still represented a sportsman's ideal of a game-keeper. He might complain about the 'despoiled' condition of the department in 1922, but he rarely indicated that he considered the settler presence a threat to wildlife.[25] Indeed, the generally pro-settler policies that

---

[21] K. Caldwell, Acting Game Warden to Editor, *Times of East Africa*, 24 June 1926, KNA KW/1/69.

[22] Lack of transport and access roads in remote areas of the country such as the Northern Reserve area were seen as the principal obstacles to the prevention of poaching. See *GDAR*, 1922, cited in Kelly, 'In Wildest Africa', 151.

[23] See ibid. and notes 20–24 in Chapter 6.

[24] J. M. MacKenzie, 'A New Introduction', in Percival, *A Game Ranger's Notebook*, xx.

[25] Kelly, 'In Wildest Africa', 151ff; and Percival, *A Game Ranger on Safari*, 244–55.

prevailed during the early 1920s were not conducive to game regulation of any sort. Added to this prevailing attitude was the Soldier Settlement Scheme, which produced an influx of undercapitalized settler farmers who frequently supplemented their farm income with trophy and meat hunting.[26] Nevertheless, this barely created a ripple in the Game Department's reckoning of game problems. Far more important in the annual reports and discussions within the department in the 1920s were two other issues: the need to control wildlife depredations in settled areas, and the control of ivory smuggling. Both of these issues would require manpower and financing which were simply not available to the department in the aftermath of war.[27] In addition, both would have important implications for the nature of the reorganized Game Department and the role of hunting in the life of the colony.

In 1923, the colonial government searched for and found the man they were looking for to develop and reorganize the Game Department. Captain A. T. A. 'Archie' Ritchie would dominate the colonial Game Department and its policies for over two decades, and in so doing would remake the relationships between hunters and wildlife, between settlers and game conservation, and between African and white hunters, in fundamental ways.[28] But, before we turn to Ritchie and his impact, it seems appropriate to take note of a little-known interim period in the leadership of the Game Department, which was also a period pregnant with crucial changes in Kenyan hunting and conservation.

Captain Caldwell and conservation

During the period between Ritchie's appointment as Chief Game Warden, as the position would henceforth be styled, and his actual arrival to take up his duties, an interim Game Warden was named. Captain Keith F. T. Caldwell would serve only until 1929 in Kenya before moving on to the international conservation scene.[29] However, during this period he would play what I believe was an extraordinary role as harbinger and transmitter of a reformulated conservationism. First, he would briefly reinstate the conservationist and scientific proclivities of Woosnam within the department before both were overtaken by the growing demand for control of wildlife. Then he would project this new conservation consciousness onto the international scene.

[26] Draft GDAR, 1919–20, KNA KW/23/173.

[27] Kelly, 'In Wildest Africa', 152–4, discusses the underfunding of the department from its earliest years, especially considered as a percentage of total expenditure and in contrast to the department's contributions to general revenues for the colony.

[28] For brief assessments of Ritchie, see Kelly, 'In Wildest Africa', 152ff; and Ofcansky, 'A History of Game Preservation', 35–6, and his *Paradise Lost*, 22–6.

[29] Caldwell initially replaced an ailing Blayney Percival as Acting Game Warden in 1922, until Ritchie's appearance in 1924, when he became Assistant Game Warden. After a brief stint in setting up the Uganda Game Department during 1925, he would be named Acting Game Warden again in 1926. On medical leave in 1927, he returned to duty in June 1928 and retired in 1929. See *Game Department Annual Report* for 1925, 1926, 1927, 1928, and 1929.

When Caldwell came to the department in 1922, he wrote what seems a remarkably impassioned confidential letter to the Society for the Preservation of the Fauna of the Empire.[30] The letter deals with the newly passed game legislation, but reveals Caldwell's commitment to wildlife conservation. Caldwell had come to the Game Department, despite his military rank of captain, directly from the civil administration of the Colony on the governor's staff. However, even there, game preservation had been his primary motive. He wrote: 'Although I have only just joined this Department ... I have been working with the Game Department ever since I came to the country. Game and its preservation originally brought me here, it is the subject in which I am intensely interested and to which I intend to entirely devote myself.'[31]

In the eleven pages that follow, he describes the ivory smuggling situation with great intensity of feeling, ending with an apology 'for the length of this letter but I am so intensely interested in Game and Game Preservation and so jealous of anything that may threaten the latter that I felt it desirable to put the whole matter before you'.[32] What I find most remarkable about this letter is the linking of his sharp analysis of the problems facing elephant conservation with an intensity of feeling that is palpable. Caldwell's passion and jealousy for animals seem utterly unlike the passion for the hunt that is so frequently the primary motive of his peers in the Game Department and among the hunter-naturalists we have encountered in previous chapters. When he represented Kenya in international conservation forums, he would point the direction for the emergence of a new international conservation consciousness.[33] Both of these would profoundly transform white and black hunting in Kenya.

Caldwell would file a report in April 1923 that, in its concern for detail, accuracy of observation, and depth of analysis, harks back to Woosnam's 1911 report on the 'Ivory Question'. Once again, the subject is the trade in ivory and, more particularly, the smuggling of ivory out of eastern Kenya's Tana and Juba River areas.[34] The report and the investigation it recounted seem to have been the result of complaints made in 1921 by the

[30] K. Caldwell to Mr Buxton, Secretary, SPFE, 19 December 1922, KNA KW/27/4.

[31] Ibid., 1.

[32] Ibid., 11.

[33] I have been unable to uncover any information on Caldwell in terms of his birth or background, education, military experience, character, or other attributes. He appears quite suddenly in the Kenya archival record and disappears just as suddenly to the international conservation scene. As far as I can discern neither Kelly's nor Ofcansky's dissertation takes note of his work with the department, with the exception of a single reference in the context of his work on game control (Kelly, 'In Wildest Africa', 233). Ofcansky's recent book mentions his work in Uganda briefly and picks him up again as a national parks advocate in 1939 (*Paradise Lost*, 39–40, 65). I can only warn the reader that he does not appear to be the same as L. Keith Caldwell, the author of *International Environmental Policy* (Durham, NC: Duke University Press, 1996 [1984]), with whom he appears to share two names and a common interest and passion for international conservation.

[34] K. Caldwell, Acting Game Warden to Acting Colonial Secretary, Nairobi, 14 April 1923, C.O. 533/295 Kenya Dispatches, June 1923. The growth of the Tana and Juba Rivers as areas of ivory smuggling goes back to at least 1916. E.g. S. H. Goldfinch to Acting Game Warden, 'Ivory in NFD', 24 January 1917, *KNA* KW/14/7, Ivory Smuggling, 1913–1924.

senior provincial commissioner of the Coast Province, who wrote: 'I would point out that the Game Department has taken little interest and no steps to stop, on the Coast and Tana River, the wholesale slaughter of vast heads [*sic*] of elephants in the past two or three years.'[35] He goes on to enumerate the large numbers of tusks (1,514) exported or stored at the coast since 1920. This gives him an estimate of 757 elephants killed, and he further estimates one-third again that number of tusks smuggled into Somaliland, giving a total of 1,000 elephants per year in the Coast and Tana districts alone. His only recommended solution to this problem is 'granting elephant licences to the best class of Arab', who he believes will have an interest in curbing the illicit slaughter.

In fact, the smuggling of ivory to Italian Somaliland was not a new problem. As early as 1913 Blayney Percival had reported on the difficulties of interdicting the trade conducted by Somali caravans in the Northern Frontier district into Somaliland.[36] The complications raised by the war and the hobbling of the Game Department had brought the situation to a crisis by 1923. After visiting the district, Caldwell reported that the development of trade routes and caravans by Somali merchants 'has caused the native hunting tribes, WaBoni, WaSanya [sic] and others, to kill for gain instead of for meat and the agricultural [Tana] river populations to devote their energies to making money by ivory poaching'.[37] Caldwell then details the source areas and maps the major smuggling routes for ivory in the northern border region. 'Practically all this contraband ivory goes over to Italian Somaliland and is openly sold on the other side of the Juba,'[38] which was the international boundary at that time. Moreover, the impending transfer of the Juba River district to Italian control had led to complicity in the trade by Italian officials anxious to capitalize on the transfer. After criticizing the government's policy on ivory purchase as leading to 'the hut tax being paid in ivory',[39] Caldwell proposes a broad programme for tightening administration, pressuring ivory dealers and runners, appointing district officers with an interest in the suppression of poaching, increasing contacts with the Boni and other hunter-foragers to encourage them to cut out Somali and other illicit buyers, and even appointing official dealers in ivory to curtail the smuggling.[40] In the last analysis, Caldwell asserts: 'There is only one real remedy for the whole question and that is for Italy to cooperate with this country'[41] in controlling the illicit trade in ivory, and with it the growing practice of Africans hunting elephant for profit.

[35] J. McClellan, Sen. Coast Commissioner to Chief Native Commissioner, 25 May 1921, KNA PC/Coast/1/10/127.

[36] Cited in R. B. Woosnam, G. W. to Chief Secretary, Nairobi, 20 March 1913, KNA KW/14/7.

[37] Caldwell to Ag. Col. Sec., 14 April 1923, 1–2, KNA KW/14/7.

[38] Ibid., 4.

[39] Ibid., 6. [40] Ibid., 8–12.

[41] Ibid., 7. Note the echoes of Woosnam's recommendation in 1913: 'The whole question of illicit trade in ivory and rhinocero's [sic] horns would be enormously simplified if an International agreement could be arrived at on the subject and the trade put a stop to by our neighbours.' Woosnam to Chief Secretary, Nairobi, 20 March 1913, KNA KW/14/7.

Caldwell's analysis of the situation, supported by Governor Northcote, was well received in the Colonial Office and would lead to Caldwell being dispatched to Rome the following year to enter into the negotiations for cooperation on controlling ivory smuggling and the poaching it encouraged.[42] At the centre of the 'Ivory Question' was the complex relationship between smuggling and poaching and, behind that, the question of the conflict between preservation and revenue generation. The heart of the matter is the acknowledgement by the colonial government of two things. The first is the recognition that the commodification of ivory and its ease of transit into international trade networks had transformed African hunting practices, even among the most conservative and isolated of hunting communities.[43] The fact that smuggling ivory across the boundary between Kenya and Tanganyika had a similar impact on Waliangulu hunters as the permeable Somali border had upon Boni and Sanye (Waata) hunters was also noted by the Customs Department at this time.[44] But this problem could be handled on an interterritorial basis within the Colonial Office without involving international diplomacy, which brings us to the second aspect of this matter: its internationalization.

Hunting by remote and isolated tribal communities, often unrecognized and unadministered locally, had international implications by the 1920s. The converse would also prove true. Actions taken in the international arena by governments and conservation-minded non-governmental bodies could and would have profound implications for the nature of hunting by Africans and whites in colonial Kenya. In many ways, Keith Caldwell's personal path would make that connection, as his local involvement in the suppression of elephant poaching and ivory trade in Jubaland would translate to international negotiations and agreements that would fundamentally alter the lives of Kenya's hunters.[45]

Captain Ritchie and game control

Captain Archie Ritchie had been recruited from Australia to preside over the transformation of the Game Department from a minuscule body of young sportsmen and a small staff of African subordinates into a disciplined, organized, and to some degree professional government department. Ritchie himself, a bluff, broad-faced man of military bearing, was a soldier and sportsman (Photo 8.1). He would always be referred to by his military title and rank as Captain Ritchie, and would instil a martial tone in the entire department, whose members were recruited for their sporting and

---

[42] E. Northcote, Governor to Duke of Devonshire, Minute Paper 11 June 1923, *C.O.* 533/295. See K. Caldwell to Game Warden, Nairobi, 5 December 1924, on his visit to Rome to arrange for cooperation in ivory control and elephant preservation.

[43] A. B. Sharpe, D.C., Digo District, 'Killing of Game by WaBoni', Kwale, 1 October 1925, and 'The Warungula Elephant Hunters of the Coast Hinterland', KNA DC/Kwale/3/4.

[44] Commissioner of Customs to Ag. Game Warden, 8 May 1923, citing D. C., Vanga District to Commissioner of Customs, 6 May 1923, KNA KW/14/7.

[45] See Chapter 9 in this volume.

soldierly qualities.[46] Although it would become a department with a reputation for corruption, this would never touch the personal integrity of Ritchie himself. In many ways, Ritchie's character would be stamped on the growing department that he attempted to create in his own image.[47]

There are two particular influences wielded by Ritchie that I wish to examine here. First, the general tone of the military spirit – if not military discipline – that Ritchie seems to have embodied was translated into a recruitment policy that privileged the martial arts and virtues such as outdoorsmanship and enthusiasm for adventure at the expense of scientific or economic concerns or values. In sharp contrast to colonial forestry departments, which had more narrowly scientific and economic objectives, the Game Department under Ritchie and his colonial successors would continue to favour officers and gentlemen and would remain somewhat suspicious of scientific and scholarly attainments.[48] This produced a senior staff who relished the aspects of their work that kept them away from their desks and out hunting in the name of conservation and progress.

Secondly, the department under Ritchie would put an increased emphasis on game control. The growing demand from settler and African farmers alike moved the Game Department to serve their interests as agriculturalists, whose chief relationship to game was a hostile and competitive one. As Ritchie put it at the end of his career: 'Game Control is an essential corollary of Game Preservation; for no human community will tolerate in its vicinity the existence – much less subscribe to the protection – of species that are a perpetual source of danger or depredation.'[49] Animals, particularly large herbivores, were a constant threat to crops, while large predators were a threat to livestock and humans. There was a steady demand for the services of Game Department employees to shoot these intruders on white farms and, from the 1930s, in African *shamba* (cultivated fields) as well.[50] A corresponding willingness on the part of the department staff to devote their time to accomplishing these tasks meant that Game Rangers were continually employed in hunting the *shamba* raiders among elephant, buffalo, baboons, bush pig, and other transgressors of the boundaries between the wild and the sown.

There were several ways in which the Game Department under Ritchie sought to answer the pressing demands for the protection of agriculture.

---

[46] Between 1925 and 1929, Ritchie's preferences for staffing the department with 'officers and gentlemen' can be seen in the military ranks attributed to four of the five staff in 1925. Former soldiers seldom made up less than 50 per cent of the department's European staff under Ritchie's administration. See Interview D/2, Ian Parker, 25 August 1987.

[47] A glowing assessment of Ritchie's influence and character can be found in K. Caldwell, draft 'Faunal Survey of Eastern and Central Africa', August 1947 (a) KENYA, 7, KNA KW/1/83.

[48] E. Steinhart, 'Hunters, Poachers and Gamekeepers: Toward a Social History of Hunting in Colonial Kenya', *Journal of African History* 30 (1989): 256. See also Interview D/2, Ian Parker, 25 August 1987.

[49] Introduction to J. A. Hunter, *Hunter* (London: Hamish Hamilton, 1952), xi. For Ritchie's views on the relationship between agricultural progress and game preservation, see *GDAR* for 1925, 18–20.

[50] Kelly, 'In Wildest Africa', 208–23 on settler attitudes to game and 223–38 on African demands for control of *shamba* raiders.

Photo 8.1
Archie Ritchie:
Game Warden

The most important and direct method was the assignment of Game Rangers to kill *shamba* raiders and 'rogues'. This took two forms. Part of the duties of all the senior (white) staff was to shoot animals 'on control' when requested to do so by white farmers or African villagers.[51] This was especially true for large and dangerous animals, especially elephants, which could not be shot without licences except by Europeans in immediate defence of life or property. Full-time 'Game and Vermin Control Officers', whose job it was to kill animals that stood in the way of agricultural progress, were employed by the department from 1929.[52] Early in the history of the colony, game rangers were used in an extermination campaign against zebras that had become a major nuisance to white farmers in the Highlands.[53] Later, attempts to remove rhino from an area designated for African settlement led to a remarkable campaign in which the professional hunter-cum-Game Ranger, J. A. Hunter, killed over 1,000 rhino in 13 months.[54] Moreover, much of the day-to-day work of the assistant wardens and control officers had become the routine killing of *shamba* raiders and carnivores preying on domestic cattle, as can be seen in the reports filed by them annually in the 1930s.[55]

The heavy damage done by elephants was always a prime concern of Kenya's Game Department. Already by the 1920s, elephant control had become such an overriding concern to the regimes in the British colonies that the new departments created to manage game were often referred to simply as 'Elephant Control Departments'. This was certainly true of the nascent department that Keith Caldwell had helped launch in Uganda, which came under the direction of Lt.-Colonel C. R. S. Pitman in 1925. Northern Rhodesia's department charged with game control and preservation was also entitled Elephant Control Department for many years.[56]

Not all of the work on control was as satisfying to the hunting urge among the Game Rangers as shooting elephants and lions. The destructive

---

51 See A. Ritchie, 'Notes on Game Control', 1–5, KNA KW/8/30; and see G. Adamson, *Bwana Game* (London: Collins and Harvill, 1968), 90–140 *passim*, for the control work done by Kenya's most famous Game Ranger and conservationist.

52 *GDAR*, 1929, 1; and A. Fowle, Monthly Reports for May, June, and October 1929, KNA KW/23/143, Mr Andrew Fowle, Monthly Reports; J. T. Oulton, 'Report for May, 1931', 'Report for December, 1931', KNA KW/23/144, Capt. J. T. Oulton, Temporary Game and Vermin Control Officer, Monthly Reports; and Capt. R. Whittet, 'Annual Report for 1935', and 'Annual Report for 1936', KNA KW/23/168, Reports of Asst. Game Warden, Meru.

53 E.g. *GDAR*, 1925, 10; and Kelly, 'In Wildest Africa', 218–19.

54 Hunter was originally hired on contract by the short-staffed department in 1928 to kill lions, but eventually became a full-time employee. On his rhino hunting, see Hunter, *Hunter*, 10, 180ff; and K. Caldwell, draft 'Faunal Survey', 7, KNA KW/1/83. In another example of extreme 'control', the Game Control Officer J. D. Bonham killed 87 elephants on control in Kwale District in 1943. *GDAR*, 1943, and Manuscript report, KNA KW/23/166, Reports and Publications.

55 E.g. Reports by Capt. R. Whittet, Mr C. G. MacArthur, and Capt. J. T. Oulton, Game and Vermin Control Officer, appended to *GDAR*, 1936, 16–21.

56 Lt.-Col. C. R. S. Pitman, *A Game Warden Takes Stock* (London: Nisbet, 1942), 1; and N. Carr, *The White Impala: The Story of A Game Ranger* (London: Collins, 1969), 25–9 and 33–47. On Caldwell's role, see *GDAR*, 1925, 2.

capacity of certain animals deemed vermin (as lions had been briefly in the early period) continued to be a source of pressure for 'control' throughout the colonial era. From the 1920s, baboons, bush pigs, and hyenas were subject to eradication campaigns in which the use of strychnine and other poisons and the setting of traps that would otherwise have been deemed unsporting and illegal were used around settled areas. The attitude toward such work, however, was at best ambivalent. Ritchie himself referred to the arsenic and strychnine used in poisoning herbivores and carnivores, respectively, as 'both loathsome substances'.[57] Partly this was because it not infrequently led to the death of jackals and other carrion eaters that were not labelled as vermin. Principally, however, it was because of the unsportsmanlike nature of the work and the painful, humiliating deaths they inflicted on their prey. Perhaps this, in addition to senior staff shortages, explains why by the 1940s Africans were being trained in techniques of administering poisons to vermin.[58] A curious expression of the ambivalent attitude towards poisoning is that the official and colourful title for those Game Department junior staff employed in this work was the melodramatic one of 'borgias'.

Even before Ritchie's arrival in Kenya, the pressure from settlers for the control of game in the white Highlands had led to a major innovation that would have important implications for hunting. The appointment of the first Honorary Game Wardens took place in 1922, and the rapid expansion in the use of amateur hunters and local sportsmen as unofficial game control officers would follow under Ritchie. From 1925, the year of Ritchie's first full annual report, the number of Honorary Wardens had risen to 31, and by 1935 had reached 74, with a further 31 'Honorary Trout Wardens'.[59] During this same period, the number of paid senior staff of Game Rangers never rose above eight, some of whom were on leave in any given year.[60] In some ways, the institution of the programme of honorary wardens would prove the 'solution' to the problem. By turning the resident hunters into gamekeepers, pressure on the limited staff of the department was reduced and the settler establishment was brought 'inside the tent'.

The list of Honorary Game Wardens reads like the 'Burke's Peerage' of the settler elite. Among the earliest appointees was Sir Northrup MacMillan, the venerable host of Theodore Roosevelt in 1909. Later appointments included the professional hunter W. H. Hoey, the early safari company organizers Alan and Henry Tarleton, and the much admired Denys Finch Hatton. The honorary wardens had high visibility, enormous prestige, and, according to Captain Ritchie, extensive powers, 'similar to my own'.[61] They were empowered to enforce the game laws

[57] A. Ritchie, 'Notes on Game Control', 5, KNA KW/8/30.

[58] T. Oulton, 'Game and Vermin Control Report', 1941, KNA KW/23/165.

[59] See *GDAR*, 1925–1932/34 under 'Honorary Game Wardens' for the official figures.

[60] Ibid.

[61] *GDAR*, 1926, 4–5. It might be noted that the first and I believe only Asian ever admitted to the ranks of the Honorary Game Wardens under Ritchie's tenure was J. Sorabjee, Esq. of Nairobi, in 1936. *GDAR*, 1936, 4. No Africans were ever enrolled as Honorary Game Wardens.

and they were 'licensed to kill' on control. Thus much of the work of controlling *shamba* raiders, including elephant, would fall to the Honorary Game Wardens. They now could not only shoot animals on their own property, but could also serve as surrogates for the professional game-keepers in shooting animals that had infringed on settled areas, farms, and properties belonging to others. In addition, an annual allocation of free ammunition to settlers for the protection of their fields and herds was also made by the department to supplement its own work in 'disciplining' the animals.[62]

By the 1930s, control had become the chief work of the Game Depart-ment, even if accomplished mainly by the auxiliary Honorary Game Wardens. The evidence of the numbers of wardens engaged in 'hunting on control' can be underscored by a cursory examination of the *Game Depart-ment Annual Reports* for this period, which discuss 'Game and Vermin Control' work in approximately five times the number of pages as it takes to cover 'Game Preservation'.[63] Ritchie himself was moved to defend the willingness of one of his gamekeepers to kill in the following terms: 'It is not bloodlust that has made him volunteer when dangerous game has had to be killed, for he never enjoyed the taking of life; it is the thrill of the hunt and the danger of it that he revels in, and the practice of skill that alone maintains the thin line which separates superman from suicide.'[64]

That the interests of the professional and auxiliary staff lay in hunting, rather than preserving, is further indicated by the difficulties that the Chief Game Warden had in getting the staff to do other aspects of their jobs. The reluctance of his staff to do the routine clerical work of issuing licences and filing reports is hardly surprising. But, as late as 1951, Ritchie's successor, William Hale, had to order all the department staff to assist forest officers in fighting fires 'even to the exclusion of control work'. After all, he commented, 'I do not want your work to be entirely control and shooting.'[65]

That the efforts of Game Wardens, honorary wardens, and contract killers to control game were insufficient to cure the problem can be seen from two continuing sources of complaint. First, among white farmers, there continued to be a considerable body of opinion in favour of extermination of all wildlife in settled areas. This was sometimes urged under the pretext of the health risks that it was asserted wild animals posed to domestic ones,[66] sometimes because of the threat to life from predators and to

---

[62] On the idea of shooting animals as a method of instilling 'discipline' in the herds, especially of elephant, see W. Hale, Chief Game Warden to Director, Coconut Research Institute, 30 October 1953, KNA KW/15/16; and A. Ritchie, 'Introduction' to Hunter, *Hunter*, xii, where he argues that animals are controlled by driving them away or by 'instilling discipline – usually by oft-reiterated and painful lessons! – so that animals will respect man his husbandry, and thereby earn a provisional tolerance'.

[63] E.g. *GDAR*, 1929, 8–13, 14–15.

[64] Ritchie, 'Introduction' to Hunter, *Hunter*, xiii.

[65] W. Hale, Game Warden to All Officers of the Game Department, 15 December 1951, KNA KW/15/16.

[66] The literature on the connections between wild animal vectors and various diseases is large and would form an important focus of the Game Department's scientific work. For

property from herbivores. Always extermination of game was proposed, with the cloak of advancing 'progress' and 'civilisation' to disguise naked self-interest. Keith Caldwell wrote in 1952, 30 years after the institution of honorary wardens and his joining the department: 'Farm owners are uncompromisingly against these animals. They feel that their presence constitutes a menace both to life and property and wish them either driven away or destroyed.'[67]

In response to complaints contained in a letter from a settler in Naro Moru to the northwest of Mount Kenya, Ritchie himself put it even more starkly:

> To all intents and purposes the plains game is completely disappeared from the Naro Moru–Nanyuki area and from most of Laikipia. It has in fact gone very largely from practically the whole of the European settled area of the Colony. The whole truth of the matter is that the vast majority of settlers are not prepared to have any quantity of game on their farms.... The suggestion that vast hoards [*sic*] of Government employees, or as you put it government slaughterers, have shot off the game has no basis in truth as far as the settled areas are concerned. Thousands of game were shot in the Nanyuki district during the war since there was a profit motive, but they were merely carrying out what the Nanyuki Farmers' Association had been trying to organise for many years before the war.[68]

The second source of complaint was African farmers, who shared many of the same concerns and fears as their white counterparts. Moreover, they were far less prepared for meeting the depredations of elephants and buffalo, pigs, and baboons than were the well-armed and experienced hunters so common among the settlers. Instead, the ability of African farmers to hunt continued to be curtailed by the spread of colonial administrative effectiveness throughout the colonial era, with only brief and temporary lessening of the administrative presence during wartime and emergency. Some voices were raised in defence of African rights to hunt as part of the process of civilization. In neighbouring Tanganyika, the Principal Medical Officer, Dr J. B. Davey, would write in 1922:

> Before the incursion of the European powers, the native carried on a ceaseless struggle against his rivals (not least of which was the large game) in the race for the survival of the fittest. The advent of the white mans [*sic*] rule abolished warfare between the various native tribes. This benefit should not be neutralised by paralysing or severely handicapping him in

---

[66] (contd) instance, see KNA KW/15/13 Game Diseases, 1933–4; KW/15/14 Rinderpest and Game, 1917–35; KW/15/17 Rinderpest Campaign, 1938; KW/8/34 International Rinderpest Conference, Nairobi, October–November 1948. On tsetse in particular, Agriculture Department Report, 'Game as Spreaders of Disease', 1929, KNA KW/6/95; E. B. Worthington, 'Science in Africa', and E. A. Lewis, 'The Tsetse Fly', KNA KW/24/47, Preservation of Game, Scientific Research (1935–47); and J. J. McKelvey, *Man Against Tsetse* (Ithaca, NY: Cornell University Press, 1973).

[67] K. Caldwell to Lt. Col. C. L. Boyle, Secretary, The Fauna Preservation Society, London, 31 January 1952, KNA KW/15/16, Administration of Game Laws, Game, and Vermin Control.

[68] A. Ritchie to Brig. A.G. Arbothnot, 27 February 1948, KNA KW/1/73.

his struggle against the rest of the animal creation. The driving back of the larger wild animals is a natural and essential process in the development of any country and should be allowed to proceed. Efforts to thwart this natural process can only impede development.[69]

Despite such pleas, even the ability to act in immediate defence of property, always recognized as a right of landowners, was denied to Kenya's African farmers. In the case of elephants, in particular, Africans were forbidden to do more than chase them from their *shambas* using the 'weapons of the weak', sticks, stones, and fire. Instead of being allowed to kill elephants in defence of their homes and fields, African farmers were encourage to call in the administration, which would dispatch a Game Ranger or Scout to hunt down the marauder after the fact. The ineffectiveness of this approach gave rise from early in the century to the question of the payment of compensation for damages to those who had been significantly and materially harmed by the failure to control wild animals.[70] This would be a source of controversy for decades,[71] and a serious source of corruption when a compensation policy was instituted after independence.

Taken together, the demands of white and black farmers alike to be protected from the depredations and competition of other species would form a powerful incentive to transform Kenya's gamekeepers from protectors of animals to controllers, managers, and ultimately killers of large numbers of wild animals.[72]

Beyond control

Although control became the heart of Game Department work in the Ritchie era, it was certainly not the only function the department administered. Beyond questions of control, the department's major functions stemmed from administering the game laws. This included licensing

[69] J. B. Davey, P. M. O., 'Memorandum on Game Preservation', 16 October 1922, PRO CO/691/57.

[70] The earliest reference to the payment of compensation I have found is contained in F. Jackson, Acting Governor to Secretary of State, Colonies, 29 June 1909, PRO Cd. 5136 (1910) Africa: Further Correspondence, in which Jackson recommends the payment of compensation to Africans and Arabs (Swahili) who have suffered 'considerable damage ... done by elephants'.

[71] M. Cowie, Warden, National Parks of Kenya to Member for Agriculture, Nairobi, 8 October 1952, KNA KW/15/16: 'I wish to advise very strongly against granting any form of direct compensation for damage by wild game.'

[72] Sample figures for one control officer for one month in 1931 can be found in T. Oulton, Report for May 1931, as follows: '8 bushbuck, 6 warthogs, 5 duiker, 4 zebra, 1 reedbuck (by mistake as they do no harm), 1 waterbuck, 1 baboon', KNA KW/23/144. An approximate annual tally for 1954 of game animals shot on control can be found in draft GDAR, 1953–4, KNA KW/23/151. It consists of: 'Elephant...223, Buffalo...56, Rhino...45, Hippo...1, Lion...10, Leopard...1, Zebra...8, Hartebeest...2, Other Antelope...261, Serval Cat...1'. This list does not include vermin 'such as baboons, hyenas, bush pig, wart hog [sic]'. However, in one extermination operation 'During this period about 371 wart hogs were killed.'

hunters and scientific specimen seekers; advising the government on revisions to the game laws and the creation of schedules of protected animals, vermin etc.;[73] and the collection of revenues from hunting, firearms, and export licences and from the sale of confiscated trophies, especially ivory seized in the course of enforcing the laws.[74] In 1926, the department named its first Assistant Warden in charge of trout fisheries, and after 1930, the work of a Fish Officer became a permanent feature of the department's responsibilities.[75] In addition to this, some amount of scientific work on animal ecology and disease was also a regular feature of the department's work and is reflected in the department's correspondence and the annual reports. In the early years, the reports often contained only anecdotal information on such things as 'zoological events of interest' that were of limited scientific value.[76] More significant in terms of science was the work done by the department's staff in assisting visiting scientific expeditions with the collection of specimens and live animals for zoos around the world. By the 1930s, the department was also assisting film-makers and photographers as well as requiring licences for scientific collecting and photographic safaris. The department also prepared exhibits of fauna for occasional imperial exhibitions such as those at Wembley in 1924 and Johannesburg in 1936.[77]

Most important in terms of the time and effort expended by the wardens, rangers, and scouts was the enforcement of the game laws, which meant the work of preventing and punishing poaching and other violations of the regulations pertaining to game preservation.[78] Aspects of this last function will be examined in the next section.

Chief among the less formal functions of the Game Warden was the popularization of Kenya as a destination for sportsmen and tourists, and then promotion of hunting internationally. This was often undertaken in the form of letters or columns in the local press, and articles written by

---

[73] In the pioneer period, licensing was often handled by district or provincial administrators (see, S. L. Hinde, PC, Coast to Ag. Chief Game Warden, 19 June 1908, KNA PC/Coast/1/1/138). Only later would the Game Department take responsibility for this central operation of the system of hunting and game regulations. Under Ritchie, returns of the numbers and types of hunting and other licences issued are reported each year under 'Revenue' in the *GDARs*.

[74] Revenue and expenditure are reported annually in the *Game Department Annual Reports*, with revenue always well in excess of expenditure. E.g. *GDAR*, 1928 which gives figures for the years 1922–8. Also K. Caldwell to Ag. Colonial Secretary, 23 January 1929 which separates revenues from ivory and licences for 1923–8; and see also *GDAR*, 1936.

[75] See *GDAR*, 1926 and 1930.

[76] *GDAR*, 1926. See reports and correspondence in KNA KW/24/40, 41, 42, 46, and 47.

[77] See N. Rothfels, 'Catching Animals', in *Animals and Human Histories*, ed. M. Henninger-Voss (Rochester, NY: Rochester University Press, 2002), 182–228; and materials in KNA KW/25/2 British Empire Exhibition, 1924; KW/25/5 Empire Exhibition – Johannesburg, 1936; and KW/25/6 Exhibitions – General.

[78] A large section of virtually every *GDAR* from 1925 to 1950 is devoted to the department's anti-poaching efforts. For the period after 1945, see Chapter 10 of this volume.

Captain Ritchie for sportsmen's magazines such as *The Field*.[79] Other occasional activities included attending international conferences on game conservation or scientific gatherings on game management or disease, etc., as well as periodic meetings with the game wardens of the other British colonies on coordination of policy between Kenya and its neighbours.[80] The Game Warden would also advise the government on proposed game legislation and changes in the different schedules that indicated how many of what types of game might be shot on the different licences.[81]

Behind all of these functions stood the ideological commitment to game preservation. However, this was a commitment so broad and vague in its application, even justifying, as we have seen, the killing of large numbers of animals 'on control', as to leave open to a wide range of interpretation just which laws required strict enforcement and which could be honoured in the breach.

The Lone Ranger and *Tonto*

The administration of the game laws constituted the enforcement functions of the Game Department. By the mid-1930s, the work of enforcement fell to a solid core of six Game Wardens of various ranks who made up the working senior staff of the department. They were supported by two clerical staff, both of Goan extraction, and a long list of between 80 and 90 Honorary Game Wardens, and an indeterminate number of African junior officers called Scouts, who worked directly under the supervision of the European senior staff. The African staff tended to be recruited from the pastoral or 'warlike' tribes, such as the Maasai, Samburu, and Kalenjin, and were selected for their military virtues of bravery and discipline, rather than for their skills as hunters or trackers. Indeed, it was their military skills that counted most in the pursuit of poachers in the field.[82]

In their role as law enforcement agents, the game wardens and scouts operating in the field under the direction of the Warden engaged in the pursuit and prosecution of poachers. This was the least popular aspect of game work, involving as it did the pursuit of individuals who shared many of the attributes, skills, and values of the hunters-turned-gamekeepers themselves. The arrest and punishment of poachers, smugglers, and law-

---

[79] E.g. A. Ritchie, 'Game in East Africa', Special East Africa Supplement of *The Times* (London), KNA KW/1/69 Miscellaneous Correspondence, June 1926–April 1928.

[80] E.g. 'Memorandum', First African Game Conference, 21–25 January 1926; 'Proceedings', Second Annual Game Conference, 11–15 January 1927, KNA KW/8/33; 'Report of Proceedings of a Conference of Game Wardens', 10 February 1939, KNA KW/8/31 Preservation of Game, Conferences and Conventions (1936–9); and various press clippings and correspondence in KNA KW/8/30, 32 and 33.

[81] Two frequent functions of game keeping – the declaration of legal closed seasons during which certain animals could not be shot, and the administration of hunting blocks, by means of which shooting areas could be temporarily closed to prevent localized over-shooting – seem not to have been functions of the Kenya Game Department until the mid-1950s. Closed seasons were suggested as early as the draft *GDAR*, 1909–10, and a closed season on birds was proclaimed in 1938. Draft *GDAR*, KNA KW/23/170; 'Proclamation 32', 1938, KNA KW/18/23 Birds, Closed Seasons.

breakers was generally viewed as a necessary, but unpleasant, aspect of the Game Department's mandate by the senior staff who patrolled the vast territories of the Colony in search of malefactors. The fact that the police aspect of the job was thought to be at the heart of conservation efforts might ease the consciences of the keepers. However, most often they appear to have resented the work of disciplining and punishing other hunters, and they were just as often resented for it.[83] The result was a broad pattern of inconsistent enforcement and contradictory policies and practices. Indeed, in the pursuit and punishment of poachers, a double standard existed that reserved for African hunters the heavy weight of the laws against poaching, while at the same time treating most European violators merely as overzealous sportsmen who fell afoul of legal technicalities.

An almost conspiratorial attitude pervades the relationship between the white gamekeepers and white poachers. In the early period when white hunters, visiting and resident, were almost invariably gentlemen and sportsmen, an attitude of status deference seems to have prevailed. Overshooting the limit on birds by a visitor might provoke nothing more than a reprimand if the shooter was 'a well-known sportsman' who seemed simply to have been overwhelmed by enthusiasm at the numbers of birds he might bag.[84] And, if the shooter was a settler, a wide range of political pressures, added to the strong policy favouring settlement, might induce the gamekeepers to turn a blind eye.

Sometimes, a settler hunter might directly request a blind eye. W. B. Aggett informed the department of his intention to hunt hogs and possibly bongo using hunting dogs, and to 'lay a bit of poison up there. So I expect you will back me up if there is any trouble about it.'[85] Ritchie's reply shows him to have entered into the spirit of conspiracy. After stating that there was no objection to using dogs to hunt hogs, 'as Hogs are not game animals', he politely suggested to Aggett, 'but please don't hunt Bongo with dogs'. Ritchie then goes on to ask, 'If you get an opportunity to capture some young hogs alive, do get me one.' Most telling of the conspiratorial spirit between sportsmen, Ritchie closes his note: 'Do be careful how you put the poison down, for neither of us has any right to use it unfortunately, and I couldn't help you much if trouble arose. Good luck.'[86]

In another incident, two European hunters, accompanied by a professional hunter, shot one elephant too many and then acquired a licence after the fact. On conviction, the tusks of the second elephant were confiscated by government and later sold to the American Museum of Natural History. No other punishment except the opprobrium of other sportsmen

---

[82] *GDAR*, 1935, 1936, and 1937 on 'Staff'.

[83] A. L. MacDonald to Editor, *East African Standard*, 5 July 1937, KNA KW/27/2.

[84] Kelly, 'In Wildest Africa', 208–33, on the influence of settlement on the Game Department.

[85] W. A. Aggett to A. Ritchie, Game Warden, 18 October 1931, KNA KW/1/15. Giant forest hog and the shy and reclusive bongo (second in size among Kenya's antelope after the eland) inhabit the forests on the upper reaches of the Aberdares and Mount Kenya.

[86] A. Ritchie to W. A. Aggett, 20 October 1931, KNA KW/1/15.

was imposed.[87] Even government officials charged with enforcing the laws might also find their poaching activities treated as peccadilloes. In 1941, 'a very experienced hunter', G. Hopkins, the District Commissioner in Machakos, took the Game Licence book on safari with him and, when he was sure he could bag an elephant, issued himself a game licence. Despite the fact that this highly irregular procedure was 'open to grave suspicion', no prosecution for poaching or fraud was suggested.[88]

The attitude of tolerance to hunting violations by gentlemen, be they farmers, visiting sportsmen, or civil servants did not extend to those who were not deemed sportsmen. Boers were clearly excluded, as were some working-class whites who might be viewed as 'meat butchers' when they hunted. Most importantly, virtually all Africans were excluded from the proper hunting set and leisure class. In describing African elephant hunters, the Game Warden wrote:

> The very speedy destruction of so many elephants carrying really large ivory … [causes] extreme dismay. Could one but believe that even one pair [of tusks] … were to remain as honoured trophies, it would alleviate the bitterness. [But they are all cut up for sale] … to provide a livelihood for those too idle to work.[89]

The irony of admiring the leisured classes who hunted for sport and trophies while at the same time condemning those as lazy who hunted for a livelihood seems to have been lost on the author and the audience. It seems quite clear that strongly class-biased attitudes towards poaching were among those 'European views on game and its uses, [which were] … superimposed on the existing pattern' of African attitudes along with European rule.[90]

Where tolerance and a blind eye prevailed as the semi-official attitude of the Game Department at all levels, the attitudes to African poaching – that is, to all African hunting without licence or 'proper' weapons – were a good deal more inconsistent and contradictory.[91] For the most part, experienced Game Wardens tended to turn a blind eye to what they considered minor infractions. Only the killing of large animals, especially the big trophy-bearing animals (elephant, rhinoceros, hippopotamus, leopard, and some of the larger antelopes) would arouse the ire of the wardens.[92] Special exemptions were made for hunting by so-called 'flesh-

---

[87] The correspondence and a clipping from the *East African Standard*, 16 December 1938, are found in KNA KW 18/19, Breaches of the Game Ordinance 1937–9. This file on 'Breaches' contains material on European violations, while African incidents are found in files on 'Poaching'.

[88] District Commissioner of Police to Game Warden, n.d., KNA KW/18/18.

[89] Appendix B, 'Situation in Kenya', Proceedings of the Second Annual Game Conference, 11–15 January 1927, KNA KW/8/33.

[90] Kelly, 'In Wildest Africa', 70–71.

[91] See Lieut. R. L. Taverner, 'Game Report, Southern Game Reserve', January–May 1925, 6; 'Extract from ADC, Kapini Annual Report, 1925', demonstrating administrative tolerance of small-game hunting; and K. Caldwell, Ag. Game Warden to Asst. Colonial Sec., Nairobi, 15 September 1926, who argues for legislation to outlaw 'killing for profit', KNA KW/23/174.

[92] See Provincial Commissioner, Central Province to Colonial Sec., Nairobi, 9 January 1937, and A. L. MacDonald to Editor, *East African Standard*, 5 July 1937, KNA KW/27/2.

eating tribes', such as the Waliangulu, and in times of drought and famine the rules were frequently relaxed, if not lifted altogether, in the interests of humanity.[93] By and large, those who tolerated the poaching of small game for the pot viewed Africans with both tolerance and an understanding that hunting was an element of their culture deserving of respect. Perhaps there was even a bit of recognition of similarities in the values held by African and European hunters, akin to the respect offered to courageous gun bearers and faithful trackers. Some individual rangers might even earn the respect of the African hunters for their willingness to be lenient in the face of continued African hunting for the pot.[94]

At the other extreme, there were those wardens who seemed to believe that any African hunting was not just a violation of law to be punished to the fullest extent, but also a violation of the natural order. They seem to have viewed themselves as guardians of public order, which allowed them to bring down the wrath of the law on those they believed violated the natural order of society. One such anti-poaching puritan was George Adamson, who through his wife's work with lions became Kenya's best-known gamekeeper of the colonial era.[95]

But, if George Adamson was a puritan, it was only in matters of game preservation. When he applied to the department on the advice of his friend, the Control Officer T. Oulton, Adamson appears to have been saved from a life of frustration and dissolution.[96] His fecklessness to that point made his conversion to a Game Ranger a turning-point in his life. As he put it: 'I found my vocation as a Game Warden.'[97] It not only provided the respectability and regular income that had been missing, but led to his marriage to Joy, an artist and scion of a wealthy Austrian family, whose own work in conservation would make the two of them internationally famous. There is no need to go into the story of the rescue, rehabilitation, and return to a life in the wild of the lioness Elsa. The true story of *Born Free* rivals the fictional account of Bambi in the romantic nature literature of the twentieth century.[98] In 1938, however, when Adamson joined the department, fame and fortune were beyond the visible horizon for the young Irishman and failed entrepreneur.

[93] A. Ritchie to Hobley, Confidential, 19 June 1936, KNA KW/8/31.

[94] See A. Ritchie to Colonial Sec., Nairobi, 16 November 1936; F. H. Clarke, Ag. Game Warden to Colonial Sec., Nairobi, 26 February 1937, KNA KW/27/2; draft *GDAR*, 1930, 11–18, KNA KW/23/145; and Henry G. Laurie, Sec., SPFE to Undersecretary of State, Colonial Office, 26 August 1938, KNA KW/27/2 for the contrasting views of the Game Department and the international conservationists of the SPFE on the question of native poaching of non-trophy animals.

[95] Joy Adamson née Gessner was the daughter of a prominent and aristocratic Austrian family and in 1942, when she met George, she was already married to Peter Bally, a botanist and member of the wealthy Swiss family. See George Adamson, *My Pride and Joy: An Autobiography* (London: Collins and Harvill, 1986), 64–70. Also Adamson, *Bwana Game*. Both autobiographies are illuminating as to George's attitudes and values regarding wildlife and poachers, and together are a major source of my evaluations of his work.

[96] Adamson, *Bwana Game*, 1–72.

[97] Ibid., 79.

[98] Joy Adamson, *Born Free: A Lioness of Two Worlds* (New York: Pantheon Books, 1960), is much less revealing of George's attitudes than his own writings.

It is hard to tell if it was the simple stability of employment that saved George Adamson or the fact that he found in game preservation something of a crusading cause, a struggle of good against evil. The tone of much of his correspondence from his early posts in the Meru and Northern Frontier District (NFD) outpost hints of his almost obsessive commitment to hunt down and punish poachers, especially Kamba and others who took large game. This shows up in his oft-expressed desire to be in the field in pursuit of the poachers whom he sees as '*shenzies*' (savages).[99] In fact, his temperament seemed to fit well with the life of relative isolation and periodic excitement of anti-poaching work. Inasmuch as this work consisted of patrolling and pursuing wrongdoers, alone or with African Game Scouts as his sole companions, he seemed to be the very image of 'The Lone Ranger'. He directly expressed the view that this was the tried and proven method by which poachers could and should be attacked. He advocated the continuance of the Game Department's traditional anti-poaching methods when these were challenged by more systematic practices of anti-poaching devised and deployed by National Park personnel in the 1950s.[100] Whether this was because the life of a 'lone ranger' suited his temperament or because he could conceive of no more effective weapon against poaching is perhaps unknowable. But his commitment to a singular and personal policy of direct action against poachers is dramatically underlined both by his own methods of pursuit during his life and by the manner of his death in a shoot-out with poachers (called bandits by the press) in August 1989, at the age of 83.[101]

Where others would almost certainly turn a blind eye to minor infractions, Adamson was relentless in his pursuit and prosecution of wrongdoers. Moreover, he was also stern in his demand for the imposition of maximum punishments for even the most trivial of offences. While serving in Meru, he would regularly seek imprisonment for violations of the game laws that was out of proportion to the damage done or the kinds of penalties imposed on Europeans committing even more serious offences. One such instance of imprisonment resulting from Adamson's zealousness came to my attention during my interviews. In this case, a Tharaka hunter was arrested, tried, and imprisoned in the Meru lockup for possession of contraband. The contraband in question, the poacher asserted, was a single squirrel skin and some hunting paraphernalia. As he put it to me:

> Even before [the Emergency] there were restrictions, on killing animals....
> If you were caught you had to be jailed.
> [*Question: Were you ever caught?*] Yes, I was one time jailed in Meru town ...
> [for] one year.... I killed an *nduru* (squirrel).... Yes, one year for an *nduru*! I was put in *tonto*.[102]

[99] G. Adamson to Game Warden, 3 September 1950, KNA KW/23/148.

[100] Ibid.

[101] Greg Neale, 'Caught in the Crossfire', *The Daily Telegraph* (London), 22 August 1989. See obituaries also in *The Times* (London), *The Guardian* (Manchester), *The Independent* (London), 22 August 1989. See also *Sunday Times* (London) 27 August 1989, p. A9.

[102] Interview C/1, Kiriamagwa, 6 September 1987 at Nkondi market, Tharaka, Meru District.

My next question elicited the information that '*tonto*' was the Meru name for the town jail.

The poacher and his son, who sat in on the interview, explained to me that this incident took place shortly after the Mau Mau emergency, probably in 1957. I suspect that the general atmosphere of violent crisis that prevailed in Meru and the neighbouring Kikuyu and Embu districts at that time may have conditioned the harshness of punishment. I then asked how he had been caught. 'I was caught coming home from my shamba with bow and arrows having killed and skinned the animal; I only had the meat.... I was caught because when they saw me with the bow and arrows they thought it was for killing elephant.' In answer to my question if it was game people (*wagaimu*) who had caught him, the old poacher replied: 'a European game warden named "Ka'ngedwa"'. The nickname indicates that the warden in question had a beard and the records show it would have been George Adamson in charge of Meru district and based in Isiolo at the time.[103]

Technically, of course, it would be the DC Meru who heard the case and pronounced sentence. But there can be little doubt that it was the initiation of the prosecution by the resident Game Ranger, ever vigilant for violations of the game laws, whose authority it was to ask for a heavy jail sentence for this infraction, which would put this poacher in *tonto*. Taken together, Adamson's intensity of feeling both in the pursuit of poachers and in the severity of punishment meted out to them makes him an exemplar of the old-fashioned Game Ranger in pursuit of these violators of nature and nature's laws as he understood them.

Well before the 1950s, Adamson's 'shoot from the hip' methods of anti-poaching were already being condemned as outmoded and ineffective. But so was the larger effort at game preservation becoming a dinosaur among the new breed of gamekeepers advocating the permanent set-aside of nature preserves as national parks. They, like Captain Ritchie, believed in the inevitability of the progress of civilization and the resultant and equally inevitable conflict with wild animals. This new faith in the prospect for saving wildlife in untrammelled nature, and the commitment to preservation of habitats it engendered, predestined Ritchie's conservation efforts and policies to failure. 'Ritchie believed the Game Department's most important duty was to prevent conflict between humans and animals.'[104] Hence the heavy emphasis on control works. But, even more significantly,

> Ritchie failed to address meaningfully the problem of preserving fauna in a society committed to European settlement and rapid economic development. This is not to suggest, however, that Ritchie was inefficient or derelict in the performance of his duties; on the contrary, he was a farsighted official who repeatedly argued for the establishment of a national park system as the only sure way of preserving Kenya's wild animals.[105]

[103] Ibid.
[104] Ofcansky, 'A History of Game Preservation', 36, and his *Paradise Lost*, 22–6.
[105] Ofcansky, 'A History of Game Preservation', 42.

But it would not be for Captain Ritchie to lead the campaign for the creation of national parks as preserves and sanctuaries for Kenya's wildlife from hunters of all sorts. That work would fall to a new generation and a new breed of keepers of the game: wildlife preservationists intent on the creation of total sanctuaries for wildlife and hence distinct in many ways from the game conservationists of Captain Ritchie's generation.

Nine

◆◆◆◆◆◆◆◆◆◆◆◆◆◆◆◆◆◆◆◆◆◆◆◆◆◆◆

International Preservationists
& the National Park Idea

1925–45

In the two decades from the mid-1920s to the end of the Second World War, the modern international conservation movement took form. At the core of this political movement for the preservation of the world's 'natural' environments was the idea of national parks. Superficially at least, this was an idea that was nurtured in the metropole, especially in the capitals of the Anglo-American world, and that spread along the sinews of empire to the farthest corners of the globe.

On closer inspection, however, we can discern a dialectical process of give and take between centre and periphery, between the ruling classes and dominant ideas of imperial Britain and the local, colonial representatives of that order. In Kenya, at least, an internal, colonial movement for the conservation of nature, especially of wildlife, would develop in parallel and in contact with the international, imperial movement for the preservation of nature. They would share two presumptions. The first is that the best guardians of nature were the imperial and colonial ruling classes, the great aristocratic hunters of the previous generation, now transformed and reincarnated as champions of game preservation. The second is that the best instrument for preservation lay in the creation of nature and wildlife sanctuaries modelled on the aristocratic hunting parks of eighteenth-century Britain and their ideological progeny, the new national parks, such as Yellowstone Park, in the United States.[1] In this

---

[1] For background on the emergence of imperial and international conservationism in the 1920s and 1930s, see M. Nicholson, *The Environmental Revolution* (New York: McGraw-Hill, 1970) and his *The New Environmental Age* (Cambridge: Cambridge University Press, 1987); L. K. Caldwell, *International Environmental Policy*, 3d ed. (Durham, NC: Duke University Press, 1996 [1984]); R. Nash, *Wilderness and the American Mind*, 3d ed. (New Haven: Yale University Press, 1982), esp. 342–78; and R. Neumann, *Imposing Wilderness* (Berkeley: University of California Press, 1998), 122–56, and his 'Dukes, Earls and Ersatz Edens: Aristocratic Nature Preservationists in Colonial Africa', *Environment and Planning. D, Society and Space* 14, 1 (1996), 79–98. See T. Ofcansky, 'A History of Game Preservation in British East Africa, 1895–1963', unpublished Ph.D. dissertation, University of West Virginia,

chapter we shall examine the parallel development of both the international and the local Kenyan national park movement to understand the crises this development would provoke for Kenya's African hunters.

Kenya and international conservation

The platform from which the international preservation efforts of the interwar years would be launched was the perennial problem of ivory smuggling from Kenya to Italian territory in East Africa. It remained a vexing problem even after the signing of a formal treaty to regulate the boundary between the two colonial territories in July 1924.[2] Captain Keith Caldwell, who had been involved in these negotiations, remained involved in the international negotiations to secure the enforcement of the agreements. He would visit Djibouti in early 1924 to examine export figures, and Rome in December 1924 to negotiate a bilateral arrangement for ivory control and elephant preservation.[3] He was central to the negotiation of a 'Note Verbale' signed by Italy in January 1926.[4] As a result, Caldwell emerged as a key figure connecting the international conservation lobby with the Kenyan game-keeping establishment.

By the time Britain signed the Note Verbale in July 1926, Governor Edward Grigg was already complaining to the Secretary of State for the Colonies of the inadequacy of Italian cooperation to control the illegal traffic.[5] The report of Captain Erskine of the Boundary Commission, described by Caldwell as 'probably the greatest authority on … the ivory trade',[6] denied that 'an enormous quantity of ivory' entered Jubaland since its cession to Italy one year before. Nonetheless, Erskine recognized that contraband passing through Somaliland ports was still considerable.[7] In April 1927, Captain Ritchie would file a memorandum on poaching 'with special reference to the Italian boundary of Kenya', in which he indicated that the still unsatisfactory situation obtaining between the two colonial powers was a result of the free purchase of ivory in Italian territory. He argued that the international situation was thwarting Kenya's efforts to control the destruction of elephant in its northern districts that had been noted by Captain Erskine on an inspection tour earlier that year. As late as April 1929, Ritchie was still complaining of the lack of good faith on the

---

[1] (contd) 1981, 164–218, for a particularly triumphalist view of the 'National Park Solution'. Contrast the more sober and mature view in his *Paradise Lost: A History of Game Preservation in East Africa* (Morgantown: West Virginia University Press, 2002), 65–92.

[2] 'Treaty between the United Kingdom and Italy', 15 July 1925. KNA KW/14/3. See also K. Caldwell, Ag. G. W. to Ag. Col. Sec., 14 April 1923, and Minute Paper, Preservation of Elephants, Ivory Traffic, 11 June 1923, in PRO C.O. 533/295, Kenya Despatches, for the background to the negotiations.

[3] K. Caldwell to Game Warden, 4 June and 5 December 1924. KNA KW/14/3.

[4] Note Verbale, 9 January 1926. KNA KW/14/3.

[5] E. Grigg, Gov. to L. S. Amery, Sec. of State for Colonies, 26 July 1926. KNA KW/14/3.

[6] Caldwell to Ag. Colonial Secretary, 17 September 1926. KNA KW/14/3.

[7] Capt. E. Erskine, Political Officer, Jubaland Boundary Commission, 'Memo on Ivory Trade in Italian Somaliland', 24 July 1926. KNA KW/14/3.

part of the Italians in controlling the smuggling of ivory through Italian territory.[8]

In all these dealings, Caldwell's central role would bring him to the attention of the men who mattered in the British conservation lobby. In the wake of his December 1922 letter of introduction sent to the Society for the Preservation of the Fauna of the Empire (SPFE), Caldwell wrote an essay for their journal on Kenya game conservation.[9] In it, he not only defended the Kenya Game Department as a worthwhile investment of funds, but he also struck a note that resonated with the aristocratic leadership of the Society. First, he blamed the native hunters for the depletion of Kenya's stock of elephant and rhino, and then for good measure threw in a dig at Kenya's Afrikaner hunters: 'Another problem', he reported, 'is the Dutchman.'[10]

However, it was Caldwell's recommendation for the creation of game reserves as 'nature sanctuaries, not shooting preserves',[11] that would be a harbinger of the direction of things to come. Although there were still differences on the status of hunting in the growing movement in the metropolis for the creation of national parks, Caldwell's evocation of the notion of sanctuaries was in keeping with the thrust of the conservation movement in England as it was developing in the 1920s.[12] British conservationists had come to see the creation of national parks as the key to game preservation in the empire, especially in Africa. But how was the creation of national parks to be accomplished on a continental stage?

Here again it would be Caldwell's experience, rooted in Kenyan realities, which would make him key. In 1926, Caldwell gave a lecture in Nairobi that was reproduced by the *Society for the Preservation of the Fauna of the Empire Journal*, in which he advocated an international agreement to stop ivory from 'bleeding' through Italian territory.[13] The following year, the *Journal* also reproduced extracts from Ritchie's 1927 memorandum on 'Illegal Killing of Elephants', urging some form of international agreement or cooperation on ivory trafficking, which was recognized as being the focus of Caldwell's labours going back to 1923.[14] Caldwell had established himself on the pages of the leading international outlet for conservation advocacy as a champion of an international agreement as the means to accomplish the preservation of wildlife. No less a figure than Leopold Amery, Secretary of State for the Colonies, would acknowledge that

---

[8] 'Memorandum, Illegal Killing of Elephants and Rhinoceros', 2 April 1927; Erskine to Game Warden, 2 January 1927. KNA KW/14/3; Ritchie to Ag. Col. Sec., 19 April 1929. KNA KW/14/4.

[9] L. K. Caldwell, 'Game Preservation: Its Aims and Objects', *Society for the Preservation of the Fauna of the Empire [SPFE] Journal* 4 (1924), 45–56. See also Caldwell to Buxton, SPFE, 19 December 1922. KNA KW/27/4.

[10] Caldwell, 'Game Preservation', 51–3.

[11] Ibid., 55.

[12] K. Caldwell to Ag. Col. Sec., 18 September 1926. KNA KW/8/33, defends the privileges of landowners to protect their property from depredation by wildlife despite its frequent abuse.

[13] L. K. Caldwell, 'Commercialisation of Game', *SPFE Journal* 7 (1927), 89–90.

[14] *SPFE Journal* 8 (1928), 80–82.

Caldwell was the source of the idea for 'promoting some form of international agreement for the protection of big game in Africa'.[15]

I have gone to some length to establish Caldwell's place in this crucial phase of the international conservation movement because he has so frequently been ignored in favour of the more important and visible work of Col. J. Stevenson-Hamilton, the man frequently credited with the 1926 creation of Kruger National Park in South Africa.[16] It is clear that Stevenson-Hamilton's work at Kruger became the model for national park administration and as such gained the recognition of the SPFE, which published his ideas in its *Journal*.[17] Although his work has been seen as crucial by numerous authorities, they generally fail to credit the crucial idea of extending that model throughout Africa by negotiated international agreements to the work of Caldwell and the influence of East African pressures.[18]

The SPFE and the parks idea

Regardless of the source of the idea within African contexts, the national park idea and the need for an international agreement to enforce preservation fell on particularly fertile ground in the London headquarters of the SPFE and its president from 1926, Lord Onslow. The reasons that the SPFE, founded in 1903, and its aristocratic leadership should become champions of wildlife and specifically of national parks have been examined recently by Roderick P. Neumann. His view is that 'the aristocratic core membership of the SPFE carried its patrician notions of private parks and elite hunting from England into the Empire'.[19] In the process, 'the SPFE reinvented sports hunters as nature preservationists'.[20] Moreover, Neumann demonstrates how this transference was a part of the efforts both to preserve 'aristocratic privilege and values' and to conserve what remained of aristocratic political power from the rise of mass politics at home.[21] In placing Lord Onslow, the aristocratic and well-placed landed nobleman, at the centre of this reactionary movement, he also demonstrates how remote

---

[15] L. Amery to E. Grigg, 24 February 1928. KNA KW/14/3.

[16] J. Carruthers, *Wildlife and Warfare: The Life of James Stevenson-Hamilton* (Pietermaritzburg: University of Natal Press, 2001), 147–98, and her 'Creating a National Park, 1910 to 1926', *Journal of Southern African Studies* 15, 2 (1989), 188–216. See also her '"Police Boys" and Poachers: Africans, Wildlife Protection and National Parks, the Transvaal 1920 to 1950', *Koedoe* 36, 2 (1993), 11–22.

[17] Col. J. Stevenson-Hamilton, 'The Management of a National Park in Africa', *SPFE Journal* 10 (n.d. [1930?]), 13–20. See also J. Carruthers, *Wildlife and Warfare*, 81–118, 131–47, which covers the life of Stevenson-Hamilton and his central role in the creation of Africa's model national parks.

[18] E.g. Nicholson, *The Environmental Revolution*, 191; Nash, *Wilderness and the American Mind*, 355–6. In contrast, see Neumann, *Imposing Wilderness*, 123, who credits Caldwell with developing 'a proposal for obtaining such an [international] agreement in 1928'.

[19] Neumann, 'Dukes, Earls and Ersatz Edens', 87.

[20] Ibid., 88.

[21] Ibid., 88–95.

from African realities that movement was in both its impulse and its experience.

In June 1928, Colonial Office discussions with the SPFE regarding the exact 'distinction between a National Park and an ordinary reserve' were already under way, along with the question of expropriation of private owners, the possible removal of the Maasai from the Southern Reserve areas in Kenya, and the inevitable clash between game preservation and 'civilisation'.[22] The idea had been raised in a letter from C. W. Hobley, a former Kenya colonial official and then secretary of the SPFE, requesting 'the Secretary of State for the Colonies submit a recommendation to the Government of Kenya that the Southern Game Reserve be raised to the status of a National Park and vested in Trustee'.[23]

That the request fell foul of the Colonial Office bureaucracy initially may stem in part from its aristocratic presumption, which clashed with the leadership of the Colonial Office directed at that time by the British socialist Lord Passfield. However, it must also have stemmed from the SPFE's own confusion about what it hoped to accomplish. As spokesmen for the new environmentalism, the leaders of the SPFE found themselves at once motivated by the attempt to preserve privilege, including the hunting privileges of the upper classes, and simultaneously convinced that wildlife preservation and the material progress of civilization were incompatible. This shows up in the confusion in the negotiations with the Colonial Office over whether national parks would be created as permanent set-asides for wildlife, or if the existing system of game reserves should be continued. Parliamentary questions raised by Lord Onslow in 1929 specifically requested the Secretary of State for the Colonies and 'His Majesty's Government' to 'use every proper and reasonable effort in its power to further the preservation of game throughout the Empire, especially by encouraging the establishment of national parks and reserves'.[24]

In March 1930, a deputation, headed by Lord Onslow representing the SPFE and including members from the Joint East African Board, a business organization, visited the Colonial Office in London to make representations for calling a joint meeting of East African Game Wardens to discuss the possibility of developing 'a common wildlife policy' and 'a national parks contingency plan'.[25] Lords Passfield and Onslow appeared to agree that the economic development of East Africa was insufficiently advanced to allow the immediate creation of national parks. Moreover, Passfield believed that such permanent alienation of lands in the interest of game was properly the decision of the individual colonial governments, and not of the respective Game Departments. He rejected the idea of a joint conference of wardens, and recommended instead that a delegation

---

[22] Minute by C. Eastwood to Earl of Onslow, 6 June 1928. *PRO* C.O. 533/378/25.

[23] C. Hobley to P. C. Mitchell, 19 May 1928. *PRO* C.O. 533/378/25.

[24] Parliamentary Debates, House of Lords, 21 November 1929, vol. 75, 21, 624. The entire debate (623–48) is also available in KNA KW/27/1. See also the 1929–30 correspondence promoting a colonial game preservation conference led by Lord Onslow in KNA KW/8/33.

[25] Ofcansky, 'A History of Game Preservation', 167.

be sent to East Africa to consult with both governments and game officials in formulating 'a list of practical policy changes to the appropriate officials in London'.[26] Onslow and a delegation – dispatched in May 1930 and headed by the experienced hunter and military officer, Major R. W. G. Hingston, accepted the proposal to look into game policy changes.[27]

It should also be noted that a parallel movement to the one under way in Britain was also going on simultaneously in the United States. There, a New York-based committee sponsored by Kermit Roosevelt, Teddy Roosevelt's son and his 1909 hunting companion in Kenya, had been established to monitor abuses of the game laws by US big-game hunters in East Africa, and to provide information of US and Canadian game protection laws.[28] In a sense, the American equivalent of a landed aristocracy and moneyed elite was also engaged in the reactionary movement to preserve privilege and power in coordination with their British and Imperial counterparts.

Major Hingston's report to the SPFE of his 'five-months whirlwind tour'[29] accomplished two things. It placed the idea of national parks firmly in the public eye by fuelling the propaganda campaign that the SPFE undertook. In addition, it brought the British government to support their 'efforts to create a national parks system by dispatching a delegation to the International Congress for the Preservation of Nature' meeting in Paris in July 1931. Prime Minister Ramsey MacDonald named Lord Onslow to head the delegation to Paris.[30] In Paris, Onslow would maintain that the responsibility for the preservation of wildlife in colonial territories lay with imperial government, but that the migratory nature of most species required international coordination 'to supplement the effects of individual governments'.[31] In furtherance of this coordination, the Paris gathering voted to convene an international conference under the terms of the International Convention of 1900, to discuss international efforts to promote wildlife preservation. The motion to convene this conference for international cooperation was made by the SPFE delegate, Captain Keith Caldwell.[32]

---

[26] Ibid., 168.

[27] Ibid., 169–71. Ofcansky also notes (169) a degree of Colonial Office resistance to what was seen as outside interference by the conservationists, who were merely propagandists with interests that were incompatible with the Colonial Office's mission.

[28] See C. Hobley to A. Ritchie, 14 March 1930; Ritchie to Hobley, 12 April 1930. KNA KW/27/1. Ritchie's efforts to assist the SPFE in coordinating its efforts with American sympathizers was halted by a Colonial Office directive to the Game Warden not to report to the SPFE as a non-governmental body. Colonial Secretary to Ritchie, 2 May 1930. KNA KW/27/1. See also Nash, *Wilderness and the American Mind*, 358ff, and Daniel J. Herman, *Hunting and the American Imagination* (Washington: Smithsonian Institution Press, 2001), 237–53, for the background to American contributions to international conservation.

[29] Ofcansky, 'A History of Game Preservation', 169. For Hingston's report see Major R. W. G. Hingston, 'Report on a Mission to East Africa for the Purpose of Investigating the Most Suitable Methods of Ensuring the Preservation of Its Indigenous Fauna', *Journal of the SPFE* NS 12 (1930), 21–57.

[30] Ibid., 171.

[31] Onslow quoted in ibid., 172.

[32] Ibid.

The London Conference of 1933

The American environmental historian Roderick Nash expressed the watershed importance of the conference that the work of Caldwell and Onslow among others had brought to fruition:

> The high point of institutionalised global nature protection before the Second World War came on October 31, 1933, when representatives of all the colonial powers ... convened in the House of Lords to open the London Conference for the Protection of African Fauna and Flora. After a week's deliberations, a nineteen-article convention emerged for final signing. It expressed a determination to increase the number of national parks and what were termed 'strict natural reserves'.[33]

The overall significance to global and international conservation of the 1933 Conference and the Convention it drew up continues to be recognized as a landmark. At the time, local opinion in Kenya also saw the conference as a 'most important event in the history of African Game Preservation'.[34] It could hardly be ignored that, after the opening articles of the draft convention on the scope of application of the convention and definitions of terms, the next five articles (3–8) of the 17-article draft all dealt with the creation and administration of national parks.[35] With Lord Onslow in the chair of the conference, which was held more than just symbolically in the House of Lords with British aristocratic and imperial influence in the ascendancy, it is no wonder that the national park idea emerged triumphant from the conference. Clearly, for Kenya the triumphant idea would represent a direct challenge to colonial officials, white settlers, and African subjects to accommodate national parks in their older ideas about the nature of wildlife conservation.

In March 1934, the Colonial Office forwarded the final draft convention coming from the conference and being considered for signature by His Majesty's Government to Governor Byrnes of Kenya for his consideration. Byrnes, in turn, sent it on to his Game Warden, Captain Ritchie.[36] Ritchie found nothing objectionable in the substantial articles 3–10 and

---

[33] Nash, *Wilderness and the American Mind*, 359–60.

[34] 'Preservation of Game', *East African Standard*, 29 November 1933. KNA KW/8/28. A 1997 American Museum of Natural History exhibition on endangered species entitled 'Endangered' ranked the Conference as one of two dozen 'land marks' between the creation of Yellowstone National Park in 1872 and the Convention on the International Trade in Endangered Species in 1975. 'Conservation Land Marks', Exhibit Board, American Museum of Natural History, April 1997.

[35] Draft Convention proposed by HMG, June 1933. KNA KW/8/28. The official version can be read in 'Agreements concluded at the International Conference for the Protection of the Fauna and Flora of Africa', London, 8 November 1933. PRO Cmd 4453 Africa (Flora and Fauna) 28, 1.

[36] Secretary of State for Colonies (Plymouth) to Gov. J. A. Byrnes, 17 March 1934, KNA KW/8/29 contains an eight-page précis of the discussions in the House of Lords as well as the final draft of the convention.

thought that there would be no need for major alterations to Kenya's game laws to bring Kenya into conformity with their provisions.[37] Moreover, Ritchie noted that the convention went further than the existing bilateral agreement with Italy and should form a new basis to gain compliance from the Italian government in fulfilling its anti-smuggling obligations. From Ritchie's perspective, the Convention accomplished what he and Caldwell had intended it to do: strengthening Kenya's hand in policing the Somaliland border against smuggling of valuable ivory, and curbing the danger this illicit trade represented to Kenya's elephant herds.[38]

But what did this mean for Kenya's policy on national parks as opposed to simple game reserves as the basis of conservation policy? In the following years, Ritchie would frequently speak in favour of the creation of national parks and was considered by many Kenya conservationists to be a strong supporter of the national parks idea.[39] However, there is little evidence of his taking this beyond verbal advocacy on his own initiative. Instead, it was left to private initiatives coming from the settler community to champion the idea of national parks and begin a public agitation in the late 1930s to see the idea realized. Nonetheless, the importance of official British governmental support and international approval of a British-initiated convention cannot be overestimated in understanding the success of private initiatives. The 1933 Convention created a global climate favourable to the idea of national parks, which could take root in local soils.

Mervyn Cowie and the Kenyan national park movement

In 1937, Sir Robert Brooke-Popham, the new governor of Kenya, was the unwitting participant in a charade whose purpose was to tip the scales in favour of the creation of Kenya's first national park on the Nairobi Commons. He was escorted to an area of the commons, an expanse of savannah grasslands abutting the new peri-urban area of Mbagathi, in order to look at lions. His guide on this short trip out of Nairobi was Mervyn Cowie, a decade-long resident of Mbagathi and a key local promoter of the national park idea. On their arrival at Lone Tree near Cowie's home, a pride of lions put in an appearance as if on cue. The purpose was to impress Brooke-Popham with the convenience and safety with which lions could be viewed in close proximity to Nairobi, and how

---

[37] Ritchie to Colonial Secretary, 5 April 1934 and 23 May 1934. KNA KW/8/29.

[38] Ritchie to Colonial Secretary, 23 May 1934, no. 2. KNA KW/8/29. See also Ritchie to Ag. Colonial Secretary, 3 August 1933, KNA KW/8/28, and L. K. Caldwell, 'The International Conference for the Protection of the Fauna and Flora of Africa', *Journal of the Society for the Preservation of the Fauna of the Empire* NS 22 (1934), 45–52, especially 49–50, in which Caldwell comments on the attempts to control traffic in ivory in the convention.

[39] Personal communication from Ian Parker, who says 'Ritchie was the advocate of National Parks.' Comments on a draft paper, n.d. (1988?), 1. See also M. Cowie, *Fly, Vulture, Fly* (London: George G. Harrap, 1961), 59 who writes 'Ritchie ... had for years been in favour of establishing National Parks in Kenya as a better method of preservation.'

the establishment of a park on the commons would be a great boon to tourism for the colony.[40] Brooke-Popham appears to have been impressed by what would turn out to have been a scam perpetrated by Cowie. Nonetheless, Cowie would soon be named to a Game Policy Committee to discuss the future of game preservation and the prospect for establishing national parks.[41] Ultimately, he would become the first Director of the National Parks of Kenya.

Who was Mervyn Cowie that, among all the experienced gamekeepers and big game hunters, he should achieve the distinction of becoming Kenya's leading game preserver? Born in 1909 to a farm family of modest means, Cowie's earliest memories of game at age 5 concerned the cracking of whips by the servants of a farm neighbour to scare away lions, when the neighbour and Cowie's father were away during the war.[42] It would be at the still impressionable age of 17 that Cowie would have what he recalled as the experiences and disappointments that diverted him from the common course of young Kenyan white men, of pursuing hunting as a vocation. He would later recall that 'This encounter with buffaloes, and another later with a rhino, put me off sport and hunting for trophies altogether.' So, although Cowie 'lived through the days when it was the accepted custom "to bash the bastard", to shoot for the sake of killing ... I never acquired this desire.... It is a form of indoctrination through which I had to pass, and I gained greatly from the experience.' But, in the wake of the emotional trauma of a failed expedition and the humiliation and near death of an Australian hunter-client, the adolescent Cowie's 'sympathies and respect shifted from the grownups to the animals'.[43]

Cowie's emotional preparation for the defence of animals was soon complemented by his formal education at Oxford University and in London. His return to Kenya in 1932 was to produce in him the shock of seeing what was perceived as a marked decline in the number of game animals, especially in the southern game reserve area around Lomita. Two events in 1933 crystallized Cowie's growing concern for the survival of the game. The Royal Commission, known as the Carter Commission, that was appointed to examine the perennial contest between the settler community and politically conscious Africans on the question of land tenure came out in support of 'the idea of converting the Nairobi Commonage into a National Park'. This had followed on the 'far-reaching decisions' of the International Conference in London, by whose terms the British government 'committed its colonies to taking steps towards the establishment of National Parks'.[44] With these pointers and with both a growing sense of the danger to wildlife and a growing familiarity with the politics of colonial and settler society gained as a lawyer practising in Nairobi, Cowie set out to organize, on behalf of 'my wild animal friends' and the Nairobi Commonage, 'my special playground'.[45]

[40] Cowie, *Fly, Vulture*, 98–100.
[41] Ibid., 82–3.
[42] Ibid., 16–17.
[43] Ibid., 30–31. For the watershed incident with a rhino, see 32–8.
[44] Ibid., 59.   [45] Ibid., 59, 73.

A special urgency was imposed on Cowie's efforts by what now appears to be a blip on the steady course towards the creation of national parks as sanctuaries. In 1937, a dispatch was received by Captain Ritchie of the Kenya Game Department in response to questions put to the Secretary of State for the Colonies, W. Ormsby-Gore. In an attempt to clarify questions of rights and public control of the parks raised by the 1933 London Conference, Ormsby-Gore offered opinions that undermined the basic idea motivating the national parks advocates in Kenya. Cowie was especially agitated by the views put forward by the Secretary of State, which he considered 'wholly unacceptable'. Ormsby-Gore had denied that the parks must necessarily be developed to attract tourists. Moreover, he flatly stated, 'a National Park is not an area in which hunting by members of the public must be entirely prohibited'. Needless to say, this dispatch, although not a public document, 'caused a lull in the enthusiasm of those who had been actively striving to establish National Parks'.[46]

From late 1937, when he was named as an Honorary Game Warden, Cowie began to work in earnest to save the animals and the Nairobi Commonage, and to fulfil the promise of creating a national park in Kenya. Cowie launched a campaign of letter writing to the local press and public meetings aimed at bringing about pressure on the government to act in defence of game and to limit the use of the Nairobi Commonage for the grazing of Somali cattle.[47]

The climax came with a public meeting at one of Nairobi's cinemas supported by the influential Nairobi Rotary Club. The meeting was to feature speeches by a distinguished list of leading settler luminaries, especially Major Jack Riddell of Kiambu, who had opened his own conservation campaign with the Kenya government. Although Riddell was taken ill, the speakers included Blayney Percival, the retired Game Warden, Mervyn Hill, a knowledgeable naturalist and amateur historian, and the redoubtable ladies' man, 'Lord Erroll, at that time a member of the Legislative Council'.[48]

When the public protests and meetings still saw the government foot-dragging on the question of national parks, Cowie had recourse to the charade at Lone Tree. I describe this incident as a charade for two reasons. First, it was planned as part of a long public campaign to gain public support for the creation of a national park in Kenya, with the focus being on the Nairobi Commons.[49] Moreover, it continued the duplicitous practices that had marked the letter-writing campaign. These efforts

---

[46] M. Cowie, 'History of the Kenya National Parks', KNA KW/1/78 no. 224, 17–18. See also M. Cowie, *Fly, Vulture*, 73, and 'Report of Proceedings of a Conference of Game Wardens', 9–10 February 1939. KNA KW 23/163.

[47] The Nairobi City Council passed restrictions on cattle grazing on the Commonage in June 1938. Appendix A, 'Interim Report of the Game Policy Committee'. KNA KW/18/2.

[48] Cowie, *Fly, Vulture*, 80. For Riddell's efforts, see Cowie, 'History of the Kenya National Parks', KNA KW/1/78 224, 18–19, and correspondence between Riddell, Ag. Game Warden Clarke, and the Colonial Secretary from May 1938 in KNA KW/27/2.

[49] Cowie, *Fly, Vulture*, 78–83.

included Cowie ghost-writing letters to the press for other settlers to sign.[50] It has also been alleged that the letter of 9 February 1938 from Elspeth Huxley, the well-known settler author, to her even better-known scientist-conservationist cousin, Julian Huxley, urging his support for local Kenyan anti-poaching efforts, may also have been a put-up job.[51] In addition, Cowie wrote one letter to the *East African Standard* signed by 'Old Settler', which offered the 'modest proposal' that 'all wild animals in Kenya' be exterminated. This effort at satire almost backfired when the Nanyuki Farmers' Association, an important settler lobby notoriously hostile to game preservation, took the letter at face value.[52]

Secondly, the Lone Tree incident was a charade because the appearance of the lions was anything but coincidental with the Governor's visit to the spot. Cowie, in fact, had been planning for it for some months by putting out meat for this particular pride of lions on a regular basis, to assure their timely entrance into his little drama. The incident was carefully staged for the benefit of Brooke-Popham.[53] As Cowie described his charade:

> I selected a triangular portion of the Game Reserve opposite my house as the best place to feed a pride of lions, so that they would be on parade each time I needed them…. With Ritchie's approval, … I started on the plan of feeding some lions. [An Ndorobo hunter was employed to] train the lions to be my publicity agents.[54]

Cowie's near taming of lions, later joined by a small group of leopards, almost backfired as well. A pride of lions who had grown 'unafraid of humans in cars or afoot' pursued a European visitor, killed an *askari* (guard), and produced an outcry in the Nairobi white community against dangerous animals so near the city. A decision was taken to kill the 'tame' lions, and in the end eleven lions were 'bashed'.[55] Fortunately for Cowie's elaborate plans, the killing of these sacrificial victims appeared to have eased the settler pressure against the park and allowed the plans to proceed.

The naming of Cowie to the 1938 Game Policy Committee under the chairmanship of a prominent settler from Trans-Nzoia, Mr A. C. Hoey, marked the triumph of the two-year-long campaign. From his position on the committee charged with recommending 'the policy to be adopted in regard to the preservation and control of game' in the colony, Cowie was well placed to see his dream of establishing the country's first national park reach fruition.[56] Moreover, the threat to create national parks as watered-

---

50 E.g. 'Inadequate Game Protection in Kenya', and the editorial, 'Game Preservation', in *East African Standard*, 25 April 1938. KNA KW/27/2. See also Cowie, 'History of the Kenya National Parks', KNA KW/1/78 224, 24.

51 E. Huxley to J. Huxley, 9 February 1938. KNA KW/27/2. The fact that this letter appears among official correspondence in a file on Preservation of Game argues against it being the purely private and informal letter it appears to be.

52 Cowie, *Fly, Vulture*, 78–9.

53 Ibid., 84–100.

54 Ibid., 84–5. 55 Ibid., 109–17.

56 The committee's membership and charge appear in 'Interim Report of the Game Policy Committee', KNA KW/18/2.

down sanctuaries or replacements for game reserves, posed by the Ormsby-Gore dispatch, had been countered by a strong statement against the Secretary's interpretations made by the Game Wardens of Kenya, Tanganyika, and Uganda at the Game Wardens' Conference held in early 1939.[57]

In fact, the deck was already stacked in favour of a strong national park solution to the question of game preservation in the committee's charge. Among its responsibilities, the committee was charged with the obligation to 'make recommendations concerning the institution in the Colony of a National Game Park or Parks, including their location, extent, constitution, control and management'.[58] The stage was set for a quick recommendation and enactment of a national park programme or, at least, the gazetting of Nairobi Commonage as the first, flagship National Park in Kenya, on terms consistent with Cowie's image of a place of total sanctuary from hunting and human interference. However, the outbreak of war in 1939 postponed the work of the Game Policy Committee, and the war itself meant that game preservation both inside and outside the boundaries of national parks was set back for almost a decade.

The impact of the Second World War

The outbreak of war brought an immediate suspension of the activities of the Game Policy Committee, as many of its members took up significant wartime appointments. It would reconvene three years later and issue its Interim Report only in October 1944.[59] The report would lay the basis for passage of a bill for the establishment of national parks and the gazetting of Nairobi National Park as Kenya's first total sanctuary for game in 1946.[60] But this meant a delay of over five years from the very promising situation in early 1939.

The war would put a temporary halt to the activities of the preservationists, but it would put paid to the big game safari and change the face of hunting in postwar Kenya. To begin with, the war cut off the flow of rich clients able to travel to Kenya for months of outdoor recreation. The difficulties of travel between Britain and Africa and across the Atlantic caused the disappearance from the Kenyan scene of those super-rich Americans and titled European nobles who had fed the lucrative 'champagne safari' of the interwar years. When the safari re-emerged after the war, it would be transformed by new modes of international transportation bringing a new clientele. These new 'tourists' were more interested in viewing 'nature' and wildlife at the newly created national

---

[57] 'Report of Proceedings of a Conference of Game Wardens', 9–10 February 1939. KNA KW 23/163.

[58] 'Interim Report of the Game Policy Committee', no. 224. KNA KW/18/2.

[59] Ibid.

[60] Colony and Protectorate of Kenya, 'A Bill to Provide for the Establishment of National Parks', KNA KW/18/2, and Cowie, 'History of the Kenya National Parks', KNA KW/1/78 no. 224, 29–32. See also Cowie, *Fly, Vulture*, 108–35.

parks and in enjoying the comforts of tourist-oriented game facilities like luxury lodges and tented camps than they were in the hunt.[61] In addition, many of the young able-bodied white hunters among young Kenyans found themselves in uniform and at war against a deadlier prey, as did game wardens, rangers, and others in the safari business.[62]

But the end of the hunting safari was not by any means the end of hunting. In one way, the paying clients of the white hunters were replaced by the influx of officers and men. As in the Great War, Kenya became a staging ground for military campaigns against Britain's, and hence the colonies', enemies. In 1939, it was no longer the German enemy who occupied territory bordering on Kenya, but the Italians, who occupied Somaliland to the east and Ethiopia to the north. Ethiopia, invaded and conquered by Mussolini's forces in 1936, would fall to British forces in 1941 with the capture of Addis Ababa, bringing the East African campaign to an early conclusion. However, very much like the experiences of 1914–19, the 'War for the Bundu' would prove to be a prolonged 'campaign safari' against Kenya's wildlife.

As early as 1940, Chief Game Warden Ritchie was registering complaints about troops shooting game on private lands without permission and issuing regulations to try to control hunting by men in uniform, including the appointment of a special Military Game Warden.[63] Nonetheless, Ritchie had to affirm the right of private landholders to permit hunters to shoot on their lands without hunting licences, 'since landowners have the right to reduce game that is a cause of loss or damage without licences'.[64] Inevitably this meant that, in certain settler districts of the country, game animals would be heavily predated during the long period in which troops on active duty were stationed there. The Game Warden would complain that soldiers had been only partially responsible for this. 'Thousands of game were shot in the Nanyuki district during the war since there was a profit motive, but they [the soldiers] were merely carrying out what the Nanyuki Farmers' Association had been trying to organize for many years before the war.'[65] However, no such excuse could be found for the practice of 'unauthorized and indiscriminate shooting of game'[66] by soldiers 'accompanying military convoys coming down from Somalia'.[67]

The end of champagne safaris put the professional white hunters temporarily out of business, which frequently freed them to join the host of soldiers-cum-hunters by donning uniforms and participating in what I

[61] See Kenya National Parks, 'National Parks in Kenya. Policy, Plans and Finance', 29 June 1949. KNA KW/1/76.
[62] B. Herne, *White Hunters* (New York: Henry Holt, 1999), 149–73.
[63] A. Ritchie, 'Kenya Game. A Plea for Sympathetic Appreciation', KNA KW/23/158; Regulation, 'Active Service Licence' no. 20. KNA KW/18/16. On the work of the Military Game Warden, see *Draft Game Department Annual Report* [*GDAR*], 1941, 2. KNA KW/23/165. The post was abolished due to staffing shortages in 1943. *GDAR* for 1943. KNA KW/23/166.
[64] A. Ritchie to Camp Commandant, Gilgil, 1 August 1940. KNA KW/18/16.
[65] A. Ritchie to Brig. A. G. Arbuthnot, Naro Moru, 27 February 1948. KNA KW/1/73.
[66] A. Ritchie to Camp Commandant, Gilgil, 1 August 1940. KNA KW/18/16.
[67] G. Adamson, Ranger's Report, KNA KW/23/167.

have called 'campaign safaris'. However, for Africans employed in the pre-war safari operations, the only option was to return to the hunting field as poachers. There is clear evidence that poaching increased during the war and that, by 1944, 'Poaching by natives in some parts of the country was severe.'[68] Despite this, the number of prosecutions under the game ordinances actually decreased during the first two years of hostilities. Ritchie would attribute the decline to 'the following reasons: (a) many persons of all races were away from home; (b) natives were nervous of going far afield on lawless expeditions; (c) offences by members of the military were … dealt with by disciplinary action and not brought to court'.[69] But this hardly explains the overall increase in poaching by Africans, merely the decrease in prosecutions.

I would attribute the increase in poaching to three factors. Inasmuch as the first line of defence against African hunting was the presence of Game Rangers, Scouts, and other government officers, their removal to military service created serious staffing shortages for the Game Department and opened up opportunities for poaching, at least near to home, that were unavailable in peacetime. Secondly, adding to the general disruption of war, 'During the years under review [1939–45] drought and the prevalence of locusts played havoc with' African agriculture.[70] The effect of this would have been to revive the time-honoured supplementation of agricultural production with the products of the hunt in the drought- and locust-stricken regions. Finally, the disappearance from the field of safari hunters left it open for others to poach unobserved and unreported to the authorities. This would include those who knew the hunting field well from having participated as guides, trackers, and other auxiliary staff for the safari companies.

The invisibility of Africans in conservation

The very idea that poaching went on beneath the threshold of observation by white outsiders again raises the question of the invisibility of Africans as hunters in much of the literature. Except when they are being condemned in general terms as the chief threat to the survival of animals,[71] African hunters only enter the purview of colonial society as crime statistics, as convictions under the game regulations. This should also warn us about another aspect of African invisibility: the absence of an African voice or presence in the Kenyan movement for conservation. The disappearance of Africans from the conservation movement can be attributed to two causes.

[68] Ibid.

[69] Draft *GDAR*, 1941. KNA KW/23/165.

[70] 'Game. 1939–1945 Inclusive'. KNA KW/23/159.

[71] See Horace S. Mazet to Chief Game Warden, 8 November 1955, enclosing 'Position of Game in Kenya – Past – Present – Future'. Mazet, a visiting American wildlife expert, states: 'In Kenya the causes of decline are really twofold – the rapid development of the Country caused by ever increasing population, and poaching by Africans.' KNA KW/1/73.

First, colonial authorities wrote them off as being without a conservation ethos of their own; their only interest was presumed to be in the exploitation of wild animals for food and profit. Secondly, and as a corollary, the Kenya conservationists pointedly ignored African opinion on conservation policy. They were not consulted on the creation or situating of Kenya's game reserves and parks, from the earliest enforced movement of Maasai pastoralists from the Southern Reserve to Laikipia and back in the first decades of the century, to the complete absence of an African voice from the Game Policy Committee's deliberations. Africans were excluded as either members or witnesses, and the district administration would stand in as the representative of African views.[72]

The resurgence of African poaching during the war, whether due to relaxed anti-poaching efforts by the Game Department or to the sheer necessity for Africans to hunt for food during the difficult wartime economy, underlines another important point too easily lost sight of during the heyday of the champagne safari. As discussed in Chapter 6, the safari was the product of transcultural production, the fusion and convergence of European expectations and African ideas and know-how. Once that transcultural construction was stopped by war and economic change, Africans returned to the kinds of hunting that had always underlain their contributions to the big game safari.

This meant a return to the traditions of hunting for the pot, which had always supplemented the agricultural and pastoral pursuits of Kamba and Kikuyu, Samburu, and Borana, as well as being the focus of Waata and Ndorobo economic life. The hunting of food animals, from dik-dik to eland, squirrels to elephants, would again come to occupy a key place in the economic and social lives of African hunters during wartime. Moreover, the hundreds of Africans employed as trackers, bearers, porters, cooks, skinners, drivers, and 'gofers' by the safari operators would now pursue those activities as their ancestors had, as part of the hunting of elephant, rhino, hippo, leopard, lion, and other trophy animals and the transportation of their skins, tusks, teeth, and claws to willing, if illegal, buyers on the Kenya coast and beyond. The continuity of these safari activities through the era of the champagne safari (and its re-emergence and modification in the post-war camera safari) reveals the fundamental – and silenced – contribution made by African hunters and hunting ideas and praxis to the creation and development of the Kenya hunting synthesis. It also raises the question of what would happen to the African hunting tradition and its bearers during the coming era of the tourist safari, the establishment of national parks, and the triumph of preservationist thinking on the place of Africa's wildlife in the modern world.

[72] See N. Kelly, 'In Wildest Africa: The Preservation of Game in Kenya, 1895–1933', unpublished Ph.D. dissertation, Simon Fraser University, 1978, v, 293–304.

Ten

National Parks
& the Poaching Crisis
1946–63

The end of the Second World War allowed for the re-emergence of the conservation effort in Kenya that was sidetracked by the outbreak of hostilities in 1939. The national parks efforts among Kenya's white settler elite had been curtailed by the war effort in East Africa, which had the further effect of producing lax law enforcement, food shortages, and a general crisis atmosphere. These, together with large numbers of men under arms, led to an increase in poaching and pressure on game during the six years of war.[1] However, the idea of conservation planning received a new impetus from the war and the need for the mobilization of resources it engendered.

The idea of planning had gained a wider currency among colonial administrators during the economic crisis of the depression years as well.[2] Soil conservation and water catchment projects were especially favoured by the colonial administration, but game preservation seems also to have benefited from the heightened awareness of the government's capacity to plan the allocation and mobilization of resources.[3] By 1937, the game

---

[1] Wartime famine seems to have been widespread in East Africa due to the disruption of communications and the inability to import foodstuffs. Personal communication, Dr Gregory H. Maddox, 20 November 1999, regarding famine conditions in Tanzania. This chapter has drawn upon my previously published essay, E.I. Steinhart, 'National Parks and Anti-poaching in Kenya, 1947–1957', *International Journal of African Historical Studies* 27, 1 (1994), 59–76, with my thanks to the editors.

[2] D. Anderson, 'Depression, Dust Bowl, Demography and Drought: The Colonial State and Soil Conservation in East Africa During the 1930s', *African Affairs* 83, 332 (July 1984), 321–43. See W. Beinart, 'Soil Erosion, Conservationism, and Ideas about Development: A Southern African Exploration, 1900–1960', *Journal of Southern African Studies* 11, 1 (October 1984), 52–83; and J. Akong'a, 'Drought and Famine Management in Kitui District, Kenya', in *Anthropology of Development and Change in East Africa*, ed. D. W. Brokensha and P. D. Little (Boulder and London: Westview, 1988), 99–120. For the growth of government activism in the area of colonial welfare in Kenya between the wars, see J. Lewis, *Empire State-Building* (Oxford: James Currey, 2000), 21–123.

[3] This seems to have been especially true in Kitui district. See M. O'Leary, *The Kitui Akamba* (Nairobi: Heinemann Educational Books, 1984), 45–8. E.g., Kitui District Annual Report,

conservation movement was also reflecting the sea change of bureaucratic muscle and governmental activism. Although the initial impetus had often come from landed aristocrats in Britain, the local Kenya preservationists, while enjoying aristocratic support, were led by commoners like Mervyn Cowie and Captain Archie Ritchie.

In 1937, in response to Cowie's initiatives, the Government of Kenya had convened a Game Policy Committee to plan the future of Kenya's wildlife.[4] The war interrupted the Committee's work, but it was reconvened and completed its charge in 1944. The recommendations for the establishment of complete sanctuaries removed from the control and influence of the government and the settler-dominated legislature might have been written by Cowie himself, who was indeed an influential member of the committee. It certainly reflected the developmentalist and activist attitudes that had come to dominate public policy on conservation during the depression and war years. When the plan was about to be implemented, it was Cowie who was chosen by the governor to become the first director of what would come to be called the National Parks of Kenya.[5] This provided him with not only a position of power from which to determine the policies of the national parks as they came into existence, but also a vital platform from which to continue to propagate his preservationist views on wildlife and wild habitat.

Nairobi National Park

The first victory for Cowie's views came quickly when, in December 1946, Nairobi National Park was gazetted on what had been the commonage on the southwest edge of Nairobi, Kenya's capital and largest city. Ken Beaton was named as the first park warden, and seems to have been a man who shared with his director the somewhat romantic and aesthetic vision of wildlife preservation as well as the delight in wildlife observation of a modern naturalist.[6] However, the establishment of Nairobi Park was a shallow victory at best. As a practical preservationist sanctuary, Nairobi had severe limitations. At first, it was so small (only 40 square miles) and so close to densely settled areas that the prospect for providing sanctuary to some animals was zero. The park had to be fenced on its northern

---

[3] (contd) 1947, KNA DC/KTI/1/1/5.

[4] M. Cowie, *Fly, Vulture, Fly* (London: George G. Harrap, 1961), 32–8, 59–100; and Chapter 8 of this volume.

[5] Game Policy Committee Interim Report, KNA KW/18/2. Cowie, *Fly, Vulture*, 124–35. The name would later be changed to the Royal National Parks of Kenya, to reflect royal patronage. I shall refer to the administration of the RNPK simply as the National Parks to avoid the misnomer of Parks Department, as it was crucial to the planners and administrators of the RNPK that they not be reduced to a department of government under the budgetary control of the colonial or imperial legislatures. In this regard, the loss of National Park independence in 1976 has been seen as a major blow against the conservationist stance in Kenya.

[6] K. Beaton, *A Warden's Diary* (2 vols.) (Nairobi: East African Standard, 1949). See also Royal National Parks of Kenya, Report, 1946–1950, 8–25, KNA KW/23/59.

perimeter, which abutted Nairobi's western suburbs of Langata and Karen. Moreover, it was simply too small to support an elephant population that could not be effectively fenced in. Secondly, it was so near populated areas that lions were frequently reported to jump the fence and prowl the streets and gardens of the fashionable adjacent suburbs, giving the well-to-do a regular topic of conversation.[7] Indeed, the threat of lions among the bougainvillea came to symbolize the objections of many in the settler community to the entire idea of preservation and national parks. The supposed incompatibility of civilization with wildlife was starkly drawn whenever a lion escaped the zoo-like enclosure of Nairobi Park.[8] It gave force to the argument that, if Kenya were to become a civilized country, the wild animals, like nudity and paganism, had to disappear into the safe precincts of history books, museums, or zoos.

Despite these limitations, Nairobi Park had quickly proven remarkably successful as a tourist attraction with perhaps the highest visitor rate of any park in Africa since the 1950s. The reasons for this are the obverse of the limitations: the prospect of seeing four of the big five game animals (rhinoceros, buffalo, lion, and leopard) after a 20-minute drive from downtown Nairobi virtually guaranteed the new park regular paying visitors from among international tourists and local residents. The convenience more than offset the small size and occasional distractions from arriving and departing jets at the neighbouring airport (now the Jomo Kenyatta International Airport). Purists would continue to ridicule the park as 'the only national park set between a drive-in theatre and a cement factory', but others would continue to visit it for its park-like beauty and its accessibility to animals of great variety. Especially when the vast herds of wildebeest migrating seasonally out of the Serengeti and Maasai Mara plains reached the unfenced southern boundaries of the park, Nairobi Park becomes an extraordinarily rich, as well as convenient, place for the observation of abundant wildlife in Kenya.

Tsavo National Park

The absence of elephants from Nairobi Park, rather than the presence of lions, was the problem that provoked the next debate in the preservationist campaign for a total sanctuary for Kenya's wildlife. Nairobi Park might admirably serve the interests of foreign tourists and day-trippers from Nairobi, but it could never be the kind of national park envisioned by the organizers of the 1933 Conference on the Preservation of Fauna and Flora or their Kenyan collaborators.[9] A search was begun to find a large area to be reserved as a total wildlife sanctuary that did not infringe on any vested

[7] Royal National Parks of Kenya, Report, 1946–1950, 1 (KNA KW/23/59); and Cowie, *Fly, Vulture*, 109–17.

[8] Beaton, *A Warden's Diary*, 108.

[9] 'Preservation of Big Game' (1930–35) (KNA KW/27/1), and Royal National Parks of Kenya, Report, 1946–50, 8, KNA KW/23/59.

interests of private individuals or governmental authorities. The elimination of any settled land or land suitable for commercial, mineral, or agricultural development left a broad swath of barren and arid territory in eastern Kenya, which the maps of the late nineteenth century had referred to as the Taru Desert. This region focused on the railway station at the Tsavo River bridge, made famous by a pair of man-eating lions and their determined exterminator, Lieut.-Colonel J. H. Patterson.[10] To the north and east of the station lay what would become Tsavo East, the vast heartland of eastern Kenya's elephant country, stretching from the railway line on the south to near the bend of the Tana River to the north. West and south of the railway line was the better-watered, more scenic region of Tsavo West, which made up for the scarcity of game by several areas of great natural beauty, including Nzima Springs, at which tourist facilities would be sited.[11] Gazetted as Tsavo National Park in April 1948, the almost 8,000 square miles would make Tsavo both Kenya's largest park and its most difficult to administer.

After a year of stagnation under an ineffective warden, Tsavo would be split into two sections along the railway line for ease of administration.[12] The vastness of Tsavo East would come under the control of David Sheldrick, a Kenya-born former military officer of youthful distinction. In taking over his responsibilities as warden of Tsavo, Sheldrick would implicitly issue a challenge to the gamekeeping establishment in Kenya, the implications of which would form the heart of a decade-long controversy over the methods and politics of game conservation.[13]

Before examining the confrontations of the 1950s, we must take a brief look at the opposition that Sheldrick and Cowie would face in the formulation of a new conservation consensus around Tsavo's elephants. Until the creation of the national parks under Cowie and Tsavo East under Sheldrick, responsibility for game conservation policy and enforcement lay entirely with the Kenya Game Department. The conflict that emerged in the 1950s, between the national parks and the Game Department, can be attributed to 'inter-service' rivalry over prestige and influence. However, I believe at root there was a far more important conflict between competing ideas about conservation of game versus preservation of wildlife. The Game Department, created shortly after the turn of the century, would be given lasting shape and direction after 1923 by Captain A. C. (Archie)

---

[10] J. H. Patterson, *The Man-eaters of Tsavo* (New York: St. Martins, 1986 [1907]). The man-eaters' story has been popularized in a Hollywood thriller entitled *The Ghost and the Darkness* (1996), starring Val Kilmer and Michael Douglas and directed by Stephen Hopkins.

[11] 'Proposed Conceptual Master Plan for Tsavo National Park', KNA KW/1/67.

[12] Minutes of Executive Committee, National Parks of Kenya, 18th meeting, 20 June 1949, KNA KW/1/76.

[13] D. Sheldrick, *The Tsavo Story* (London: Collins and Harvill, 1973); and N. Simon, 'The Elephants of Tsavo', unpublished ms., 1983, David Sheldrick Wildlife Trust Archive, Langata, Kenya. My thanks to Daphne Sheldrick, administrator of the trust and its archive, for allowing me access to this invaluable collection and for her personal insights into the character of her late husband. Interview D/7, Daphne Sheldrick, 14 February 1991.

Ritchie, who was brought in as Chief Game Warden.[14] Although game preservation work received much attention in the annual reports, in Captain Ritchie's scheme, the bulk of the department's day-to-day work went towards fulfilling its other functions. The first priority was the licensing of sports hunting by residents and visiting sportsmen, which provided the government with an important source of revenue; and the second was the control of game and vermin in settled and tribal reserve areas, which provided Kenya's settlers and peasant farmers with a modicum of relief from the depredation of their crops and fields by wildlife. Such conservation work as was done focused on the protection of trophy animals, especially elephant and rhinoceros, from commercial poaching and the smuggling of ivory and horn to markets outside East Africa. This effort was as much a concern of the Treasury Department over the loss of ivory export revenues to smugglers as it was a matter of saving the game.[15] The war interrupted even that limited conservation role of the Game Department after 1939, and by 1950, with the illness and retirement of Captain Ritchie, the Game Department's conservation efforts appear to have been leaderless and adrift.[16]

In this situation of lassitude, the energies and initiatives of David Sheldrick and the National Parks leadership would appear as both a challenge and a threat to the Game Department. Initially, at least, the newcomers were greeted with some scepticism, if not derision. In April 1949, Sheldrick and his newly appointed assistant warden, 19-year-old Bill Woodley, were instructed to survey the remote areas of Tsavo East. After a briefing that emphasized the 'scientific' nature of their endeavour, Woodley was dispatched to make 'comprehensive nature notes on all species' found in the park.[17] In addition to this wildlife survey, Sheldrick and Woodley were told to look for places to site facilities, roads, and stations from which the park could be accessed by tourists, visitors, and conservation personnel. This 'familiarization tour' would lead the two gamekeepers to what they felt was a shocking discovery. In the course of their travels, they found a large number of fresh elephant kills, tusks removed but most of the meat left to rot. Their Kamba tracker, Elui Nthengi, a knowledgeable former poacher, explained to the incredulous wardens the significance of their finds.

---

[14] See Chapter 8, pp. 158–65.

[15] See E. I. Steinhart, 'Hunters, Poachers and Gamekeepers: Toward a Social History of Hunting in Colonial Kenya', *Journal of African History* 30 (1989), 255–8; and Chapter 8 in this volume. Also A. C. Ritchie to Ag. Col. Sec., 3 August 1933 (KNA KW/8/28) and correspondence in 'Ivory and Rhino Horn, Smuggling of (1924–35)', KNA KW/14/3, 4 and 5.

[16] William Hale was appointed to replace Ritchie, from the ranks of the provincial administration where he had reached the highest likely level of advancement in his civil service career. He appears to have lacked the energy, experience, and public respect that Ritchie had earned. Nor did he have the disposition to lead the Game Department on a major departure in conservation methods or ideology. *Game Department Annual Report* (*GDAR*), 1950, 1–10; and Interview D/2, Ian Parker, 25 August 1987.

[17] D. Holman, *The Elephant People* (London: John Murray, 1967), 9.

In brief, what Nthengi explained is that the elephant kills were the result of poaching operations carried out on foot by Waata hunters using their preferred weapon: a long bow and poisoned arrows.[18] Although the evidence of bow-and-arrow kills was plentiful, Sheldrick and Woodley were initially sceptical since they shared the conventional wisdom that this was an inefficient, dangerous, and *ipso facto* a marginal form of elephant hunting. However, their scepticism was nothing compared to the positive disbelief and ridicule their findings received when reported to both the National Parks Director and the Game Department.[19]

Nevertheless, eventually Sheldrick would convince his bosses not only that the Waata and the Kamba bow-and-arrow hunters who inhabited the areas surrounding Tsavo East[20] were highly effective elephant hunters, despite using 'primitive' techniques, but that they represented a significant threat to the survival of the herds and the park that Sheldrick had been employed to protect.[21]

In the months that followed this 'discovery' of Waata poaching, a debate emerged, muffled and often at cross purposes, between the parks personnel on one side and the old guard of the Game Department on the other, regarding how to treat this 'new' threat to the survival of the elephant in Tsavo. Some of this debate may have represented divergent institutional interests between the new boys on the block, namely Sheldrick, Woodley, and even Cowie at the National Parks on the one hand, and the career gamekeepers in the understaffed, underpaid, and under-appreciated Game Department on the other. Certainly, as the decade of the 1950s advanced, the sense of mission and of privilege demonstrated by the National Parks personnel made a sharp contrast to the demoralized Game Department personnel. This contrast extended right down to the snappy new uniforms worn by the hand-picked subordinate field staff of African Rangers who patrolled the parks when compared to the poorly turned out, underpaid,

[18] Holman, *Elephant People*, 57–69, and I. Parker and M. Amin, *Ivory Crisis* (London: Chatto and Windus, 1983), 24–56. See also E. Steinhart, 'Kenya Ivory Hunters: 1850–1950', unpublished paper, American Society for Ethnohistory, Chicago, IL, 2–5 November 1989; and Chapter 1 in this volume.

[19] See Tsavo National Park East, Warden's Monthly Report for July 1949 and August 1949 KNA KW/23/31; Holman, *Elephant People*, 27–42.

[20] Approximately 2,000 Waata lived on the arid eastern margins of the Park, where their Mijikenda neighbours called them *Waliangulu* (those who eat meat). The Kamba I refer to here are Kitui Akamba, who inhabited the western and northern portions of Tsavo East and the abutting areas of Kitui district. See K. Jackson, 'An Ethnohistorical Study of the Oral Traditions of the Akamba of Kenya', unpublished Ph.D. dissertation, University of California, Los Angeles, 1972; O'Leary, *The Kitui Akamba*.

[21] Although I agree that previously the impact of the bow hunters had been seriously under-estimated, I remain unconvinced that a centuries-long symbiotic relationship between hunter and prey had been so thoroughly upset by commercial motives as to represent a credible threat to the survival of elephants in eastern Kenya. Indeed, I tend to believe that poaching alone, under conditions such as prevailed in the 1950s, constituted an insignificant threat of endangerment to elephants or the park environment. See J. D. Alladay, 'Elephants and Their Interactions with People in the Tana River Region of Kenya', unpublished Ph.D. dissertation, Cornell University, 1979, 270–73; and, although they have since recanted these views, see Parker and Amin, *Ivory Crisis*, 169–75.

and ill-disciplined African Scouts of the Game Department. An attitude of elitism and modern sophistication came to characterize the Parks staff, which, added to their freedom from the restraints of government-imposed budget accountability, gave them an *esprit de corps* totally lacking in the Game Department, which was seen both from outside and within as 'just another government department'.[22] Moreover, there may have been generational and class differences that separated the champions of the two sides in the debates. At core, however, what was being contested was the ideological terrain over which the struggle for a conservation policy, adapted to the needs of a new Kenyan society, was to be played out.

New poaching challenges

Once the problem of Waata and, to a lesser extent, Kamba poaching was understood, the efforts at countering them began. 'The accepted method of counteracting poaching ... had always been to operate from a series of outposts,... but in Tsavo this system was proving a dismal failure.'[23] Posts had been created in the park, and Ranger patrols had begun to pursue poachers who entered the park in violation of the law and in pursuit of elephant. But, faced with experienced and locally knowledgeable poachers and applying the time-honoured techniques of the gamekeeper's art, the white Wardens and African Rangers, drawn from the northern pastoral tribes with a reputation for hardiness and warlike qualities, proved no match.

When the Game Department was approached for advice, Senior Game Ranger George Adamson simply reasserted the old verities. Adamson was then the Senior Game Ranger in title as well as experience, having patrolled the Northern Game Reserve since being employed by the department in the mid-1930s.[24] In 1950, his response to the poaching crisis in Meru district – which he describes as 'one of the worst poaching areas in Kenya and a hotbed of illegal trade in leopard skins' – was to increase the frequency and intensity of patrolling the district from headquarters in Isiolo, from which he also patrolled the vast reaches of the Northern Frontier District.

> It is a job that requires a special officer whose sole occupation for a year would be to harry the Meru and Kamba poachers.... In my opinion the easiest way to put a check on the illegal traffic in trophies, is to get at its source, that is to deal with the shenzies [savages] who actually obtain the trophies by hunting and trapping. The sophisticated trader who buys the loot, is a much more difficult and expensive bird to catch.[25]

The kind of 'special officer' that Adamson himself was, and whose role

---

[22] Interview D/2, Ian Parker, 25 August 1987.

[23] Sheldrick, *Tsavo Story*, 43.

[24] For a characterization of Adamson, see Chapter 8 in this volume. On his attitudes and methods at this time, see G. Adamson to D.C., Meru, 1 July 1949; Adamson to Game Warden, 5 July, 6 August, and 6 September 1949, KNA KW/23/175.

[25] G. Adamson to Game Warden, 3 September 1950, KNA KW/23/148.

he saw as central to game keeping, was a kind of 'Lone Ranger' in pursuit of bands of poaching desperadoes. Increasing patrols to harass the poachers and catching them red-handed on information received from informants would avoid the problems created by arresting and prosecuting the illegal receivers and smugglers, whose wealth, sophistication, and capacity for corrupting the authorities had caused the Game and Treasury Departments so much grief over the decades.[26] The Mau Mau Emergency relied on the tried and proven methods that Adamson clearly believed had held poaching in check for decades before 1950. In addition, it relied on the kind of special skills and aptitudes, dedication, and determination that he himself possessed in abundance.[27]

It is difficult to determine if Adamson's 'lone ranger' approach held the day at the Game Department because of his forcefulness in advocacy, or if mere entropy and failure to appreciate the changed nature of the challenge was responsible. In any case, the outbreak of the Mau Mau Emergency in 1952 would have brought an end to whatever anti-poaching programmes had been in operation at the time.

Hunting Mau Mau

As it turned out, the Emergency and its suppression would have a profound influence on the subsequent anti-poaching campaign that would take place in Tsavo. It was far more than a hiatus in the anti-poaching efforts and the careers of Sheldrick, Woodley, and the other Kenya game-keepers. It proved a school and training ground for the key personnel and may well have helped inspire the strategies and prepare the ground for the next phase of anti-poaching operations. But, initially at least, the call-up of able-bodied white men into the ranks of the local 'anti-terrorist' levies depleted the ranks of the Game Department's Rangers and the Parks' junior Wardens.[28] Like others who were left in the field, George Adamson in the Northern Frontier District would report that he was 'now becoming heavily involved in emergency duties.... It is not going to leave me much time to attend to game matters, but ... the Emergency must come first.'[29]

Young Bill Woodley answered the call and saw active duty in the forests of Central Province, 'hunting' Mau Mau guerrillas. He gained vital experience in bush warfare, against an enemy who had the advantage of superior knowledge of the terrain and the ability to survive in the bush.[30]

[26] On the history of ivory smuggling, see Chapter 7 of this volume, and R. B. Woosnam to Colonial Secretary, 20 March 1913 (KNA KW/14/27); A. C. Ritchie, 'Memorandum', 2 April 1927, KNA KW/14/3. See Parker and Amin, *Ivory Crisis*, 118–21.

[27] Adamson's two autobiographies, *Bwana Game: The Life Story of George Adamson*, (London: Collins and Harvill, 1968) and *My Pride and Joy: An Autobiography* (London: Collins and Harvill, 1986), provide eloquent testimony to his character as a 'lone ranger'.

[28] See Mau Mau files in the Game Department materials in KNA KW/23/135 and 175.

[29] G. Adamson to Game Warden, 2 August 1954, KNA KW/23/175.

[30] Sheldrick, *Tsavo Story*, 59–60.

The analogy between anti-Mau Mau operations and hunting was not lost on the military authorities. Mau Mau fighters were instructed that '[t]he qualities which must be developed in troops engaged against the Mau Mau are … those required to track down and shoot shy game'.[31] We should also recognize that the techniques of counter-insurgency, although not formalized until after the British Malay campaign of the late 1950s, would also play a role in the formulation of an anti-poaching strategy in the wake of the suppression of the insurrection in Kenya.

David Sheldrick was refused leave due to his age and seniority and stayed at his warden's job during the Emergency, although he volunteered during his leaves for active duty with the 'mounted section of the Security Forces'.[32] He was already an experienced military officer, having served with distinction during the Second World War. A brilliant career as an intelligence officer had been predicted for him, and his decision to leave the service to take up employment as a gamekeeper had been regretted by his superiors in the Kenyan military. Virtually all of the other white officers who would serve with Sheldrick and Woodley on the anti-poaching campaign were experienced counter-insurgency warriors and veterans of the Mau Mau war.

The anti-poaching campaign in Tsavo

Just as Mau Mau has been characterized as a struggle over land, a peasant revolt by landless and land-hungry peasants against the export-oriented settler agriculture of the white highlands,[33] the anti-poaching campaign can be similarly characterized as a struggle over wildlife between the few remaining black hunters and a colonial state representing the local and international conservationist vision of wildlife sanctuaries. With the one struggle ending in 1955, the time was right for the final act in the other.

The death of one of the African Rangers in Tsavo East on 15 January 1955, at the hands of a cornered Waata poacher, led directly to the formation of the key instrument of the new anti-poaching strategy, the Voi Field Force.[34] Initially, the Voi Field Force was an operation within the National Park administration headquartered at Voi on the southern edge of Tsavo East. In April 1955, the Voi Field Force was in operation and enjoyed initial success in finding and apprehending both Waata and Kamba poachers. However, in October 1956, Park Director Mervyn

---

[31] Government of Kenya, *A Handbook on Anti-Mau Mau Operations* (Nairobi: Government Printing Office, n.d. [1954?]), 11. My thanks to John Lonsdale of Trinity College, Cambridge for making this citation available.

[32] Sheldrick, *Tsavo Story*, 60.

[33] Donald Barnett and Karari Njama, *Mau Mau From Within; Autobiography and Analysis of Kenya's Peasant Revolt* (New York: Monthly Review Press, 1966); and Tabitha Kanogo, *Squatters and the Roots of Mau Mau* (London: James Currey, 1987).

[34] Tsavo Royal National Park East. Warden's Quarterly Report for the Period 1st January–31st March 1955, KNA KW/23/31. See also Holman, *Elephant People*, 89–100.

Cowie convened a meeting that including top-ranking Police and Game Department officials. A decision was taken to begin a joint, all-out operation against the Tsavo poachers and to create two more field forces of 100 men each. Moreover, African Game Rangers would be specially recruited and commanded by Game and Parks field officers under the control of David Sheldrick. The force would have access to transportation, including a police spotter plane, and the newly recruited African staff would undergo a three-month training period in the new anti-poaching techniques.[35] Indeed, after October 1956 and for the next 15 months, the combined force achieved unprecedented success in curtailing the activities of the poaching fraternity in the Tsavo region, making the operation, in the words of one of its key Game Department officers, Ian Parker, 'the only successful anti-poaching operation in the history of colonial Africa'.[36] It is also the most carefully documented anti-poaching campaign, thanks to the meticulous reporting of the Parks' wardens in monthly and quarterly reports throughout the period of intense field operations, which were declared a success and wound up in December 1957.[37]

What accounts for the success and novelty of this anti-poaching operation, which would become the model for the postcolonial anti-poaching units created with World Bank assistance and operated in Kenya from the late 1960s to the present?[38] I believe that there were three practices adapted to the special purposes of the Voi Field Force that gave it its novelty and capacity for dealing with a difficult poaching problem. First, there was the matter of intelligence gathering and its application to the apprehension and prosecution of poachers. Secondly, there was the tactical application of police and anti-Mau Mau techniques to the needs of anti-poaching. Finally, there was the gradual transformation of the African and European personnel from the 'lone ranger' model that had so dominated previous efforts at the control of poaching to the less romantic – but highly effective – use of former poachers as local spies, informants, and game rangers in the effort to round up and destroy the poachers' support network and access to local resources. That is to say, the campaign succeeded in turning the poachers into gamekeepers. Let us look at

[35] Simon, 'The Elephants of Tsavo'; and Sheldrick, *Tsavo Story*, 43–5. 'Anti-Poaching Operations in Kenya', Press Office Hand Out No. 1203, KNA MTW/1/302 and other documents in this deposit.

[36] Interview D/2, Ian Parker, 25 August 1987. Mr Parker was closely involved with the anti-poaching campaign, and his assistance in clarifying my own views in this and other matters relating to the Waata and their fate is most gratefully and respectfully acknowledged.

[37] See Warden's Quarterly Report, Royal Tsavo National Park, 1 October–31 December 1956 (KNA KW/23/31) which contains a list by name and offence of some 43 Wakamba and Waata convicted of poaching during the first three months of the campaign. Summaries of events are available in the published annual reports by the trustees (written by Mervyn Cowie) during this period and are also available in the National Archives (KW/23/59ff).

[38] Simon, 'The Elephants of Tsavo', 76–8, on the establishment of the Voi Anti-Poaching Unit; and 'Anti-Poaching Operations in Kenya', KNA MTW/1/302. See also Daphne Sheldrick, personal communication, 24 January 1991; and Interview D/7, Daphne Sheldrick, 14 February 1991.

how this worked and then examine the ideological underpinnings of this transformation.

The key to the first new practice was the files. Starting in 1955 and working retrospectively, Sheldrick began to collect 'rap sheets' on the Tsavo poaching fraternity, eventually producing an extensive 'rogues' gallery' of poacher biographies. Both criminal activities and a wide range of personal data regarding family background, habits, haunts, and idiosyncrasies on each of the 200 to 300 Kamba and Waata hunters, and especially the handful of 'aces', or specially talented and experienced poachers, were collected, collated, and kept on file at the Voi headquarters.

Not only did this provide the gamekeepers with a profile of each of the hunters, complete with 'mug shot' when available, it also provided anecdotal information on alleged but unproven illegal activities, which would become especially useful in interrogating suspects. The adaptation of this police technique to the poaching problem was novel, but in and of itself could not win the struggle against the poachers. However, in combination with other police tactics, the 'intelligence files' would prove crucial to breaking up the poaching network.[39]

The second new practice was the mounting of pre-dawn raids on the homes, hide-outs, and haunts of the poachers, from information collected in the rogues' gallery about their habits. This was a significant departure from the anti-poaching sweeps made by the Game Department Rangers and Scouts. Prior to the 1955–7 campaign, arrests for poaching could only be made if the poachers were caught red-handed in the bush with weapons and the evidence of recent kills. This put the wardens at a disadvantage, as the poachers were able to use all their accumulated skills at bushcraft, tracking, and stealth to avoid pursuit and capture. Charges of possession of contraband game products or arrow poison, which carried only mild penalties, were the only ones that could result from capturing poachers outside the parks or at home.

The campaign made several important changes in this. First, the rangers of the Voi Field Force were empowered from 1956 to operate both inside and outside the park, against the haunts and hide-outs in the dense bush used by Waata and the hilltop camps favoured by Kamba poachers on the outskirts and the remote areas of the Tsavo vastness. Previously, only the Game Department had jurisdiction outside the park boundaries.[40] Secondly, penalties for the lesser offence of possession of contraband were increased by the courts, on the directive of the Attorney-

[39] These files on 3" x 5" index cards are the property of Daphne Sheldrick, the widow of David and at the time of the campaign, the wife of Bill Woodley. My thanks to Ian Parker, who is using them to write a collective biography of the Waata hunters, for allowing me to examine them and for his generous sharing of his experiences with the Voi Field Force. Interview D/2 Ian Parker, 25 August 1987; Simon, 'The Elephants of Tsavo', 70–92; and Sheldrick, *Tsavo Story*, 67–8, 77–8.

[40] As a corollary of this, it had become possible, after some discussion within government, for the National Parks to retain ownership of confiscated trophies, i.e. ivory, and sell it to benefit the National Parks accounts instead of the General Treasury as happened to ivory seized by the Game Department. See KNA KW/17/12.

General, to the same level as for poaching itself.[41] This gave the Voi Field Force important leverage in dealing with suspects caught in the pre-dawn raids. Finally, Sheldrick and Woodley in particular made effective use of the rogues' gallery in gaining confessions and valuable information on other poachers from those caught in the raids.

To understand this last, it is necessary to recognize the disorienting situation in which Waata and other '*washenzi*' poachers were caught. Roused from sleep by armed men bursting into a camp or hut, the suspect would be threatened with arrest for possession of poison or contraband and confronted with accusations about his past activities. Effective use was made of gossip and other information about the poacher's previous criminal activities or personal life in an effort to persuade him that the interrogators already knew everything. He was encouraged to confess his recent poaching escapades and implicate his contacts and collaborators in crime. Promised lenient treatment, and in some cases recruited then and there to the Voi Field Force as trackers, some poachers were turned into gamekeepers by this method.[42]

Many questions are raised by this 'police state' tactic. First, the possibility of abuse by the interrogators is clear. No search warrants were needed, but then none had been required of Game Department personnel at any time in the history of the colony. No legal counsel was permitted to be present and no 'Miranda rights' were read to the suspects. Physical abuse of suspects did occur, especially at the hands of the seconded police and Game Department officers of the force. However, in the hands of interrogators like Sheldrick and Woodley, the intimidation achieved by the knowledge of intimate details of the suspects' lives proved more effective than physical coercion in extracting confessions and information.[43]

We must also ask ourselves, why did the poachers succumb so readily to the browbeating and blandishments of the interrogators? To begin with, we must understand that these hunters were a particularly unsophisticated group of people in terms of their familiarity with the workings of the colonial regime. Knowledge of the outside world, of the workings of colonial law (as opposed to colonial prisons), and of the protections it afforded was negligible. No poacher would have known to request a lawyer even if he could afford to hire one. Although Kamba herders would organize effective protests against cattle culling and the forced marketing of their animals,[44] no such capacity for organization can be found among

---

[41] Attorney General's Directives Nos. 1 and 22 for 1956, Governor's Circulars, KNA KW/3/8.

[42] Holman, *Elephant People*, 143–65; Attorney General's Directives Nos. 1 and 22 for 1956, Governor's Circulars, KNA KW/3/8.

[43] Interview D/2, Ian Parker, 25 August 1987; and Holman, *Elephant People*, 143ff. Given the widespread use of force by Game Department staff and law enforcement agents in Kenya, I believe that the use of 'moral coercion' by Sheldrick and Woodley was the exception rather than the rule in these encounters. Still, there is no direct evidence that the anti-poaching campaign sanctioned the use of torture or physical coercion in these interrogations.

[44] Robert Tignor, *The Colonial Transformation of Kenya* (Princeton: Princeton University Press, 1976), 331–54.

the loose-knit fraternity of hunters. Moreover, the poaching fraternity, although extremely small (with perhaps 200 Waata, 250 Kamba, and 50 'other tribes' operating in the Tsavo East area[45]), were highly individualistic and competitive. They saw no shame or betrayal in turning in their rivals among the other Waata or Kamba hunters if it helped them lessen their punishment or secure the rewards of employment as trackers and scouts for the gamekeepers. No sense of ethnic or guild solidarity or *esprit de corps* seemed to have operated among the poachers. This greatly facilitated the work of the field forces in gathering additional intelligence on the habits, operations, and plans of the poachers remaining at liberty. By late 1957, virtually the entire Waata poaching fraternity and a large number of the Kamba had been run to ground by these methods, directed by Bill Woodley, Ian Parker, and the other Voi Field Force officers.[46]

The last new practice that grew out of this campaign was the recruitment of Waata and Kamba poachers into the ranks of the junior (i.e. African) staff of scouts and rangers for the Parks and Game Department. Originally, the Field Force was composed of six European Officers (Woodley from Parks; David McCabe, Dennis Kearney, and Ian Parker from Game; David Brown from Administration; and Major Hugh Massey from Police), and African rangers recruited from the northern warlike tribes (Turkana, Samburu, Somali, and Orma).[47] Increasingly, as former poachers were recruited to serve with the Force, it began to develop a local character. This gave the gamekeepers better information on the terrain, methods of operation, and habits of the Tsavo poachers.

The recruitment of Kamba was not without its difficulties. On more than one occasion, Kamba Rangers were dismissed for conniving in the escape of prisoners or for misleading the European officers to protect their friends or kinsmen.[48] The dangers of setting reformed poachers to catch others weighed on the Field Force leadership. Counterbalancing this disadvantage was the well-established reputation of the Kamba as 'Soldiers of the Queen',[49] due to their early recruitment and preference for military service by the colonial authorities. In this regard they simply added a new uniformed service to the list of acceptable, even prestigious, occupations preferred by young Kamba men.

After the campaign, many of the newly recruited Waata remained with the Parks or Game Department, allowing them to continue the outdoor life that they knew, hunting down the hunters of the game that they had once pursued themselves. By 1958, the former way of life of Waata and

---

[45] Holman, *Elephant People*; and Interview D/2, Ian Parker, 25 August 1987.

[46] In addition to the detailed account of Woodley found in Holman, *Elephant People*, chaps. 13 and 14, supplemental accounts can be found in Sheldrick, *Tsavo Story*, chap. 6; Parker and Amin, *Ivory Crisis*, chaps. 1 and 5; and in the Monthly and Quarterly Warden's Reports for 1955 through 1957 in KNA KW/23/31.

[47] Sheldrick, *Tsavo Story*, 43–5, 76.

[48] E.g. Tsavo Royal National Park East, Warden's Quarterly Report for 1st July–30 September 1955, KNA KW/23/31.

[49] See T. H. Parsons, '"Wakamba Warriors Are Soldiers of the Queen": The Evolution of the Kamba as a Martial Race, 1890–1970', *Ethnohistory* 46, 4 (1999), 671–701.

many Kamba hunters had been eradicated.[50] Poaching by Tsavo's indigenous hunting peoples no longer represented a threat to the survival of the elephant herds in whose interests the cultural survival of the Waata had been sacrificed. The way of life of the hunter-foragers was at an end, and with it new cultural and conservation problems would emerge.

The end of the game hunters

The success of the 1956–7 anti-poaching campaign was not merely a triumph for the conservationists. It also represented the coming of age of an ideology of conservation based on the bureaucratic and administrative model of African change and development that had already triumphed in many other spheres of Kenyan life. The change of gamekeeping personnel and the emergence of the National Parks administration as the leading force in wildlife conservation was, at base, I believe a reflection of the transformation of colonial society in Kenya. The pioneer settlers and big game hunters had largely passed from the scene with Lord Delamere, Baron Bror Blixen, and Denys Finch Hatton in the 1930s, although in the white hunter clique certain figures from the 1920s heyday would manage, like J. A. Hunter, to make the transition to modern gamekeeper.[51] Among the gamekeepers, the social sea change was reflected in the change from the ideals and values of hunter-game wardens like Captain Archie Ritchie and George Adamson to those of the non-hunting preservationists like Mervyn Cowie and Noel Simon.[52] Can this be seen to symbolize the change from the romantic and aristocratic game conservation ideology suited to the Kenya of the pioneer settlers, to that of the modern preservationist ethos espoused by its mid-century colonial leaders? Even more symbolic, not to say ironic, is the fact that, during the Mau Mau Emergency, Mervyn Cowie served as the colony's Director of European Manpower, a position that was held a decade earlier during the Second World War by that exemplar of aristocratic hauteur and Kenyan settler decadence, Lord Erroll.[53]

However, for the African hunters of Tsavo, the end of the game was a more frightening and demoralizing experience. The Wakamba who lived

---

[50] Although it was possible during my fieldwork in 1987 to find individuals who were identified by others as Waata, it was no longer possible to find a surviving community with a collective life that represented a hunter-forager cultural survival.

[51] E. Trzebinski, *The Kenya Pioneers* (New York: Norton, 1985) is a collective biography of the settler pioneers. Individual biographies include E. Trzebinski, *Silence Will Speak* (Chicago: University of Chicago Press, 1977) on Finch Hatton; E. Huxley, *White Man's Country*, 2 vols. (London: Chatto and Windus, 1980 [1935]) on Delamere; and U. Aschan, *The Man Whom Women Loved: The Life of Bror Blixen* (New York: St. Martins, 1987) on Bror Blixen. J. A. Hunter's autobiography, *Hunter* (London: Hamish Hamilton, 1952), traces his career from 'professional white hunter' to professional gamekeeper.

[52] Cowie, *Fly, Vulture;* and N. Simon, *Between the Sunlight and the Thunder: The Wild Life of Kenya* (Boston: Houghton Mifflin, 1962).

[53] Cowie, *Fly, Vulture*, 94–5; J. Fox, *White Mischief. The Murder of Lord Erroll* (New York: Random House, 1982), 48 on Erroll's wartime service.

on the fringes of the park might hope to continue hunting by scrupulously avoiding the precincts of the park itself, even in search of honey.[54] Most found it increasingly necessary to seek other forms of employment in agriculture, herding, or wage earning, especially in the police, military, and uniformed services of the National Parks and Game Department.

For the pure hunters among the Waata, 'The very heavy hand of the anti-poaching campaign has ... left its mark and the Wata remain confused and to some extent bitter.'[55] Mercilessly hounded in the bush and at home during the course of the anti-poaching operation, 'nearly every Wata male went to prison'.[56] Left without a means of supporting themselves or their families after their release, many would drift back into poaching, avoiding the parks if at all possible. Efforts to impose cultivation, tried unsuccessfully in the 1920s, began to take effect. 'The young men make it quite clear that it is only their fathers and grandfathers who want to continue hunting. These youngsters queue up to become askari [police].'[57] Others, as we have seen, would be briefly recruited as informers and agents of the anti-poaching task force. Lacking even rudimentary formal education or employment skills, their efforts at anything except gamekeeping were doomed from the outset. Better results were hoped for from the only concerted effort to find employment for the hapless Waata by the government: the Galana River Management Scheme.[58]

In 1959, Ian Parker was selected to head a government-sponsored scheme that would turn the now disorganized and despondent former Waata poachers into gamekeepers and elephant hunters, to 'control', by scientifically managed culling, the same elephant population they once threatened. Armed with modern rifles instead of their far more effective bows and *Acocanthera*-poisoned arrows, the Waata were established in a community and employed to cull elephants along the Galana River as part of a wildlife management scheme. Despite some initial successes, the Waata proved to be difficult to convince of the superiority of 'modern' methods of hunting, and difficult to accommodate to an authoritarian management style imposed by the administration. Despite Parker's efforts

---

[54] Interview B/7, Mwaniki Vila and Kilungu Musyoka, 24 April 1987; Interview B/8, Musemi Mulaki, 24 April 1987. These informants from Kyome and Kasivumi villages in Kanziko location, on the western edge of the park, were among the most bitter and sullen of informants I encountered, reflecting the well-known hostility to the parks and the Game Department of those living near the parks, documented by J. Akama, 'A Political-Ecological Analysis of Wildlife Conservation in Kenya', unpublished Ph.D. dissertation, Southern Illinois University, 1993.

[55] W. H. Thompson, Annual Report, Tana River, 1958–1959, Rhodes House, Mss.Afr. s.839, 5.

[56] Ibid. Their treatment in prison may well be imagined from reports of Kamba informants: 'The poachers who were caught or rather arrested by the game rangers were beaten almost to death and some even killed.' Interview B/9, King'oku Kaluku, 24 April 1987.

[57] W. H. Thompson, Annual Report, Tana River, 1958–1959, Rhodes House, Mss.Afr. s.839, 4.

[58] Interview D/2, Ian Parker, 25 August 1987. The entire collection of 303 documents relating to the operation of the Galana River Management Scheme are located in KNA MTW/1/187.

to allow some leeway for Waata beliefs and practices and to persuade government to allow the revenues generated by the Galana project to be maintained in the area, the central administration would not yield any local autonomy to the Scheme. Ultimately, it failed because of bureaucratic inefficiency and authoritarian values, a profit orientation on the part of the central government regarding ivory revenues, and the inability or unwillingness of the Waata to be 'managed'.[59]

The need for the Galana River Scheme stemmed from the fact that from the mid-1950s until the time of Kenyan independence a combination of drought, decline in predation, and natural growth of the herds had led to so serious an increase in the elephant herds of eastern Kenya that the chief threat to the survival of the herds was no longer from poachers but from the degradation of the environment caused by an overpopulation of elephants. The culling of elephants and rhinoceros by white hunters employed by the National Parks and Game Department became a major source of embarrassment as well as real concern to the ideologists of preservation and wildlife management, who were by then firmly in charge of Kenya's conservation establishment.[60] As independence for Kenya approached in the first years of the 1960s, the concern was that the highly visible culling of elephants in the parks – contrary to the ideology of total sanctuary that the parks were established to create – would lead Kenya's new African leaders to treat the ideas of sanctuary as so much hypocrisy, an expression of a continuing colonial desire to have it all for themselves.[61]

The locus of struggle

The struggle over the ownership of wildlife in eastern Kenya shifted by the time of independence. The class of independent producers of game products for subsistence use who controlled their own means of production, most Kamba and Waata, Meru and Tharaka, Digo and Duruma, had been either proletarianized or sedentarized and turned to wage labour, peasant agriculture or mixed farming. Those who might still occasionally enter the bush in search of game did so often as acts of defiance against a regime, colonial or postcolonial, that seemed remote and often opposed to their interests as hunters for food and sport. Perhaps their romantic, backward-looking reaction can be seen as a throw-back to the English gentlemen poachers of the early modern era, acting in response to their exclusion from the hunting fields? The locus of struggle was now between

---

[59] Parker and Amin, *Ivory Crisis*, 52–6. See Simon, 'The Elephants of Tsavo', 92–104.

[60] David Sheldrick, 'The Elephant Problem', Memorandum, 23 October 1964; I. Parker, 'Galana Game Management Scheme', Annual Report, 1 April 1960–30 June 1961. On the ecological crisis of the 1960s, see David Sheldrick, 'Notes of Meetings held 11 July, 1962, 14 Sept. 1962 and 12 May 1965 at the Kenya National Parks Headquarters', Sheldrick Wildlife Trust Archive, Langata, Kenya.

[61] Informal interview with Daphne Sheldrick, Langata, 24 January 1991. See also Edward Steinhart, 'David Sheldrick and the "Elephant Problem" in Kenya: 1956–1964', unpublished paper, African Studies Association Meeting, Nashville, 16–19 Nov. 2000.

peasants and the state, between workers and capital, both local and international. It resided both in the safari-based tourist industry and beyond, in Kenya's dependent economy. Any dreams of an independent life outside the global economy had been shattered by the 1950s conservation-inspired anti-poaching campaign that brought about the end of subsistence as well as elephant hunting by Kenya Africans. As we shall see in the epilogue, the poaching crises of the 1970s and 1980s would be based on a very different set of class forces and economic and political struggles.

Conclusions & Epilogue

It has been over a century since Kenya came under colonial rule, and four decades since that era ended. During that brief period in the history of hunting in Kenya, several vital transformations took place in the relationship of hunters to prey and of humanity to nature. Most significantly for us, the colonial era saw a transformation of the relationship of African hunters to the Europeans who came to pursue game and eventually, as a consequence of the desire to pursue, to preserve wildlife. This was a small part of the history of colonial relations, but I believe it was one especially fraught with significance for our understanding of the histories of Kenya and of colonialism.

This study has been offered as a social history. Its focus has been on hunting as a social activity and its role in building and transforming the social order. Of course, hunting is much more than this. It is also an economic activity with important ecological implications. It would become an issue of political import within Kenyan society as well as within British imperial society. It also raised crucial cultural questions of gender and values, and basic ideas about nature and religion, conservation, and international politics. Despite that, or perhaps even because of the endless complexities of the subject, this book is, in its design and research, its structure and argument, a social history. As such, I have often raised questions for which economic, cultural, or environmental historians would have provided different, more complex, and lengthier answers. I apologize if I have raised expectations that I would consider those important questions of economic impacts, cultural representations, and landscape and environmental change more thoroughly than I have. I believe that we have learned much from the social history research presented here about hunting, about colonialism, and about the Kenyan past.

The history of colonial Kenya, like the history of most societies, has been a history of struggle. The struggle over hunting and the control of wildlife in Kenya always took second place to the struggle over land. For most Kenyan Africans, indeed for almost all pre-industrial, pre-capitalist societies, land and water resources were fundamental in determining the economic life of the community. Control of animal resources, both domestic and wild, was also an important part of that struggle. As we have seen in the early chapters of this book, the struggle over game was intensified by the important position that hunting held in the lives of Kenyan communities on the eve of colonization. That is the concern of our first set of conclusions.

The place of African hunting

In the course of this study, I came to recognize that the role hunting played in the lives of Kenya's farmers and herders, as well as the country's scattered and sparse population of hunter-foragers, has been persistently denied, denigrated, and dismissed. The core of the problem has been the persistent undervaluation of hunting by subsistence farmers in the ethnographic and historical literature on African agricultural societies, and of the role that hunting has played in producing both economic and cultural values. I believe that the reasons for this denial of African hunting are in part benign and in part grossly prejudicial, rooted in the preconceptions of the meanings of hunting that attached to the practices of European cultures since the Middle Ages.

How are we to understand the wilful blindness represented by the denial of the African hunter as a social category by European observers? In part – the benign part – it is a result of what Steven Feierman has called 'invisible histories', part of the process by which 'African narratives had been silenced in colonial histories' and ethnographies.[1]

In this manner, colonizers and their historians saw African hunting practice as one of those 'particular domains of African life' considered to be irrational, the kind of behaviour that was out of character and therefore made no sense to the colonizer. Just as colonial writers marginalized Feierman's 'public healers', excluding them from history as it was understood by the colonizers, they have also seen hunting as something on the fringe of African society, inappropriate to the class and culture imputed to the 'natives' as stereotypical 'peasants' in the colonial mind-set.

In a larger sense, hunting was more than marginalized and ignored. Its very absence served to allow the colonizers and their apologists to reconstruct a mythic African peasant, more to their liking than the reality of the African hunters whom they could not 'see' or understand. This was due to the practice by some colonizers 'to destroy some forms of practice within the African societies they governed', or 'to suppress deeply rooted African traditions'.[2] However, there is more than denial and ignorance at work here. Beyond 'the historical occultation' of the practices of African

---

[1] S. Feierman, 'Colonizers, Scholars, and the Creation of Invisible Histories', in *Beyond the Cultural Turn*, ed. V. Bonnell and L. Hunt (Berkeley: University of California Press, 1999), 183.

[2] Ibid., 186.

hunting, there was also the creation of a positive image of the African. However 'mythic' and false, this image enabled the colonizer to create an imagined history, a semiotic system for understanding an African world that appeared to them more rational and in keeping with what the world should be.[3]

What I have done in the first chapters of this book is attempt to demythologize African hunting. Although the hunting praxis that I have examined is rooted in an ancient culture of hunter-foragers, I have shown it to be highly malleable over space and time. Although I speak of hunting traditions, I have found nothing that corresponds to 'traditional hunting' being practised in colonial Kenya, either among the Waata, who held closest to the ancient tools and techniques, or among the subsistence hunters within the Bantu-speaking farming communities in Meru, Kwale, or Kitui districts. Instead what I have tried to represent, despite the absence of chronological specificity, is a changing, adaptive, and inventive hunting praxis that proved capable of responding to market opportunities in the nineteenth century and of accommodating to colonial demands for labour and skills in the twentieth. Among the Kamba of Kitui district, as well as the Tharaka and many other hunting practitioners, we can see not the unyielding conservatism of the colonizers' stereotypical peasant, but a commitment to the development and improvement of their skills in the interests of their own and their community's well-being. Instead of the rigidity of custom so often encountered in colonial descriptions, there is a fluidity of practice, a variety of forms and a range of prey, changing hunting fields, and developing profitable (and commercial) uses of hunting skills and the products of hunting. The individuality of the Waata 'aces' and the entrepreneurship of the Kitui ivory hunters should help us un-define the idea of African hunter from its colonial strait-jacket and demystify the image of rural African stasis and conservatism.

The dynamics of class and the hunting synthesis

David Cannadine has recently reminded us that, 'We should never forget that the British Empire was first and foremost a class act, where individual social ordering often took precedence over collective racial othering.'[4] For Cannadine it was the performance of class relations that provided the fundamental dynamic to imperial relations. Neither should we forget the important roles played by racial othering (or more plainly by racism) or that played by gender hierarchy and expectations in shaping British perceptions and practices overseas. In the recent literature on Kenya and African society in general, race and gender have claimed pride of place in historical and ethnographic analysis. The examination of hunting in

---

[3] Here I draw on my reading of Philip Dine's *Images of the Algerian War* (Oxford: Clarendon Press, 1994), especially 8–12, which in turn is based on the analysis of *mythologies* by Roland Barthes.

[4] David Cannadine, *Ornamentalism: How the British Saw Their Empire* (Oxford: Oxford University Press, 2001), 10.

colonial Kenya in this book should serve to remind us of the centrality of class in maintaining the three-legged balance, alongside race and gender, in the analysis of colonial societies. Cannadine's 'class act' was intended as much as a play on the word 'act' as a reminder of the importance of class in the history of the British Empire. As the title of the Cannadine's book, *Ornamentalism*, impiously suggests, and as George Orwell vividly described in his short story, 'Shooting an Elephant', empire was an act, a theatrical performance staged before a captive audience of millions of colonized subjects.[5]

The colonization of Kenya in the 1890s by British imperial statesmen and soldiers, and its settlement by British gentlemen and ladies, imported into Kenya not just ideas of government and commerce, land ownership, and ethnic identity, but a whole culture of new class relations. One of the distinctive signs of this new imperial cultural complex was the peculiar role that hunting played in representing and dramatizing class relations. The pioneer hunters and the settler hunters did their best to maintain the purity and aristocratic lineage of the hunting 'traditions' they carried with them. However, class relations and their cultural manifestations cannot be as easily transplanted and bred in a new environment as, say, maize seeds or Holstein cattle. The introduction of the imperial hunting tradition laid the basis for the creation of a transcultural form of hunting, the big game safari.

Through interaction with coastal merchants and safari organizers and leaders, the first European pioneers began the process of cultural miscegenation. The hunting expeditions of Charles Stigand or 'Karamoja' Bell looked to all intents and purposes like a nineteenth-century Swahili trading safari. Even more clearly, the hunting and trading ventures of A. Arkell-Hardwick or Arthur Neumann resembled these merchant endeavours. Moreover, they were outfitted and organized by the same coastal agents, and accompanied and staffed by the same Kamba (or Nyamwezi or Yao) porters and safari workers, as had been their Arab-Swahili prototypes. By the time imperial soldiers and administrators like Richard Meinertzhagen and Frederick Jackson came along, they could do little more than take their place at the head of the long column of 'dark companions' who were the co-inventors of the safari.

The Kenya settlers would adapt the safari to their own purposes, and conform their own expectations to local hunting realities. Aristocrat land-owners like Lord Delamere would make efforts to translocate the aristocratic ideals of the hunt from England and the Continent to the grasslands and forests of Kenya. Even fox-hunting and trout fishing would be introduced to Happy Valley and the slopes of Mount Kenya. Trout could be caught, brought out, and released in the mountain streams; for foxes the settler hunter might substitute the local equivalent, the silver-backed jackal. It was far more difficult to re-create the social drama, to re-enact the hunt, to replicate the relations of class authority and sub-

---

[5] George Orwell, 'Shooting an Elephant', in *Shooting an Elephant and Other Essays* (New York: Harcourt Brace, 1945), 3–12.

ordination. Here, the substitution of deferential African peasants, Kikuyu and Kamba, Maasai, and Samburu, would prove both essential and difficult. The 'rules of the game' could not simply be imported and stocked like a trout stream. Nor would Kamba hunters so easily fill the roles of crofters and cottagers. In the processes of struggle and adaptation, new social relations distinctive to the big game safari would emerge. The gun bearer, the camp cook, and later, the driver and mechanic would emerge as part of the panoply of new characters and new social types associated with the transcultural safari. And, although their voices are silent in the written record and they are seen but dimly or at a distance, this itself is the mute testimony to the struggle between the different visions of the hunt that was under way.

With the emergence of the visiting hunter, the big game safari became Kenya's distinctive contribution to twentieth-century sports and promoted to the Western world the image of Kenya abroad as a veritable Garden of Eden. Like the settlers and pioneers, the visiting hunters shared a common cultural expectation that hunting was the activity of gentlemen and ladies, however differently they might define that status. The organization of the safari was designed to cater to that expectation. Ultimately, it was this expectation that required the emergence of the professional white hunter (PWH) as the pivotal figure in the changing dramatization of class. The African monopoly of local knowledge at the beginning of the century was filtered through the personae of local reputed white hunters. These safari leaders were drawn from the ranks of the settler hunters like Cuninghame, Finch Hatton, and von Blixen, or, less frequently, from among the hunting members of officialdom who could be seconded to the visitor's safari. They were men with local experience and expertise learned on safari with African hunters who knew the territory. In both cases, the proto-PWH possessed several assets that were essential to their calling. First, they knew a modicum of Swahili, the language of trade and of safari work throughout East Africa. Secondly, they were experienced in hunting local species and in local terrain, also learned on safaris with African staff recruited locally. Finally, they were familiar with the means of recruitment of a safari staff of gun bearers and guides, porters and drivers, tanners and skinners. Using all three of these acquired skills, the emergent PWH was a mediator, both a commercial middleman and an interpreter of local lore and practice to the visiting client/hunter. This required knowledge of the flora and fauna, the landscape, and terrain, as well as familiarity with the culture of the African hunters, who were the collaborators in the enactment of the hunting drama.

By the late 1920s and 1930s, the professional white hunter was the key figure among Kenya settlers in the newly invented transcultural safari tradition. As skilled in telling stories for the edification of his clients as he was in tracking game, the real role of the PWH was in creating and maintaining the image of white racial and class superiority: the white leader (*bwana*) of the safari was a proper gentlemen (*pukka sahib*). The corollary of this was that the African companions on safari were imagined as a suitable underclass of servants, an appreciative audience to the staging of a drama that would re-create the class relations of colonialism.[6]

But behind the scenes and beneath the façade of whiteness, the safari was the product of African local knowledge, African hunting values and practices and African adaptation to the imposition and negotiation of colonial rule. There can be little doubt that the contribution of African labour to the safari was as crucial as it was to other colonial enterprise, such as commercial mining or factory production of textiles. But, unlike those industries, in which a pattern of class relationship could be trans-located from Europe where they already existed and adapted to local conditions, in the case of the safari industry, not just the labour but the models, methods, and ideas were already firmly in place on African soil and in African minds. I would argue that the result, unlike any other colonial enterprise, was transcultural at its deepest levels.

The professionalization and commercialization of safari leadership in the hands of local white hunters was one aspect of the transcultural formation of the big game safari. Just as the safari organization was becoming a business enterprise with its own professional code of conduct, etc., other elements of twentieth-century technological change were making their impact. The introduction of wheeled transport and the attempts to limit its destructive impact on both wildlife and the drama of the hunt was the first of these elements. The use of aircraft in the hunting field and, even more importantly, as a means to get to the hunting field would also begin to change the class content of the safari. The introduction of the camera as a substitute rather than a supplement for the gun would also foreshadow and encourage a change in the class nature of the big game safari. However, what would ultimately undermine the hunting safari was a change that came from within Kenya's hunting culture as well as from without. The struggle over who owns the animals would reach a crescendo and be decided by a new local and international elite and their commitment to ideas of wildlife conservation.

Who owns the animals?

While the struggle between Africans and settlers over land has captured the attention of Kenya's historians for three generations, the continuing struggle over the control of animals, and especially wildlife, has largely been ignored. Moreover, the processes of marginalization of indigenous forms of hunting and the hybridization of imperial hunting by the trans-cultural production of the big game safari did nothing to resolve the conflict. The struggle continued at the margins in the efforts to suppress indigenous African hunting and, at the centre, beneath the stage on which the imperial drama of safari hunting was being enacted.

---

[6] Cannadine, *Ornamentalism*, 11–23, and 28–40 and *passim* for the attempts by the settlers 'to recreate their leisured, landed, and privileged lives in the White Highlands of Kenya' (39).

The reason for this is simple enough to understand: there was funda-mental agreement among African, imperial, and safari hunters that the hunter owned the prey. He might own it via possession and once the prey had been killed. No hunter appears to have recognized any other claim to ownership, although they might recognize the rights of landowners, political authorities, or the state to limit their access to animals. Nature itself had no rights of ownership. Neither did posterity.

The hunting consensus meant that Africans and Europeans might compete over the ownership of particular animals in the wild, but they did so by applying rules to regulate access and punish offenders against those restrictions. This is self-evident in the use of game laws, licensing fees, and regulations to control access. It is less evident, but equally real, in the regulations and controls exercised by means of ritual and initiation into the hunting societies such as the *waathi* in Tharaka and by the authority of the *athiani* hunting leaders among the Kamba. Most important to understand is that, as a result of this consensus, neither white hunting nor white settle-ment and consequent habitat destruction 'drove out' African hunting. The destruction of habitat by the spread of both white settlers and African cultivators may have marginalized hunting by moving the bulk of hunting for the large trophy animals, especially elephant, to the peripheries of settled areas. However, hunting persisted beneath and beyond the view of game rangers and colonial authorities down at least to the end of the colonial era. It would not suddenly begin again in the 1940s and 1950s, but would simply once again come onto the government's radar. Why should this be?

I have argued that a transformation took place in the basic ideas about the conservation of nature and wildlife during the colonial era. From early in the century, issues of game conservation came under game wardens whose job it was to ensure the long-term access of the sporting public to game by regulating hunting, imposing licences, and policing the borders of human settlement, where unregulated contact with animals could lead to mutual destruction. Gradually, this conservationist ethos that gave rise to game reserves came to be challenged by a new preservationist view. This was true on the ground in Kenya among a certain segment of white society, but it was also part of a larger movement of thought that changed game conservation (for future use by hunters) to wildlife preservation (for future, non-consumptive use by 'posterity'). This shift has often been presented in a triumphalist manner in terms of the growth of humanitarian sentiments and sensibility towards the welfare of animals. Here it has been described instead as the result of changes in the class position and relations of hunters to a wider society, such as their incorporation into the safari industry and their recruitment to service in the Game Department and National Parks service. Certain enabling changes in technologies associated with the hunting safari (e.g. automotive and air transport and photography) also facilitated this transformation. In Kenya, the shift in sensibility manifested itself in a political movement for the creation of national parks as wildlife preserves, rather than the regulation of hunting through the use of game reserves.

The creation of national parks in the post-Second World War era was, in my view, far more than just a change in conservation techniques or policies. It introduced a new combatant into the struggle over the ownership of animals. The wildlife preservationist was not simply a more humane conservationist, although many conservationists would personally make the leap to preservationism, at least at the level of championing national parks. Wildlife preservation's ultimate purpose was to redefine the ownership of animals as a sacred trust owed by the living generations to the future. Where conservationists were content to create reserves in which hunting was to be closely controlled and game animals reserved for future consumption, the preservationists' ideal was to establish a 'total sanctuary', to invent a wilderness free of human intrusion, occupation, or influence. A national park was to be a place where nature could be observed without being changed. This ideal of re-creating a Garden of Eden is still very much a part of the international conservation and environmental ethos, despite its utopian taint.

In practice, the establishment of Kenya's first large-scale national park based on the ideal of preserving wildlife, especially the endangered elephant, was to lead to the first real battle between whites and Africans over the ownership of nature and wildlife. Kenya's premier gamekeepers came to be the wardens of Tsavo National Park, conceived of as the key-stone to a new elephant preservation policy. It was the perceived threat to elephants by bow-and-arrow hunters, who had exploited the elephants of Tsavo for meat and ivory for generations, that would lead to a major anti-poaching campaign. It would be these few subsistence hunters who would fall victim to the new keepers of the game, acting in the name of posterity.

This struggle involved a combination of old and new anti-poaching techniques, but at its core was the notion that each and every elephant (within the boundaries of the park) deserved protection from those hunters who 'took' animals without having rights of ownership. African hunters, who had been confined and constrained by game reserves, game laws, game licences, and a myriad of legal restraints under conservationist policies, were now the 'Black Poachers' of this book's title. Poaching too had undergone a metamorphosis, from the simple violation of game limits and licence controls by whites to the creation of a whole class of black outlaws, vilified by the press and public as impinging on the rights of humanity and of posterity. In the end, it was the conservationists who ended all three of Kenya's hunting traditions – African subsistence, imperial, and safari hunting – and made every hunter a poacher.

I don't mean to excuse the practices of those who kill animals simply for profit or who use brutal and wanton methods in their pursuit of gain rather than game. But by turning the struggle over the ownership of animals into a Manichean battle fought in the name of humanity and posterity, we have distorted and demeaned the pursuit of game by both white and black hunters in Kenya. In so doing, we have also created an impossible ideal of 'total' sanctuaries and wildlife preservation policies from which we are only now turning away. It is my hope and ideal that something of the traditions of hunting by both blacks and whites can survive into the future along with the animals that sustain hunting cultures.

How can we as a species obtain this double objective of sustaining the prey and the predation? It seems highly unlikely that there is a single silver bullet that can hit both targets. But a mixture of the changing practices of the colonial past with new methods and tactics seems to me more hopeful. This may involve developing sustainable national parks for the non-consumptive observation and enjoyment of seeing animals obeying their own dictates. It may involve reintroducing big game hunting on licence for both foreign visitors and African residents. This would have to be carefully done so as not to reintroduce a system in which wealth, class, or race determined access to, if not ownership of, the game. By working in the direction of new policies of sustainable and manageable wildlife utilization, both consumptive and non-consumptive, in community-based wildlife programmes aimed at providing African users of wildlife both significant input and meaningful returns,[7] we may yet bring about a *modus vivendi* with nature (if not a Garden of Eden) and prevent the long-anticipated and much-feared 'end of the game'.

Epilogue: after Independence

The winds of change that blew so violently across Kenya in the 1950s brought a sudden and unexpected calm after the transfer of power in 1963. Even the desegregation of the leadership of the Game Department with the appointment of Dr Perez Olindo, the first warden trained as an ecologist, was hardly a revolutionary transformation.[8] There was much continuity in the scientific aspects of game keeping, which had begun in earnest with the first scientifically organized faunal surveys in the late 1940s, and increased after the 1956 Game Policy Committee Report with the creation of the Wildlife Research Unit and a standing committee on game policy.[9] One of the results of better information on game numbers

---

[7] For recent comments on community-based wildlife programmes, see Clark Gibson, *Politicians and Poachers* (Cambridge: Cambridge University Press, 1999); C. C. Gibson and S. A. Marks, 'Transforming Rural Hunters into Conservationists: An Assessment of Community Based Wildlife Management Programs in Africa,' *World Development* 23, 6 (1995), 941–57; and Stuart A. Marks, 'Back to the Future: Some Unintended Consequences of Zambia's Community Based Wildlife Program', *Africa Today* 48, 1 (2002), 121–41.

[8] Interview D/5, Dr Perez Olindo, Director of Wildlife, WCMD Headquarters, Langata, 26 October 1987. See P. Olindo, 'The Old Man of Nature Tourism: Kenya', in *Nature Tourism*, ed. T. Whelan (Washington, DC: Island Press, 1991), 23–38.

[9] Interview D/4, J. P. Oriero, Asst. Director, Conservation, WCMD Headquarters, Langata, 19 October 1987. The Faunal Survey of 1947, conducted under the auspices of the SPFE, was in fact headed by none other than Keith Caldwell near the end of his career as an international conservation leader. Capt. K. Caldwell, 'Faunal Survey of Eastern and Central Africa', August 1947 (*KNA* KW/1/83); and his 'Report of a Further Faunal Survey in East Africa', *SPFE Journal* NS, Part 61 (1950), 15–22. Colony and Protectorate of Kenya, Sessional Paper No. 1 of 1959/60 'A Game Policy for Kenya', Official Publications Library [OPL] CO/544/88.

and distribution was the Game Department's policy, from the late 1950s, of establishing clearly demarcated hunting blocks and rotating licensed hunting so as to 'rest' hard-pressed areas, which seemed to work reasonably well in managing the country's wildlife resources outside the parks.[10]

The wildlife sanctuary provided for animals inside the parks appears to have led to an increase in game numbers as elephants, in particular, drifted into the protected areas of eastern Kenya's national parks and reserves, such as Tsavo, Amboseli, Meru, and others, as they were created during the years immediately after independence. However, the resurgence of game numbers inside and outside the parks was not destined to last. Not only would the natural cycle of population growth and decline play a part, but the workings of the business cycle and international conflicts would also contribute to the end of hunting, if not the end of the game, in Kenya.

The final chapter in the history of Kenya hunting may be said to have been the direct result of the resurgence of poaching in the 1970s. As the price of ivory sky-rocketed and new non-traditional poachers entered the game with new methods, weapons, and logistical support, a new and wholly unprecedented challenge faced Kenya's African and white hunters and gamekeepers alike. Three seemingly unrelated events lie behind the new wave of poaching at this time. The Arab oil embargo, declared in 1973, was a key event in a global inflationary spiral that saw the prices of ivory as well as the prices of oil and gold rise dramatically. At the same time, the end of a prolonged war between Ethiopia and Somalia created a glut of young men with military experience and few opportunities for employment in the Horn of Africa. Using the weapons of war, chiefly AK-47 semi-automatic rifles,[11] and military transport, Somali poachers began a new wave of poaching in the mid-1970s. Finally, there were frequent reports of growing corruption on the part of high officials in the administration of President Jomo Kenyatta. These included suspicions that the president's wife, Mama Ngina, and others in top positions were in collusion with the ivory poachers and smugglers.[12] If nothing else, there was 'chaos and confusion that surrounded the issue of trophy licences and export permits'[13] for ivory.

This new challenge evoked two responses from the Government of Kenya. First, in 1976 it merged the Game Department and the Royal National Parks of Kenya, creating a single government department under ministerial control. The autonomy of the National Parks, so central to the

---

[10] Interview D/3, Jack Barrah, Wildlife Conservation and Management Department Headquarters, Langata, 5 October 1987. For an examination of the problems of poaching and preservation in the independence era, see Gibson, *Politicians and Poachers*.

[11] For the impact of new weapons on politics elsewhere in East Africa, see M. Mirzeler and C. Young, 'Pastoral Politics in the Northeastern Periphery of Uganda', *Journal of Modern African Studies* 33, 3 (2000), 407–29.

[12] The only published analysis of this dark period in Kenya's conservation history that I have found is I. M. Hughes, *Black Moon, Jade Sea* (Wimbledon, UK: Clifford Frost, 1988), 175–224.

[13] Ibid., 206.

thinking of an earlier generation of gamekeepers and conservationists, was at an end. At the same time, Dr Perez Olindo, the widely respected head of the Game Department, was eased out of his post by the amalgamation.[14]

Secondly, in response to the growing crisis in ivory poaching and smuggling, the government took the dramatic action of announcing a total ban on legal, licensed hunting in May 1977. 'Well meaning international conservation organizations had brought their considerable pressure to bear on the Government to impose the ban.'[15] But why would a ban on legal hunting, following as it did a ban on ivory exports, be expected to influence the Somali poachers and their smuggling partners? Even on the face of it, a ban on the legal hunting and export of ivory was likely to drive ivory prices higher in the grey markets of Asia and the West and prove a windfall for the poachers. According to Ian Hughes and others, 'there is strong evidence to suggest that the hunting ban exacerbated rather than eased the poaching pressure in Kenya'.[16]

The intentions of the international conservationists were no doubt well meaning, if somewhat naive and fervent.[17] More sober analysis of both the hunting and trading bans would argue effectively that these intentions were worse than misguided.[18] Real cynicism, however, was reserved for those who sought explanations of the government's motives in banning legal hunting in a positive effort to promote poaching. According to the late Glen Cottar, a professional hunter and tour guide and a knowledgeable, if cynical informant, there was a hidden scenario for the total ban on hunting.[19]

Cottar believed that in the face of government ineffectiveness in suppressing poaching, professional white hunters had begun to take matters into their own hands. Frustrated at seeing their own paying clients beaten to the game by poachers in total disregard of the hunting blocks that had been assigned to the PWHs, they began to actively report poaching to the game and legal authorities in a futile effort to at least curb illegal hunting in their hunting blocks. Some white hunters began to shoot at the poachers themselves. Their efforts to report poachers for arrest, Cottar believed, were thwarted by the courts, which were releasing poachers without penalties returning them to the bush. Rumours among the PWHs were that the magistrates were acting on orders from 'Nairobi'. The same rumours suggested that highly placed government officials ('Nairobi') were issuing false export permits to allow confiscated ivory to be effectively smuggled out of Kenya, with the proceeds enriching the officials. Mama Ngina was seen as the kingpin in this corrupt operation.[20]

---

14 Interview D/1, Glenn Cottar, 16 July 1987.

15 Hughes, *Black Moon*, 223.

16 Ibid.; see also Interview D/1, Glen Cottar, 16 July 1987.

17 See I. and O. Douglas-Hamilton, *Among the Elephants* (New York: Viking, 1975) for an example of the best-intended conservationist attitudes.

18 R. Bonner, *At the Hand of Man* (New York: Alfred A. Knopf, 1993), and his 'Crying Wolf Over Elephants', *New York Times Magazine*, 7 February 1993, 17ff.

19 Interview D/1, Glenn Cottar, 16 July 1987.

20 This is confirmed to some degree by Hughes, *Black Moon*, 203–6, 223–4.

Cottar went on to suggest that, with the PWHs effectively interfering in poaching operations, the government was persuaded by the corrupt elements within it to accede to the World Bank's and international conservationists' well-meaning pressures to ban hunting and then, some months later, to ban ivory and other trophy exports. This had the immediate effect of clearing the licensed hunters and their clients from the hunting fields, leaving them free of legitimate hunters, licensed and hunting in game department-approved hunting blocks. Instead, only the poachers would have free rein to hunt elephants and rhino with their AK–47s, cut out the tusks or horns, leaving the meat to rot, and load their valuable trophies on lorries, drive them to Somalia and from there smuggle them onto the international market, using false Kenyan export papers.

It is unlikely that either the PWHs were as successful in curbing poaching as Glen Cottar seemed to believe, or that there were not, within the government and Kenyan gamekeeping community, some sincere supporters of the idea of a ban on hunting and ivory exports as a potential cure for the poaching crisis. However, one cannot dismiss the idea that, to the extent that good hunting was interfering with poaching, it had become a target of the corrupt and collusive elements in 'high places'. Regardless of the motives, the result of the total ban on hunting in Kenya was the startling irony of what might be termed a Gresham's law of Wildlife Management: bad hunting will drive out good hunting.

A century-long history of colonial hunting in Kenya was brought to an end between 1946 and 1963. What remained of that tradition of transcultural hunting in independent Kenya would be ended within a decade and a half by a new kind of poaching crisis that reflected Kenya's place in a shrinking global environment and the conflicting claims of hunters, conservationists, and government over who owns the animals.

Bibliography

Archival sources

Kenya National Archives, Nairobi (KNA)

A large number of files from the Game Department and National Parks filed under the KW/ (Game Department), MTW (Ministry of Tourism and Wildlife) and WRS/ (Wildlife Research Service) deposit rubrics were consulted, as well as Eastern, Southern, and Coastal Province and selected District archival deposits. These include:

Ministry of Wildlife and Tourism, Deposit 1
    KW/1/15–86 Administration
    KW/3/8 Circulars
    KW/5/43–48 Societies, Clubs and Associations
    KW/6/85–91, 95 Boards and Committee Minutes
    KW/8/7, 28–34 Conferences and Seminars
    KW/12/8 Export and Import
    KW/13/45, 162 National Parks and Game Reserves
    KW/14/1–7 Game Trophies
    KW/15/1–19 Game and Vermin Control
    KW/17/3–4, 12–13 Hunting and Poaching
    KW/18/2, 6, 12–28 Legislation
    KW/20/3, 19–20 Press Cuttings
    KW/22/14 Publications
    KW/23/17, 29–31, 59–79, 124, 130, 135, 140–76 Reports
    KW/24/40–42, 47 Research
    KW/24/46 Zaphiro Aerial Counts
    KW/25/2, 5–6 Shows and Exhibitions
    KW/27/1–4 Game Preservation
    KW/27–24 Circulars

Ministry of Tourism and Wildlife, Deposits 2, 4
    MTW/1/182–9, 194–6, 210, 227–8, 255, 257, 266, 278, 281, 284, 294, 298, 301–2, 546, 768
    KW/10/1
    KW/16/2
    KL/12/22/63/01 and 02
    KL/13/2; 26/2; 27/14; 28/4
    KL/13/A/5/14
    KL/18/1–8
    KL/26/1–2
    KL/27/7–12
    KL/28/1–4
    KM/1–12
    MTW/4/1–61
    BM/1–4
    WRS/PROJ/IV 1977 Banning Circular

Provincial Commissioner, Coast Province Files
    PC/Coast/1/1/129, 132, 136, 138
    PC/Coast/1/8/1, 2, 5, 8, 12, 16
    PC/Coast/1/10/3, 30, 42, 59, 62, 80, 127, 164

PC/Coast/1/17/13
PC/Coast/1/19/36, 89, 118, 138
PC/Coast/1/20/9, 19, 22, 60, 68, 106, 109
PC/Coast/1/22/21
PC/Coast/2/5/15, 17
PC/Coast/2/12/2; 13/22; 15/1–5

Provincial Commissioner, Eastern Province Files
PC/EST/1/1/20 Kitui Handing Over Reports 1956–60
PC/EST/1/2/11 Kitui Honey and Beeswax Production
PC/EST/1/3/17 Kitui District Annual Reports 1963–8
PC/EST/1/3/20 Kitui District Annual Report 1955

Provincial Commissioner, Southern Province Files
PC/SP.1/4/1 Kitui District Annual Reports 1948–9
PC/SP.1/4/2 Kitui District Annual Reports 1952–6
PC/SP.1/4/3–6 Kitui District Annual Reports 1957–60
PC/SP.4/1/1 Memoranda, 1910
PC/SP.5/1/1 1956 Game Policy Committee, Papers
PC/SP.5/1/2 1956 Game Policy Committee, Final Report

Provincial Commissioner, Central Province Files
PC/CENT/2/1/3 Native Council Minutes
PC/CENT/2/1/11 Lambert Report, Meru

District Commissioner, Kitui Files
DC/KTI/1/1/1 Annual Reports 1909–20
DC/KTI/1/1/2 Annual Reports 1920–30
DC/KTI/1/1/3 Annual Reports 1920–30 (dupl.)
DC/KTI/1/1/4 Annual Reports 1931–42
DC/KTI/1/1/5 Annual Reports 1942–8
DC/KTI/1/1/6 Annual Report 1949
DC/KTI/1/1/7 Annual Report 1950
DC/KTI/1/2/1 Ukamba Province Annual Reports 1915–21
DC/KTI/2/1 Handing Over Reports 1930–48
DC/KTI/2/2 Handing Over Reports 1949–52
DC/KTI/3/10/1 Game, Claims for Compensation
DC/KTI/3/10/2 Game, Destruction of
DC/KTI/6/2/1 W. E. H. Stanner, 'The Kitui Kamba'
DC/KTI/7/1–5 Political Record Books
DC/KTI/8/1 Prov. Comm.'s Inspection Reports 1910–18

District Commissioner, Meru Files
DC/MRU/1/1 Annual Reports 1912–24
DC/MRU/1/2 Annual Reports 1925–36
DC/MRU/1/3–4 Annual Reports 1937–49
DC/MRU/1/5/1 Annual Report 1950
DC/MRU/1/6, 8–11/1 Annual Reports 1951–5
DC/MRU/1/7 Central Province Annual Reports, 1952–7
DC/MRU/1/11/1–2 Annual Report 1955
DC/MRU/1/12/1–2 Annual Report 1956
DC/MRU/1/13 Annual Report 1957
DC/MRU/1/14 Annual Report 1958
DC/MRU/1/15 Annual Report 1959
DC/MRU/1/16 Annual Report 1960
DC/MRU/2/1 Tharaka Murder
DC/MRU/2/2–3 Tharaka Safari Reports 1948–53
DC/MRU/3/1–10 Handing Over Reports 1935–50
DC/MRU/3/11–14 Handing Over Reports 1953–8

DC/MRU/4/4 Political Record Books 1930–50
DC/MRU/4/5 Chuka Political Records
DC/MRU/7/1–2 Reconstruction 1955
DC/MRU/8/1 Revenue Handbook
Meru District Socio-Cultural Profiles, Draft Report, n.d.
Embu District Socio-Cultural Profiles, Draft Report, n.d.

District Commissioner, Kwale Files
DC/KWL/1 Annual Reports
DC/KWL/2 Handing Over Reports
DC/KWL/3 Political Record Books
DC/KWL/4 Law and Order
DC/KWL/5 Diaries
DC/KWL/6 Correspondence
DC/KWL/7 Gazettes
DC/KWL/8 Roads
DC/KWL/9 Population
DC/KWL/10 Economy
DC/KWL/11 Letter Book
Kwale District Socio-Cultural Profiles, Draft Report, February 1986
Kwale District, Environmental Assessment, Draft Report, September 1985

In addition, the manuscript collections and Africana materials from the following archives, collections and libraries were consulted:
British Museum Library, London
David Sheldrick Wildlife Trust, Langata, Kenya
East African Collection, Kenyatta Library, University of Nairobi
Kenya Wildlife Research Service Library, Nairobi
Official Publications Library, London
Public Record Office (PRO), London
Rhodes House, Oxford
Royal Commonwealth Society Library, London
School of Oriental and African Studies Library, University of London

Interviews

All the interviews were conducted at the homes of the respondents unless otherwise indicated. Tape recordings were made unless otherwise indicated and transcripts were made with the assistance of research assistants as indicated. Typed transcripts were deposited with the National Archives of Kenya and the Institute of African Studies at the University of Nairobi in keeping with the requirements of the research permit issued by the Office of the President of Kenya.

Series A: Kwale District
Interviews in this series were conducted in various locales in Kwale and Mombasa districts from 28 February to 12 March 1987. Most were done with the assistance of a recent school-leaver from Kwale Secondary School, Mr Kalinga Mgandi.

A/1   Subject: Hamisi Ndiyani
    Place: Mwanzuani, Kwale   Date: 28 February 1987
    Asst: Salim J. Mwahaga
    Comment: Subject was a local farmer and stock raiser, age *c.* 58 years. The Assistant, a fourth-form student at Kwale Secondary School, was a substitute for Mr Mgandi, who was unavailable.
A/2   Subject: Harrison Bemwagandi wa Musinda
    Place: Kibanda Ongo, Kinongo   Date: 1 March 1987
    Asst: Kalinga Mgandi

Comment: No tape was made of the interview, as the subject was unwilling to be recorded. Despite this reservation, the subject, age *c.* 65, was cooperative and informative.

A/3   Subject: Kilute Dalu
Place: Puma, Kinango   Date: 1 March 1987
Asst: Kalinga Mgandi
Comment: This long interview involved contributions from members of Mr Dalu's household, especially Dalu Benzara and Msinda Muhupa, both nephews of the subject, who helped dramatize the stalking, shooting, and 'butchering' of animals in the Duruma tradition.

A/4   Subject: Nganawa Mwijo
Place: Kinango town   Date: 1 March 1987
Asst: Kalinga Mgandi
Comment: A useful interview on techniques and equipment in Duruma hunting from a 59-year-old farmer.

A/5   Subject: Juma M. Dzilla
Place: Golini, Kwale   Date: 3 March 1987
Asst: Kalinga Mgandi
Comment: This interview was with a younger (c. age 53) informant who still actively hunts for garden-raiding wild pig.

A/6   Subject: Omari Njama
Place: Kiruku, Kikoneni   Date: 5 March 1987
Asst: Kalinga Mgandi (with arrangements and help from Ali Swalehe)
Comment: The oldest in Kwale district, this informant was very helpful, dressing himself in traditional Digo hunting outfit and demonstrating hunting techniques, etc. He was reluctantly assisted by a neighbour, Mohammed Samba, who was knowledgeable, but wanted compensation for his help.

A/7   Subject: Nasoro Njama
Place: Kikoneni town   Date: 5 March 1987
Asst: K. Mgandi
Comment: The informant, age *c.* 74, was supported by his brother, Abdullah Njama, and was anxious to help arrange for us to accompany a local group hunt for pigs, pending permission from local authorities, which could not be obtained.

A/8   Subject: Ali Shehe Rungwa
Place: Magoborani, Kikoneni   Date: 5 March 1987
Asst: Kalinga Mgandi
Comment: This subject, age *c.* 65, provided basic biographical material on his own hunting experiences in southern Kwale District.

A/9   Subject: Nasoro Njama (follow-up interview)
Place: Kikoneni town   Date: 8 March 1987
Asst: Kalinga Mgandi
Comment: We returned in order to observe a permitted hunt, but having failed to get permission from the District Officer, Msambweni. Instead we were allowed to observe the subject in the preparation of arrows and a bow, which I was able to purchase.

A/10 Subject: Rashid Omar Mwakutunza
Place: Golini, Kwale   Date: 10 March 1987
Asst: Kalinga Mgandi
Comment: The younger subject, age *c.* 51, was useful on hunting in the vicinity of Kwale town.

A/11 Subject: Richard Wilding
Place: Ft. Jesus Museum, Mombasa   Date: 11 March 1987
Asst: None (In English, no tape recording)
Comment: The subject was an anthropologist and curator of the Ft. Jesus Museum. We spoke of his work on the hunting practices and material culture of Boran pastoralists.

A/12 Subject: Joseph Wamae
Place: Headquarters   Date: 12 March 1987
                            Shimba Hills National Park

Asst: None (In English, no tape recording)

Comment: The subject was the game warden for the National Park and our discussions covered hunting and conservation policy and the identities of Waata employees of the park.

A/13　Subject: Wilfred Aligula

　　　　Place: Entrance gate　　　　　　　　　　　Date: 12 March 1987

　　　　Shimba Hills National Park

　　　　Asst: Kalinga Mgandi (In English, no tape recording)

　　　　Comment: The subject was a recent employee of the parks and was questioned on the impact of conservation on local hunting.

Series B: Kitui District

Interviews were conducted in three locations in this very large district: Kitui town and Migwani in the centre, Mutomo and environs in the southern areas near the boundary of Tsavo East National Park, and in the northern area around Mwingi township. A Mutomo-based schoolteacher, Mr Joshua Kaluku, conducted one additional interview after my departure from the district for which special thanks are given. My research assistant in this district was Mr Steven Nyaa, age 19 and Head Boy of Kitui High School, occasionally assisted by Mr Charles Nding'o, a school friend from a prominent Kitui family. My thanks to Mr J. Musomba, Deputy Headmaster, and Mr Maluki Mwinzi, History Master, at Kitui High for making it possible for Mr Nyaa to assist me.

B/1　Subject: J. M. Munyoki Kieti

　　　　Place: Valasani, Matinyani Loc.　　　　　　Date: 13 April 1987

　　　　Asst: Steven Nyaa with Charles Nding'o

　　　　Comment: A very cooperative informant, age 73, who voluntarily brought his hunting kit for us to examine and freely offered information on his 60 years as a hunter.

B/2　Subject: Kitonga Kusewa

　　　　Place: Mutuni, Changwitha Loc.　　　　　　Date: 14 April 1987

　　　　Asst: Steven Nyaa with Charles Nding'o

　　　　Comment: Both Mr Kusewa, age *c.* 70, and his wife were present and offered material on both hunting and preparation of meats.

B/3　Subject: Julius Ndiulu Kimau

　　　　Place: Ndalani, Matinyani Loc.　　　　　　Date: 15 April 1987

　　　　Asst: Steven Nyaa with Charles Nding'o

　　　　Comment: This informant, age *c.* 91, hunted in the early part of the century and related personal experiences.

B/4　Subject: Kioko Mulanga

　　　　Place: Ngiini, Changwithe Loc.　　　　　　Date: 16 April 1987

　　　　Asst: Steven Nyaa with Charles Nding'o

　　　　Comment: Aged *c.* 88, the informant, after requesting payment, provided much material on hunting by boys and young men. Arrangements were made to purchase a specimen bow and arrows.

B/5　Subject: Ndambuki Ndeve

　　　　Place: Kyome, Mutomo Loc.　　　　　　　Date: 23 April 1987

　　　　Asst: Steven Nyaa and William Wandebe, Dist. Office driver

　　　　Comment: This man, age *c.* 89, was an elephant hunter and helped with the methods particular to that pursuit.

B/6　Subject: Nzenge Kitoi

　　　　Place: Kandai, Mutomo Loc.　　　　　　　Date: 23 April 1987

　　　　Asst: Steven Nyaa

　　　　Comment: Directed to this blind informant by the location chief, William Muliki, we found him to be most useful on elephant and leopard hunting and weapons.

B/7　Subject: Mwaniki Vila and Kilungu Musyoka

　　　　Place: Kyome, Kanziko Loc.　　　　　　　Date: 24 April 1987

　　　　Asst: Steven Nyaa with William Ndeve

　　　　Comment: The informants were age mates who hunted together and expressed useful views on the role of Game Wardens and Scouts; reasons for the end of hunting.

B/8　Subject: Musembi Mulaki

Place: Kasivumi, Kanziko Loc.   Date: 24 April 1987
Asst: Steven Nyaa
Comment: After a fruitless search for recommended informants, we arranged an impromptu interview with this reluctant and less than candid local *mzee*, who lived near the Tsavo boundary.

B/9   Subject: King'oku Kaluku
        Place: Kasivuni, Kanziko Loc.   Date: 24 April 1987
        Asst: Steven Nyaa
        Comment: After listening to the previous interview, this subject offered to help and presented a very useful monologue history of southern Kitui hunting and honey-gathering.

B/10   Subject: Kathukya Kikwai
        Place: Kyamboo, Migwani Loc.   Date: 28 April 1987
        Asst: Steven Nyaa, introduced by Maluki Mwinzi
        Comment: This infirm *mzee* proved a very lively and helpful informant on elephant hunting, prices, small game, hunting in central Kitui and Tana River Valley; and attitudes to rangers and scouts.

B/11   Subject: Petero Kitheng'e, Paulo Ngutu Ngutha, and Musila Muli
        Place: Home of M. Mwinzi, Migwani   Date: 28 April 1987
        Asst: Steven Nyaa and Maluki Mwinzi
        Comment: Mr Mwinzi, my host and a history teacher, gathered these age mates from among his elders in Migwani. The three men include the father of the then Director of Tourism, David Muli. Their testimony was comprehensive and especially useful for central Kitui.

B/12   Subject: Kikuli Mutulya
        Place: Bondoni, Mwingi Loc.   Date: 30 April 1987
        Asst: Steven Nyaa with his father, Samson Nyaa
        Comment: A lengthy and invaluable interview on northern Kitui and Tana River elephant hunting expeditions *c.* 1900 with graphic detail on methods, tactics, magic, and structure of hunt.

B/13   Subject: Kitema Ngumbi
        Place: Mwingi Loc.   Date: 30 April 1987
        Asst: Steven Nyaa with Samson Nyaa and Kiluli Mutulya
        Comment: Useful informant on hunting during the famine of Ngomanisye (1898–9) and prices, marketing, and attitudes to game people.

B/14   Subject: Samson Nyaa
        Place: Kyome, Migwani Loc.   Date: 30 April 1987
        Asst: Steven Nyaa
        Comment: The informant had assisted his son in locating and interviewing other subjects and proved invaluable in providing vernacular names for game animals.

B/15   Subject: Vetelo Kituva Nzee
        Place: Ngwani, Ikanga Loc.   Date: May 1987
        Asst: Joshua N. Kiluku
        Comment: The informant, a well-known old hunter of south Kitui, was interviewed from a question schedule prepared by Mr Kiluku, a local history teacher. He helped confirm information on hunting methods, poison, sale of ivory, weapons, *athiani* and *anake*, and the impact of game people.

Series C: Meru District

Interviews were focused on two locations and required two research assistants/interpreters. First, I based myself in Nkondi Location in the Kitharaka-speaking area in the southeastern corner of the district bordering the Tana River and the southern end of Meru National Park. Here my interpreter was Mr Julius Mucee Kairanya, a recent A-level graduate of Kakamega High School. His parents, Mr and Mrs Eugene M'kairanya, were kind enough to provide accommodation at their farm near Nkondi market. The good offices of Mr Joseph Mugao Kibunjia, a local headmaster, were invaluable in finding informants and arranging my induction into the Tharaka hunter's society. (A note on the spelling and pronunciation of Kitharaka names: at circumcision into an age set, young men are given names which begin with the syllable *mta* which is written either *M'* or *M'ta*. Hence *M'kirebu* is pronounced as mta-kirebu.) Next, I based myself in Kangeta Location in Igembe Division where Mr David Nguthari Maore was my interpreter. Additional help was provided by Mr Samson Koome, a University of Nairobi undergraduate home on holiday, who accompanied us on some of the interviews and provided useful advice and local information. Special thanks also to Dr John Nkinyangi and his family in Kangeta for providing me with generous hospitality.

C/1 Subject: Kiriamagwa
Place: Nkondi, Tharaka Loc.   Date: 6 September 1987
Asst: Mucee Kairanya
Comment: An exceptionally long and useful interview covering hunting by young men; weapons, poison and traps; prayers and magic; and a statement on the role of game people. The subject also makes bows and arrows for sale, samples of which I purchased.

C/2 Subject: M'kirebu Mukangau, M'giakanu M'tomaige, M'takwenga N'takarichi, Joseph Mugao Kibunjia, and John Livingstone Mate
Singers: Njeru M'takwenda, Mushomba M'tamuthuri, Rugendo M'beria, Nderi Kimbo, and Danieli Mwinzi
Place: Nkondi, Tharaka Div.   Date: 7 September 1987
Asst: Mr Kibunjia acted as translator and sponsor
Comment: This collective interview was both performance and initiation ceremony. The singing of hunting songs by a chorus of younger men was followed by an induction rite into the *Waathi* society conducted by Mr M'kirebu Mukangao and then a symbolic hunting demonstration. Payment was made for *uki* (honey-beer) and a he-goat as initiation fee. A discussion completed the four-hour interview.

C/3 Subject: Franklin J. M. Kanampiu
Place: County Hotel, Meru Town   Date: 8 September 1987
Asst: Mr Kibunjia provided introductions
Comment: The subject, an assistant chief in Mutino Loc., Chuka Division, was introduced by chance and provided spontaneous information on Tharaka hunting equipment and the social role of hunting in Tharaka.

C/4 Subject: Kimwere M'tamangara
Place: Maranthiu, Tharaka Div.   Date: 9 September 1987
Asst: Mucee Kairanya with J. Kibunjia and subject's son Julius Kimwere
Comment: This exceptionally well-informed subject, age *c.* 88, provided a wide range of firsthand information on hunting in the Tana River valley, where he claimed to still be an active hunter.

C/5 Subject: Kabete M'kagorwe
Place: Mukothima market, Kanjoro Loc.   Date: 10 September 1987
Asst: Mucee Kairanya
Comment: Useful information on both his and his father's generation and on relations with local administration for whom he worked as a hunting guide (*kilongozi*).

C/6 Subject: Eugene M'kairanya
Place: Nkondi, Tharaka Div.   Date: 10 September 1987
Asst: Mucee Kairanya
Comment: This interview was dedicated to identifying the major animal and bird species by their Kitharaka names. The subject was *c.* 57 years and had first hunted in 1944.

C/7 Subject: John Livingstone Mate
Place: Nkondi, Tharaka Div.   Date: 11 September 1987
Asst: Mucee Kairanya
Comment: Mr Mate was an educated man and retired civil servant who had hunted an a young man and had both firsthand experience and informed opinions on the history of hunting in Tharaka.

C/8 Subject: Joseph Mugao Kibunjia
Place: Nkondi, Tharaka Div.   Date: 11 September 1987
Asst: Mucee Kairanya
Comment: Mr Kibunjia acted as my sponsor for initiation into the Waathi society and to facilitate my visit. Thanks are due to his son, Mzalendo Kibunjia, a graduate student in archaeology, for introducing us. The interview resulted from a request for

help with Kitharaka animal names, but extended well beyond that into a history of local administration.

C/9   Subject: M'mutiga Kaumbuthu
Place: Mukothima, Kanjoro Loc.   Date: 12 September 1987
Asst: Mucee Kairanya
Comment: A knowledgeable informant who had hunted until recently outside the southern end of Meru Park and related his experiences of conflict with Game and Park wardens.

C/9b   Subject: David Kirema, David Muthani and Daniel Murithi
Place: Mutothima, Kanjoro Loc.   Date: 12 September 1987
Asst: Mucee Kairanya
Comment: While I was waiting in Mukothima market, a group of teenaged boys began to examine my field guide to East African birds, i.e. J. G. Williams and N. Arlott, *A Field Guide to the Birds of East Africa* (London: Collins, 1963). I began to question them about their knowledge of local birds and the result was an impromptu interview to identify bird names in Kitharaka.

C/10   Subject: Paul Kubai, Lawrence Mbabu and Julius Thuranira
Place: Kangeta market, Igembe Div.   Date: 24 September 1987
Asst: None
Comment: Having just arrived in Kangeta, I conducted this interview with some young men and a few elders (*wazee*) in the market square to gather the Kigembe names of animals and birds using field guide illustrations in J. G. Williams, *A Field Guide to the National Parks of East Africa* (London: Collins, 1967) to make identifications.

C/11   Subject: Isaac Kabura
Place: Muringene market, Igembe Div.   Date: 25 September 1987
Asst: David Maore
Comment: A useful interview on Igembe use of poison (*ubai*) and traps, including a demonstration of weapons.

C/12   Subject: Francis Kibunja
Place: Maua Town, Igembe Div.   Date: 26 September 1987
Asst: David Maore
Comment: This informant, age *c.* 62, was very helpful on arrow poison, relations with game officers, and hunting in the plateau area north of Igembe (*ruanda* or desert).

C/13   Subject: M'imbere M'Limbere
Place: Milu Tatu, Igembe Div.   Date: 26 September 1987
Asst: David Maore and Samson Koome
Comment: This informant was a blacksmith and fletcher and focused on arrow making and materials. The interview included an off-microphone discussion of the impact of game regulations on local hunting.

C/14   Subject: Kinjuki M'mbuiria with Charles M'tabari and Henry Kiunga
Place: Burieruri, Igembe Loc.   Date: 28 September 1987
Asst: David Maore and Samson Koome
Comment: This youthful informant (age *c.* 36) provided useful material on subsistence hunting, the protocol of sharing, and the reduction in game availability.

C/15   Subject: Joseph Thuranira
Place: Kangeta market, Igembe Div.   Date: 28 September 1987
Asst: None
Comment: The informant after participating in Interview C/1 had drawn up his own list of bird names, using a pen I had given him as a gift (*chai*, literally tea). We spent some time checking his list against the field guide and listening to kibitzers in the market, attracted by the book.

C/16   Subject: Stefano Mwenda
Place: Kangeta market, Igembe Div.   Date: 29 September 1987
Asst: David Maore
Comment: This experienced hunter (age c. 48) provided much detail on arrow poison, preferred prey, anti-poaching impact and reduction in game.

Series D: Nairobi Interviews

These interviews were conducted with retired and active Game Department personnel, professional white hunters, and others closely associated with hunting, game keeping, or conservation during the colonial era. In general, I preferred to use official records or more contemporary accounts by white hunters and other firsthand participants, etc., to the collection of reminiscences from them years later. However, in a number of cases, these interviews proved invaluable in both fleshing out written accounts and providing commentaries and interpretations of the intentions and beliefs behind the events discussed in the contemporary record. All interviews were in English.

D/1   Subject: Glen Cottar
      Place: Karen, Nairobi Dist.   Date: 16 July 1987
      Asst: None
      Comment: The subject runs a safari company and game-viewing camp. He was a professional hunter like his father and grandfather before him and provided useful information on safari hunting, poaching, and outsider attitudes to game keeping.

D/2   Subject: Ian Parker
      Place: Mbagathi, Nairobi Dist.   Date: 25 August 1987
      Asst: None
      Comment: Now a nature writer, the subject was a Game Ranger, and director of the Galana Scheme to employ Waata as elephant hunters. He has been a wildlife consultant and cropping expert and is the author of two books on wildlife. His firsthand information on Waata hunters, elephants and ivory, and the workings of the Game Department, has been invaluable.

D/3   Subject: Jack Barrah
      Place: Wildlife Conservation and Management Department (WCMD) Headquarters, Langata   Date: 5 October 1987
      Asst: Dr E. S. Atieno Odhiambo
      Comment: Now a Wildlife Consultant with the Kenya WCMD, Mr Barrah joined the Game Department in 1956 and was helpful on official attitudes and the organization of game keeping, controlled sport hunting, and anti-poaching operations.

D/4   Subject: J. P. Oriero
      Place: WCMD Headquarters, Langata   Date: 19 October 1987
      Asst: None
      Comment: The subject was Assistant Director for Conservation and provided useful information about the department's organization and programmes and historical material on wildlife research and controlled hunting and regulation in the 1950s.

D/5   Subject: Perez M. Olindo
      Place: WCMD Headquarters, Langata   Date: 26 October 1987
      Asst: None
      Comment: Dr Olindo was appointed Director of the WCMD in January, 1987 and had been Director of the National Parks from 1966 to 1976. He was most helpful on establishing both official and current popular views on hunting, conservation and the role of the Game Department historically.

D/6   Subject: Oscar T. Owre
      Place: Biology Department   Date: 12 April, 1988
      University of Miami, Coral Gables, Florida
      Asst: None
      Comment: Dr Owre is a research ornithologist and led the 1958 Maytag Expedition to Lake Turkana (Rudolph) sponsored by the University of Miami. He provided useful insights on the relationship between hunting and scientific data collecting. My thanks to Dr Steven Green of the Biology Department at Miami for making this introduction.

D/7   Subject: Daphne Sheldrick
      Place: David Sheldrick Wildlife Trust   Date: 14 February 1991
      Langata Gate, Nairobi National Park
      Asst: None
      Comment: Well known internationally for her work in wildlife preservation, the subject is the widow of David Sheldrick. She not only provided essential insights into the character and ideas of her late husband and his work as Park Warden, she also

allowed me to have access to his private files relating to anti-poaching and the elephant crisis of the 1960s. Special thanks to Ms Bernice Gordon for the introduction.

Published works

Books and articles

Abercrombie and Kent, *Africa*, advertising brochure, 2003.

Ackerman, D. 'A High Life and a Wild One'. *New York Times Book Review*, 23 August 1987.

Adams, Chuck. The *Complete Book of Bowhunting*. New York: Winchester Press, 1978.

Adams, Jonathan S. and Thomas O. McShane. *The Myth of Wild Africa*. New York: Norton, 1992.

Adamson, George. *Bwana Game: The Life Story of George Adamson*. London: Collins and Harvill, 1968.

——. *My Pride and Joy. An Autobiography*. London: Collins and Harvill, 1986.

Adamson, Joy. *Born Free: A Lioness of Two Worlds*. New York: Pantheon Books, 1960.

Akeley, Carl. 'Gorillas—Real and Mythical'. *Natural History* 23, 5 (1923).

——. *In Brightest Africa*. Garden City, NY: Garden City Publishing, 1925.

Akeley, Delia J. *Jungle Portraits*. New York: Macmillan, 1930.

Akeley, Mary L. Jobe. *Carl Akeley's Africa*. New York: Dodd, Mead, 1930.

——. 'In the Land of His Dreams'. *Natural History* 27, 6 (1927).

——. *Rumble of a Distant Drum*. New York: Dodd, Mead, 1946.

——. *The Wilderness Lives Again*. New York: Dodd, Mead, 1946 [orig. pub. 1940].

Akong'a, Joshua. 'Drought and Famine Management in Kitui District, Kenya'. In *Anthropology of Development and Change in East Africa*, ed. David W. Brokensha and P. D. Little. Boulder and London: Westview, 1988.

—— (ed.). *Kenya District Socio-Cultural Profiles, Kitui District*. Draft Report, Institute of African Studies, University of Nairobi, 1986.

Allman, J., S. Geiger and N. Musoke (eds). *Women in African Colonial Histories*. Bloomington: Indiana University Press, 2002.

Alpers, Edward A. *Ivory and Slaves in Eastern Africa*. London: Oxford University Press, 1975.

——. 'The Ivory Trade in Africa: An Historical Overview'. In *Elephant: The Animal and Its Ivory in African Culture* (catalogue). Los Angeles: Fowler Museum, 1993.

Ambler, Charles H. *Kenyan Communities in the Age of Imperialism*. New Haven and London: Yale University Press, 1988.

——. 'Population Movement, Social Formation and Exchange: Central Kenya in the 19th Century'. *International Journal of African Historical Studies* 18, 2 (1985).

Anderson, David M. 'Depression, Dust Bowl, Demography and Drought: The Colonial State and Soil Conservation in East Africa During the 1930s'. *African Affairs* 83, 332 (July 1984).

——. 'Policing the Settler State: Colonial Hegemony in Kenya, 1900–1952'. In *Contesting Colonial Hegemony*, ed. Dagmar Engels and Shula Marks. London: British Academic Press, 1994.

——. 'Visions of the Vanquished'. In *Revealing Prophets*, ed. D. M. Anderson and D. H. Johnson. London: James Currey, 1995.

—— and Richard Grove (eds). *Conservation in Africa. Peoples, Policies and Practice*. Cambridge: Cambridge University Press, 1987.

—— and David Killingray (eds). *Policing the Empire*. Manchester: Manchester University Press, 1991.

—— and David Throup. 'Africans and Agricultural Production in Colonial Kenya'. *Journal of African History* 26 (1985).

Anderson, J. K. *Hunting in the Ancient World*. Berkeley: University of California Press, 1985.

Anonymous. *Meru*. Nairobi: Consolata Fathers, n.d.

Appiah, K. A. 'White Mischief'. *Transition* 62 (1993).

Arkell-Hardwick, Alfred. *An Ivory Trader in North Kenia*. London: Longmans, Green, 1903.

Aschan, Ulf. *The Man Whom Women Loved: The Life of Bror Blixen*. New York: St. Martins, 1987.

Baden-Powell, R. S. S. *Sport and War*. London: Heinemann, 1900.

Bailey, Robert and Robert Aunger, Jr., 'New Hunters vs. Archers: Variations in Women's

Bibliography

Subsistence Strategies in the Ituri Forest'. *Human Ecology* 17, 3 (1989).

Baker, Carlos. *Ernest Hemingway. A Life Story*. New York: Charles Scribner's Sons, 1969.

——. *Hemingway: The Writer as Artist*. Princeton: Princeton University Press, 1963.

Balneaves, Elizabeth. *Elephant Valley*. London: Butterworth Press, 1962.

Barnett, Donald L. and Karari Njama. *Mau Mau from Within; Autobiography and Analysis of Kenya's Peasant Revolt*. New York: Monthly Review Press, 1966.

Barringer, Judith M. *The Hunt in Ancient Greece*. Baltimore: The Johns Hopkins University Press, 2002.

Bass, George F. 'Oldest Known Shipwreck Reveals Treasures of the Bronze Age'. *National Geographic* 172 (December 1987).

Bassi, Marco. 'Hunter and Pastoralists in East Africa: The Case of the Waata and the Oromo-Borana'. In *Dynamics of Populations, Movements and Responses to Climatic Change in Africa*, ed. B. E. Barich and M. C. Gatto. Rome: Bonsignore Editore, 1997.

Baxter, E. H. (ed.). *From Shikar to Safari. A Big Game Anthology*. London: A. C. Black, 1931.

Beachey, R. W. 'The East African Ivory Trade in the Nineteenth Century'. *Journal of African History* 8, 2 (1967).

Beard, Peter. *The End of the Game*. London: Collins, 1978.

Beaton, K. de P. *A Warden's Diary*. (2 vols) July to December. Nairobi: East African Standard, 1949.

Bederman, Gail. *Manliness and Civilization*. Chicago: University of Chicago Press, 1995.

Beinart, William. 'African History and Environmental History'. *African Affairs* 99, 395 (2000).

——. 'Empire, Hunting and Ecological Change in Africa'. *Past and Present* 128 (August 1990).

——. 'Introduction: The Politics of Colonial Conservation'. *Journal of Southern African Studies* 15, 2 (1989).

——. 'Soil Erosion, Conservationism, and Ideas about Development: A Southern African Exploration, 1900–1960'. *Journal of Southern African Studies* 11, 1 (October 1984).

Bell, W. D. M. *Bell of Africa*. London: N. Spearman, 1960 [Republication of *The Wanderings of an Elephant Hunter* with a new introduction by Col. Townsend Whelan].

——. *The Wanderings of an Elephant Hunter*. London: Country Life, 1923 and New York: Charles Scribner's Sons, 1923.

Bennet, E. *Shots and Snapshots in British East Africa*. London: Longmans, Green, 1914.

Bennett, Gavin. 'Out of Her Africa, Out of Her Mind'. *AutoNews* (Nairobi), March 1986.

Berman, Bruce. *Control and Crisis in Colonial Kenya*. London: James Currey, 1990.

—— and John Lonsdale. *Unhappy Valley*. London: James Currey, 1992.

Bernard, Frank Edward. *East of Mount Kenya: Meru Agriculture in Transition*, Afrika Studies 75. Munich: Weltform Verlag, 1972.

Bernardi, B. *The Mugwe: A Failing Prophet*. London: Oxford University Press, 1959.

Biesele, M. *Women Like Meat*. Johannesburg: Witwatersrand University Press, 1993.

Binks, H. K. *African Rainbow*. London: Sidgwick and Jackson, 1959.

Bird-David, Nurit. 'Beyond "The Original Affluent Society": A Culturalist Reformulation'. *Current Anthropology* 33, 1 (1992).

Blixen, Bror. *The Africa Letters*, trans. and intro. by G. F. V. Kleen. New York: St. Martins, 1988.

Bodry-Sanders, Penelope. *Carl Akeley: Africa's Collector, Africa's Savior*. New York: Paragon House, 1991.

Bonner, Raymond. *At the Hand of Man*. New York: Alfred A. Knopf, 1993.

——. 'Crying Wolf Over Elephants'. *New York Times Magazine*, 7 February 1993.

Boteler, T. *Narrative of a Voyage of Discovery to Africa and Arabia*. London: Richard Bentley, 1835.

Bradley Martin, Esmond and Chryssee. *Run Rhino Run*. London: Chatto and Windus, 1982.

—— and Lucy Vigne. 'Rhino Poaching and Conservation'. *Swara* 9 (1986).

Brander, Michael. *Hunting and Shooting*. New York: G. P. Putnam's Sons, 1971.

Brett, Rob. 'Are Kenya's Rhino Recovering?' *Swara* 14, 1 (1991).

Bridges, Roy. 'Elephants, Ivory and the History of the Ivory Trade in East Africa'. In *The Exploitation of Animals in Africa*, ed. Jeffrey C. Stone. Aberdeen: Aberdeen University, African Studies Group, 1988.

Brockington, Dan. *Fortress Conservation: The Preservation of the Mkomazi game Reserve, Tanzania*. Oxford: James Currey, 2002.

Brokensha, D. and B. Riley. *The Ethnobotany of Mbeere*. Lanham, MD: University Press of America, 1988.

Burton, Antoinette (ed.). *Gender, Sexuality and Colonial Modernities*. London: Routledge, 1999.

Burton, Richard. *Zanzibar: City, Island, and Coast*. 2 vols. London: Tinsley Brothers, 1872.

Bush, Barbara. *Imperialism, Race and Resistance: Africa and Britain, 1919–1945*. London: Routledge, 1999.

Caldwell, L. Keith. 'Commercialisation of Game'. *Society for the Preservation of the Fauna of the Empire [SPFE] Journal* 7 (1927).

——. 'Game Preservation: Its Aims and Objects'. *Society for the Preservation of the Fauna of the Empire [SPFE] Journal* 4 (1924).

——. 'The International Conference for the Protection of the Fauna and Flora of Africa'. *Journal of the Society for the Preservation of the Fauna of the Empire* NS 22 (1934).

——. *International Environmental Policy*. 3d ed. Durham, NC: Duke University Press, 1996 [1984].

Cameron, Kenneth M. *Into Africa. The Story of the East African Safari*. London: Constable, 1990.

Cameron, Verney L. *Across Africa*. New York: Negro Universities Press, 1969 [1877].

Cannadine, David. *The Decline and Fall of the British Aristocracy*. New Haven: Yale University Press, 1990.

——. *Ornamentalism. How the British Saw Their Empire*. Oxford: Oxford University Press, 2001.

Capstick, Peter Hathaway. *Death in the Long Grass*. London: Cassell, 1977.

——. *Safari: The Last Adventure*. New York: St. Martins, 1984.

Carr, Norman. *The White Impala. The Story of a Game Ranger*. London: Collins, 1969.

Carruthers, Jane. 'Creating a National Park, 1910 to 1926'. *Journal of Southern African Studies* 15, 2 (1989).

——. 'Game Protection in the Transvaal, 1900–1910'. *South African Historical Journal* 20 (1988).

——. '"Police Boys" and Poachers: Africans, Wildlife Protection and National Parks, the Transvaal 1902 to 1950'. *Koedoe* 36, 2 (1993).

——. *Wildlife and Warfare: The Life of James Stevenson-Hamilton*. Pietermaritzburg: University of Natal Press, 2001.

Carter, Nick. *The Arm'd Rhinoceros*. London: Andre Deutsch, 1965.

Cartmill, Matt. *A View to a Death in the Morning*. Cambridge, MA: Harvard University Press, 1993.

Casson, Lionel. *The Periplus Maris Erythraei*. Princeton: Princeton University Press, 1989.

Caughley, Graeme. 'The Elephant Problem – An Alternative Hypothesis'. *East African Wildlife Journal* 14 (1976).

Cerulli, E. 'The Wáttá: A Low Caste of Hunters'. *Harvard African Studies* 3 (1922).

Champion, Arthur M. 'The Atharaka'. *Journal of the Royal Anthropological Institute* 42 (1912).

——. 'Some Notes on the Wasanye'. Reprinted journal article (n.p., n.d.), located in Africana Collection, University of Nairobi Library.

Champion de Crespigny, Sir Claude. *Forty Years of a Sportsman's Life*. London: Mills and Boon, 1925.

Chanler, W. A. *Through Jungle and Desert: Travels in Eastern Africa*. New York: Macmillan, 1896.

Chapman, Abel. *On Safari. Big Game Hunting in British East Africa*. London: Edward Arnold, 1908.

Chase, Ilka. *Elephants Arrive at Half-Past Five*. London: W. H. Allen, 1964.

Chenevix Trench, Charles. *The Men Who Ruled Kenya. The Kenya Administration, 1892–1963*. London: Radcliffe, 1993.

——. *The Poacher and the Squire. A History of Poaching and Game Preservation in England*. London: Longman, 1967.

Chittick, H. Neville and Robert I. Rotberg (eds). *East Africa and the Orient. Cultural Synthesis in Pre-Colonial Times*. New York and London: Africana Publishing Co., 1975.

Churchill, Winston. *My African Journey*. London: Hodder and Stoughton, 1908 and New York: Doubleday, Doran, 1909.

Clark, Carolyn. 'Land and Food, Women and Power in Nineteenth Century Kikuyuland'. *Africa* 50, 4 (1980).

Clignet, Remi. 'A Critical Evaluation of Concomitant Variation Studies'. In *A Handbook of Method in Cultural Anthropology*, ed. R. Naroll and R. Cohen. Garden City, NY: Natural History Press, 1970.

Cockerell, Nancy. 'Air Transport in Sub-Saharan Africa'. *Interavia* 4/5 (1978).

Coquery-Vidrovitch, Catherine. *African Women: A Modern History*. Boulder: Westview Press, 1997.

Cornwall, A. and N. Lindisfarne (eds). *Dislocating Masculinities*. New York: Routledge, 1994.

Courtney, Roger. *Claws of Africa. Experiences of a Professional Big-Game Hunter*. London: George G. Harrap, 1934.

Cowie, Mervyn. *Fly, Vulture, Fly*. London: George G. Harrap, 1961.

——. 'The Royal National Parks of Kenya'. *Corona* 9 (1957).

Cranworth, Lord. *A Colony in the Making, or Sport and Profit in British East Africa*. London: Macmillan, 1912.

——. 'Game Preservation in East Africa'. *National Review* (May 1907).

——. *Kenya Chronicles*. London: Macmillan, 1939.

Cronon, William. *Changes in the Land*. New York: Hill and Wang, 1983.

Cullen, Anthony. *Downey's Africa*. London: Cassell, 1959.

—— and Sydney Downey. *Saving the Game*. London: Jarrolds, 1960.

Cummings, Robert. 'The Early Development of Akamba Local Trade History, c. 1780–1820'. *Kenya Historical Review* 4 (1976).

——. 'Wage Labor in Kenya in the Nineteenth Century'. In *The Workers of African Trade*, ed. C. Coquery-Vidrovitch and P. Lovejoy. Beverly Hills: Sage Publications, 1985.

Cuninghame, R. J. 'Big Game Shooting. Safaris'. In *Handbook of British East Africa, 1912*. Nairobi: Caxton (B. E. A.) Printing and Publishing, 1912.

Curtis, Arnold. *Memories of Kenya. Stories from the Pioneers*. London: Evans Brothers, 1986.

Curtis, Charles. *Hunting in Africa East and West*. Boston, MA: Houghton Mifflin, 1925.

Cutright, Paul. *Theodore Roosevelt, the Naturalist*. New York: Harper Bros., 1956.

Dalleo, Peter J. 'The Somali Role in Organized Poaching in North-Eastern Kenya, c.1909–1937'. *International Journal of African Historical Studies* 12 (1979).

Daly, Marcus. *Big Game Hunting and Adventure 1897–1936*. London: Macmillan, 1937.

Darling, F. Fraser. *Wild Life in an African Territory. A Study Made for the Game and Tsetse Control Department of Northern Rhodesia*. London: Oxford University Press, 1960.

Davidson, F. T. 'Elephants, Lions and Airplanes'. *Natural History* 34, 2 (1934).

de Watteville, Vivienne (see Watteville).

Dickinson, F. A. *Big Game Shooting on the Equator*. London: John Lane, 1908.

Dine, Philip. *Images of the Algerian War*. Oxford: Clarendon Press, 1994.

Dinesen, Isak. *Letters from Africa, 1914–1931*. London: Picador, 1983.

——. *Out of Africa and Shadows on the Grass*. New York: Vintage, 1985 [1938, 1960].

Douglas, Robert Dick, Jr., David R. Martin, Jr., and Douglas L. Oliver. *Three Boy Scouts in Africa. On Safari with Martin Johnson*, school ed. New York and London: G. P. Putnam's Sons, 1929.

Douglas-Hamilton, Iain and Oria. *Among the Elephants*. New York: Viking, 1975.

Duffy, Rosaleen. *Killing for Conservation: Wildlife Policy in Zimbabwe*. Oxford: James Currey, 2000.

Dundas, Charles, Hon. 'History of Kitui'. *Journal of the Royal Anthropological Institute* 43 (1913).

Dyer, Anthony. *The East African Hunters*. Clinton, NJ: Amwell, 1979.

Eastman, G. *Chronicles of an African Trip*. Rochester, NY: Priv. pub. for the author, 1927.

——. *Chronicle of a Second African Trip*. Rochester, NY: Friends of the University of Rochester Libraries, 1987.

——. 'A Safari in Africa'. *Natural History* 27, 6 (1927).

Edward VIII, King of Great Britain. *Sport and Travel in East Africa: An Account of Two Visits 1928 and 1930*, compiled by Patrick R. Chalmers from the private diaries of H.R.H. The Prince of Wales. New York: E. P. Dutton, n.d. [1931?].

Eggan, Fred. 'The Method of Controlled Comparison'. *American Anthropologist* 56 (1954).

Eliot, Sir Charles. *The East African Protectorate*. New York: Barnes and Noble, 1905.

Eltringham, S. K. *Wildlife Resources and Economic Development*. New York: John Wiley and Sons, 1984.

Estioko-Griffin, A. , and P. Bion Griffin. 'Woman the Hunter: The Agta'. In *Woman the Gatherer*, ed. Frances Dahlberg. New Haven: Yale University Press, 1981.

Fadiman, Jeffrey A. 'Early History of the Meru of Mt. Kenya'. *Journal of African History* 14, 1 (1973).

——. 'The Meru People'. In *Kenya Before 1900*, ed. B. A. Ogot. Nairobi: East African

Publishing House, 1976.
——. *Mountain Warriors. The Pre-Colonial Meru of Mt. Kenya*, African Series No. 27. Athens, OH: Ohio University Center for International Studies, 1976.
Farrant, L. *The Legendary Grogan*. London: H. Hamilton, 1981.
Feierman, Steven. 'Africa in History: The End of Universal Narratives'. In *After Colonialism: Imperial Histories and Postcolonial Displacements*, ed. Gyan Prakash. Princeton: Princeton University Press, 1995.
——. 'Colonizers, Scholars, and the Creation of Invisible Histories'. In *Beyond the Cultural Turn*, ed. V. Bonnell and L. Hunt. Berkeley: University of California Press, 1999.
Fetner, P. Jay. *The African Safari*. New York: St. Martins, 1987.
Fitzgerald, W. W. A. *Travels in the Coastlands of British East Africa*. London: Chapman and Hall, 1898.
Foà, Édouard. *After Big Game in Central Africa*. New York: St. Martins, 1989 [1899].
Foran, W. Robert. *A Breath of the Wilds*. London: Robert Hale, 1958.
——. *A Hunter's Saga*. London: Robert Hale, 1961.
——. *The Kenya Police, 1887–1960*. London: Robert Hale, 1962.
——. *With Roosevelt in Africa*. London: Robert Hale, 1924.
Fox, James. 'Not Quite the Only Begetter'. *The Spectator*, 1 August 1987.
——. *White Mischief. The Murder of Lord Erroll*. New York: Random House, 1982.
Frankland, Noble. *Witness of a Century: The Life and Times of Prince Arthur, Duke of Connaught, 1850–1942*. London: Shepheard-Walvyn, 1993.
Galbraith, John S. *MacKinnon and East Africa 1878–1895*. Cambridge: Cambridge University Press, 1972.
Gallman, Kuki. *I Dreamed of Africa*. New York: Penguin Books, 1991.
Gandar Dower, Kenneth. *The Spotted Lion*. Boston, MA: Little Brown, 1937.
Gerlach, Luther P. 'Nutrition in its Sociocultural Matrix: Food Getting and Using Along the East African Coast'. In *Ecology and Economic Development in Tropical Africa*, ed. David Brokensha. Berkeley: Institute of International Studies, 1965.
——. 'Traders on Bicycle: A Study of Entrepreneurship and Culture Change among the Digo and Duruma of Kenya'. *Sociologies* 13 (1963).
Giblin, James. 'Trypanosomiasis Control in African History: An Evaded Issue?' *Journal of African History* 31 (1990).
Gibson, Clark C. *Politicians and Poachers*. Cambridge: Cambridge University Press, 1999.
Gibson, C. C. and S. A. Marks. 'Transforming Rural Hunters into Conservationists: An Assessment of Community Based Wildlife Management Programs in Africa'. *World Development* 23, 6 (1995).
Government of Kenya. *A Handbook on Anti-Mau Mau Operations*. Nairobi: Government Printing Office, n.d. [1954?].
Graham, A. D. *The Gardeners of Eden*. London: George Allen and Unwin, 1973.
Green, Fitzhugh. *Martin Johnson, Lion Hunter*. New York and London: G. P. Putnam's Sons, 1928.
Greenwood, James. *Wild Sports of the World*. London: S. O. Beaton, n.d. [1862?].
Griffiths, J. B. 'Glimpses of the Nyika Tribe (Waduruma)'. *Journal of the Royal Anthropological Institute* 65 (1935).
Grogan, E. S. and A. H. Sharp. *From the Cape to Cairo*. London: Hurst and Blacklett, 1902.
Grove, Richard H. *Ecology, Climate and Empire*. Cambridge: White Horse Press, 1997.
Hanawalt, Barbara A. 'Men's Games, King's Deer: Poaching in Medieval England'. *Journal of Medieval and Renaissance Studies* 18, 2 (1988).
Haraway, Donna. *Primate Visions*. New York: Routledge, 1989.
——. 'Teddy Bear Patriarchy'. In D. Haraway, *Primate Visions*. New York: Routledge, 1989.
Hardin, Blaine. 'The Last Safari'. *New York Times Magazine*, 4 June 2000.
Harms, Robert. *Games Against Nature: An Ecocultural History of the Nono of Equatorial Africa*. Cambridge: Cambridge University Press, 1987.
Hay, Douglas. 'Poaching and the Game Laws on Cannock Chase'. In *Albion's Fatal Tree*, ed. D. Hay, P. Linebaugh, and E. P. Thompson. London: Allen Lane, 1975.
Hays, Samuel P. *Beauty, Health, and Permanence. Environmental Politics in the United States, 1955–1985*. Cambridge: Cambridge University Press, 1987.
Healey, Christopher. *Maring Hunters and Traders. Production and Exchange in the Papua New Guinea*

Bibliography

Highlands. Berkeley and Los Angeles: University of California Press, 1990.

Hemingway, Ernest. *Fifth Column and the First Forty-Nine Stories*. New York: Scribner, 1938.

——. *Green Hills of Africa*. New York: Charles Scribner's Sons, 1935.

——. *True at First Light*. New York: Scribner, 1999.

Hemsing, Jan. *Ker and Downey Safaris. The Inside Story*. Nairobi: Ker and Downey Safaris, 1989.

Henninger-Voss, Mary (ed.). *Animals and Human Histories*. Rochester, NY: University of Rochester Press, 2002.

Hepburn, A. B. *The Story of an Outing*. New York: Harper and Bros., 1913.

Herbert, Eugenia. *Iron, Gender and Power*. Bloomington: Indiana University Press, 1993.

——. *Red Gold of Africa*. Madison: University of Wisconsin Press, 1984.

Herlehy, Thomas J. 'Ties That Bind: Palm Wine and Blood-Brotherhood at the Kenya Coast During the Nineteenth Century'. *International Journal of African Historical Studies* 17, 2 (1984).

Herman, Daniel J. *Hunting and the American Imagination*. Washington: Smithsonian Institution Press, 2001.

Herne, Brian. *White Hunters*. New York: Henry Holt, 1999.

Hibbert, Christopher. *Africa Explored*. New York: W. W. Norton and Co., 1982.

Higham, Robin. *Britain's Imperial Air Routes 1918 to 1939*. Hamden, CT: Shoe String Press, 1961.

Hill, Kevin A. 'Zimbabwe's Wildlife Utilization Programs: Grassroots Democracy or an Extension of State Power?' *Africa Studies Review* 39, 1 (1996).

Hinde, Mrs S. L. 'Man-hunting by Lions'. *Blackwood's Magazine* 178 (1905).

Hinde, S. L. and H. Hinde. *The Last of the Masai*. London: W. Heinemann, 1901.

Hindlip, Lord. *British East Africa: Past, Present and Future*. London: T. Fisher Unwin, 1905.

Hingston, Major R. W. G. 'Report on a Mission to East Africa for the Purpose of Investigating the Most Suitable Methods of Ensuring the Preservation of Its Indigenous Fauna'. *Journal of the Society for the Preservation of the Fauna of the Empire* [*SPFE*] NS 12 (1930).

Hobley, Charles W. *Bantu Beliefs and Magic*. New York: Barnes and Noble, 1967 [new impression of 2nd edition, 1938; 1st edition, 1922].

——. *Ethnology of A-Kamba and Other East African Tribes*. London: Frank Cass, 1971 [orig pub. Cambridge: Cambridge University Press, 1910].

——. *Kenya: From Charter Company to Crown Colony*. 2d ed. London: Frank Cass, 1970 [1929].

——. 'Native Trapping Methods'. *Journal of the Society for the Preservation of the Fauna of the Empire* NS 23 (1934).

——. 'Notes on the Wa-Sania'. *Journal of the Royal Anthropological Institute* 41 (1911).

——. 'The Wa-Langulu or Ariangulu of the Taru Desert'. *Man* 8–9 (1912).

Holman, Dennis. *The Elephant People*. London: John Murray, 1967.

——. *Inside Safari Hunting with Eric Rundgren*. New York: Putnam, 1970.

——. *Massacre of the Elephants*. New York: Holt, Rinehart, and Winston, 1967.

Hopkins, Harry. *The Long Affray. The Poaching Wars 1760–1914*. London: Secker and Warburg, 1985.

Host, Emily. 'The Professional Hunters of East Africa'. *East African Annual* (1951–2).

Hudson, Robert J., K. R. Drew, and L. M. Baskin (eds). *Wildlife Production Systems. Economic Utilisation of Wild Ungulates*. Cambridge: Cambridge University Press, 1989.

Hughes, Ian Meredith. *Black Moon, Jade Sea*. Wimbledon: Clifford Frost, 1988.

Hunter, J. A. *Hunter*. London: Hamish Hamilton, 1952.

——. *Hunter's Tracks*, assisted by Alan Wykes. New York: Appleton-Century-Crofts, 1957.

Hutchinson, Horace G. (ed.). *Big Game Shooting*. Vol. 2. London: Country Life, 1905.

Huxley, Elspeth. *The Flame Trees of Thika*. New York: Weidenfeld and Nicolson, 1987 [1959].

——. 'Memoir'. In *Nellie*, Nellie Grant. London: Weidenfeld and Nicolson, 1984.

——. *Murder on Safari*. New York: Viking, 1989 [1938].

——. *Out in the Midday Sun*. Harmondsworth: Penguin Books, 1987.

——. *Settlers of Kenya*. Westport, CT: Greenwood, 1975 [1948].

——. *White Man's Country*. 2 vols. London: Chatto and Windus, 1980 [1935].

—— and Arnold Curtis. *Pioneer's Scrapbook: Reminiscence of Kenya 1890 to 1968*. London: Evans Brothers, 1980.

Huxley, J. S. *The Conservation of Wildlife and Natural Habitats in Central and East Africa*. Paris: UNESCO, 1961.

Imperato, Pascal James. *Quest for the Jade Sea*. Boulder, CO: Westview Press, 1998.

Bibliography

Ingold, Tim. *Hunters, Pastoralists and Ranchers*, Cambridge Studies in Social Anthropology. Cambridge: Cambridge University Press, 1980.

Itzkowitz, David C. *Peculiar Privilege. A Social History of English Foxhunting 1753–1885*. Hassocks: Harvester Press, 1977.

Jackson, F. *Early Days in East Africa*. London: Dawsons, 1969.

Jackson, Kenell [sic] A., Jr. 'Ngotho (The Ivory Armlet)'. *Kenya Historical Review* 5, 1 (1977).

James, Wendy. 'Antelope as Self-Image Among the Uduk'. In *Signifying Animals. Human Meaning in the Natural World*, ed. Roy Willis. London: Unwin Hyman, 1990.

Jessen, B. H. *W. N. MacMillan's Expeditions and Big Game Hunting in Southern Sudan, Abyssinia, and East Africa*. London: Marchant Singer, 1906.

Johnson, D. H. and D. Anderson (eds). *The Ecology of Survival*. Boulder: Westview, 1988.

Johnson, Marion. 'Elephants and Imperialists'. In *The Exploitation of Animals in Africa*, ed. Jeffrey C. Stone. Aberdeen: Aberdeen University African Studies Group, 1988.

Johnson, Martin. *Camera Trails in Africa*. New York: Grosset and Dunlop, 1924.

——. *Lion: African Adventures with the King of Beasts*. New York: G. P. Putnam's Sons, 1929.

——. *Over African Jungles*. New York: Harcourt, Brace, 1935.

——. *Safari*. New York and London: G. P. Putnam's Sons, 1928.

Jordan, John A. *Mongaso: Man Who Is Always Moving*. As told to John Prebble. London: Nicholas Kaye, 1956.

Kael, Pauline. 'The Current Cinema: Sacred Monsters'. *New Yorker*, 30 December 1985.

Kanogo, Tabitha. *Squatters and the Roots of Mau Mau, 1905–1963*. London: James Currey, 1987.

Karsner, Douglas. '"Now Hawaii is only hours away!" The Airlines Alter Tourism'. *Essays in Economic and Business History* 18, 1 (1999).

Kayamba, H. M. T. 'Notes on the Wadigo'. *Tanganyika Notes and Records* 23 (1947).

Kennedy, Dane. *Islands of White: Settler Society and Culture in Kenya and Southern Rhodesia, 1890–1939*. Durham, NC: Duke University Press, 1987.

Kenny, Michael. 'A Mirror in the Forest: The Darobe Hunter-Gatherers as an Image of the Other'. *Africa* 51, 1 (1981).

Kent, Susan, 'Cross-cultural Perceptions of Farmers as Hunters and the Value of Meat'. In *Farmers as Hunters*, ed. Susan Kent. Cambridge: Cambridge University Press, 1989.

Kerasote, Ted. *Bloodties: Nature, Culture and the Hunt*. New York: Random House, 1993.

Kimambo, Isariah. 'The Economic History of the Kamba'. *Hadith* 2 (1969).

Kittenberger, Kálmán. *Big Game Hunting and Collecting in East Africa 1903–1926*. London: Longmans, Green, 1929.

Koenig, Oskar. *Pori Tupu*. New York: McGraw-Hill, 1954.

Krapf, J. Lewis (Johann Ludwig) and J. Rebmann. *Travels, Researches, and Missionary Labours During an Eighteen Years' Residence in Eastern Africa*. 2nd ed. London: Frank Cass, 1968 [1st ed. Boston, MA, 1860].

Kratz, Corinne A. *Affecting Performance*. Washington: Smithsonian Institution Press, 1994.

——. 'Ethnic Interaction, Economic Diversification, and Language Use'. *SUGIA* 7, 2 (1986).

Lamphear, John. 'The Kamba and the Northern Mrima Coast'. In *Precolonial African Trade*, ed. R. Gray and D. Birmingham. Oxford: Clarendon, 1970.

——. 'The Persistence of Hunting and Gathering in a "Pastoral" World'. *SUGIA* 7, 2 (1986).

Landau, Paul S. 'With Camera and Gun in Southern Africa: Inventing the Image of the Bushman, c.1880 to 1935'. In *Miscast: Negotiating the Presence of the Bushman*, ed. Pippa Skotnes. Cape Town: University of Cape Town Press, 1996.

Lee, Richard B. *The !Kung San. Men, Women and Work in a Foraging Society*. Cambridge: Cambridge University Press, 1979.

Lee, Richard B. and Richard Daly (eds). *The Cambridge Encyclopedia of Hunters and Gatherers*. Cambridge: Cambridge University Press, 1999.

Lee, Richard and Irven DeVore (eds). *Man, the Hunter*. Chicago: Aldine, 1968.

Lewis, Joanna. *Empire State-Building*. Oxford: James Currey, 2000.

Lindblom, Gerhard. *The Akamba in British East Africa*. 2nd ed. enlarged. Uppsala: Archives D'Études Orientales, 1920 [1st edition, University Thesis, 1916].

——. *Notes of Kamba Grammar*. Uppsala: Appelbergs, Boktryckeri Aktiebolag, 1926.

Lord, J. *Duty, Honor, Empire*. New York: Random House, 1970.

Bibliography

Lovell, Mary S. *Straight on Till Morning. The Biography of Beryl Markham.* London: Hutchinson, 1987.

Lugard, F. *The Diaries of Lord Lugard.* 2 vols. Evanston: Northwestern University Press, 1959.

———. *The Rise of Our East African Empire.* 2 vols. Edinburgh: Blackwood and Sons, 1893.

Lyall, S. 'Elspeth Huxley, 89. Chronicler of Colonial Kenya, Dies', obituary, *New York Times,* 17 January 1997, 13.

Lyell, Denis D. *African Adventure. Letters from Famous Big-Game Hunters.* New York: St. Martins, 1988 [1935].

———. *Memories of an African Hunter.* London: T. Fisher Unwin, 1923.

Lynn, Kenneth S. *Hemingway.* New York: Simon and Schuster, 1987.

Lyons, Maryinez. *The Colonial Disease. A Social History of Sleeping Sickness in Northern Zaire, 1900–1940.* Cambridge: Cambridge University Press, 1992.

MacDonald, Major J. R. L. *Soldiering and Surveying in British East Africa 1891–1894.* Folkestone and London: Dawsons of Pall Mall, 1973 [orig. pub. 1897].

MacKenzie, John M. 'Chivalry, Social Darwinism, and Ritualised Killing'. In *Conservation in Africa,* ed. D. Anderson and R. Grove. Cambridge: Cambridge University Press, 1987.

———. 'Empire and the Ecological Apocalypse'. In *Ecology and Empire,* ed. T. Griffeths and Libby Robin. Seattle: University of Washington Press, 1997.

———. *The Empire of Nature. Hunting, Conservation and the British Empire.* Manchester and New York: Manchester University Press, 1988.

——— (ed.). *Imperialism and the Natural World.* Manchester: Manchester University Press, 1990.

———. 'The Imperial Pioneer and Hunter and the British Masculine Stereotype in Late Victorian and Edwardian Times'. In *Manliness and Morality,* ed. J. A. Mangan and James Walvin. Manchester: Manchester University Press, 1987.

Madeira, Percy C. *Hunting in British East Africa.* Philadelphia: J. B. Lippincott, 1909.

Mandiringana, E. and T. J. Stapleton. 'The Literary Legacy of Frederick Courtney Selous'. *History in Africa* 25 (1998).

Manning, R. B. *Hunters and Poachers.* Oxford: Clarendon Press, 1993.

Markham, Beryl. *West with the Night.* Boston, MA: Houghton Mifflin, 1942.

Marks, Stuart A. 'Back to the Future: Some Unintended Consequences of Zambia's Community Based Wildlife Program'. *Africa Today* 48, 1 (2002).

———. *The Imperial Lion. Human Dimensions of Wildlife Management in Central Africa.* Boulder: Westview, 1983.

———. *Large Mammals and a Brave People. Subsistence Hunters in Zambia.* Seattle and London: University of Washington Press, 1976.

———. 'Prey Selection and Annual Harvest of Game in a Rural Zambian Community'. *East African Wildlife Journal* 11 (1973).

———. 'Small-Scale Hunting Economies in the Tropics'. In *Wildlife Production Systems,* ed. Robert J. Hudson, K. R. Drew, and L. M. Baskin. Cambridge: Cambridge University Press, 1989.

———. 'Some Reflections on Participation and Co-management from Zambia's Central Luangwa Valley'. In *Resident Peoples and National Parks: Social Dilemmas and Strategies in International Conservation,* ed. Patrick W. West and Steven R. Brechin. Tucson: University of Arizona Press, 1991.

———. *Southern Hunting in Black and White. Nature, History, and Ritual in a Carolina Community.* Princeton: Princeton University Press, 1991.

Mathew, G. 'The Coast'. In *History of East Africa.* Vol. 1. Edited by R. Oliver and G. Mathew. Oxford: Clarendon, 1963.

Matson, A. T. *Nandi Resistance to British Rule, 1890–1906.* Nairobi: East African Publishing House, 1970.

Matthiessen, Peter. *African Silences.* New York: Random House, 1991.

———. *Sand Rivers.* New York: Viking, 1981.

Maxon, R. M. *John Ainsworth and the Making of Kenya.* Washington: University Press of America, 1980.

Mazet, Horace S. *Wild Ivory.* London: Robert Hale, 1971.

Mbithi, P. and P. Wisner. 'Drought and Famine in Kenya'. *Journal of Eastern African Research and Development* 3 (1973).

Mbiti, John S. *English-Kamba Vocabulary.* Nairobi: Kenya Literature Bureau, n.d. [1958?].

Bibliography

McCann, James C. *Green Land, Brown Land, Black Land*. Portsmouth, NH: Heinemann, 1999.

McClintock, A. *Imperial Leather*. New York: Routledge, 1996.

McCormack, Robert L. 'Airlines and Empires: Great Britain and the "Scramble for Africa": 1919–1932'. *Canadian Journal of African Studies* 10, 1 (1976).

——. 'Imperialism, Air Transport and Colonial Development: Kenya, 1920–46'. *Journal of Imperial and Commonwealth History* 17, 3 (1989).

——. 'War and Change: Air Transport in British Africa, 1939–1946'. *Canadian Journal of History* 24 (1989).

McKelvey, J. J. *Man Against Tsetse*. Ithaca, NY: Cornell University Press, 1973.

Meinertzhagen, Col. Richard. *Kenya Diary 1902–1906*. Edinburgh and London: Oliver and Boyd, 1957.

Michael, George. *African Fury*. London: Travel Book Club, 1955.

Midgley, Clare (ed.). *Gender and Imperialism*. New York: Manchester University Press, 1998.

Millais, J. G. *Life of Frederick Courtenay Selous, D.S.O.* New York: Longmans, Green, 1919.

Miller, Charles. *The Lunatic Express*. New York: Macmillan, 1971.

Milliken, Tom. 'The African Elephant'. *Swara* 17, 5 (1994).

Mirzeler, M. and C. Young. 'Pastoral Politics in the Northeastern Periphery of Uganda'. *Journal of Modern African Studies* 33, 3 (2000).

Mosley, P. *The Settler Economies: Studies in the Economic History of Kenya and Rhodesia 1900–1963*. Cambridge: Cambridge University Press, 1983.

Moss, Cynthia. *Elephant Memories. 13 Years in the Life of an Elephant Family*. New York: William Morrow, 1988.

Mullin, Molly H. 'Mirrors and Windows: Sociocultural Studies of Human–Animal Relationships'. *Annual Review of Anthropology, 1999*.

Mungeam, G. H. *British Rule in Kenya, 1895–1912*. Oxford: Clarendon, 1966.

Munro, J. Forbes. *Colonial Rule and the Kamba. Social Change in the Kenya Highlands 1889–1939*. Oxford: Clarendon, 1975.

Munsche, P. B. *Gentlemen and Poachers: The English Game Laws, 1671–1831*. Cambridge: Cambridge University Press, 1981.

Muriuki, Godfrey. *A History of the Kikuyu, 1500–1900*. Nairobi: Oxford University Press, 1974.

Murphy, John F. 'Legitimation and Paternalism: The Colonial State in Kenya'. *African Studies Review* 29, 3 (1986).

Mutwira, Roben. 'Southern Rhodesian Wildlife Policy'. *Journal of Southern African Studies* 15, 2 (1989).

Mwangudza, Johnson A. *Kenya's People: Mijikenda*. London: Evans Bros., 1983.

Mwaniki, H. K. S. *The Living History of the Embu and Mbeere*. Nairobi: East African Literature Bureau, 1973.

Nash, Roderick F. *The Rights of Nature. A History of Environmental Ethics*. Madison: University of Wisconsin Press, 1989.

——. *Wilderness and the American Mind*, 3rd ed. New Haven: Yale University Press, 1982.

Ndeti, K. *Elements of Akamba Life*. Nairobi: East African Publishing House, 1972.

Ndoo, Kasina. *The Life Story of a Kenya Chief as told to J. B. Carson*. London: Evans Bros., 1958.

Needham, Rodney. 'The Left Hand of the Mugwe: An Analytical Note on the Structure of Meru Symbolism'. *Africa* 30, 1 (1960).

Neil, Henry. *Roosevelt's Thrilling Experiences in the Wilds of Africa*. n.p. [Chicago?]: A. Hamming, 1910.

Neumann, Arthur H. *Elephant Hunting in East Equatorial Africa*. London: Rowland Ward, 1898.

Neumann, Roderick P. 'Dukes, Earls and Ersatz Edens: Aristocratic Nature Preservationists in Colonial Africa'. *Environment and Planning. D, Society and Space* 14, 1 (1996).

——. *Imposing Wilderness*. Berkeley: University of California Press, 1998.

New, Charles. *Life, Wanderings and Laborers in Eastern Africa*. London: Frank Cass, 1971 [orig. pub. 1873].

Nicholls, C. S. *The Swahili Coast*. London: Oxford University Press, 1971.

Nicholson, Max. *The Environmental Revolution*. New York: McGraw-Hill, 1970.

——. *The New Environmental Age*. Cambridge: Cambridge University Press, 1987.

Nitecki, Matthew and Doris V. Nitecki (eds). *The Evolution of Human Hunting*. New York and London: Plenum, 1987.

Noss, A., and B. Hewlett, 'The Contexts of Female Hunting in Central Africa'. *American*

Anthropologist 103, 4 (2001).

Nyamweru, Celia. 'Environment and Civil Society in Kenya'. *Africa Notes* (Cornell University) (March 1998).

———. 'Sacred Groves Threatened by Development, The Kaya Forests of Kenya'. *Cultural Survival Quarterly* (Fall 1996).

Nyeki, Daniel Musili. *Wildlife Conservation and Tourism in Kenya*. Nairobi: Jacaranda, 1993.

Nzioki, Sammy. *Kenya's People: Akamba*. London: Evans Bros., 1982.

Ofcansky. Thomas P. *Paradise Lost: A History of Game Preservation in East Africa*. Morgantown: West Virginia University Press, 2002.

Ogot, Bethwell A. *Ecology and History in East Africa. Hadith 7*. Nairobi: Kenya Literature Bureau, 1979.

———. *Economic and Social History of East Africa. Hadith 5*. Nairobi: Kenya Literature Bureau, 1976.

———. (ed.). *Kenya Before 1900. Eight Regional Studies*. Nairobi: East African Publishing House, 1976.

———. *Zamani. A Survey of East African History*. New York: Humanities Press, 1968.

Ogutu, M. A. and C. Kratz, 'Hunting and Gathering'. In *Kenya Socio-cultural Profiles: Narok District*, Draft Report. Nairobi: Ministry of Planning and National Development, and African Studies Institute, University of Nairobi, 1987.

O'Leary, Michael F. *The Kitui Akamba*. Nairobi: Heinemann Educational Books, 1984.

Olindo, Perez. 'The Old Man of Nature Tourism: Kenya'. In *Nature Tourism*, ed. Tensie Whelan. Washington, DC: Island Press, 1991.

Oliver, Roland A. and Gervase Mathew (eds). *History of East Africa*. Vol. 1. Oxford: Clarendon, 1963.

Orde-Brown, G. St. J. *The Vanishing Tribes of Kenya*. Westport, CT: Negro Universities Press, 1970 [orig. pub. 1925].

Ortega y Gasset, Jose. *Meditations on Hunting*. New York: Charles Scribner's Sons, 1972.

Orwell, George. 'Shooting an Elephant'. In *Shooting an Elephant and Other Essays*. New York: Harcourt Brace, 1945.

Osborn, H. F. 'Vanishing Wild Life of Africa.' *Natural History* 27, 6 (1927).

Overton, John D. 'The Origins of the Kikuyu Land Problem: Land Alienation and Land Use in Kiambu, Kenya, 1895–1920.' *African Studies Review* 31, 2 (1988).

———. 'War and Economic Development: Settlers in Kenya 1914–1918'. *Journal of African History* 27, 1 (1986).

Owen, W. F. W. *Narrative of Voyages to Explore the Shores of Africa, Arabia and Madagascar*. London: Richard Bentley, 1833.

Paice, Edward. *Lost Lion of Empire: The Life of 'Cape to Cairo' Grogan*. London: Harper Collins, 2001.

Pakenham, Valerie. *Out in the Noonday Sun. Edwardians in the Tropics*. New York: Random House, 1985.

Parker, Ian. *Oh Quagga!. Thoughts on People, Pets, Loving Animals, Shooting Them and Conservation*. Nairobi: Ian Parker, 1983.

——— and Mohammed Amin. *Ivory Crisis*. London: Chatto and Windus, 1983.

Parkin, David J. *Palms, Wine, and Witnesses*. San Francisco: Chanler, 1972.

Parsons, Timothy. *The African Rank and File*. Portsmouth, NH: Heinemann, 1999.

———. '"Wakamba Warriors Are Soldiers of the Queen": The Evolution of the Kamba as a Martial Race, 1890–1970'. *Ethnohistory* 46, 4 (1999).

Patterson, Lt. Colonel J. H. *The Man-eaters of Tsavo*. New York: St. Martins, 1986 [orig. pub. London: Macmillan, 1907].

Pavitt, Nigel. *Kenya. The First Explorers*. New York: St. Martins, 1989.

Percival, A. B. *A Game Ranger on Safari*. London: Nisbet, 1928.

———. *A Game Ranger's Notebook*. London: Nisbet, 1924. Reprinted with an introduction by J. MacKenzie in 1987 at Camden, NC.

Percival, Philip H. *Hunting, Settling and Remembering*. Agoura, CA: Trophy Room Books, 1997.

Peterhans, Julian Kerbis, Chapurukha Kusimba, Thomas Gnoske, Samuel Andanje, and Bruce Patterson, 'Man-eaters of Tsavo'. *Natural History* (November 1998).

Pierson, Ruth, and Napur Chaudhuri (eds). *Nation, Empire, Colony: Historicizing Gender and Race*. Bloomington: Indiana University Press, 1998.

Pitman, Lt.-Colonel C. R. S. *A Game Warden Takes Stock.* London: Nisbet, 1942.

Powell-Cotton, P. H. G. *In Unknown Africa.* Nendeln: Kraus Reprint, 1973 [orig. London: Hurst and Blackett, Ltd, 1904].

Powys, Llewelyn. *Black Laughter.* New York: Harcourt, Brace, 1924.

Pratt, M. L. *Imperial Eyes.* London: Routledge, 1992.

Prins, A. H. J. *The Coastal Tribes of the Northeastern Bantu.* London: International African Institute, 1952.

Ranger, Terence O. 'The Invention of Tradition in Colonial Africa'. In *The Invention of Tradition,* ed. Eric Hobsbawm and T. O. Ranger. Cambridge: Cambridge University Press, 1983.

——. *Voices from the Rocks,* Oxford: James Currey, 1999.

——. 'Whose Heritage? The Case of the Matobo National Park'. *Journal of Southern African Studies* 15, 2 (1989).

Redfern, A. W. 'Camera in Place of Rifle'. *SPFE Journal,* 37 (1939).

Reiger, John F. *American Sportsmen and the Origins of Conservation.* New York: Winchester Press, 1975 [rev. ed. Norman, OK: University of Oklahoma Press, 1986].

Richards, Audrey. *Hunger and Work in a Savage Community.* Glencoe: Free Press, 1948.

——. *Land Labour and Diet in Northern Rhodesia.* London: Oxford University for International Institute of African Languages and Cultures by Oxford University Press, 1939.

Richards, Audrey I. (ed.). *Economic Development and Tribal Change.* Cambridge: W. Heffer and Sons (n.d., *c.* 1953).

Richards, Paul. *Indigenous Agricultural Revolution. Ecology and Food Production in West Africa.* London: Hutchinson, 1985.

Rigby, Peter. *Cattle, Capitalism, and Class.* Philadelphia: Temple University Press, 1992.

——. *Persistent Pastoralists.* London: Zed, 1985.

Ritvo, Harriet. *The Animal Estate.* Cambridge, MA and London: Harvard University Press, 1987.

——. 'Animals in Nineteenth-century Britain: Complicated Attitudes and Competing Categories'. In *Animals and Human Society,* ed. A. Manning and J. Serpell. London: Routledge, 1994.

Rockel, Stephen. '"A Nation of Porters": The Nyamwezi and the Labour Market in Nineteenth-Century Tanzania'. *Journal of African History* 41 (2000).

——. 'Wage Labor and the Culture of Porterage in Nineteenth-Century Tanzania: The Central Caravan Routes'. *Comparative Studies of South Asia, Africa, and the Middle East* 15, 2 (1995).

Roosevelt, Kermit (b. 1889). *The Happy Hunting-Grounds.* New York: Charles Scribner's Sons, 1921.

——. *The Long Trail.* New York: Review of Reviews, 1921.

Roosevelt, Kermit (b. 1916). *A Sentimental Safari.* New York: Alfred A. Knopf, 1963.

Roosevelt, Theodore. *African Game Trails. An Account of the African Wanderings of an American Hunter-Naturalist.* New York: Charles Scribner's Sons, 1910.

Rosaldo, Renato. *Culture and Truth.* Boston, MA: Beacon, 1989.

Rotberg, Robert I. (ed.). *Africa and Its Explorers.* Cambridge, MA and London: Harvard University Press, 1970.

——. *Imperialism, Colonialism and Hunger in East and Central Africa.* Lexington, MA: Lexington Books, 1983.

——. 'Joseph Thomson'. In *Africa and its Explorers,* ed. R. I. Rotberg. Cambridge, MA and London: Harvard University Press, 1970.

Rothfels, Nigel. 'Catching Animals'. In *Animals and Human Histories,* ed. M. Henninger-Voss. Rochester, NY: Rochester University Press, 2002.

Rottland, Franz and Rainer Vossen (eds). *African Hunter-Gatherers.* Vol. 1. International Symposium, *SUGIA,* Band 7.1, 1986.

Routledge, W. S. and K. *With a Prehistoric People.* London: Frank Cass, 1968 [1910].

Ruark, Robert C. *Horn of the Hunter.* Garden City, NY: Doubleday, 1953.

——. *Use Enough Gun [On Hunting Big Game].* London: Corgi Books, 1969 [orig. pub. 1967].

Ryan, James R. *Picturing Empire.* Chicago: University of Chicago Press, 1997.

Sahlins, Marshall. *Stone Age Economics.* Chicago: Aldine, 1972.

Sassoon, Siegfried. *Memoirs of a Fox-Hunting Man.* New York: Coward-McCann, 1929.

Bibliography

Schama, Simon. *Landscape and Memory*. New York: Vintage, 1995.

Scott, Robert Lee. *Between the Elephant's Eyes!* New York: Ballentine Books, 1957 [1954].

Seaton, Henry. *Lion in the Morning*. London: John Murray, 1963.

Selous, Frederick Courtney. *African Nature Notes and Reminiscences*, with a foreword by President Roosevelt. London: Macmillan, 1908.

——. *A Hunter's Wanderings in Africa*. London: Richard Bentley and Son, 1890.

Shanklin, Eugenia. 'Sustenance and Symbol: Anthropological Studies of Domesticated Animals'. *Annual Review of Anthropology* 14 (1985).

Sheldrick, Daphne. 'Raising a Baby Rhino'. *Swara* 10, 5 (1987).

——. *The Tsavo Story*. London: Collins and Harvill, 1973.

Shepard, Paul. *The Tender Carnivore and the Sacred Game*. New York: Charles Scribner's Sons, 1973.

Sheriff, Abdul A. *Slaves, Spices and Ivory in Zanzibar*. London: James Currey, 1987.

Shire, C. 'Men Don't Go to the Moon'. In *Dislocating Masculinities*, ed. A. Cornwall and N. Lindisfarne. New York: Routledge, 1994.

Showers, Kate B. 'The Ivory Story, Africans and Africanists'. *Issue* 22, 1 (1994).

Sikes, Sylvia K. *The Natural History of the African Elephant*. London: Weidenfeld and Nicolson, 1971.

Simon, Noel. *Between the Sunlight and the Thunder: The Wild Life of Kenya*. Boston, MA: Houghton Mifflin, 1962.

Sleeman, Col. Sir James L. *From Rifle to Camera: The Reformation of a Big Game Hunter*. London: Jarrolds, n.d. [1947?].

Spear, Thomas. *The Kaya Complex. A History of the Mijikenda Peoples of the Kenya Coast to 1900*. Nairobi: Kenya Literature Bureau, 1978.

——. *Kenya's Past*. London: Longmans, 1981.

Spear, Thomas and Richard Waller (eds). *Being Maasai*. London: James Currey, 1993.

Sperling, David. 'The Coastal Hinterland and Interior of East Africa'. In *The History of Islam in Africa*, ed. N. Levtzion and R. Pouwels. Oxford: James Currey, 2000.

Steinhart, Edward I. 'Hunters, Poachers and Gamekeepers: Toward a Social History of Hunting in Colonial Kenya'. *Journal of African History* 30 (1989).

——. 'The Imperial Hunting Tradition in Kenya'. In *Animals in Human Histories*, ed. M. Henninger-Voss. Rochester, NY: University of Rochester Press, 2002.

——. 'National Parks and Anti-poaching in Kenya, 1947–1957'. *International Journal of African Historical Studies* 27, 1 (1994).

Stevenson-Hamilton, Col. J. 'The Management of a National Park in Africa'. *Society for the Preservation of the Fauna of the Empire [SPFE] Journal* 10 (n.d. [1930?]).

Stigand, Captain C. H. *Central African Game and Its Spoor*. London: Harper Cox, 1906.

——. *The Game of British East Africa*. 2nd ed. London: Harper Cox, 1913.

——. *Hunting the Elephant in Africa*. New York: Macmillan, 1913.

Stiles, Daniel. 'Hunters of the Northern East African Coast: Origins and Historical Processes'. *Africa* 51, 4 (1981).

Stockley, Lt.-Col. C. H. *African Camera Hunts*. London: Country Life, 1948.

——. 'Camera Stalking'. *Society for the Preservation of the Fauna of the Empire [SPFE] Journal* 33 (1938).

Stoddart, Brian. 'Sport, Cultural Imperialism, and the Colonial Response in the British Empire'. *Comparative Studies in Society and History* 30, 4 (1988).

Stone, Jeffrey C. (ed.). *The Exploitation of Animals in Africa. Proceedings of a Colloquium at the University of Aberdeen, March 1987*. Aberdeen: Aberdeen University African Studies Group, 1988.

Stone, Michael L. 'Organized Poaching in Kitui District: A Failure in District Authority, 1900 to 1960'. *International Journal of African Historical Studies* 5, 3 (1972).

Stoneham, C. T. *Hunting Wild Beasts with Rifle and Camera*. London: Thomas Nelson and Sons, n.d. [1932?].

Storey, William K. 'Big Cats and Imperialism: Lion and Tiger Hunting in Kenya and Northern India, 1898–1930'. *Journal of World History* 2, 2 (1991).

Streeter, Daniel W. *Denatured Africa*. New York and London: G. P. Putnam's Sons, 1926.

Tate, H. 'Notes on the Kikuyu and Kamba Tribes of British East Africa'. *Journal of the Royal Anthropological Society* 34 (1904).

Bibliography

Taylor, John. *Pondoro – Last of the Ivory Hunters*. London: Frederick Muller, 1956.

Thomas, Keith. *Man and the Natural World*. New York: Pantheon, 1983.

Thompson, E. P. *Whigs and Hunters. The Origin of the Black Act*. London: Allen Lane, 1975.

Thomson, Joseph. *Through Masai Land*. London: Frank Cass, 1968 [orig. pub. 1885, 2d ed. 1887].

Thurman, Judith. *Isak Dinesen: The Life of a Storyteller*. New York: St. Martins, 1982.

Tidrick, Kathryn. *Empire and the English Character*. London: Tauris, 1990.

Tignor, Robert. *The Colonial Transformation of Kenya*. Princeton: Princeton University Press, 1976.

Trzebinski, Errol. *The Kenya Pioneers*. New York: Norton, 1985.

——. *The Lives of Beryl Markham*. New York: Norton, 1993.

——. *Silence Will Speak*. Chicago: University of Chicago Press, 1977.

Tucker, A. *Eighteen Years in Uganda and East Africa*. 2 vols. London: Edward Arnold, 1908.

Turnbull, Colin. *The Forest People*. New York: Simon and Schuster, 1962.

Turner, James. *Reckoning with the Beast*. Baltimore: Johns Hopkins University Press, 1980.

Turner, V. W. *Schisms and Continuity in an African Society*. Manchester: Manchester University Press, 1957.

Unger, F. W. *Roosevelt's Hunting Trip in Africa*. Chicago: Charles Thompson, 1909.

van Lawick, Hugo. *Among Predators and Prey*. San Francisco: Sierra Club Books, 1986.

Vansina, Jan. *Paths in the Rainforest. Toward a History of Political Tradition in Equatorial Africa*. Madison: University of Wisconsin Press, 1990.

van Sittert, Lance. '"Keeping the Enemy at Bay": The Extermination of Wild Carnivora in the Cape Colony, 1889–1910'. *Environmental History* 3, 3 (1998).

van Zwanenberg, Roger. 'Dorobo Hunting and Gathering: A Way of Life or a Mode of Production?' *African Economic History* 2 (1976).

—— and Ann King. *Economic History of Kenya and Uganda*. Nairobi: East African Publishing House, 1975.

Vaughn-Jones, T. G. G. *A Short Survey of the Aims and Functions of the Department of Game and Tsetse Control*. Lusaka: Government Printer, 1948.

von Blixen-Finecke, Baron Bror. *African Hunter*. New York: St. Martins, 1986 [1938].

von Hohnel, Ludwig (Lieut.) *Discovery of Lakes Rudolf and Stefanie*. 2 vols. London: Longmans, Green, 1894.

Walker, Dennis A. 'Giriama Arrow Poison'. *Central African Journal of Medicine* 3, 6 (1957).

Waller, Richard. '*Emutai*: Crisis and Response in Maasailand, 1883–1902'. In *The Ecology of Survival*, ed. Douglas H. Johnson and David M. Anderson. Boulder, CO: Westview, 1988.

——. 'Interaction and Identity on the Periphery: The Trans-Mara Maasai'. *International Journal of African Historical Studies* 17, 2 (1984).

——. 'Tsetse Fly in Western Narok, Kenya'. *Journal of African History* 31 (1990).

Walsh, Martin. 'The Degere: Forgotten Hunter-gatherers of the East African Coast'. *Cambridge Anthropology* 14, 3 (1990).

——. 'Elephant Shrews and Arrow Poison'. *East African Natural History Bulletin* 22 (1992).

Warren, Louis S. *The Hunter's Game*. New Haven: Yale University Press, 1997.

Watt, Rachel. *In the Heart of Savagedom*. London, Edinburgh and New York: Marshall Bros., n.d. [1922?].

Watteville, Vivienne de. *Speak to the Earth*. New York: Penguin, 1988 [1935].

Werner, Alice. 'The Bantu Coast Tribes of the East African Protectorate'. *Journal of the Royal Anthropological Society* 45 (1915).

——. 'A Few Notes on the Wasanye'. *Man* 13 (1913).

West, Nicholas. *Happy Valley: The Story of the English in Kenya*. London: Secker and Warburg, 1979.

Western, David. 'Amboseli National Park: Enlisting Landowners to Conserve Migratory Wildlife'. *Ambio* 11 (1982).

——. 'Ecosystem Conservation and Rural Development: The Case of Amboseli'. In *Natural Connections: Perspectives in Community-based Conservation*, ed. D. Western and R. M. Wright. Washington, DC: Island Press, 1994.

White, C. M. N. 'The Role of Hunting and Fishing in Luvale Society'. *African Studies* 15, 2 (1956).

White, Landeg. *Magomero: Portrait of an African Village*. Cambridge: Cambridge University Press, 1987.

White, Luise. 'Women's Domestic Labor in Colonial Kenya: Prostitution in Nairobi, 1909–1950'. African Studies Center Working Paper No. 30, Boston University, 1980.

White, Stewart Edward. *The Land of Footprints*. Garden City, NY: Doubleday, Page, 1913.

Whitehouse, George Fitzhugh. 'To Lake Rudolph and Beyond'. In *Hunting and Conservation*, ed. George Bird Grinnell and Charles Sheldon. New York: Arno and New York Times, 1970 [1925].

Wienholt, Arnold. *The Story of a Lion Hunt*. London: Melrose, n.d. [1922].

Williams, Heathcote. *Sacred Elephant*. London: Jonathan Cape, 1989.

Williams, John G. *A Field Guide to the National Parks of East Africa*. London: Collins, 1967.

—— and N. Arlott. *A Field Guide to the Birds of East Africa*. London: Collins, 1963.

Wilmsen, Edwin. *Land Full of Flies*. Chicago: University of Chicago Press, 1989.

—— and James Denbow, 'Paradigmatic History of San-speaking Peoples and Current Attempts at Revision'. *Current Anthropology* 31, 5 (1990).

Wood, J. 'The Lion King', *New York Review of Books*, 11 July 1999, 15.

Woodburn, James. 'Egalitarian Societies'. *Man* 17 (1982).

Worster, Donald. *Nature's Economy*. 2d ed. Cambridge: Cambridge University Press, 1994.

Yeager, Rodger and Norman N. Miller. *Wildlife, Wild Death*. Albany, NY: State University of New York Press, 1986.

Dissertations and theses

Akama, John S. 'A Political-Ecological Analysis of Wildlife Conservation in Kenya'. Ph.D. dissertation, Southern Illinois University, 1993.

Alladay, James D. 'Elephants and Their Interactions with People in the Tana River Region of Kenya'. Ph.D. dissertation, Cornell University, 1979.

Ambler, Charles H. 'Central Kenya in the Late Nineteenth Century: Small Communities in a Regional System'. Ph.D. dissertation, Yale University, 1983.

Anderson, David M. 'Herder, Settler and Colonial Rule: A History of the Peoples of the Bovingo Plains, Kenya: 1890–1940'. Ph.D. dissertation, Cambridge University, 1982.

Casada, James A. 'The Imperialism of Exploration: British Explorers and East Africa, 1856–1890'. Ph.D. dissertation, Vanderbilt University, 1972.

Cummings, Robert J. 'Aspects of Human Porterage with Special Reference to the Akamba of Kenya: Towards an Economic History, 1820–1920'. Ph.D. dissertation, University of California, Los Angeles, 1975.

Fadiman, Jeffrey A. 'Traditional Warfare among the Meru of Mt. Kenya'. Ph.D. dissertation, University of Wisconsin, 1973.

Gerlach, L.P. 'The Social Organization of the Digo of Kenya'. Ph.D. dissertation, University of London, 1961.

Jackson, K.A. Jr. 'An Ethnohistorical Study of the Oral Traditions of the Akamba of Kenya'. Ph.D. dissertation, University of California, Los Angeles, 1972.

Kelly, Nora. 'In Wildest Africa: The Preservation of Game in Kenya, 1895–1933'. Ph.D. dissertation, Simon Fraser University, 1978.

Lehmann, Nancy Beth. 'Poaching for Profit'. Masters thesis, University of Texas, Austin, 1979.

Lowenthal, Richard A. 'Tharaka Age-Organization and the Theory of Age-Set Systems'. Ph.D. dissertation, University of Illinois, 1973.

McKay, William F. 'A Precolonial History of the Southern Kenya Coast'. Ph.D. dissertation, Boston University, 1975.

Muthamia, E. J. M'muthrui. 'History of Political Organization in Meru: A Study of Political Development among the Meru of Kenya to 1973'. Ph.D. dissertation, University of Nairobi, 1974.

Mwaniki, H. S. K. 'A Political History of the Embu'. Master's thesis, University of Nairobi, 1973.

Neumann, Roderick P. 'The Social Origins of Natural Resource Conflict in Arusha National Park, Tanzania'. Ph.D. dissertation, University of California, Berkeley, 1992.

Ofcansky, Thomas P. 'A History of Game Preservation in British East Africa, 1895–1963'. Ph.D. dissertation, University of West Virginia, 1981.

Overton, John D. 'Spatial Differentiation in the Colonial Economy of Kenya: Africans, Settlers and the State, 1900–1920'. Ph.D. dissertation, University of Cambridge, 1983.

Sperling, David C. 'Some Aspects of the Islamization of East Africa with Particular Reference to the Digo of Southern Kenya'. Ph.D. dissertation, University of Nairobi, 1970.

Summary, Rebecca M. 'The Role of Tourism in the Economic Growth of Kenya and Barbados: A Comparative Study'. Ph.D. dissertation, University of Illinois, Urbana, 1983.

Journals consulted

East African Agricultural and Forestry Journal, 1935
East African Natural History Bulletin, 1970–
East African Wildlife Journal (later *African Journal of Ecology*), 1963–
Focus, Newsletter of the World Wildlife Fund
Oryx (previously *Journal of the Society for the Preservation of the Fauna of the Empire*, Old Series 1904–21; New Series 1921–48)
Swara, Journal of the East African Wildlife Society

Unpublished materials and papers

Ambler, Charles, H. 'The Great Famine in East Central Kenya, 1897–1900: A Regional View'. Unpublished paper, Kenya Historical Association, Nairobi, August 1977.

Anderson, David M. 'Ecology, Culture and Cattle among the Kalenjin'. Unpublished paper, African Studies Association, Chicago, 27–31 October 1988.

Askwith, T. G. 'Memoirs'. Unpublished typescript, Rhodes House, Oxford, 1963.

Bell, R. H. V. and E. McShane-Coluzi. 'Conservation and Wildlife Management in Africa'. Proceedings of a workshop organized by the US Peace Corps at Kasingu National Park, Malawi, October 1984.

Cable, Charles. 'Forager–Farmer Interaction in Kenya Pre-History'. Staff seminar paper No. 5. University of Nairobi, History Department, Nairobi, 1987.

Carruthers, Jane. 'Dissecting the Myth: Paul Kruger and the Kruger National Park'. Seminar paper, African Studies seminar, St Antony's College, Oxford, May 1993.

Cashmore, T. R. 'Your Obedient Servant'. 2 vols. Unpublished ms., Rhodes House, Oxford, 1964.

Chenevix Trench, Charles. Papers, Northern Frontier District. Unpublished ms. Rhodes House, Oxford, n.d.

Collett, David and Joan Knowles. 'Parks, Pastoralists and Peregrinators. Images and Reality in Kenya Masailand'. Unpublished typescript, n.d.

Conn, B. E. 'Ecology in Historical Perspective: An East African Example'. Unpublished conference paper, Historical Association of Kenya, 1972.

Cowie, Mervyn H. 'History of the Royal National Parks of Kenya'. Unpublished typescript, National Archives of Kenya, 1946.

Elkington, Margaret. 'Recollections'. Unpublished typescript, Rhodes House, Oxford, n.d.

Galaty, J. G. 'East African Hunters: "So-Calling" Some Historical Myths'. Conference paper, American Anthropological Association, Houston, 3 December 1977.

Gipta, Desh. 'A Brief Economic History of the Akamba, with Particular Reference to Labour Supplies'. Unpublished typescript, University of Nairobi, n.d.

Girouard, Sir Percy (E. P. C.). 'Memoirs, Etc.'. Unpublished ms. Rhodes House, Oxford, n.d.

Grogan, Quentin O. 'Papers of Quentin O. Grogan'. Unpublished ms. Rhodes House, Oxford, n.d.

Institute of African Studies. 'Kenya District Socio-Cultural Profiles, Kitui District'. Draft report, Project of the Ministry of Planning and Development and the Institute of African Studies, University of Nairobi, Prof. G. Were, General Editor, Dr J. Akanga, Coordinator, 1986.

Kratz, Corinne. 'Are the Okiek Really Masai? or Kipsigis? or Kikuyu?' Unpublished paper, African Studies Association, Baltimore, MD, November 1978.

MacKenzie, A. Fiona D. 'Contested Ground: Colonial Narratives and the Kenyan Environment, 1920–1945'. Unpublished paper, Conference on 'African Environments, Past and Present'. Oxford, July 1999.

MacKenzie, John. 'Hunting in East and Central Africa in the Late Nineteenth Century, with Special Reference to Zimbabwe'. Draft essay, July 1993.

———. 'Poachers and Preservers: Game Law in British Colonial Africa'. Unpublished typescript, n.d.

Marks, Stuart A. 'Snaring Wildlife – A Hidden Transcript'. Unpublished essay, December 1994.

Middleton, J. 'Tourism in Kenya: Fantasies of the Other'. Unpublished draft essay, May 1997.

Mulongo, A. H. 'Land Use Conflicts on Lochinvar'. Unpublished paper, University of Zambia History Department, 1979–80.

Oates, John. 'From Collecting to Conservation'. Chapter 2 of unpublished manuscript, 'Myth and Reality in the Rain Forest: Conservation Lessons from Africa and India'. n.d.

Sanjee, Sultan. 'Material Culture in Ukambani'. Unpublished seminar paper No. 67, Institute of African Studies, University of Nairobi, 8 July 1976.

Simon, Noel. 'The Elephants of Tsavo'. Unpublished ms., David Sheldrick Wildlife Trust Archive, Langata, 1983.

Sobania, Neal. 'Exchange and Ethnicity in Northern Kenya'. Unpublished paper, African Studies Association, Chicago, 27–31 October 1988.

Sperling, David. 'Some Aspects of Islamization in East Africa with Particular Reference to the Digo of Southern Kenya'. Seminar paper, University of Nairobi Department of History, 1970.

Steinhart, Edward. 'David Sheldrick and the "Elephant Problem" in Kenya: 1956–1964'. Unpublished paper, African Studies Association Annual Meeting, Nashville, TN, 16–19 November 2000.

———. 'Kenya Ivory Hunters: 1850–1950'. Unpublished paper, American Society for Ethnohistory, Chicago, 2–5 November 1989.

———. 'White Hunters in Kenya: 1895–1909, The Ivory Harvesters and Pioneers'. African Studies Association Annual Meeting, Toronto, Ontario, 2–6 November 1994.

Trapido, Stanley. 'Poachers, Proletarians and Gentry in the Early Twentieth Century Transvaal'. Unpublished seminar paper, Institute of Commonwealth Studies, University of London, 18 October 1983.

Ueda, Hitoshi. 'The Power of Hunting Leaders Among the Kamba'. Unpublished paper No. 116, Institute of African Studies, University of Nairobi, 1979.

———. 'Wathi Ritual Among the Kamba'. Working paper No. 115. Institute of African Studies, University of Nairobi, 1979.

Waller, Richard. 'Age, Wealth and Authority within Pastoralist Society'. Unpublished paper. African Studies Association, Chicago, 27–31 October 1988.

White, Luise. 'Tsetse Visions: Popular Culture and Imperial Science in Colonial Northern Zambia, 1931–1937'. Draft ms., 1992.

Young, S. J. 'Changes in Diet and Production in Southern Moçambique 1855–1960'. Unpublished paper. African Studies Association of the United Kingdom, Durham, UK, 1976.

Index

'aces', Waata 25-8 *passim*, 199, 208
Adamson, George 114, 170-2, 195-6, 202
Adamson, Joy 170
administrators, colonial 9, 69, 78-82, 89, 90, 97
Afrikaner hunters 176 *see also* Boers
Aggett, W.B. 168
agriculture 5, 21-4 *passim*, 36-7, 66, 67, 150, 159, 161, 163-4, 187, 193, 197, 204, 212
agropastoralism 7, 44
air reconnaissance 144
air transport 144-6, 211
Aka 4
Akeley, Carl 123-5, 131, 141
Akeley, Mary Jobe 124, 143
Amboseli National Park 215
American Museum of Natural History 123, 141, 143, 144, 168
Americans 3, 18, 115-19, 122-5, 128-30, 134, 141-2, 145-6, 185 *see also individual entries*
Amery, Leopold 176
Anderson, David 12
anene 50
animals, ownership of 11, 13, 211-14, 217
antelope 22, 35, 76, 79, 96, 169
Arabs 9, 25, 48-50, 54, 113, 157, 209, 215
aristocracy 62-3, 66, 69, 91-9, 120, 177, 209
Arkell-Hardwick, A. 73-5, 209
Atkinson, Dr 93
athiani (hunting leaders) 40, 47, 52-4, 212
Azania 18-19

baboons 5, 86-7, 159, 162, 164
Bagge, Stephen 90

Bambuti 4, 5n8
ban, on hunting 1, 3, 32, 216-17
Bantu-speakers 7, 19, 24, 26, 30, 31, 46n15, 208
Baringo Game Reserve 95
Beaton, Ken 190
beekeeping 44-5
Bell, Walter D.M. 70-2 *passim*, 209
Berman, Bruce 80
Bernard, Frank 36
Black, Tom 104
Blixen, Baron Bror 99, 104-6 *passim*, 121, 127, 129, 132, 133, 144, 202, 210
Blixen, Karen (Isak Dinesen) 99, 102, 105, 121, 127
blocks, hunting 215-17 *passim*
Boer settlers 97, 98, 169
bongo 76, 168
Boni 17, 157, 158
Boran 19, 34, 188
Botswana 23
bow-and-arrow hunters 7, 19, 26-8, 30, 32, 35-7 *passim*, 39, 44, 72, 194, 213
boys 6, 20, 22, 32
Bridges, Alan 67
Britain/British 2, 5, 9, 17, 63-7, 91-109, 174-6 *passim*, 208-9 *see also* colonial era; England
British East Africa Company 78, 81
British East African Protectorate 17-18
Brooke-Popham, Sir Robert 181-2, 184
Brown, David 201
buffalo 98, 159, 164
Burton, Sir Richard 71
bushbuck 32, 37
bush craft 76, 114
Byrnes, Governor J.A 180

Caldwell, Capt. Keith F.T. 155-8, 161, 164, 175-81 *passim*
cameras 9, 122-6, 138-42, 146, 211
Cameron, V.L. 78
Cannadine, David 2, 208-11
Cape Colony 70
caravan, hunting 114-15 *see also* safaris; trade 9, 36, 42, 46, 47, 49-51, 54, 56, 78, 113
Carter Commission 182
Champion de Crespigny, Sir Claude 84
Chapman, Abel 72
Chenevix Trench, Charles 81
Churchill, Winston 115
class 2-4 *passim*, 6, 9, 11, 13, 20, 63, 72, 89-90, 133, 142, 145, 146, 169, 208-11 *passim*, 214
Cole, Berkeley and Galbraith 97, 99, 101
Cole, Florence 95
collecting 9, 123-5, 166, 169
colonial era 1-3, 7-13, 17-20, 28-9, 34, 43, 53, 55-8, 80, 90, 149-72 *passim*, 189, 206-14; pre 2, 47-51, 56; post 214-17
Colonial Office 80, 158, 178, 180
compensation, for wildlife damage 165
Conference for the Protection of African Flora and Fauna 180-3 *passim*, 191
Congo 4
Connaught, Duke and Duchess of 125
conservation/conservationists 2, 3, 10-13 *passim*, 73, 81, 85, 93, 95, 116, 124, 140, 144, 146, 149-89; *passim*, 192, 193, 202, 206, 211-16 *passim*; and Africans 12-13, 187-8; international 175-7
Convention for Protection of African Fauna and Flora 180-1
cooks 75, 77, 84, 128, 133, 137, 188, 210
corruption 121, 159, 165, 196, 215, 216
Cottar, C..W. (Budd) 136, 140
Cottar, Glen 136n85, 216-17
Cottar's Safari Service 134
Courtney, Roger 134
Cowie, Mervyn 181-5, 190, 194, 197-8, 202
Cranworth, Lord 79, 93, 96-9
culture 2, 3, 9, 20, 32-3, 37-40, 45, 92, 93, 120, 170, 202, 206, 209
Cumming, R.G.G. 70
Cummings, Robert 47, 51
Cuninghame, R.J. 116, 131, 210

Dahalo 17
Dara brothers 25
Davey, Dr J.B. 164-5
Davidson, Frederick T. 144
Degere 31
Delamere, Lord 93, 95-6, 101, 115, 118, 119, 121, 202, 209
Digo 7, 9, 24, 30-4 *passim*, 204

dik-dik 32, 37, 188
Dinesen, Isak *see* Blixen, Karen
dogs, hunting 33n14, 96, 168
Dorobo 17, 20, 21, 23-4, 35, 75, 77, 188; fallacy 23
drivers 133, 188, 210
drought 43, 47, 54, 170, 187
Duruma 7, 9, 24, 30-4 *passim*, 204

East African Professional Hunters Association 136, 145
East African Society for Prevention of Cruelty to Animals 140
Eastman, George 122, 141
Eastman-Pomerey-Akeley expedition 122-5, 143
eland 32, 85, 188
elephants 9, 18, 25-9 *passim*, 43-56, 69-74 *passim*, 77, 79, 81, 83, 85, 95, 98, 99, 104, 150-7 *passim*, 161, 163-5 *passim*, 168-9, 175, 176, 181, 191-4, 202-4, 212-15 *passim;* and ivory 9, 18, 42, 45-51 *passim*, 53, 54, 72, 150-7 *passim*, 181
El-Hakim 74
Eliot, Sir Charles 91, 95, 150
Elkington, James and Margaret 104
Embu 19, 36
employment 56-8 *passim*, 203 *see also* safaris, staff
England/English 9, 63-7
environmental factors 36-7
Erroll, Lord 121, 183, 202
Erskine, Captain 175
Ethiopia 7, 186, 215
Europe/Europeans 3-5 *passim*, 9, 18, 55, 61-109 *passim*, 113, 185, 206, 207
explorers/exploration 9, 66, 70-1, 77-8, 113
exports, ivory 18, 44, 46, 151, 215, 216; ban on 216, 217; permits 215, 216

famine 22, 43, 47, 51, 54, 170, 189n1
farmers, African 2, 5, 7, 20, 21, 23, 30, 31, 164-5, 193, 207
Feierman, Steven 207
films 67, 141-2, 166
Finch Hatton, Denys 10, 99, 104-7 *passim*, 121, 127, 132, 133, 144, 162, 202, 210
Foran, Major W. Robert 82-4
foxhunting 4, 65-6, 104, 209
France 67

Galana River Management Scheme 203-4
game 2-3, 6, 7, 13, 17-21 *passim*, 31, 37, 46, 67-77, 85, 99, 120, 154-5; control 158-65; laws 55, 61, 63-5 *passim*, 81, 91, 134, 143, 150, 156, 163, 165-7, 171, 212, 213; preservation 95, 97, 98, 151, 152, 159, 167, 170-88 *passim*, 202;

reserves 7, 85, 95, 96, 144, 176, 178, 212, 213

Game Department 82, 121, 134, 136, 140, 146, 149-51, 154-73 *passim*, 176, 183, 187, 192-6, 199-201 *passim*, 203, 206, 212-16 *passim*

Game Policy Committee 184-5, 188, 190, 214

Game Rangers 149-51 *passim*, 154, 159, 161, 162, 165, 170-2, 195-6; African 195, 197-9 *passim*, 201

Game Scouts 151, 165, 167, 171, 187, 195, 199, 201

Game Wardens 155, 163, 166-7, 169-70, 195 *see also individual entries*; Honorary 162-3, 167; Military 186

gamekeepers 2, 13, 64, 81, 136, 146, 149-73, 194, 199, 202, 203, 213

gazelle 32

gender issues 4-6, 22, 208

gentlemen/gentry 2, 63-5 *passim*, 67, 99-102, 169, 209, 210

giraffe 35, 79, 85, 96

Giriama 19

girls 22

Gloucester, Duke of 91, 104, 105, 125-7

goats 37

'gofers' 188

Goldfinch, S.H. 104

Grigg, Governor Edward 175

Grogan, Ewart 100-2 *passim*, 121

Grogan, Quentin 102

Grove, Richard 12

guides 72, 75, 77, 137

gun bearers 55, 57, 75, 77, 83-4, 128, 143, 170, 188, 210

habitat destruction 99

Hadza 23

Haggard, Rider 79

Hale, William 163, 193n16

Hamisi 83

Handbook of British East Africa 131

Happy Valley 122, 209

Haraway, Donna 124

Harris, William C. 70

hartebeest 79

health risks, animal 163

Hemingway, Ernest 6, 18, 105, 122, 128-30

herders 2, 20-2 *passim*, 200

Heyburn, A. Barton 115

hides 21, 22, 29

Hill, Mervyn 183

Hinde, S.L. 80-1

Hindlip, Lord 96

Hingston, Major R.W.G. 179

hippopotamus 169

Hobley, C.W. 178

Hoey, A..C. 184

Hoey, W.H. 162

Hood, Robin 62

Hopkins, J.G. 81, 169

hospitality 116, 118-19

Hughes, Ian 216

Hunter, J.A. 18, 114, 161, 202

hunters, African 1-7 *passim*, 11, 17-58, 75-7, 114, 149, 158, 168-70, 187-8, 202-3, 206-13 *passim*; 'aces' 25-8 *passim*, 199, 208; bow-and-arrow 7, 19, 26-8, 30, 32, 35-9 *passim*, 44, 72, 194, 213; subsistence 2, 37, 45-6, 56, 98, 188, 204, 205, 208, 213 *see also* hunter-foragers; 'pure' 2, 24, 70-7; white 1-3 *passim*, 6, 11, 61-109, 114, 122, 131-7, 168, 202, 213, 216; pioneer 69-77, 93, 209; professional 6, 9, 11, 102, 116, 121, 127, 129-37, 140, 186, 210, 216-17; settler 2, 91-109, 202, 209, 210; sports 132, 177

hunter-foragers/gatherers 2, 4, 5, 17, 19, 20, 23, 36, 37, 157, 202, 207, 208

hunting 1-13; by Africans 1-3, 6, 7, 17-58, 75-6, 114, 158, 164, 169-70, 207-8, 214; ban on 1, 3, 32, 56, 216-17; by Europeans 2, 3, 5, 9, 55, 61-109, 122, 132, 133; and gender 4-6; and historiography 10-13; history 7-10, 17-19, 61-7; military associations 63, 67, 84-90; promotion of 166-7; safari 2-3, 6, 9-10, 54, 56-8, 91, 104-5, 113-46, 185-7, 209-12 *passim;* sport 2, 69, 78-80, 83, 92, 97, 115-19, 132, 177; by visitors 2, 3, 18, 91, 115-19, 122, 128-30, 132-4, 140-6, 185-6, 210, 214

Huxley, Elspeth 92, 93, 96, 100, 102-4 *passim*, 118, 184

Huxley, Julian 184

hyena 85, 162

ideology 2, 3, 20, 21, 90, 167, 202

Igembe 30, 34-6

impala 32, 79

imperialism 2-4 *passim*, 9, 10, 12, 68-77, 90, 208

India/Indians 10, 54, 67, 101

industrialism 66

initiation ceremonies 38-40, 212

International Convention for the Preservation of Nature 179, 180-82

Islam 31-4 *passim*

Italy 157, 175, 176, 181, 186

Itzkowitz, David 65

ivory 7, 9, 18, 25-6, 28, 31, 34, 36, 42, 44-50 *passim*, 53, 54, 69-74 *passim*, 77, 83, 98, 99, 150-8 *passim*, 175, 215-17; exports 18, 44, 46, 150, 215, 216; ban on 153, 216, 217; government purchase

of 152-3,157; harvesters 47-51, 69, 73-7, 83, 150; smuggling 152-3, 155-8, 175, 176, 181, 193, 215-17; trade 7, 25, 31, 36, 42, 45-51 *passim*, 53, 54, 74-5, 99, 152-3, 156-7, 175, 181; ban on 153
Jackson, Frederick 78-80, 209
Jodhpur, Maharajah of 126, 138n1
Johnson, Martin 122, 130, 141, 144
Johnson, Osa 6, 122, 130, 141
Johnston, Sir Harry 79, 95, 96, 149
Joint East African Board 178
Jubaland 156-8, 175

Kafonde, Galogalo 25
Kalenjin 167
Kamba 7, 9, 10, 19, 26, 28, 31, 35, 38, 42-58, *57*, 108, 109,113, 114, 134, 171, 188, 194, 195, 197-204 *passim*, 208, 210, 212
Kearney, Dennis 201
Kenya, Mount 7, 24, 30, 35, 37, 209
Kenyatta, Jomo 147, 215
Kenyatta, Mama Ngina 215, 216
Ker and Dopwney 134
Kibunjia, Joseph 33, 39, 41
Kikuyu 19, 20, 44n9, 134, 188, 210
Kitui district 7, 9, 30, 42-58, 208
Koitalel 87-9
Kolb, Dr 73
Krapf, Johannes L. 48, 49, 107
kudu 79
kuthuua system 43, 47
Kwale district 7, 25, 30-4, 208

ladies 2, 4, 102-5, 209, 210
Laikipia 164, 188
land 10, 12, 13, 182, 197, 206-7, 211
Landau, P. 142
laws, game 55, 61, 63-5 *passim*, 81, 91, 134, 143, 150, 156, 163, 165-7, 171, 212, 213
leopard 35, 169, 184
licences, hunting 1, 81, 96, 98, 141, 150, 151, 153, 157, 161, 163, 166-8 *passim*, 193, 212-14 *passim*
Lindblom, Gerhard 108, 109
lions 21, 32, 46, 81-2, 85, 96, 150, 162, 181, 182, 184, 191
liver 46
locusts 187
Lone Tree incident 181-4 *passim*
Lugard, Frederick 78

Maasai 19, 21-2, 29, 80, 167, 178, 188, 210
MacDonald Major R. 84
MacDonald, Ramsay 179
Machakos 30, 41, 43, 44
MacKenzie, John 10-11, 77-8

MacMillan, Lucie 100
MacMillan, Sir Northrup 100-1, 108, 118, 121, 162
Madeira, Percy 115
Mahupa, Msinda 32
Markham, Beryl 5, 100, 102-5 *passim*, 121, 126, 144
Markham, Mansfield 104
Marks, Stuart 11
Marxism 3
Massey, Major Hugh 201
Mate, John 38, 39, 41
Matobo National Park 12
Mau escarpment 24, 88
Mau Mau 196-7, 202
Mbeere 36
Mbooni 43
McCabe, David 201
McCormack, Robert 145
meat 20, 21, 25, 29, 31-2, 37, 78, 79, 109, 115, 120
Meinertzhagen, Capt. Richard 80, 84-90, 209
merchants 9, 47, 113, 209
Meru district 5, 7, 8, 19, 30, 34-6, 195, 204, 208; National Park 35, 215
middle classes 66
migration 44, 47
Mijikenda 7, 119, 24, 25, 27, 30-4 *passim*
missionaries 69, 107-8
mobility 43, 56
Mokena, Mr 39
moran 21, 22
motor cars 142-4
Mozambique 70
Mukangau, M'Kirebu 38
Mutulya, Kikuli 51-3
Mwenda, Kivoi 48-9
Mwijo, Nganyawa 15

Nairobi National Park 147, 185, 190-1
Nandi 19, 84-90 *passim*, 103
Nanyuki Farmers' Association 184, 186
Nash, Roderick 180
Neumann, Arthur H. 72-3, 209
Neumann, Roderick 12, 13, 177
Newland and Tarleton 116, 118, 131
nobility, European 4, 62-3, 120, 185
Norfolk, Duke of 125, 138n1
Northcote, Governor E.158
Northern Rhodesia 161
N'takarichi, M'takwenda 39
Nthengi, Elui 193-4
Nyambeni hills 30, 34-5
Nzima Springs 192

occultation 2, 56, 207-8
oil embargo 215

Okiek 17, 24
Olindo, Perez 214, 216
Onslow, Lord 177-80 *passim*
Orma 26, 34, 201
Ormsby-Gore, W. 183
Orwell, George 209
Oulton, T. 170
ownership, of animals/wildlife 11, 13, 61, 211-14, 217

Parker, Ian 3, 27, 198, 201
parks, national 3, 7, 10, 12, 28, 39, 85, 95, 144, 149, 152, 171-206, 213-16 *passim;* exclusion of Africans from 12
Passfield, Lord 178
pastoralists 2, 21-2, 24, 31
patronage 49
Patterson, Col. J.H. 81-2, 151, 192
peasants 20, 61-3 *passim*, 205, 207, 210
Pease, Sir Alfred 118
Percival, A. Blayney 18, 85, 97, 150, 151, 154, 157, 183
Percival, Philip *57*, 116, 129-37 *passim, 135*
photography 122-6, 138-42, 146, 166, 188, 211, 213
pig, wild 32, 33, 159, 162, 164
pioneer hunters 69-77
pitfalls 31, 37
Pitman, Lt.-Col. C.R.S. 161
planning 189
poachers/poaching 3, 20, 62-5, 82, 98, 114, 154, 157-8, 167-73, 189, 194-205, 213, 215-17; African 168-73, 187, 188, 194-202, 213; anti- campaign 3, 28, 65, 167-73, 184, 196-205; 'motor' 143; white 168-9; in England 63-4
poison 162, 168; acocanthera 26-8, 32-3, 36, 37, 44, 194, ban on use of 26
Pokomo 19, 36
police 9, 56, 82-4, 90
Pomeroy, Daniel E. 123
porters/porterage 44, 50, 56, 57, 75, 77, 84, 113-15 *passim*, 128, 133, 137, 143, 188, 209, 210
poverty 36
Pratt, Mary Louise 114
preservationism 212-14 *passim see also* wildlife
Prince of Wales 91, 122, 125-7
professional white hunters (PWH) 6, 9-11 *passim*, 102, 116, 121, 127, 129-37 *passim*, 140, 186, 210, 216, 217; Association 136, 14 5

racism 13, 76, 125, 133, 208, 214
Rainey, Paul 96
Ranger, Terence 12
Redfern, A.W. 141

regulation, game 155 *see also* laws, game; hunting 69, 212, 213
religion 32-3
Renoir, Jean 67
reserves, game 7, 85, 95, 96, 144, 176, 178, 212, 213
revenues, colonial 150-1, 153, 154, 166
rhinoceros 74, 83, 85, 161, 169, 176, 193; horn 31, 69, 73, 193
Riddell, Major Jack 183
riding to hounds 9, 65, 104
Ridley, Mervyn 104
rinderpest 98
Ritchie, Capt. A.T. 134, 146, 155, 158-67, *160*, 172-6 *passim*, 180-1, 183, 186-7, 190, 192-3, 202
ritual 21, 22, 32, 38-9, 212
Roosevelt, Kermit 82, 116, 117
Roosevelt, Theodore 9, 18, 75, 82, 91, 102, 111, 113, 115-19, *117*, 122-4 *passim*, 131, 132, 162
Ruark, Robert 6, 18, 130n68, 136

safari, big game/hunting 2-3, 6, 9-10, 54, 56-8, 91, 104, 105, 113-46, 185-7, 209-12 *passim;* camera 122-6 *passim*, 138-42, 146, 166, 188; 'campaign' 186-7; champagne 9, 119-27, 185, 188; literary 9, 128-30; royal 125-7; scientific 122-5; staff 55, 57-8, *57*, 75, 77, 83, 84, 113, 128, 133, 137, 170, 188, 209-10; tourist 142-6, 185-6
safari, trade 9, 113, 209
Samburu 19, 21, 34, 167, 188, 201, 210
San (Basarwa) 4, 23
sanctuaries 3, 7, 85, 173, 174, 176, 185, 190, 204, 213, 214
Sanye 24, 158
Schumacher, Raoul 104
scientific work 9, 116-17, 122-5, 141, 166
Selous, Frederick 70, 116-18 *passim*, 131
settlers 2, 4, 9-11 *passim*, 13, 18, 20, 66, 69, 85, 91-109, 118, 121, 146, 150, 154-5, 162-4, 168, 181-3; *passim*, 202, 209, 212; elite 4, 62-3, 66, 69, 91-107
Sheldrick, David 192-4, 196-200
Shimba hills 30, 31, 34; National Park 7, 31
shooting parties 4, 9, 65, 120
Simon, Noel 202
skinners 55, 57, 75, 77, 84, 133, 137, 188, 210
skins, horn etc. 21, 22
slaughtering, of animals 32-3
Sleeman, James 140-1
Smithsonian Institution 116, 117
smuggling, ivory 152-3, 155-8, 175, 176, 181, 193, 215-17
social hierarchy 20, 61-4

socialization 6, 20, 22
Society for the Preservation of Fauna of the Empire 98, 156, 176-9; *Journal* 176, 177
soil conservation 189
soldiers 2, 9, 56, 84-90; Soldier Settlement Scheme 92, 155
Somali/Somalia 7, 19, 54, 93, 201, 215
Somaliland, Italian 157, 175, 181, 186
South Africa 67, 70, 72, 177; Kruger National Park 177
sport 2, 7, 69, 78-80, 83, 92, 97, 115, 132, 177
squirearchy 64-5
Stevenson-Hamilton, Col. J. 177
Stigand, Capt. Charles H. 75-7, 209
stone age 18, 24
Stoneham, C.T. 139
strike, 137
Swahili 9, 19, 25, 48-50 *passim*, 54, 113, 209
Switzerland 67

Tana River 35-7 *passim*, 46, 56
Tanganyika 12, 18, 78, 144, 164
Tanzania 22
Tarleton, Alan and Henry 162
Taru desert 192
techniques, hunting 2, 7, 25-9, 31-2, 35-7, 51-5, 109
technology 10, 138-46, 185
Teleki, Count 79
Tharaka 5, 7, 30, 34-41 *passim*, 56, 171-2, 204, 208, 212
Thomson, Joseph 18, 71, 73, 78
Tigania 36
tourism 142-6, 185-6, 205
trackers 55, 57-8, *57*, 77, 83, 84, 128, 137, 170, 217
trade 9, 36, 42-4, 54, 99, 113; ivory 7, 25 31, 36, 42, 44, 47-51 *passim*, 53, 54, 74-5, 99, 152-3, 156-7, 175, 181; ban on 153
tradition, hunting 2, 3, 7, 18-19, 24, 30, 44-7, 61-9, 147, 188, 208, 209; European 2, 3, 5, 61-7; English 63-7
transculturation 2, 9, 114-37, 188, 209-11, 217
transport 9, 142-6, 185, 211 213
Transvaal 70
traps 31, 36, 37, 162
Treasury Department 150, 193, 196
treaty, Britain-Italy 175
tribes 28-9
trophies 69, 70, 90, 115, 139
trout fisheries 166, 209
Trzebinski, Errol 10, 92
Tsavo National Park 10, 56, 191-202, 213, 215
Tsavo River 81-2

Tucker, Bishop Alfred 107
Turkana 19, 201
tusks 21, 22, 29, 53, 153

Uasin Gishu plateau 97
Ueda, Hitoshi 51
Uganda 17, 101, 144, 161; Railway *94*, 95, 98
Ukambani 48-58 *passim*, 108-9
United States 67, 174, 179; Yellowstone Park 174

Van Lawick, Hugo 21
Vanderbilt, Alfred 105
Vanderbilt, George 134
vermin 9, 26, 70, 150, 161-3 *passim*, 193
Voi Field Force 197-201 *passim*

Waata (Waliangulu) 5, 7, 10, 24-31, 33, 36, 44, 72, 158, 170, 188, 194, 195, 198-204 *passim*, 208
Waathi society 38-41, 50, 53, 212
Wameru 7
war; Ethiopia-Somalia 215; First World (Great) 64, 66, 120-1, 154; Second World 56, 185-7, 189, 193
warthogs 32
water 207; catchment projects 189
Watt, Rachel 108
Watt, Reverend Stuart 108-9
weapons 19, 26-9, 32, 35-7 *passim*, 39, 44, 55-6, 109, 215
White, Stewart and Billy 115
wildebeest 191
wilderness 3, 12, 67, 213
wildlife 7, 10, 12, 61, 83, 93, 98, 99, 123, 124, 139, 146, 161-3 *passim*, 188, 193, 197, 204-13; ownership of 211-14, 217; preservation 3, 10, 12, 13, 69, 85, 97, 146, 149-72, 178, 192, 212-14 *passim*; Research Unit 214
Wilson Airways 144
women 4-6, 25, 68, 102-5, 116, 129-30 *see also* ladies
Woodley, Bill 193-4, 196-7, 200, 201
Woosnam, R.B. 151-5 *passim*
World Bank 217

Yak 113
Yatta plateau 46, 55
York, Duke and Duchess of 82, 91, 125
young men 20, 21, 31, 56-7, 203 *see also moran*

Zambia 11
Zanzibar 113
zebra 32, 35, 96, 161
Zimbabwe 11, 12